THE JEWISH OREGON STORY

Ellen Eisenberg

THE JEWISH OREGON STORY

1950–2010

LIBRARY OF
CONGRESS
SURPLUS
DUPLICATE

Oregon State University Press   Corvallis

Published in cooperation with the Oregon Jewish Museum
and Center for Holocaust Education

Library of Congress Cataloging-in-Publication Data

Names: Eisenberg, Ellen, author.
Title: The Jewish Oregon story, 1950-2010 / Ellen Eisenberg.
Description: Corvallis : Oregon State University Press, [2016] | "Published in
    cooperation with the Oregon Jewish Museum and Center for Holocaust
    Education."
Identifiers: LCCN 2016023605 | ISBN 9780870718694 (paperback)
Subjects: LCSH: Jews—Oregon—History. | Oregon—Ethnic relations. | BISAC:
    HISTORY / Jewish.
Classification: LCC F885.J4 E38 2016 | DDC 979.5/04924—dc23
LC record available at https://lccn.loc.gov/2016023605

♾ This paper meets the requirements of ANSI/NISO Z39.48-1992
(Permanence of Paper).

First published in 2016 by Oregon State University Press, in cooperation with the
Oregon Jewish Museum and Center for Holocaust Education
Printed in the United States of America

OSU
Oregon State
UNIVERSITY
OSU Press

Oregon State University Press
121 The Valley Library
Corvallis OR 97331-4501
541-737-3166 • fax 541-737-3170
www.osupress.oregonstate.edu

Dedicated to Rabbi Joshua Stampfer

CONTENTS

ACKNOWLEDGMENTS

It is no exaggeration to say that this book would not exist without Rabbi Joshua Stampfer. Rabbi Stampfer determined in 2012 that there should be a book charting Oregon Jewish history from 1950 to 2010—a volume to follow Steven Lowenstein's *The Jews of Oregon, 1850–1950*, commissioned in the mid-1980s by the Jewish Historical Society of Oregon (JHSO). In short order, Rabbi Stampfer gathered a committee, invited proposals, and enlisted sponsors. Long before 2012, he laid the groundwork for such a volume by founding a series of organizations including the JHSO and its successor, the Oregon Jewish Museum. The work that these organizations, their staffs, and their legions of volunteers have conducted over decades to preserve and interpret Oregon Jewish history has been absolutely essential to this project.

The Book Committee established by Rabbi Stampfer has been an engaged and supportive group. The committee's members—Elaine Cogan, Sylvia Frankel, Gayle Marger, Judy Margles, Alice Meyer, David Newman, and Paul Schlesinger—have been generous with their time, sage in their advice, and mindful of their boundaries. From my initial interview with them, through our final meeting as I completed revisions on the manuscript and selected images, they have been a pleasure to work with.

To Rabbi Stampfer's call for sponsors, a remarkable group of donors responded with lightning speed. I am very grateful for major support from Harold & Arlene Schnitzer CARE Foundation/Arlene Schnitzer & Jordan Schnitzer, Renee and Irwin Holzman/Holzman Foundation Inc., Ralph and Bunny Schlesinger Foundation, Leonard and Lois Schnitzer Family Fund of OJCF, Jay & Diane Zidell Charitable Foundation, Jerry and Helen Stern, Elizabeth and Ruben Menashe, Sol & Rosalyn Menashe Family Fund of OJCF, and Lora and James Meyer. Additional support was provided by Jewish Federation of Greater Portland, Judith and Garry Kahn, Stan and Ethel Katz Briller Jewish Education Fund of OJCF, Diane and David Rosencrantz, Eric

& Tiffany Rosenfeld Fund of OJCF, Mrs. Moe Tonkon Fund of OJCF, Gerel Blauer, and Julie Diamond. I thank all who contributed for their faith in this project.

If Rabbi Stampfer was the spiritual and inspirational leader for this project, Alice Meyer was the chief logistics officer. Alice worked tirelessly on arrangements ranging from the sponsor reception (generously hosted in her home) to periodic book committee meetings. She managed systems of feedback that allowed committee members to share ideas and concerns, without overwhelming the process (or me). She has been outstanding as the chief communications officer and as a sounding board. She is an exemplar of the "professional volunteers" about whom I write in chapter 3—the women who work behind the scenes in the community and are seldom acknowledged, but without whom nothing would ever get done.

Paul Meyer played a critical role as well, assisting with logistics (and, of course, cohosting the reception for sponsors). He and Bob Conklin played a key role as special advisors, working on the copublication agreement with Oregon State University Press. Paul also was a helpful informant as I explored the politics of the Portland Jewish community during the key period from the 1960s to the 1980s.

One of the joys of this project was the opportunity it gave me for an extended period of research at the Oregon Jewish Museum (OJM; it became the Oregon Jewish Museum and Center for Holocaust Education, OJMCHE, as this book was in progress). Beginning in May 2014, I came to the museum weekly for about a year to work in the archives. Executive Director Judy Margles, Curator Anne LeVant Prahl, and Archivist Pete Asch were all wonderful resources on the collections and the community, and discussions with them helped shape my thinking about the project. Likewise, Sura Rubenstein, who was simultaneously working on a project of her own at the museum, was a key contact, always willing to share relevant sources and information. Discussions with her were helpful to my thinking about South Portland, religious life, and other key topics. She was also generous in reading and providing feedback on an early chapter for this project.

Judy, Anne, and Pete opened all collections to me and allowed me to roam freely through the archives—catalogued or not. In addition, they allowed me full remote access to photo collections, and even provided me with a full copy of the nearly five-hundred digitized oral histories. This was a researcher's dream arrangement for archival access, for which I am extremely grateful. The entire staff of the OJMCHE was unfailingly welcoming and friendly. I was happy to join their lunch circle on my weekly visits, to engage with them, and to be made to feel like part of their extended family.

When I first visited the Oregon Jewish Museum in the early 1990s, the archives were kept in a small storage facility at the back of an office. There was no physical museum at all. I did my research sifting through unsorted cartons of materials while sitting on the floor. That situation has changed dramatically—the museum now has a place of its own, with a well-organized archive and workspace. On nearly every visit I was reminded of the many volunteers and interns, past and present, who have contributed to these changes. As I worked, volunteers were often at the next table, sorting through the Congregation Beth Israel Collection, while interns transcribed oral histories. All of those interns and volunteers—past and present—as well as those who have provided the financial resources to support a building, a permanent collection, and a professional staff, deserve recognition as contributors to this project.

I had the great privilege as a part of this project to engage with two Willamette undergraduates. During the summer of 2014, Willamette's Liberal Arts Research Collaborative (LARC, a Mellon-funded program) enabled me to work with Camille Debreczeny and Cathryn "Caty" Priebe as they developed their own focused research projects on Jews in Oregon, also based on the archival resources of the OJMCHE. Camille's project on Jewish women's engagement in interethnic coalitions and Caty's project on attitudes toward Israel and Zionism informed parts of chapter 3 through chapter 5 of this volume. Driving back and forth from Portland weekly during the summer, discussing our interrelated research in the car, over ice cream, and in our formal group meetings provided a great synergy among our projects. The discussions of our larger "research community," which also included my colleague David Gutterman and his student Noor Amr, enhanced my understanding of the broader literature on religion in the Pacific Northwest.

As I drafted chapters, Judy Margles was invariably my first reader, and my work (on this project as with all my earlier work on Jews in Oregon) has benefited greatly from her insights, suggestions, and encouragement. Sylvia Frankel also generously offered to read the full manuscript and provided useful feedback. Camille Debreczeny and April Slabosheski both assisted with editing, and Camille also greatly aided my work with the oral history collection. Ultimately, a number of members of the Book Committee read all or part of the manuscript and provided helpful suggestions. Many more suggestions came from members of audiences, as I presented portions of the work in progress in Cannon Beach, Portland, and Salem.

While engaged with the final revisions on this manuscript, I was saddened to learn of the passing of William "Bill" Toll. Bill was truly the pioneer historian of the Portland Jewish community, and his monograph, *The Making of an Ethnic Middle Class: Portland Jewry over Four Generations*, published in 1982, remains a critical work on the topic. I am grateful that I had the opportunity to work closely with Bill, and with fellow western Jewish historian Ava F. Kahn, for several years on our coauthored volume, *Jews of the Pacific Coast: Reinventing Community on America's Edge.* That project, and my many conversations with Bill and Ava, fundamentally shaped my views on western Jewish history and greatly inform this book.

Over the past several years, I've had the opportunity to work with the staff at Oregon State University Press both as an author and as a member of the press faculty advisory editorial board. I continue to be impressed with their professionalism, excellent insights, willingness to go the extra mile, and enthusiasm for their projects. Their personal touch and commitment has enabled them to craft an impressive collection, and I am very proud that this volume will be a part of that list.

My work, as always, has benefited tremendously from the support I receive as the holder of the Dwight and Margaret Lear Chair in American History at Willamette University. Through a sabbatical leave, I was able to devote myself full time to this project during the 2014–2015 academic year. I remain grateful to be part of a faculty and department where I count not only many wonderful colleagues, but many longtime and dear friends.

And finally, thanks go to my family—my parents, Meyer and Carolyn Eisenberg; my sons, Alex and Ben Korsunsky; and, most especially, my husband, Ami Korsunsky.

PREFACE

As I embarked on this study, after coauthoring a book on Jews in the Pacific West and writing another on the history of Jewish Oregon to 1950, I expected few surprises. I originally thought that the subject of this book, the post-1950 evolution of Oregon's Jewish communities, would be the final chapter of what became *Embracing a Western Identity: Jewish Oregonians, 1849–1950*, rather than a separate volume. When a committee formed by Rabbi Joshua Stampfer invited me to submit a book proposal on Jewish Oregonians since 1950, I hesitated to participate, not sure how much more I had to say on the topic.

Rabbi Stampfer's committee included a number of longtime leaders of what was then the Oregon Jewish Museum and its predecessor group, the Jewish Historical Society of Oregon. That organization, in the mid-1980s, had published Steven Lowenstein's *The Jews of Oregon, 1850–1950*.[1] Now, more than twenty-five years later, they were eager to commission a second volume to serve as a sequel to Lowenstein's book. I have long relied on Lowenstein's work for my research—I have *two* dog-eared and much underlined copies, one in my office and the other at home. Yet I had no real desire to write a sequel. I was nearing the end of *Embracing a Western Identity* (a volume that I soon came to refer to as "book one") and, although I relied very heavily on the same archive and oral history collection used by Lowenstein, my approach was quite different from his. Rather than a chronological community history with an emphasis on key institutions and leaders, my "book one" was thematic, and made more effort to look outside of the Oregon Jewish community to the larger regional and national context, linking communal evolution to broader themes in American Jewish and Oregon history. Fortunately, I was encouraged by members of the committee to submit a proposal that, instead of being a sequel modeled on Lowenstein's book, enabled me to continue my thematic approach. As I developed the proposal over the next several weeks and then interviewed with the committee, I became increasingly excited about the idea of extending my project and transforming my ideas for a sweeping, single postwar chapter into a more developed volume of its own.

Looking back now at the proposal I submitted in 2013, a number of themes I anticipated do play a prominent role in the finished volume. It seemed obvious from the start that changing gender roles would be a rich vein to tap. As expected, examination of organizational records, the community press, and the oral histories of approximately five hundred community members (recorded between the 1970s and the 2010s) revealed dramatic changes in women's participation in the workforce, in community institutions, and in religious life. What I did not fully expect was the poignancy of these voices: Shirley (Soble) Nudelman[2] publicly wrestling in her newspaper column with her longing to go back to work; Eve (Overbeck) Rosenfeld, a professional social worker who found that her voice on the Jewish Family and Child Services board was ignored; Rosemarie (Frei) Rosenfeld, who fretted about how to earn money for her donation to the Federation Women's Division in an era when housewives were discouraged from working; and the many women, such as Evelyn (Asher) Maizels and Laurie (David) Rogoway, who built on their extensive experiences volunteering in the community to transition into professional positions.

I knew that I wanted to continue to explore regional Jewish identity by looking at the changing ways in which Jewish Oregonians have presented their past, yet I could not have anticipated finding a script for a homegrown musical called *Whatever Happened to Old South Portland?* The musical serves as an excellent window into the meaning of the historic immigrant neighborhood for Jewish Portlanders, vividly demonstrating the ways that they fused local and national history and myth to express what it meant to be a Jewish Oregonian. Although I had a sense that there was a story worth telling about the relationship between the Jewish community and the emergence over the last several decades of a local hipster/foodie/environmentalist ethos embodied in the television comedy *Portlandia*, I had no idea that my exploration of that theme would lead to a discussion of a mikvah (ritual bath) in a yurt, or the emergence of Oregon as a center for post-denominational, and particularly Renewal, Judaism.

Also unexpected were discoveries that bridged the thematic chapters. As a resident of Salem, I had no intention of producing such a Portland-centric work. During the years I spent on the Oregon Jewish Museum board, 1999 to 2008, when there were never more than two or three of us from outside the metropolitan area, I made it my personal mission to see that the board remember the rest of the state. Every time someone would mistakenly say "Portland Jewish community," "Portland history," or (on occasion) "Portland Jewish Museum," I would pipe up with a loud "OREGON!" And yet, in both of my Oregon books, it has been difficult to maintain such geographic balance. Although Jews lived in scattered small settlements throughout the state during the pioneer period, when all sorts of unlikely small towns had main streets lined by Jewish stores, by the turn of the twentieth century, the Oregon Jewish story was increasingly a Portland story. This was even truer in the mid-twentieth century. Not until the 1970s and 1980s did Willamette Valley Jewish communities such as Salem and Eugene begin to experience significant growth; that growth would expand to a few towns on the east side of the Cascades, the coast, and Southern Oregon in the 1990s and the early twenty-first century.

The most unexpected overarching motif was one of timing. Again and again, I found myself returning to the late 1960s and early 1970s as a turning point. As any student of American Jewish history knows, this is, in part, a national phenomenon—1967 is widely seen as a watershed moment in American Jewish history. That year's Six-Day War in the Middle East represented an existential crisis for Israel, and, by extension, for world Jewry. It coincided with the fragmentation of the American Civil Rights coalition of the 1960s, as many Jews and other white liberals became alienated by the Black Power/ Black Nationalist movement. The result was that American Jews "turned inward," focusing less on the interethnic coalitions of a few years earlier and more on specifically Jewish programming, centered largely on Israel and, later, on Soviet Jewry.

For Oregon Jewry, this national watershed coincided with a local turning point: the razing—as part of an urban renewal plan—of the historic South Portland neighborhood, which had housed the majority of Jewish Oregonians earlier in the century and remained the institutional center of the community. Thus, the Portland Jewish community came to terms with the national shift in Jewish priorities and identity just as they were facing wrenching questions about their past and their future. How would they remember the old neighborhood and their communal and familial experiences there? Where would the institutions go? What would be the geography of the Jewish community? Given the new level of acceptance and integration, should there be a Jewish center at all, and, if so, of what would it consist?

Beyond this communal crisis, the same period in the late 1960s and early 1970s was also a turning point in Oregon history. At midcentury, Oregon and Portland were conservative, even stodgy. The reputation for progressivism, thoughtful development, and an environmental ethos now so associated with the region began to emerge during this period, and was hotly contested in some quarters of the state. A dramatic political shift led to the embrace of policies that drove Oregon and Portland's reputations as leaders in regional and urban planning, and attracted many people to an area increasingly viewed as a model of livability. The shift had a profound impact on Jewish Oregonians and played an important role in shaping communal identity. Individual community members as well as communal institutions and organizations participated in, contributed to, and reflected these shifts. Increasing numbers of newcomers found themselves drawn to Oregon in part because of them.

After decades of communal stability—some would say stagnation—the number of Jewish Oregonians began to grow, part of a larger group of migrants to the region who were young, well educated, and notably secular. Beginning in the 1970s and 1980s and accelerating dramatically in the 1990s and 2000s, their arrival brought new challenges to the community and shaped its character. The Oregon Jewish community in the early twenty-first century is significantly larger than it was in the 1960s, 1970s, or 1980s. It is also less attached to communal institutions, more diverse, and less geographically concentrated. In many ways, it presents the type of profile that most worries American Jewish leaders; with high intermarriage and low affiliation rates, it seems unsustainable. At the same time, it has been ahead of the curve in terms of outreach programming and particularly receptive to post-denominational religious approaches like Renewal Judaism.

This volume attempts to frame and examine this period of local and national change through six chapters. Chapter 1, "The Shape of Community: Jewish Oregonians in a Changing State," focuses on the broad trajectories of geographic and demographic development. Placing the geographic shift triggered by the razing of the South Portland neighborhood in the larger context of Oregon's shifting politics, it provides an introduction to the era with a focus on the period in the late 1960s and early 1970s that was such a turning point for the state of Oregon, the city of Portland, and the Jewish community.

Chapter 2, "*Whatever Happened to Old South Portland?* Constructing a New Oregon Jewish History," follows up on the urban renewal story from Chapter One, examining how Portland Jews memorialized their historic neighborhood, and in so doing constructed a new Oregon Jewish identity that connected them to the iconic Jewish immigration story of the Lower East Side and *Fiddler on the Roof*. Demonstrating the ways in which communal memory and identity are shaped to meet contemporary needs, the chapter traces the continued evolution of Oregon Jewish history, as it incorporated Sephardim, Holocaust survivors, and others into the communal story.

That the musical *Whatever Happened to Old South Portland?* and so many of the various exhibits and historical projects that followed were largely the work of women suggests their key role, performing voluntary labor in the community. Chapter 3, "A Woman's Place . . ." focuses on the ways in which the community, and the women themselves, were affected by changing gender roles as they entered the workforce in increasing numbers and began to win acceptance as equals in organizational and ritual life. Institutional records and the community press open a window on the gradual transformation of women's roles in ways big and small, while the rich collection of oral histories provides insights into individual women's (and men's) perceptions of this process.

Chapter 4, "Looking Outward: Minority Consciousness and Civic Engagement," and chapter 5, "Looking Inward: Oregonians and the Jewish World," focus on two major spheres of Jewish communal engagement. The first examines the activity of Jewish Oregonians—and the posture of the organized community—in the local and state arena. Broader histories of American Jewry make clear that the 1950s and 1960s were a time of tremendous Jewish involvement in what was then called intergroup work, as Jewish Americans embraced the idea that fighting anti-Semitism meant fighting prejudice in all its forms. Coalitions with other ethnic minorities, especially African Americans, and engagement in liberal politics became central to the agenda of Jewish communities. Chapter 4 examines how these alliances played out in Oregon, a state with a troubled racial history and where, in the 1950s, Jews still faced professional and social exclusions. The continued engagement in local civic issues after the oft-cited turn inward of the late 1960s is also explored; along with a renewed, vigorous engagement on the issue of gay rights at the turn of the twenty-first century. Chapter 5, "Looking Inward: Oregonians and the Jewish World," begins with a focus on the impact of the Six-Day War locally—an impact magnified by the personal experiences of the state's two leading rabbis, Joshua Stampfer and Emanuel Rose, both of whom happened to be in Israel during the war. The chapter charts the increased communal focus on Israel and the Jewish world, including the local campaign for Soviet Jewry and resettlement efforts. This chapter also examines the growing division within the Jewish community over Israeli politics in the 1980s and beyond.

The pronounced local discord over Israel in recent decades is a reflection, in part, of the shifting demographics of the Oregon Jewish community and of the larger progressive context of the state. Chapter 6, "The *Jewish* Oregon Story," returns to the question of demographics, focusing on the most recent decades and zeroing in on the impact of Oregon and Portland's emergence as a progressive stronghold. This chapter examines the composition of the early twenty-first-century community based on recent local and national studies, demonstrating the impact of selective migration and local context on the shape of community. Exploring the embrace of post-denominational Jewry, spirituality, an environmentalist ethos, and a commitment to sustainability, this chapter looks at some of the emerging responses to an expanding and changing Jewish population.

There is a danger common to both ethnic history and regional history; focusing on a particular group or a specific region can easily lead to uncritical exceptionalism. The historian is tempted to highlight distinctiveness: What is it about Jewish community that differentiates it from another ethnic or religious group? What are the "special" contributions of Jews to the larger city or state? Or, what is singular about the experience of the community in Oregon? How are Oregon's Jewish communities unique? As David Peterson del Mar points out in discussing Oregon history, so-called distinctive features "almost always turn out to be much less peculiar than one had thought," and focusing on such features can easily lead to a tendency to overlook important themes that are common to other groups or places.[3]

In this volume I have tried to resist these tendencies and strike a balance, recognizing factors that are unique, such as the particular impact of urban renewal on Portland Jewish identity, and those that are not, like the general pattern toward suburbanization among American Jews. Jewish Oregonians experienced national and international events that turned Jewish communities "inward" and shifting gender norms that altered the fabric of families, synagogues, and communities, but they experienced these events in a particular place with its own history and dynamics. Just as they responded to calls for interracial cooperation in the context of a city and state with a particular history of race relations, they heard about the Six-Day War not only through the press but also through the words of their own rabbis, huddled in shelters in Israel with their families. Both their broader experiences as American Jews and their particular circumstances as Oregonians shaped their responses; through these, we can learn much about the texture of regional and Jewish community identity.

THE JEWISH OREGON STORY

CHAPTER ONE

The Shape of Community
Jewish Oregonians in a Changing State

For the Oregon Jewish community 1971 was a banner year. In the Portland metropolitan area, home to over 85 percent of the state's Jews,[1] the highlight was the completion of an expansive new Jewish Community Center. In advance of the opening, tours were offered of the "magnificent" new building. Community leaders touted the new JCC as "more than just a beautiful, impressive edifice," claiming it would be "the spirit and hub of Jewish activities, Jewish cultural and social functions, and Jewish education," and "the symbol and the reality of Portland Jewish Community life . . . filled with fun, warmth and innovation."[2]

Offering vast recreational, health, cultural, social, and educational opportunities for community members from infants to seniors, the center was designed to be "a second home for the entire Jewish community and its friends for generations to come," according to Julius Zell, chair of the building campaign.[3] Only two miles from the Robison Jewish Home for the Aged and boasting a campus that included new facilities for the community-wide Portland Hebrew School, the JCC promised to provide the glue that would ensure continuity into the future. Harold Schnitzer, chair of the JCC building committee, explained, "The Community Center has become the focal point of the whole community. It used to be the synagogue was the focal point, but there has been a shift of emphasis to the social aspect of our daily living as opposed to the religious centrality of the religious theme."[4]

The new JCC (it became the Mittleman Jewish Community Center, or MJCC, in honor of Helen Mittleman in 1976, after her husband, real estate developer Harry Mittleman, paid off the mortgage) not only offered capacious and modern facilities, but anchored an emerging new community hub in Southwest Portland, approximately four miles from the historic South Portland neighborhood that had been the community's center since the early twentieth century. Less than a mile from the new JCC, on the newly named Peaceful Lane, stood the impressive six-year-old building of Congregation

A bird's-eye view of the Jewish Community Center in Southwest Portland, 1994.
Courtesy OJMCHE

Neveh Shalom (Conservative), with its enormous façade in the shape of the Ten Commandments. With a congregation of eight hundred families and sanctuary seating for nine hundred, the building could amply accommodate the growing congregation, formed through the merger of Neveh Zedek and Ahavai Sholom. The *Jewish Review* reported just after that building's opening in November 1964, "all of the activities of the Congregation have experienced significant growth ever since the move to the new location."[5] Similarly, Portland Hebrew School's relocation from its quarters in the old South Portland neighborhood to the new JCC campus significantly boosted enrollment. The combination of improved facilities and proximity to the public schools with the highest concentrations of Jewish students led to a 40 percent growth in the student body in the first month at the new location.

Over the next several decades, the new cluster in Southwest Portland included additional Jewish institutions, such as the Portland Jewish Academy day school; a Chabad-Lubavitch center,[6] including a synagogue, preschool, and, eventually, a day school; and commercial establishments offering kosher food. Nearby, the May Terrace Apartments, dedicated in 1981, offered an independent retirement living option adjacent to the Robison Home; the campus, now called Cedar Sinai Park, later added Rose Schnitzer Manor (assisted living, 1998) and Rose Schnitzer Tower (independent living, 2007), as well as adult day services. A second cluster, in Portland's near Northwest—home

Rabbi Joshua Stampfer
blowing a shofar in front of
Congregation Neveh Shalom's
building on Peaceful Lane,
dedicated in April 1965.
Courtesy OJMCHE

since 1927 to the venerable Congregation Beth Israel (Reform)—also began to develop in this period, with the erection of a new building for Shaarie Torah (Traditional) in 1965. Decades later, Congregations Beth Israel and Shaarie Torah were joined in their Northwest neighborhood by Congregation Havurah Shalom (Reconstructionist) and the Oregon Jewish Museum. The unprecedented fundraising campaigns and resulting spacious, modern facilities for the older congregations, along with the creation of new institutions, suggested not only the rapid growth of the Jewish community in the final decades of the twentieth century, but also a sense of optimism for the future.

Even as these projects began in the 1960s and early 1970s, there were concerning signs amid the ambitious community projects and celebrations of progress. The new buildings were initially motivated less by community growth than by a combination of neighborhood degradation, poor facilities, and displacement by urban renewal and freeway construction. In the late 1950s, as Portland struggled with sluggish growth, the city embraced a program of urban renewal as the key to future development. The strategy was to build up the downtown core as a business and entertainment center for the metropolitan area by "sanitizing untidy transitional blocks on the downtown fringe," and clearing much of the low-rise housing and small businesses located there to make way for highways, parking, and high-rise development.[7] Fringe areas—including those like the South Portland neighborhood that had been the center of the immigrant Jewish community earlier in the century—were maligned as dilapidated and crime-ridden; a Portland renewal promotional piece from 1962 was titled "Meet Creepy Blight." A major urban renewal project of the era, the South Auditorium Project, proposed clearing over one hundred "economically isolated" acres in South Portland "to turn this old 'stopover' neighborhood into a place of offices and businesses."[8] The new I-405 freeway paved over adjacent areas, razing the neighborhood and, with it, much of the infrastructure of the Jewish community.

Doubly affected by these developments, Shaarie Torah, the city's oldest Orthodox congregation, was forced to move from its First Street location by urban renewal. In 1960, the congregation dedicated its new building on Park Avenue and announced the selection of Rabbi Yonah Geller. According to Geller, "The very next day in the paper, they announced a new freeway [was] going to go right through the synagogue. It was an anti-Semitic freeway, it took away Shaarie Torah, it took away Neveh Shalom [sic], and it took away the Jewish Community Center."[9] As Shaarie Torah relocated again, this time to Northwest Portland, the congregation absorbed Linath Hazedek, a small Orthodox synagogue that had fallen victim to dwindling membership and urban renewal. Ahavai Sholom's move to Peaceful Lane was also forced by freeway development, which compelled the congregation to leave the building at Southwest Thirteenth and Market that they had dedicated scarcely a decade earlier. It was this challenge that led to Ahavai Sholom's merger with congregation Neveh Zedek to form Neveh Shalom. Like Linath Hazedek, Neveh Zedek had been struggling to survive prior to urban renewal; poor facilities in the deteriorating neighborhood made it difficult for these congregations to attract younger members, and their core populations were aging. As Abe "English" Rosenberg, a member of Neveh Zedek, recalled, "the average age of the members was in their seventies and it got so that we were dying on the vine."[10] The mergers make clear that, despite the optimism suggested by the JCC and other building projects, the number of congregations was actually shrinking as the combination of urban renewal and dwindling memberships made the smaller, aging congregations unsustainable.[11]

Urban renewal also forced the Sephardic Ahavath Achim to leave its historic South Portland location in 1962, a move that caused great consternation among the tight-knit community. The congregation fought the city in court, with the transcripts revealing their particular concern about moving away from the neighborhood that housed the thirteen elderly members who still walked to Sabbath services, as was traditional. Though few in number, these members were, according to synagogue president Ralph Funes, "the heart and soul of our synagogue."[12] Consternation turned to grief when their building was irreparably damaged during an effort to move it to a newly purchased site on Southwest Barbur Boulevard.

In contrast, the expansion of Portland State University came as a boon for the JCC. According to Barry Itkin, who served as president 1966–1968, the center "was on the verge of financial collapse. People were not using the Center because the building was old and run down and there weren't enough physical facilities."[13] In this case, the desire of the Portland Development Commission (the entity created in 1958 to lead the city's "redevelopment and civic promotion")[14] to buy the property to facilitate the expansion of Portland State was a "lucky coincidence," according to Itkin.

Thus, the much-heralded development of new Jewish institutional clusters in Southwest and Northwest Portland in the late twentieth century was more the result of pushes than of pulls. Although there had been a long-standing migration of families out of the deteriorating South Portland neighborhood, prior to these moves there was no emerging Jewish center or obvious destination. In fact, several congregations considered sites on the east side of the Willamette River (which divides Portland) before settling in Southwest or Northwest, and their decisions to remain on the Westside were contested, often bitterly, by Eastsiders. The eventual building sites were chosen more for financial than strategic reasons, and many in the community expressed qualms about their suitability and lack of centrality. According to Milt Carl, charged with identifying a site for the JCC in the wake of Portland State's expansion, "We had to look for another location. I was charged with the responsibility of finding a proper location. That's the reason we ended up where we're at. There's ten acres that were available. And there was a partnership, one of the partners were Jewish. And we were able to buy that ten acres and then we negotiated with the state for the sale of our building."[15] Promotional material for the JCC touted many aspects of the new building, but its failure to highlight the location as an asset is evidence that the cluster emerging in Southwest Portland was not at the forefront of the planners' minds.[16] The struggle over the location of Ahavai Sholom (prior to its decision to merge with Neveh Zedek) was particularly bitter, with substantial contingents in favor of building on the Eastside or in a more central, downtown location. Ultimately, it would take two different building committees, two years of debate, and two congregational votes to approve the Peaceful Lane site.[17]

The outpouring of nostalgia for the Old South Portland neighborhood makes clear that these institutional moves to more suburban, southwest locations were generally seen as a *loss* of the historic, concentrated community.[18] Although the new *buildings* were proudly touted, the new *locations* were described in the context of residential dispersal rather than as the beginning of new Jewish neighborhoods. The JCC was framed not only in terms of the shiny new facilities, but also as part of an effort to grapple with the scattering of the Jewish population, a shift seen as a threat to traditional community. Across America, Jewish movement to the suburbs signaled professional and

Ahavath Achim sitting alone amid the rubble left by Urban Renewal (above);
the effort to move the building in 1962 resulted in its destruction (opposite).
All courtesy OJMCHE

residential acceptance into mainstream, middle-class life that, while welcome, had the potential to erode Jewish identity. As historian Edward Shapiro explains,

> The problems of postwar American Jewry were primarily the problems of suburbia. The diffusion of Jewish population into the suburbs and exurbs diluted Jewish identity. In the compacted Jewish neighborhoods of the cities, Jewish identity was absorbed through osmosis. In suburbia, it had to be nurtured. Jewish suburbanites lived in localities where, in contrast to the city, most of the people were not Jews, the local store did not sell Jewish newspapers, there were no kosher butchers, synagogues were not numerous and corned beef sandwiches were not readily available.[19]

In addition to the broad challenges of suburbanization and assimilation facing Jews nationwide, Portland Jewry also had to contend with discouraging demographic trends. The year that the new JCC opened, the Jewish Welfare Federation of Portland (Federation)[20] conducted a survey designed to scientifically study the community. The 1971 study reported that 7,750 Jews lived in the Portland metropolitan area, down from the 7,832 in 1957; in contrast, the general population of the area grew over 20 percent just between 1960 and 1970. In fact, since World War II, Jewish population growth in Oregon generally and in Portland specifically had been "much slower than the general population."[21] Lack of growth was not the only cause for anxiety. Most notable among the concerns raised by the 1971 survey was the finding that young Jewish adults tended to migrate out of the area: although there were plenty of teenagers, "something happens at age twenty . . . and people start leaving."[22] This pattern contributed to the community's low fertility rate, creating anxiety about future growth. Along with worries about the numbers, the report noted that the "basis of identity in Jewish religious ritual is rapidly eroding"[23] (emphasis in original).

The report's conclusion sounded an alarm. There were, it emphasized, "at least four" "possible sources of danger or threat to the community, its integrity and vitality." First among these was demographic: "If institutional size and strength, economic and moral, do depend upon a certain population base, there is cause for concern," due to the low fertility rate and the tendency of young adults to leave town. Second, the report expressed worry over the geographic dispersal of the community across the metropolitan area, and raised a question about the extent to which "a Jewish milieu located in distinctive neighborhoods with their visible Jewish enterprises is important as a factor in preserving the integrity of the community." Third, the authors noted the clear lack of knowledge of or interest in Jewish history and culture, and warned that this trend of disinterest suggested that "a key resource for unity and identity is disappearing." The report concluded, "In both the attitudinal and behavioral categories of evaluating the religious practice in terms of traditional standards, there is little possibility of avoiding the conclusion that religion as a force is weakening among Portland's Jews, as it is among other populations in contemporary America."[24] The closing admonition follows:

> This lack of a common core of religious belief and identity will not necessarily lead to the immediate demise of the Portland Jewish Community. There is enough evidence that the momentum of the past alone will carry the community into the immediate future. But if this is a condition of "coasting" on the accumulated "cultural capital" of the past, without the adequate program of renewal to bolster it, there can be no guarantee of survival.[25]

Although initiated well before the publication of the study, the ambitious building projects of the 1960s and early 1970s—those in Southwest Portland, as well as the new facilities for congregations in other areas of the city—spoke to the same concerns about engagement and attempted to provide the called-for "program of renewal." These projects also suggested an optimism unwarranted by the report. If the community was losing its base of young adults and had not seen any real growth since the early decades of the century, wasn't there a danger that these building projects were unrealistic? If the population had not grown in decades, and if those remaining were increasingly scattered and disinclined to affiliate, then who would populate the new sanctuaries, classrooms, and gymnasiums?

Yet the optimism inherent in the building projects was, ultimately, justified. When the new facilities were built, Jews *did* come. After a period of stagnation in the 1950s and 1960s, Oregon's Jewish population (still overwhelmingly concentrated in Portland) began to grow in the 1970s at a rate that matched statewide growth. In subsequent decades, Jewish population accelerated further, exceeding the general rate of growth in the state. Not only would the ample buildings erected in the 1960s and 1970s fill, they would have to be expanded to accommodate growing memberships and would be joined by an array of new organizations catering to the growing numbers of Jewish Oregonians.

Who were these new Jewish Oregonians, and how did their arrival impact the existing community? As the Jewish population increased, how did its geography and institutions change? This chapter traces the demographic and geographic evolution of the Jewish community against the backdrop of the movement triggered by urban renewal, and places it within the larger context of Oregon's quickly evolving demographic, cultural, and political landscape. With a focus on Portland, it will lay the groundwork for the examination, continued in subsequent chapters, of the ways population shifts and a changing zeitgeist affected Jewish institutions, and of how the influx of self-selected newcomers shaped the innovative and creative new groups in the Jewish community and beyond. After decades of population stability and institutional consolidation in the immediate postwar decades, Oregon Jewry became increasingly dynamic in ways that reflected both the energy of a growing population and the ethos of its Pacific Northwest setting as it transitioned into the twenty-first century.

1950s–1960s: Population Stability and the Challenges of Urban Renewal

During Oregon's early years of settlement, Jewish individuals—and in some cases small Jewish communities—could be found in the far-flung corners of the state. Even isolated towns such as Jacksonville and Baker had enough Jews to mark occasions together and think of themselves as a community (although still lacking a formally organized synagogue). By the early twentieth century, however, most of the state's small-town Jews had either intermarried and assimilated, or moved to Portland.[26] In contrast to other parts of the country, where newly arriving East European immigrants revitalized small-town Jewish life, few such immigrants came to Oregon's smaller towns. By the mid-twentieth century, with a few exceptions in the Willamette Valley, there was little Jewish communal life outside of the Rose City (Portland's nickname). Although Baker had a small Jewish community in the nineteenth century, when Robert Neuberger was growing up there in the 1950s and 1960s, his was the only Jewish family in the area with children. When it came time for his bar mitzvah, in 1966,

> We had come to Corvallis . . . to pick up my older sister, Pat [from Oregon State University]. . . . So my father just, on the way back, just pulled in at the Shaarie Torah Synagogue [in Portland] right around, you know, *minyan* time and went in and made arrangements. And when he came out, I was told that I would be coming back in a week and was going to be living with so and so. . . . And so I spent one three-week session and another two-week session with a family on Everett, NW Everett, between 21st and 22nd.[27]

Following this training, Neuberger celebrated his bar mitzvah at Shaarie Torah.

Jacksonville in Southern Oregon was home to one of Oregon's first Jewish communities. During the mining boom of the 1850s, Jewish businesses had a substantial presence, lining the town's main street.[28] Jacksonville was also the site of the first Jewish religious service in Oregon, although no synagogue was established. Yet, by the 1870s, the mining boom had passed and only a few merchants remained; families either relocated or assimilated into the general population. North of Jacksonville, a brief experiment in agrarian communal settlement brought several dozen Russian Jewish idealists to Douglas County to settle New Odessa in the early 1880s.[29] After that community's dissolution in 1885, although scattered Jewish individuals or families could be found in various Southern Oregon towns, there was no community as such for nearly a century. Not until the 1970s and 1980s did small Jewish communities reemerge in Ashland, Medford, and other towns in the area.

The north coast town of Astoria, which, like Jacksonville, had a substantial core of Jewish merchants early in its history, was somewhat anomalous, experiencing a small influx of East European Jews at the turn of the century, and growing again at midcentury, likely due to the expansion of military bases nearby. A congregation functioned there beginning in 1940 and lasted until 1963. During much of the period, when pharmacist Harry Steinbock served four terms (starting in 1959) as Astoria's third Jewish mayor, there was no organized Jewish communal life. Even in Salem, which became home to the only purpose-built synagogue outside of Portland in 1948, the community was too small to support even a part-time rabbi until the late 1980s. Instead, Salem's Temple Beth Sholom hosted occasional visiting clergy, mostly from Portland, for life cycle events and major holidays.

In Portland, where well over 90 percent of the state's Jews lived at midcentury, the community had experienced no real growth in several decades. In 1953, Rabbi Joshua Stampfer, hoping to explore "the frontier of Jewish life in America,"[30] accepted the call to assume the pulpit at congregation Ahavai Sholom (eight years before its merger with Neveh Zedek). In 1960, Rabbis Emanuel Rose and Yonah Geller took their positions in Portland congregations Beth Israel and Shaarie Torah, respectively. The three young rabbis found in the Rose City a community that was "insular," with a population that had been virtually "stagnant" for decades. The community reflected the larger city, which, according to Rabbi Rose, had scarcely any new buildings downtown. Furthermore, it was provincial, particularly for the Roses, who had relocated from New York City and experienced "culture shock." When Rabbi Rose's wife, Lorraine (Wilson) Rose, went out on her first day in Portland to have a cappuccino, she discovered that nothing was available in Portland other than "regular coffee."[31] Although the Stampfers, Roses, and Gellers could not have anticipated it at the time, their arrival would mark the beginning of the end of a long period of torpor in Portland's Jewish community.

The three rabbis worked, each within the stream of a different movement, to modernize congregations described by Rose as "stodgy" and "old fashioned," and by Stampfer as "static." Geller had been asked by Yeshiva University to consider moving to Portland because Shaarie Torah, the Orthodox congregation, was "going under" and "needed real leadership."[32] Arriving just as the challenges of residential dispersal, urban renewal, and congregational angst were challenging the community, the three determined to reverse earlier discord by working together on common issues through the Oregon Board

Rabbi Yonah Geller of Shaarie Torah soon after his arrival in Portland. Like his colleagues Rabbi Joshua Stampfer (Neveh Shalom) and Rabbi Emanuel Rose (Beth Israel), Geller would serve his congregation until the turn of the twenty-first century. Courtesy OJMCHE

of Rabbis. By the time they completed their long tenures as Portland's "three rabbis" in the early twenty-first century, the city and its Jewish community had transitioned from stodginess to innovation. Portland—and Oregon— would offer a menu of Jewish organizational and lifestyle options in the early twenty-first century that rivaled its selection of coffee houses.

A series of three studies provides an opportunity to examine Portland Jewry during the 1950s and 1960s. Prior to the 1971 census, the Portland Jewish Welfare Federation had conducted a population study in 1957. Like Jewish community surveys from other parts of the country, both Federation studies were based on lists of Jews who were affiliated with synagogues, the JCC, or who had contributed to community fundraising campaigns.[33] Between these two studies, Oregon State University student Jack Segal completed a 1965 master's thesis titled "The Jews of Portland, Oregon: Their Religious Practices and Beliefs." Segal conducted detailed interviews with 262 individuals who were members of synagogues.[34]

The 1957 Jewish community census is a useful baseline for examining postwar demographic trends. Conducted via telephone interviews over sixteen evenings, the study found that over a ten-year period, the Jewish population had increased by just under 10 percent, from 7,128 to 7,832 individuals. Oregon had grown by 30 percent in the same period, so this increase was "much slower than [that of] the general population." The Jewish share in the state's population was declining. The survey found evidence of communal stability, not only in size, but also in composition. With the exception of a relatively small number of wartime and postwar refugees, the vast majority of the foreign born—roughly a quarter of the Jewish population—were elderly Jews who had arrived in Portland early in the century, and had been among the East European and eastern Mediterranean (Sephardic) immigrants residing in South Portland. Nearly half of the community was composed of their children and the descendants of earlier Jewish settlers; native Oregonians made up 47 percent of the population. Only about a quarter of the Jewish population were newcomers from elsewhere in the United States—a relatively small proportion given the city's rapid growth during the war years.[35] As in the prewar period, the 1957 census found that much of the community—nearly half—was self-employed, compared to only 12 percent of the total labor force of Portland. Although this too continued a pattern established in the first half of the century, the self-employed were now as likely to be professionals as merchants. The community remained largely endogamous: only 6 percent of couples included a non-Jewish partner, a rate of intermarriage slightly below that of Jews nationally.[36]

Demographic stagnation continued through the 1960s, with the total number of Jews counted in 1971 slightly lower than in 1957.[37] Family structure reinforced a sense of steadiness: the population was overwhelmingly married, with an intermarriage rate of only 5 percent in 1971.[38] Seniors were overrepresented in comparison to Jewish communities in other cities.[39] Only among young adults was there more movement, with many native-born twenty-somethings leaving the state, only to be replaced by newcomers from elsewhere.[40]

Both the 1965 master's thesis and the 1971 census asked detailed questions about observance and religious attitudes. Responses suggest low levels of ritual observance. For example, in the 1965 study, even among respondents who self-identified as Orthodox, fewer than 40 percent observed *kashrut* (Jewish dietary laws) in the home.[41] Rates of observance of dietary laws were considerably lower among Portland Jews than among those in Washington, DC, and Milwaukee, Wisconsin, two similarly sized communities. For example, 62 percent of Orthodox in Milwaukee and 66 percent in Washington, DC, had separate sets of dishes for meat and dairy, in comparison to just under 40 percent of Portland's Orthodox. Whereas over a third of Milwaukee's Orthodox kept kosher outside of their homes, only a quarter of Portland's Orthodox did so.[42]

Indeed, Portland seemed to present an exaggerated picture of precisely those trends that most concerned national and local Jewish leaders worried about the impact of assimilation and the long-term viability of the Jewish community in the United States. A large percentage of the Portland Jewish community professed pride in identity, asserted the value of tradition, and participated in family-centered, infrequent rituals, but they were not particularly knowledgeable about Jewish heritage nor inclined to observe more demanding daily and holiday practices. In the 1965 study, nearly 98 percent of all respondents across denominations attended a Seder, yet over 20 percent of the Orthodox—and well over 50 percent of the Reform—brought bread products into their homes on Passover.[43] Likewise, in the 1971 survey, although 80 percent of respondents stated that traditional values and practices were very or moderately important, only 8 percent reported buying kosher meat and 24 percent admitted serving bacon or ham "more or less regularly." Even among those who identified as Orthodox, 29 percent reported that they occasionally served bacon or ham in their homes.[44]

Not surprisingly, the younger generation was less observant than their parents: "Both husbands and wives report[ed] that their parents were more observant of traditional Jewish practices than they themselves currently are."[45] As in national surveys, both the 1965 and 1971 studies demonstrated that Portland Jews who identified as Orthodox tended to be older—a factor that helps to account for the dwindling memberships of traditional congregations like Linath Hazedek and the sole Eastside synagogue, Tifereth Israel, as members of that generation passed away. Yet the 1971 study also suggested that generational differences may have been exacerbated by the coming and going of young adults, with natives leaving and migrants from elsewhere arriving. As the study's authors explained, there were "almost as many migrants as natives of Portland in the 25–44 age group," and, among those in this group over age thirty, "the overwhelming majority has moved here from somewhere else."[46] Among these young adults, only about 65 percent believed that belonging to a congregation was very or moderately important, compared to 84 percent of the over 65 group.[47]

Unlike their predecessors in earlier decades, young adults arriving in the 1960s and early 1970s were doing little to shore up traditional congregations. In the past, whether early in the century or immediately after World War II, new arrivals had been a conservative force. In the 1910s and 1920s, waves of migrants, Sephardim coming directly from the eastern Mediterranean and East European immigrants arriving after sojourns elsewhere in the United States, tended to bolster—or found—the more traditional (Orthodox or Conservative) congregations. Shaarie Torah, the first Orthodox congregation in Portland, formed when traditionally oriented Russian immigrants split from the more progressive Neveh Zedek in 1902. The two smaller Orthodox congregations, Linath Hazedek and Kesser Israel, were also founded by newcomers, in 1914 and 1916, respectively. After World War II, the arrival of German refugees had a similar conservative influence. According to poet and historian Gary Miranda, the trend at Ahavai Sholom had been toward liberalism reminiscent of that at the historic Reform congregation, Beth Israel, but with the arrival of the wartime refugees, the newcomers became "the dominant element in the Sabbath morning service, both in numbers and in influence over the manner in which it was conducted."[48] In both the early and midcentury cases, the fact that many of the migrants came to Portland due to family or community ties tended to reinforce religious institutions. Richard Matza, a future leader of the Sephardic congregation Ahavath Achim, was the son of wartime immigrants. His mother, Julia Beneviste, a native of Rhodes, was brought to Portland in 1939 by her sister and brother-in-law. In Portland, she met Aaron Matza, then serving in the U.S. Army, at a dance at the Jewish Community Center. Although Richard Matza describes his father as relatively secular and without a strong Jewish education, his aunt and uncle lived next door and were pillars of the Ahavath Achim community. It was through the sponsoring aunt and uncle that a strong tie to the congregation, and a strong tradition of leadership, was cultivated in the younger generation.[49]

The arrival of the war refugees, even when they lacked familial connections, was often facilitated by a local Jewish group, such as the Oregon Émigré Committee (OEC), or later, the Service for New Americans (a constituent agency of the Jewish Welfare Federation). In the early 1950s, the OEC received annual allocations just over $20,000, making it second only to the Jewish Educational Association among the Federation's constituent agencies.[50] The OEC assisted immigrant Jews in finding housing, employment, and social services, and encouraged newcomers to get involved in communal organizations. In an era when sponsorship was crucial to potential immigrants hoping to secure visas, the OEC helped to arrange local sponsors for desperate would-be immigrants. For example, Karl Bettman was able to leave Germany just before the war, when Anselm Boskowitz, chair of the OEC, arranged for him to take a "fictitious job as a cleric" at Shaarie Torah, enabling him to get a visa as a clergyman. Bettman subsequently became sexton at Ahavai Sholom, and a "dominant force" in shifting the congregation "toward a more traditional, European tone."[51] After the war, Bettman played a key role in the Portland Friendship Club, a mutual support, social, and cultural group for German Jewish émigrés, active into the 1970s.[52] Similarly, when Holocaust survivors Lydia "Libby" (Lax) and Bernard "Barry" Brown arrived in Portland in 1951, the Service for New Americans assisted them with housing, employment, and medical care. "The Service for New Americans gave us twenty-five dollars a week and paid the rent for us until Barry found work," Libby Brown recalled in a 1975 oral history, "Without them we couldn't have made it."[53] The Browns became active in the Orthodox congregation Kesser Israel and were among the founders of Portland's first Jewish day school, the Hillel Academy. Joy and Joe Alkalay, also Holocaust survivors, were similarly aided by the Service for New Americans, living briefly in an apartment kept by the service for that purpose. Both of them were assisted in finding work at Jewish-owned firms within the community.[54]

In contrast to these refugees and survivors arriving in the 1940s and 1950s, the young adults coming to Oregon in the 1950s, 1960s, and beyond arrived independently.[55] Rather than selecting Portland because of family ties or communal sponsorship, the overwhelming majority of these young adult newcomers were college-educated American-born Jews, drawn to Oregon by professional opportunities. Working in the office of Congregation Beth Israel, Joy (Levi) Alkalay was well positioned to observe this influx of newcomers.

Interviewed in 1981, she explained that the new, younger members of Beth Israel who had arrived over the previous decade were "not children of older congregants," but "children who have moved here from California or New York or from the East Coast. . . . A lot of younger people have come to Oregon in search of whatever: work, new horizons. Young professionals, young lawyers, lots of young people have come."[56] Those among them who opted to affiliate, like other American Jews of their generation, were far more likely to choose the Conservative or Reform congregation than an Orthodox one.

Beyond Portland, a few of these young professionals ventured into communities such as Salem, the state's capital, or Eugene, home of the University of Oregon. Leon Gabinet, a University of Chicago–trained lawyer, arrived in 1953 to serve a clerkship at the Supreme Court; and Brooklyn native Martin Acker, a University of Chicago and New York University–trained counselor, was recruited by the University of Oregon in 1961, after a stint at Stanford. Acker connected to the small Eugene Jewish community mostly through secular activities, rather than through the local synagogue. "The people involved with me in the civil rights movement, the faculty people involved with me, were Jewish for the most part," he recalled.[57] Gabinet, in contrast, found life in Salem—where there was a synagogue but not a rabbi—too isolating. The promise of a more extensive Jewish cultural and social network drew him to relocate from Salem to Portland.[58]

Even among those who were not observant, or who considered themselves more cultural/secular than religious Jews, community connections were a priority, even a necessity, because of professional and social exclusions in the 1950s and 1960s. Exclusions were often first experienced in high school, where Jewish teens found fraternities and sororities closed to them. In response, they established their own clubs and youth groups. As Renee (Rosenberg) Holzman explained,

> I would say that my academic life was obviously at Grant High School. But my social life was more with the Jewish community. At that time we were really excluded from even the service clubs. I remember speaking to my mother about it and she said, "Renee, it's their loss, not yours." She said absolutely the right thing. Those of us who grew up in the "alternate universe" as I called it, learned a lot about leadership. We really had the opportunity to do the same kinds of things they were doing in the social clubs at Grant High School that we were excluded from. On certain days, the girls at Grant wore their little sorority pins or their little uniforms or whatever, and there is no question that the Jewish kids felt very excluded.[59]

Exclusions were just as keenly felt by adults. In an era when many social clubs and private professional firms were closed to Jews, communal organizations and clubs provided the networks critical to employment. In Portland, where prominent social clubs refused to admit Jews until the late 1950s

(Multnomah Athletic Club), 1960s (University Club and Arlington Club), and even the early 1970s (Waverly Country Club),[60] access to athletic facilities— and, in the case of professionals, country club golf courses and dining rooms— necessitated membership in the JCC or the Tualatin Country Club, a Jewish club founded in response to the exclusions at the other country clubs. Oral histories of young professionals arriving in the state in the postwar period provide ample evidence of the importance of Jewish social and professional connections, even among those disinterested in religion. Henry Blauer, whose religious and judgmental grandfather had turned Henry's father very much against religion, felt a social/cultural need to get involved in the Jewish community when he moved from New York to Oregon. In New York, he recalled, "you didn't have to do anything to be Jewish; everybody was Jewish." Yet, "when I came to Portland the first thing that happened was that my cousin Meyer said to me, 'You have got to join the Jewish Community Center.'" Blauer quickly found that in the relatively small Portland Jewish community, his skills as an accountant were much in demand:

> The Jewish community really needed somebody with the kinds of skills that an accountant has. Serving on one board, I would be serving with somebody who also served on another board, and they would say, "Hey we need you." All of the boards have term limits so people get rotated off. When Frank Eiseman was rotated off the Temple Board, I was on the Temple Board and so on. For the first time, then, I really became Jewish. . . . Living in New York the emphasis had been on Americanization. "Become an American." In Portland it was taken for granted that you were an American and having served in the [military] Service, I didn't have to prove anything anymore. Contributing to the welfare of the Jewish community became very important.[61]

Involvement in Federation, the congregations, B'nai B'rith, and other Jewish organizations provided men like Blauer opportunities to give meaningful service, socialize, and build professional networks. Jewish networks enabled Blauer to find work with Ben Sussman who, along with Jack Olds, was one of the first Jewish CPAs in Oregon—"between them, they had most of the Jewish business, especially in retail and wholesale."[62]

The recruitment and grooming of new leaders became institutionalized by the mid-1960s. Federation leaders (lay and professional) such as Hal Saltzman and Cliff Josephson encouraged young professionals, including lawyer Arden Shenker, to become involved. Shenker, a Portland native who had returned to the city in 1962 after completing Yale Law School, recalled being one of thirty-five young men invited to a meeting by Saltzman and Josephson, aimed at instituting a leadership development program. Shenker quickly stepped up, not only soliciting in the annual campaign, but also joining local and national boards of organizations including the Council of Jewish Federations, the United Jewish Appeal, and others.[63]

The continued—and increasing—responsibilities of organizational life put a strain on those willing to serve on boards and committees. With a stable population well into the 1970s, the founding of a number of Jewish civic and social groups outside of the synagogues, and the increasing need for the Federation to raise funds to support projects like the new JCC and to meet the needs of Jews worldwide, demand for board service could be heavy. As Leonard Goldberg, who served as board president of both the Jewish Family and Child Services (JFCS) and the Federation recalled, "There was a big problem in getting people to serve on the boards. What happened was that people like me and Alvin Rackner and Arden [Shenker] and Jack Schwartz and others belonged to more than one board at one time. You would walk into a room and say, 'Which board are we today?' It's true."[64] Rabbi Emanuel Rose addressed this issue in a 1981 interview, explaining, "I think you end up seeing the same people involved in the same things all the time and part of it is due to the fact that we don't have enough troops out there, out of which the new leadership can emerge, because there is so much going on all the time. . . . It's to a point of wearing people out . . . and I must ascribe that to the smallness of our community."[65]

Although the pursuit of professional ties pushed newcomers in the 1950s and early 1960s toward the organized Jewish community, their residential choices often pulled in the opposite direction. At that time, despite the fact that the JCC and nearly all the congregations were still located in the historic South Portland neighborhood, as they started new families, neither native Oregonians nor newcomers chose to settle there. Even before the 1958 advent of urban renewal, South Portland was increasingly seen as blighted. Many families had relocated to more prosperous areas, like the still affordable Eastside neighborhoods that had begun attracting successful Jewish businessmen decades earlier.[66] Sura Rubenstein, a self-proclaimed member of the "last generation of Jewish kids to be raised in Old South Portland . . . when it was still a Jewish community, or, at least, the remnants of one," recalled that, in the 1950s, "families already had begun to move out and 'up' to other, more affluent/more Americanized neighborhoods."[67] William "Bill" Gordon, a University of Chicago graduate with experience in Jewish social services in the South and Midwest, was recruited in 1953 to head programming at the JCC. At the time, he recalled, many elderly people still lived in South Portland, but their grown children's families tended to reside in Northeast, often in the Irvington District, and "to a lesser extent" the Southeast. Most Jewish teens attended Grant and Cleveland high schools on the Eastside. Lila Goodman recalled that there was only a "remnant" of the Jewish community at Lincoln High in South Portland in the 1950s, and "although it had a fairly sizeable Jewish population, it wasn't the eye of the thing. That was at Grant. If you were Jewish and you wanted to be in the Jewish mix, you had to go to Grant."

Her contact with many of her Jewish peers, who became "our friends for life," took place at the JCC.[68]

After the construction of Neveh Shalom and the relocation of the JCC and the Portland Hebrew School to Southwest Portland, increasing numbers of families opted to live in that area. By the time he was interviewed in the mid-1970s, Gordon noted the change: "As far as the younger families, the vast majority live on this [the West] side," with "the largest concentration of Jewish kids," at Wilson, Sunset, and Beaverton high schools, and, "to a much lesser extent, Lincoln."[69] But for the first Jewish families who had moved decades earlier to outer southwest Portland neighborhoods such as Raleigh Hills, it would have been difficult to imagine that the area would eventually become a Jewish center. When Shirley (Georges) Gittlesohn grew up there in the 1930s, it "was not Raleigh Hills . . . it was Raleigh. It was the country." Her family raised chickens and cows, and she and her siblings met other Jewish children mostly at Sunday school and the JCC.[70] In the early 1950s, however, her father subdivided his land, creating plots for each of his (now adult) children and their families, and also offering others to friends. As Ernie Bonyhadi recalled,

> When I got out of law school, Tom Georges, Ossie's and Shirley's father, called us and said, "I am subdividing my 30 acres in Raleigh Hills and would like you to buy one of the lots? They are all half an acre. All my kids are going to get one and I want you and Ilo to go out there and have kids." So far only Tommy, his oldest son, was out there. So we bought a lot, half an acre for $1800 bucks. And we built a house there in 1953. Bill and Shirley [Gittlesohn] built their house two houses away in 1954. Ossie [Georges] built a house six months before we built ours. So we were out there, in an area where Maurine Neuberger used to call "Hadassah Acres."[71]

The 1957 survey suggested the degree to which the community had already begun dispersing. Dividing the city only into Northeast, North, Northwest, Southwest, and Southeast, this study did not clearly distinguish between the historic South Portland neighborhood (also, technically, in Southwest Portland) and areas farther southwest such as Raleigh Hills. Even so broadly defined, the Southwest was home to just under a third (32 percent) of the metropolitan Jewish population. Interestingly, more Jews resided in Northeast Portland (36 percent) and another nearly 20 percent in Southeast—putting the majority of the community on the Eastside (55 percent), despite its dearth of Jewish institutions. Even at Shaarie Torah, originally an Orthodox congregation which, in the postwar era, gradually transitioned to calling itself "traditional," a 1957 roster of officers and trustees shows that many more members of the board of directors lived in Northeast Portland than in the Westside neighborhood that had long been home to the congregation. Only

Table 1: Residential Distribution

	Southwest (including suburbs)	Northwest	Southeast	Near Northeast/ North	Far Eastside & Clackamas, Clark Cos., WA/Other
1957 Survey	2534 (32%)	651 (8%)	1503 (19%)	2880 (36%)	318 (4%)
1960–1 Hebrew School families	62 (34%)	7 (4%)	49 (27%)	57 (31%)	6 (3%)
1971 JWF Survey*	49%	5%	10%	14%	23%

*The 1971 survey used a sampling method to ensure that the geographic spread of those surveyed was representative of the known Jewish community. To determine geographic sampling proportions, they used the zip codes of households known either by virtue of congregational or JCC membership, or Federation donations, not the actual count—therefore, only the percentages appear here, and these figures were predetermined based on a population of Federation donors, favoring areas where Jews were more likely to affiliate.

two members lived in the more upscale Northwest neighborhood to which it would move less than a decade later.[72] This is particularly striking in an Orthodox/traditional congregation, where walking to synagogue on holidays and the Sabbath would, presumably, be the norm.

A Portland Hebrew School roster from 1960–1961 confirms the pattern of residential dispersion within the city. The 226 enrolled children represented 180 families from across denominational boundaries, with the majority of families affiliated with either Ahavai Sholom (76) or Beth Israel (53), and smaller numbers coming from Shaarie Torah (17), Tifereth Israel (3), and Neveh Zedek (13). Nineteen of the families were not affiliated with any synagogue. Like the 1957 survey, the roster suggests considerable residential scattering, with a larger number of families living on the east than west side. Those students whose families did reside in Southwest Portland in 1960–1961 were clustered in the area that would become home to Neveh Shalom and the JCC.

The strong presence of families from the Eastside helps to explain the bitter fights at both Neveh Shalom and Ahavath Achim over the location of facilities. Prior to the 1961 merger with Ahavai Sholom, Neveh Zedek went through a controversial, and ultimately fruitless, discussion over building on the Eastside. After the merger, the site selection process that ultimately landed them on Peaceful Lane was "anything but peaceful," as competing factions advocated for Eastside and downtown sites, rather than the Southwest location that was eventually chosen.[73] At Ahavath Achim, five years after first receiving notice from the city, the congregation continued to debate prospective sites, with several locations on the Eastside still on the table.

It was only as these separate decisions were made to relocate institutions on the Westside that the community's geographic center shifted in that direction. Although only a third of the community lived in Southwest in the early 1960s, by 1971, nearly half of the community resided there. The trend would be reinforced over the next several decades by the developing institutional clusters as Southwest Portland became the clear focal point of the metropolitan Jewish community, centered on the JCC. Yet shiny new buildings alone did not cement community. As the number of first generation immigrants shrank, and the number of well educated, American-born professionals ballooned, needs evolved. To stay viable, institutions would need to be responsive to the changing population.[74]

Programming for a New Generation

Following the 1971 survey, the Federation established a series of task forces to address community needs and concerns about engagement. Various subgroups dealt with issues of aging, the changing Jewish family, resources, the relationship between congregations and the Federation, and education. The strategies developed through this process would set the course for communal development in the coming decades. The new JCC was central to those plans. Motivated by the 1971 study's conclusion that there was little "knowledge or interest in Jewish history and culture," in the community, and that this deficit could pose severe consequences for community survival, the Federation's Task Force on the Transmission of Jewish Heritage began meeting in the mid-1970s. In January 1977, the Task Force brought Jacob Fried, a Portland State University professor of cultural anthropology who had worked on the 1971 study, to "speak on the methods by which cultures transmit their heritage." Fried emphasized the need to "create environments where networks of Jews are preserved and formed."[75] Morris Engleson, who participated in these meetings and served as chair of the Bureau of Jewish Education planning committee, wrote (apparently in preparation for a presentation to the Federation),

> The concept of the center involves both plant and programs. We envisage an area where various activities, of a Jewish nature, are available to the Jewish family. This could include such diverse aspects as a kosher restaurant or a formal school. We encourage a diversity of programs to serve those of differing philosophical and religious persuasion as well as different types of families. The common denominator in all of this is physical proximity among the housing of the programs, Jewish content of the programs, and emphasis on the family. Thus, a full time Jewish day school would not only educate the children but would recognize that parents also participate in classroom instruction. . . .We further recommend that the growth of a Jewish neighborhood around the JCC be encouraged. We

believe that the best way to transmit our heritage is for Jews to mix with, live among, and learn from other Jews in the normal environment of daily living.[76]

The task force concluded that "establishing Jewish neighborhoods would be extremely important in terms of providing constant reinforcement of Jewish behaviors. Isolation may be the most important barrier against transmitting Jewish heritage."[77]

Education was also seen as critical to the community's future, and centralized, quality educational offerings were perceived as a residential draw that would aid in fostering the growth of a "Jewish neighborhood." Given the particular concern about newly arriving young families and future generations, it is not surprising that one outcome of discussions in the early 1970s was a series of evolving task forces and committees focusing on Jewish education. A Bureau of Jewish Education began meeting in May 1973, following the recommendation of an ad hoc committee chaired by Dr. Victor Menashe of the Federation's Education Committee. The bureau included representatives of the Federation, the JCC, the Jewish Education Association (JEA), and Hillel Academy (the day school housed at Shaarie Torah). Their goals included coordination of planning for Jewish education for the entire community (with an eye toward developing comprehensive programming for all ages), improving standards, and expanding the number of children getting "intensive Jewish education."[78] In September 1973, the group issued a position paper, identifying "key problems" in Portland, including the large number of Jewish children not receiving any Jewish education or attending only once a week, the small number registered in Hebrew school, and the frequent practice of ending Jewish education after bar mitzvah. The paper lamented that only a "small saving remnant" start study of Hebrew early enough and continue through high school. After calculating the time spent by the typical student in Hebrew school, it was concluded that "the best program, taught by the best available teachers, can hardly make a dent in the armor of Am-Ha'aratzut (ignorance)."[79] The group emphasized the need to work with the three major synagogues, each of which ran its own Sunday school, as well as addressing the possible consolidation of the afternoon community Hebrew school run by the JEA and the Hillel day school.[80]

Over the next several years, the group strove to coordinate community education. One key difficulty lay in the fact that Hillel Academy was a sectarian school—affiliated with the Orthodox movement—while the Portland Hebrew School had always operated as a community-wide organization. A decade earlier, it took months of discussion before Hillel Academy was approved as a Federation agency; and as the new JCC took shape in 1971, there was no willingness to build classrooms for Hillel as part of that facility.[81] Coordination was also challenged by turf issues between the Federation and the congregations, each of which asserted autonomy in running its own school. The congregations, united in a new organization called SCORE (Synagogue Council on Religious Education), ultimately came to an agreement with the Federation's Bureau of Jewish Education to form yet another organization, the Council of Jewish Education, with representation from both congregations and communal educational institutions.[82] By April 1975, a plan to coordinate JEA afternoon Hebrew school and Hillel day school was drafted, specifying that the "coordinated" facility share a building, "preferably on the grounds of the Jewish Community Center," as well as share staff and administration. By 1977, a full plan for a "merger" of the two had been articulated, although each school's existing ideology would be maintained. Hillel continued to be traditional in focus while the Portland Hebrew School remained "acceptable to the major religious movements in Jewish life," providing the Hebrew component for each of the separate synagogue's education programs.[83] Still, the process stalled, complicated by administrative and financing challenges; in addition, there was increasing interest in a more broadly defined, nondenominational day school. A Federation planning group, setting the community agenda for 1977–1980, listed a Jewish Day School as one of the top five priorities.[84] A feasibility study in 1984 demonstrated "affirmative interest in the development of a communal education facility on the grounds adjacent to the Jewish community center . . . as well as for an afternoon Hebrew school, a high school program and Jewish Adult Studies." Soon after, the Federation's executive committee endorsed a plan for a reorganized day school "to be available and open to all branches of Judaism and the non-affiliates within the community" and a plan emerged for construction of a new educational complex at the Mittleman Jewish Community Center for such a school.[85] The Portland Jewish Academy finally opened in a newly constructed wing of the MJCC in 1987.

Jewish camping provided yet another venue for the cultivation of identity. B'nai B'rith Camp (known as BB Camp) was founded by Portland's B'nai B'rith Lodge earlier in the century as a philanthropic effort, providing opportunities for South Portland's Jewish and non-Jewish children. Modeled on YMCA summer camps, with a focus on athletics, health, and moral development, the camp has operated since 1928 at a Devil's Lake site near the coast, donated by Julius Meier. Critical support for camp operations came from a long-running, annual "Men's Camp" that provided an opportunity for men (many of them former campers) to return to camp for an immersive experience, bond with one another, and pledge support for camp facilities and camp scholarships for disadvantaged children.[86]

In the 1960s and 1970s, as part of the effort to respond to concerns about communal drift, camping opportunities expanded. Rabbi Stampfer, who himself had found Jewish summer camp a life-changing experience, believed that camping could provide the "joyous experience" at the heart of the "most effective education" for children. However, he realized that Oregon's BB Camp was not an option for his children, because it was not kosher; this led him to dedicate himself to establishing a "new Jewish educational camp," modeled on the Brandeis Camp, which he had attended. Working together with a Conservative rabbi from Seattle, Rabbi Stampfer founded Camp Solomon Schechter in 1955 as a one-week camp. Gradually expanding the camping season over the course of several years at various temporary locations, Camp Solomon Schechter grew to a full summer camp. In 1968, it moved to a newly purchased site in Tumwater, Washington. Rabbi and Goldie (Goncher) Stampfer personally ran the camp for twenty-five years.[87]

Although some plans—particularly those in the area of Jewish education—took decades to evolve, the broader strategy of reinvigorating Jewish life using the JCC as a "living room" anchoring a physical community took root more quickly. In addition to the Portland Hebrew School and, eventually, the Portland Jewish Academy, a preschool, and an expanded menu of summer day camps became central programs at the JCC. As early as 1977, MJCC director Bill Gordon observed, "Many families deliberately look for housing because they want to be close to the Center and this is particularly true of young families and particularly true of people moving into the area. They start looking for a place, the fact that we are located where we are is a reason for their wanting to move close by."[88] Longtime Northeast resident Irene Balk, interviewed in 1981, agreed: "Well let's face it, the Jewish Community Center and all the larger synagogues are on the Westside and I can certainly see why people would want to move there, if they felt more Jewish, so be it." Despite her family's long-standing residence on the Eastside and involvement in Tifereth Israel (including organizing a group for young adults in the 1950s and her husband's term as congregation president), they changed their affiliation to Neveh Shalom to access better religious education for their children.[89]

Beyond the congregations and the JCC, new community groups (many of them conceived and encouraged by Neveh Shalom's Rabbi Stampfer) met a growing demand for Jewish cultural, artistic, and academic programming. For example, in the mid-1970s, Stampfer's vision led to the creation of the Jewish Historical Society of Oregon. In addition to memorializing the South Portland neighborhood recently obliterated by urban renewal and freeway construction, the group focused on collecting oral histories, creating an archive of materials, and presenting that history, both within the community and through historical conferences and journals.[90] Eventually, the group evolved into the Oregon Jewish Museum and became the community's premier venue for Jewish cultural, artistic, and historical exhibits.

Another such group, also founded by Stampfer, was the Institute for Judaic Studies. Beginning in the early 1980s, it organized a variety of conferences, readings, films, scholar-in-residence programs, and lectures, some of which later became institutionalized in its annual Roscoe C. Nelson Jr. Memorial Lectures, the Weekend in Quest Scholar in Residence Program, the Portland Jewish Film Festival, and the Writers and Scholars Lecture Series. The institute also played a major role in supporting the introduction of Judaic studies on local campuses: by the mid-1980s, private donations led to the establishment of the Moe and Izetta Tonkon Chair in Jewish Studies at Reed College; in later decades, the Harold and Arlene Schnitzer CARE Foundation endowed Judaic studies programs at both Portland State University and the University of Oregon.[91] The Oregon Holocaust Resource Center, also founded in the early 1980s, was just one of several additional organizations focusing on historic preservation, education, and outreach in this period. For the highly educated professionals who joined the community in the 1980s, 1990s, and beyond, there was now an array of educational and cultural opportunities within the Jewish community.

Jews and the Making of the Oregon Story

The migration of young, well-educated Jewish newcomers into the Portland metropolitan area that began slowly in the 1950s and 1960s accelerated dramatically in the decades that followed. These new arrivals joined Oregon-born peers who, in contrast to the earlier pattern, increasingly chose to remain in the area, as the West became the region of the country most likely to retain its young Jewish adults. The transition from stagnation to rapid growth was closely tied to a broader migration of young, well-educated adults to Portland as it morphed from a fairly conservative and provincial city into one associated with progressive values, sustainability efforts, and creative growth. Portland's transformation, in turn, was part of a statewide "Oregon Story" that highlighted the state's "innovation and regeneration" and its emergence as a leader in environmentally sensitive planning.[92] And Jewish Oregonians— both the newly arrived and the old timers—were affected by that transition, and played a role in driving it.

Beginning in the late 1960s, Oregon became associated with a unique brand of development, emphasizing cautious growth with attention to preservation of natural resources and quality of life. More than anyone else, Governor Tom McCall (1967–1975) embodied and promoted this ethos, emphasizing a doctrine of "environmental awareness years ahead of fashion, of reason above politics, and of caution before consumption."[93] Known as a maverick politician, a moderate Republican who valued independence and stewardship over Oregon's eden, McCall articulated a model of development at odds with the excesses of the 1950s and earlier 1960s. Observing the scars on the state's land and water left by postwar development, McCall, a journalist before his entry into state politics, dramatically boosted his political fortunes through his role in a television documentary on pollution in the Willamette River, *Pollution in Paradise* (1962). As governor, he proclaimed, "We are not willing to take any industry at any price. The industry must come here on our terms, play the game by our environmental rules and be members of the Oregon family."[94] His signature measures—the country's first bottle bill, a beach bill that kept the coast open and accessible to the public, and a land use planning system that imposed strict urban growth boundaries—propelled the state to national attention. To those drawn to Oregon by articles in the national press, such as *Newsweek*'s 1974 feature titled "Where the Future Works," McCall's vision of cautious growth was evident in his quip, "Come visit us again and again. This is a state of excitement. But for heaven's sake, don't come here to live."[95] McCall's successor, Democrat Bob Straub (1975–1979), also an early advocate of environmental legislation and a strong supporter of the Beach Bill and other landmark environmental legislation, perpetuated this concept as well. A subsequent downturn in the economy led some to turn away from this vision. McCall was unable to win the Republican nomination when he tried to run for governor again in 1978.[96] Yet the Oregon Story endured. Although strongly opposed in the state's conservative, rural areas, among liberals it continued to offer "a compelling vision of a state in which quality of life was defined broadly, where citizens chose preservation and sustainability over evanescent riches and quick fixes."[97]

Given the notable engagement of Jews in liberal politics and civic organizations in this era, it should be no surprise that members of the Jewish community were among the key shapers of this emerging Oregon Story. Many of the Jewish individuals and organizations that championed measures like the Oregon Civil Rights Act and Portland school desegregation[98] were involved in a broader array of progressive causes that became central to the emerging vision of Oregon. While some contributed to a growing arts and progressive business community, others focused on efforts to reform land use and city planning, with an eye toward balancing development with stewardship for the state's natural resources.

Richard "Dick" Neuberger was an early Jewish leader in what became the state's environmental movement and served as a "political role model" for McCall. The two journalists-turned-politicians "shared basic values: a desire to protect Oregon and a determination to lift up the underdog," according to McCall's biographer, Brent Walth. Walth argues that Neuberger's early death in 1960 from cancer "created a political vacuum" for McCall. Similarly, Oregon environmental historian William Robbins features Neuberger and McCall as the two central personalities in the state's conservation movement.[99] Like McCall, Neuberger celebrated the natural beauty of Oregon, while emphasizing the importance of carefully managed development for the benefit of the public. Believing in planning and government activism, Neuberger was a staunch conservationist; in the words of Robbins, "Neuberger wanted to win all these battles: to vanquish private-power interests, to build huge dams in scenic canyons, and in the same breath to offer his support for wilderness preservation."[100] Neuberger fought private development of dams while supporting public power. Likewise, in the face of the termination of the Klamath Tribe, he championed a bill calling for federal purchase of tribal forests, believing that federal management of the land would protect it from sale to private interests and eventual clear-cutting.[101] Although Neuberger's conservationism—and his dealings with the Klamath Tribe—would likely draw considerable criticism from early twenty-first-century progressive Oregonians, like McCall, he is remembered as a key early contributor to the state's emerging reputation for a balanced environmental approach and a willingness to take a strong stand against rapacious private development.

Just as Neuberger was a key shaper of the environmental ethos so central to the emerging, state-level Oregon Story, Neil Goldschmidt was critical to a dramatic shift in Portland, and its emergence as "the city that works." Stepping onto the political stage in 1970 with grassroots support from a growing coalition of reformers motivated by issues of urban livability, Goldschmidt was elected to the city council. Two years later, at thirty-two, he became Portland's youngest mayor. Goldschmidt ultimately served two terms as mayor, one as governor and one as US secretary of transportation in the Carter administration. For decades afterward, until it was revealed in 2004 that he sexually abused a fourteen-year-old girl during his first term as mayor, he was viewed as the golden boy of Portland politics, and of Oregon's Jewish community.[102]

Goldschmidt's rise heralded a turn from the urban renewal philosophies of past decades to an embrace of new attitudes about city planning and development, much in line with those of Governor McCall on the state level. In the 1950s, the city had fallen "head over heels for urban development" in the form of razing neighborhoods and constructing office buildings, freeways, and parking lots.[103] At that time, those suggesting the sort of pedestrian- and bicycle-friendly projects that would later be embraced as the city's signature were dismissed out of hand. In his first job in the city planning department in 1959, Arnold Cogan worked on a project that would later be realized as Pioneer Courthouse Square—only at the time, he recalled, "we called it the Meier and Frank parking lot." The initial proposal for what became known as "Portland's living room"—"the revolutionary idea . . . of tearing all that parking down and building an open space in downtown Portland," was, according to Cogan, treated as "somewhere between heresy and communism." The older attitudes were still in evidence in 1967, when Cogan, then working on planning under Governor McCall, approached city officials with the idea of removing Harbor Drive, the thoroughfare along the Willamette River in downtown Portland: "Their mouths just absolutely dropped . . . they were totally stunned." [104]

Neighborhood activist and Kesser Israel stalwart Augusta "Gussie" Reinhardt poses with Mayor Neil Goldschmidt at a 1976 Jewish National Fund dinner. Courtesy OJMCHE

Goldschmidt's ascendance to city hall was indicative of the growing core of advocates beginning to change the city's approach to urban renewal. The shift started as a grassroots movement led by neighborhood activists. Among them was longtime South Portland resident Gussie Reinhardt. Fueled by indignation about the razing of South Portland, Reinhardt headed the fight to save the Lair Hill neighborhood, home to Neighborhood House and Kesser Israel, the last remaining synagogue in the historic neighborhood. Appointed by the National Council of Jewish Women's Portland section—which had founded and still owned Neighborhood House—Reinhardt led a group of neighborhood volunteers in a campaign to "stop an urban renewal clearance project," which was successful several years later in getting Lair Hill recognized as Portland's first residential historic conservation district.[105] Similarly, in August 1969, a group calling itself Riverfront for People staged a picnic on a strip between two riverfront roadways, demanding development of a park rather than the expansion of Harbor Drive. Soon, grassroots efforts to stop further highway and renewal projects were proliferating throughout the city. According to Portland historian Carl Abbott, "in the half dozen years between 1966 and 1972, largely self-defined community organizations sprang up in every quadrant of the city to fight vigorously for neighborhood conservation in the face of urban renewal and highway construction."[106] A new phase in urban development began, focused on "preservation of Portland's neighborhoods and a vital downtown," including livable urban neighborhoods with a mix of residences and businesses.[107]

The new activism signaled a fundamental reorientation of civic life. It both drove and reflected shifting demographics as increasing numbers of young people moved to the city. Replacing older leaders whose principal concern had been stability, the expanding electorate "fueled a 'revolutionary' transition in leadership" by electing significantly younger candidates who brought with them a "sense of possibility rather than limits."[108] Of this new leadership group, Goldschmidt was the most notable and influential. Starting his career as a legal aid lawyer, he developed many contacts among neighborhood activists. As city commissioner and later as mayor, he frequented neighborhood meetings and strove to empower neighborhood associations. A 1971 *Jewish Review* article noted that he and his young family had moved into a house in Northeast Portland "in an area where the problems of city neglect of neighborhood areas has begun to be apparent," making clear that when he went out to visit similar neighborhoods in his role as commissioner, he could relate personally to residents' concerns. Goldschmidt stood out at city hall, not only for his youth, but for his fresh ideas—initially, still very much in the minority; he was often the lone dissenter in commission votes during his first term. The *Review* piece established a clear linkage between Goldschmidt's Jewish heritage, his liberal politics, and his commitment to urban reform, pointing to a stint in Israel, work on the 1964 Mississippi voter registration project, and his commitment to the disadvantaged. "I feel my being Jewish and a child of my parents has played a large part in my commitment to the community," the paper quoted him as saying. "Jews know what it's like to be unsure, both physically and emotionally, of survival. We don't necessarily look different, but we know what it's like to be treated differently, so we can empathize with the blacks, the chicanos [*sic*], the poor."[109] Engagement of the city's diverse neighborhoods would be a hallmark of his mayoral administration; his implementation of the much-heralded 1972 Downtown Plan was "deeply rooted in citizens' advisory committees," and the creation of the Office of Neighborhood Associations "to provide technical support and training to these new citizens' groups" was a signature accomplishment.[110]

Embracing and embodying the emerging ethos, with its emphasis on livability, Goldschmidt's plans called for enhanced public transportation and the revitalization of both downtown and the neighborhoods. He became "the chief symbol and beneficiary of the political transition."[111] Goldschmidt is considered "the driving force behind the revitalization of the city's downtown—an undertaking that made Portland a model for cities across the nation."[112] Goldschmidt helped make Portland a magnet for newcomers.

A 1976 *Willamette Week* article titled "The Goldschmidt Era" summed up Goldschmidt's tenure as mayor succinctly:

Portland never had a better mayor.

Without Neil Goldschmidt, there would be no light rail, no transit mall, no Pioneer Courthouse Square, no Waterfront Park.

There would be no Nordstrom's downtown. . . . We'd have thousands of parking spaces downtown where buildings still sit today. There'd be no Hooper Detox center and we might still be throwing drunks and addicts in jail. There would be no neighborhood-association office in City Hall and neighborhoods would have far less to say about land use planning.[113]

Although Goldschmidt's emphasis on public transportation—particularly on the development of light rail—over freeway expansion was often framed in terms of "livability" or "beauty," it also spoke to environmental concerns and to what would later become known as sustainability. The push to reverse planned freeway construction—which succeeded in replacing Harbor Drive with Tom McCall Waterfront Park and in scrapping highway construction plans that would have cut through downtown—was motivated in part by increasing concern about air and water pollution. The same combination of concerns led to the emergence of Portland's bike culture in this era: in 1971 Oregon's Bicycle Bill ensured funding from the state gas tax for infrastructure such as bike trails. In the same year, City Commissioner Goldschmidt led a bike rally involving over 1,200 riders as part of an effort by a group called the Bike Lobby to call for a range of bike-friendly measures including bike lanes and parking, bike racks on city buses, and consideration for bicyclists' needs in city planning.[114]

Goldschmidt was the most prominent Portlander—and most prominent member of the Jewish community—involved in these efforts, but he was, of course, joined by many others. Among the key community participants was Elaine (Rosenberg) Cogan. In the 1960s, she emerged as a leader in Portland's Model Cities program, part of President Lyndon Johnson's Great Society programming that aimed at increasing citizen involvement through "maximum feasible participation." She explained in an oral history, the Model Cities program "was citizen driven from the very beginning. And I mean the kind of thing that we boast about in Portland now. But then it was very unusual." Subsequently, she served on the Portland Development Commission (PDC), becoming that body's first female chair soon after Goldschmidt was sworn in as mayor. On the PDC, she drew on her Model Cities experience of working with grassroots leaders from diverse communities, and played an important role in shifting the commission's focus from "tearing down buildings and putting up prettier ones," to a broader vision of development that included attention to health, social service, and education factors. As chair, she worked to open meetings to encourage true public engagement, and became known as an expert on public involvement and communications. Cogan's husband, Arnold, played a key role in this era, working at the state level under Governor McCall as planning coordinator and the first director of the Department of Land Conservation and Development.[115] During the same period, Fred Rosenbaum ran the Portland Housing Authority and Mildred Schwab served on the city commission. Schwab was appointed to complete Goldschmidt's term when he was elected mayor, and was later named by Goldschmidt to head the new Bureau of Neighborhood Associations, established to implement plans for incorporation of neighborhood groups into city planning processes.[116] She was reelected to her commission post three times.

Another Jewish figure critical to progressive development on the state and city level was Vera (Pistrak) Katz. Raised in New York in a German Jewish family that fled Nazism for France in 1933 (when she was an infant), and was again forced to flee from the Vichy government in 1940, Katz had a strong sense of her obligation to fight for all citizens. Elected to the Oregon legislature in 1972, she immediately became involved in equal rights efforts, helping to ensure ratification of the Equal Rights Amendment in the Oregon House. She sponsored a successful bill to prohibit discrimination based on gender or marital status and a bill to prohibit employment discrimination based on sexual orientation, which did not pass.[117] She went on to serve nine two-year terms. In 1985, she became the first female Speaker of the Oregon House. Elected to the first of three terms as mayor of Portland in 1992, Katz, like Goldschmidt, championed public transportation and continued the focus on downtown and neighborhood livability. A non-driver, Katz famously used public transportation to commute to work as mayor, and endorsed the Yellow Bike Project, one of the first community bike programs in the country, garnering much attention for Portland as a bike-friendly city.[118]

Along with the enhanced livability presented by parks, bike lanes, public "living rooms," and thriving neighborhoods, Portland experienced a cultural revolution that strongly shaped the Jewish community. In 1950, Portland was anything but cosmopolitan. Overwhelmingly white, with conservative politics, the city's cultural offerings were rather staid. Although home to the oldest art museum in the Pacific Northwest, there was little in the way of a Portland arts scene. The city boasted no significant galleries and little in the way of professional theater and music; its emergence as a center of food culture would have been difficult to predict. The recollections of community members who arrived in the 1950s and early 1960s make clear how provincial Portland was at the time. Like Lorraine Rose, who could find nothing but "regular coffee" when she and her husband, Rabbi Rose, arrived in Portland in 1960, Paul Meyer, who arrived in 1953 (also from New York) discovered that "the only theater available was Portland Civic Theater. . . . The productions were, for the most part amateur." Likewise the Portland Opera Association would not be incorporated as a professional company until 1964. The Oregon Symphony—then called the Portland Symphony—had a history going back to the nineteenth century, but had fallen victim to the Great Depression. Reconstituted in 1947, it was still in the early days of its comeback when Meyer arrived. Likewise, the Portland Symphonic Choir, also incorporated in 1947, was very much in its infancy; for several summers in the early 1950s, it performed light operas in the Holladay Bowl, an amphitheater constructed for this purpose in the pit that had been dug decades earlier for a luxury hotel that was never built. As their incorporation dates suggest, the infrastructure for a professional performing arts scene was laid during the postwar period. A number of members of the Jewish community, including newcomers like Meyer and longtime members of the community such as Roscoe Nelson Jr. and Jack Schwartz, participated in this expansion, serving on the boards of these arts organizations.[119]

In addition, several well-known and emerging Jewish artists in various fields chose to make Oregon their home in this period. Swiss-born Ernest Bloch, recognized as one of the foremost American composers of classical and Jewish music, fell in love with the Oregon Coast in 1941 and purchased a house in Agate Beach. He spent the remaining years of his life composing there, completing about a third of his repertoire while living on the coast. In 1990, thirty years after his passing, the coastal city of Newport established the Ernest Bloch Music Festival.[120] In the early 1960s, visual artist Mel Katz (then married to future mayor, Vera Katz) moved from New York to Portland, anticipating a one-year stay. Leaving behind the "art world capital," he embraced the freedom he found in a city with "sparse galleries, few art writers and a museum that wasn't keeping up with the contemporary art scene at the time."[121] Katz, the son of a New York garment worker, saw echoes of his father's work with clothing patterns in his abstract steel sculptures.[122] Teaching at Portland State University for over thirty years, Katz, according to Hallie Ford Museum director John Olbrantz, became influential in the region and was "a catalyst for bringing contemporary artists and new ideas to Portland."[123]

In the decades to come, these artists and arts supporters, among many others, would transform Oregon, and especially Portland, into a rising creative center. Among the notable Jewish community members who took part in that transition were Evelyn (Scher) Georges, whose White Bird Gallery in Cannon Beach, founded in 1971, became the first major gallery on the Oregon Coast. Focusing on local and regional artists and craftspeople, it provided a venue that helped bring to prominence members of the nascent artist colony located in the quiet beach town.

Without question, however, the greatest contribution to the emerging art scene came from the Schnitzer family. Harold and Arlene (Director) Schnitzer, and their son, Jordan Schnitzer, emerged as perhaps the most significant art philanthropists in the state. Both Arlene and Harold were born (she in Salem, he in South Portland) to Russian immigrant families, part of an interrelated group that came to Oregon in a chain migration. Starting in junk collecting, the Schnitzers turned a scrap metal business into Schnitzer Steel. Harold, one of five sons, sold off his share of the steel business in 1950 and used it to start a real estate investment firm, Harsch Investment Properties, with which he would make his fortune.

It was largely Arlene's influence that turned that fortune toward support for the arts. When she was growing up, her parents owned a furniture store in Portland. Arlene frequently went along on buying trips with her mother, Helen Director, who ran the interior decoration department and offered design services to clients. Although she recalls knowing nothing about art at that time, Arlene developed a sharp eye that would serve her well in her gallery and private collecting in later years. Her first formal involvement with art came in 1958 when she enrolled in classes at the Portland Art Museum school; a young mother, she "wanted something to do, and the hours fit." Although she did not complete that training, it lit a fire in her: "I walked into art school and that was it for me," she recalled. "It was like I got home and found myself. I'd never been touched by anything like that." With very few venues in town for local artists, she offered to use her real estate connections to assist a group of the school's faculty in setting up a co-op gallery in 1960, but was turned down by artists who saw her offer as "'nothing but junk wealth'... an anti-Semitic-edged reference to Harold Schnitzer's family's roots in the scrap-metal business."[124] She established her own gallery. Arlene Schnitzer's Fountain Gallery opened in 1961, and became Portland's "first truly professional gallery," ultimately bringing any number of local and regional artists to prominence while leading the emergence of Portland as an arts center. "The gallery," according to Portland Art Museum director Brian Ferriso, "served as the foundation for a visual arts ecosystem that sustained and invested in some of the region's most significant modernists, many of whom resisted the urge to move to the epicenter of the art world in New York."[125] Through the gallery, Schnitzer took an active role not only in promoting "her" artists, but also in making public art more visible in the city. She recalled in a 2014 interview,

> I think the one thing I really contributed as a gallery owner was pioneering putting the work of good artists of the region into major corporations, businesses, banks, lobbies. My goal was to take down all the framed prints of ducks flying out of the swamp from magazine pages and those calendar pictures that were prevalent at the time. When I started the Gallery, there really were hardly any businesses that had real art on the walls.[126]

By 1967, Arlene was serving on the board of the Portland Art Museum; Harold joined that board in 1990. Together, they became the institution's largest donors, providing endowments for the Northwest and Asian collections, for an Asian art curatorship, for capital investments, and for special exhibits, membership, and operations, in addition to donations of art from their private collections. Their philanthropy in the arts extended well beyond visual art, as they became major supporters of the Oregon Symphony, the Portland Opera, and the Oregon Ballet, and of the premier performance venue in Portland, the Arlene Schnitzer Concert Hall, popularly known as "The Schnitz." Their son, Jordan, a passionate collector of prints, would continue his parents' tradition of arts giving, donating generously to the Portland Art Museum and becoming the principal benefactor of the art museum at the University of Oregon, his alma mater. In 2005, following an extensive renovation and expansion, the Eugene institution was renamed the Jordan Schnitzer Museum of Art. In addition, the Jordan Schnitzer Family Foundation makes his and the foundation's extensive collection of prints available for exhibits around the country.

The emergence of a lively cultural scene in Oregon—and Jewish participation in helping to create that scene—was not limited to the highbrow. Harry Glickman, who grew up in South Portland playing basketball at the JCC and

Portland Trailblazers owner Harry Glickman shaking hands with forward Buck Williams. Courtesy OJMCHE

Lincoln High School, brought professional sports to Portland. Carving out a career in sporting promotions, Glickman began with boxing, and then brought preseason National Football League games, the Harlem Globetrotters, and National Basketball Association all-star games to Portland beginning in the mid-1950s. Yet, as early as 1954, he aspired to bring a professional basketball team to the Rose City. By 1960 he was a founder of the Portland Buckaroos, a very successful minor league hockey team that lasted thirteen years (until the league folded). In 1970, Glickman raised funds for a new NBA expansion team, founding the Portland Trailblazers, and serving as general manager until his retirement in 1987. In 1977, the Blazers beat the Philadelphia Seventy-Sixers for the national championship, igniting a phenomenon that became known as Blazermania. As Glickman himself recounted it, Blazermania was "a love affair between a team and its fans, an entire city and state." The final game won an unprecedented 96 percent share of the television audience in Oregon, shortened church sermons, and interrupted graduations. As the *Oregonian* wrote, "It was like the fall of Rome, the opening of the West, and the discovery of atomic power." The coming of the Blazers to Portland and the city's embrace of the moniker "Rip City," like the expansion of the art scene and the embrace of sustainability, were additional signs of Portland's emerging identity and recognition as a notably attractive and livable city.[127]

Yet, perhaps even more than for its sports and arts scenes, the state—and particularly Eugene, Portland, and rural areas in the western valleys—became known in the 1960s and 1970s as a center of the counterculture. Oregon's profile among those questioning mainstream values was raised through its connection with novelist Ken Kesey, whose property outside Eugene became the final resting place for the bus *Further* after the Merry Prankster's famous, LSD-fueled cross-country trip, documented in Tom Wolfe's *The Electric Kool-Aid Acid Test*. The annual Country Fair in nearby Veneta, first held in 1969 and for many years headlined by the Grateful Dead, also contributed to the state's reputation as a refuge for the offbeat. James Kopp, whose *Eden within Eden* documents utopian experiments in the state, counts over 250 communal settlements from 1965 to 2009; beginning in the 1960s, the area from San Francisco to British Columbia was home to the largest number of such settlements in the country.[128]

Hippie culture combined with antiwar student activism in the areas around the Portland State and University of Oregon campuses. Both became strongly identified with the countercultural movement, and the presence of hippies generated much angst, leading to police monitoring and crackdowns, including the violent suppression of an antiwar protest in Portland's Park Blocks in 1970. Yet Oregon's most famous effort to deal with the supposed threat of the counterculture was relatively friendly and, characteristically, offbeat: fearing major protests against an American Legion convention, Governor McCall's staff planned a state-sponsored rock festival called Vortex that attracted the would-be protestors away from downtown, and then looked the other way as they shed their clothing and smoked pot in McIver State Park.[129] At the city level, Mayor Goldschmidt, himself recently regarded as somewhat of a hippie, "welcomed the young activists into civic life, codified and to some degree co-opted the energy of the social movements."[130] If, on the one hand, some of the old power brokers in Portland feared that Goldschmidt was bringing in "a houseful of hippies,"[131] the message taken by those who identified with activists and the "movement" in one way or another was far more welcoming, and many flocked to the region both during the heyday of the movement and in subsequent years. Among them was Stew Albert, an early member of the Yippies and unindicted coconspirator in the Chicago Seven trial. In 1985 he moved to Portland, where he remained true to his radical politics while becoming involved in the Jewish community. In addition to serving on the Portland Jewish Federation's Community Relations Council (CRC)—the arm of the Federation focused on intergroup relations and issues such as civil rights—Albert became an early advocate of territorial compromise as a solution to the Israeli-Palestinian conflict and served as a leader in the local chapter of the progressive New Jewish Agenda, a group that emerged in the early 1980s and was notable for breaking with the American Jewish consensus by openly criticizing the Israeli government on issues such as West Bank settlements. Albert was also a local leader in efforts to promote gay rights and Jewish-Muslim dialogue on the Middle East.[132]

Covering the evolving cultural and political scene, in addition to traditional daily newspapers, was the *Willamette Week*, an independent weekly paper founded in 1974 and purchased in 1983 by Mark Zusman and Richard Meeker, both members of the Portland Jewish community. As publisher and editor, respectively, the two built one of the premier weekly alternative papers in the country. *Willamette Week* became particularly well known for its arts and culture coverage, capturing the progressive Portland scene and, in doing so, the attention of young adults. It also was responsible for breaking two of the most significant Oregon political stories of the past quarter century: the 2004 exposé on Neil Goldschmidt's abuse of a teenage girl during his mayoral term and the investigation in 2014–15 that led to the resignation of Governor John Kitzhaber. The former story was recognized with a 2005 Pulitzer Prize for investigative reporting, making the paper the only alternative weekly news-paper to be so recognized.[133]

An Expanded Community

The dramatic changes in the city and state that were part of the Oregon Story drew increasing numbers of college-educated young adults, creative inno-vators, and professionals, particularly in the 1990s and early twenty-first century. Among these newcomers were increasing numbers of Jews. After lagging behind at midcentury, Jewish population growth began to outpace Oregon's general population growth.[134] Oregon's Jewish population, having reached 10,000 by the late 1970s, doubled by the mid-1990s. By the end of that decade, it increased by another 50 percent to just over 30,000, with Portland alone reporting an increase from 17,500 to 25,000 between 1998 and 1999. The *American Jewish Yearbook* noted in its annual demographic review, "The com-munity reporting the largest population gain in 1999 was Portland, Oregon, up 7,500 to 25,000."[135] In 2010, a new study estimated that 42,000 Jews lived in Portland and over 48,000 statewide. These figures were much disputed, and were subsequently revised downward to 36,400 and 40,650, respectively. Even using the lower figures, Oregon's Jewish population had risen over 462 percent, from 8,785 in 1970 to 40,650 in 2011.[136]

The influx was part of a broader migration of Jews to the Pacific West; in 1930, Jews were only half as likely as Americans generally to live in the Pacific West; by 1971 they were nearly as likely to do so (12.3 percent vs. 13 per-cent), but by 1990, Jews were more likely than the general population to live in the Far West (16.3 percent vs. 15.7 percent).[137] By 2012, fully 24.1 percent of American Jews lived in the West—19.7 percent in the three Pacific Coast states alone, compared to 23.4 and 16.2 percent, respectively, of the general population.[138] Many of the newcomers came from the Northeast and Midwest, regions experiencing significant Jewish population declines, resulting, according to demographers Sidney and Alice Goldstein, in a "massive redistribution of Jews among the major regions of the United States."[139]

Clearly, those moving to the West in general, and to Oregon in particular, were not just a random selection of Jewish individuals. Rather, as among their non-Jewish counterparts, professionals and others with college degrees were overrepresented. In terms of Jewish identity, there is strong evidence to indicate that the self-selection process favored individuals who were less embedded in Jewish communal organizations, less traditional, and less likely to define themselves as religious than as cultural or secular Jews. This trend is clearly reflected in Jewish population studies from the 1990s and early 2000s, which demonstrate a pronounced secularism in the region. Jews who identify as secular (as opposed to "Jews by religion") are consistently overrepresented in the West; in the 1990 national Jewish population survey, 36.6 percent of those who identified as secular Jews lived in the West, compared to only 19.7 percent of Jews by religion.[140] In the same survey, 43 percent of secular Jews who moved from one region to another moved to the West.[141] This is due, in part, to the fact that the most traditional individuals in a community—the Orthodox, the in-married, those with the highest levels of ritual observance and religious education—are the least likely to leave their home community.[142]

There is also evidence that in addition to secular Jews being drawn to the West, those newcomers who are more observant may adapt to the community norms by embracing a more "northwestern" attitude toward religion.[143] Oregon has long been a destination attractive to those who identify as secular (whether Jewish or otherwise), because of its location in what religious sociologists call the Pacific Northwest "unchurched belt" or the "None Zone"—the area of the country in which people are most likely to answer "none of the above" to a question about religious orientation.[144] The "open religious environment" of the region translates into tremendous individual freedom to define religious identity, with minimal social pressure to affiliate with formal religious institutions. This results in a region in which about two-thirds of adults hold a religious identity (they identify themselves as Jews, Catholics, etc.), but only about half of that number join a religious institution—a rate of affiliation roughly half the national rate.[145] This regional trend is reflected in the Jewish community: only 30 percent of western Jews in the 2000–01 National Jewish Population Survey belonged to a synagogue, compared to 44 percent in the Northeast and 47 percent in the Midwest.[146] The greater Portland metropolitan community was identified in a 2001 study as one of the ten Jewish communities (of the largest fifty) with the lowest synagogue densities.[147] Even with the enormous growth in population during the final decades of the twentieth century, Oregon Jewish communities still face formidable challenges.

In the 1970s, faced with dire reports of stagnant population, declining observance, and loss of the community's physical center, Jewish institutions in Portland responded with building campaigns, shoring up traditional institutions, and outreach efforts, particularly through educational and cultural programming. Those efforts were largely successful; the new buildings filled, the new programs and organizations grew and prospered, and the community bounced back. By the 1980s, whether measured by school enrollment, breadth of programming, or money raised for local and international Jewish causes, the Portland Jewish community was thriving. Yet as word of the Oregon Story spread, and Portland emerged as one of the most attractive cities in the country for young people, new challenges emerged.

Despite the tremendous growth centered in Portland, the emergence of a "Jewish neighborhood" in Southwest Portland, and the proliferation of religious and cultural institutions, the MJCC found itself facing an existential crisis in the early twenty-first century. In April 2004, the *Jewish Review* reported that the MJCC, "Jewish Portland's living room," was facing financial disaster—nearly three million dollars in debt, the MJCC was "broke." Quickly, two of the community's most influential leaders, Jay Zidell and Jordan Schnitzer, stepped into the fray. Like Harry Mittleman, who had paid off the JCC's mortgage in 1976, both Zidell and Schnitzer came from Portland families that began the twentieth century as junk dealers and, within a generation, became some of the community's most generous philanthropists. Sam Zidell, a "guiding light of the Jewish community,"[148] had given generously to the Federation, the Robison Home, the Portland Jewish Academy (housed in the Min Zidell Education Building), and many other community causes; in addition to their extensive philanthropy in the Jewish community and the arts, Jordan's father, Harold Schnitzer, had chaired the building committee for the Southwest Portland JCC. Like the elder Schnitzer, who had recognized in the early 1970s the community's shift from synagogue-based religious life to a more diverse social, cultural, and ethnic interests, Jordan Schnitzer, Jay Zidell, and the many other community leaders who responded to the crisis recognized the evolving needs of a community that was much larger and more diverse than it had been thirty or fifty years before.[149] After several years of belt tightening, particularly in the athletic and fitness programs, a variety of fora to focus the community on changing needs, a successful capital campaign, and a major remodel, the MJCC emerged from the crisis. In the spring of 2007, the community celebrated the center's "rebirth," dedicating its renovated and expanded facilities on a campus now called the Schnitzer Family Campus.

An expanded campus in Southwest Portland was one step. Yet an increasingly educated, cosmopolitan, diverse, young, and secular Jewish population required new forms of outreach in the early twenty-first century. Communal institutions—in Portland and in emerging centers such as Ashland and Bend—would face the challenges brought by growing numbers of twenty-first-century Jewish Oregonians, whose needs and desires were shaped by their sensibilities as Oregonians and as Jews.

CHAPTER TWO

Whatever Happened to Old South Portland?
Constructing a New Oregon Jewish History

"Battle Hymie of South Portland"
I'm singing you a ballad of the merchants of the past
We'll cruise through old South Portland catching flavors while they last . . .
You'll see them as they were before the demolition's blast
Like—Himmelfarb's Garage.
Halperin and Colistro's grocery
Rotenberg Rosumny's bakery
Get your shave from Wolff the barber
Why should mama shlep?
Try some meat from Fry and Koessel, buy your eggs from Geller's grocery.
Tom Stern's Garage for gassing up machines.
Why should mama schlep?
Get your flaysh from Sam the Butcher. You will know that it is kosher.
Sugerman will sell you salt bag.
Why should mama shlep? . . .
Mrs. Levine for Shabbos she has fish and chicken too
Then on to Mr. Mosler he's got hallah quite a few
From there you go to Weinstein—Mogan David oh so true
So why should mama shlep?
Now towers rise and fountains flow, o'er streets where pushcarts rolled
The Neighborhood is lovelier at least that's what we're told
But how can time erase the golden memories of old.
We will not let them die.
—*Whatever Happened to Old South Portland?* (1969)[1]

For three nights in the spring of 1969, the auditorium of the Jewish Community Center on Southwest Thirteenth Avenue was filled with the sights and sounds of the historic immigrant neighborhood, as community members performed an original musical production, *Whatever Happened to Old South Portland?*

In the words of director and writer Shirley (Blum) Tanzer, "What began as a sophisticated and satiric musical review . . . evolved into a mixed media musical *mishegas* with a universal spirit which permeates everyone involved in the show: Jew and non-Jew, committed and uncommitted, old South Portland residents, Irvington residents, New Yorker, Californian, Canadian and Seattleite."[2] Invoking the names of familiar businesses, schools, and individuals, the production strove to evoke the historic ethnic neighborhood, recently paved over by urban renewal and freeway construction, while conveying a universal message about the immigrant struggle in America.

In remembering South Portland, the musical tapped into many tropes broadly familiar to American Jews, but not particular to Portland or the Northwest. Among the twenty-three original songs in the production were several that recalled "neighborhood" foods like rye bread, kosher pickles, lox, and bagels—foods that had an authenticity when eaten in "Old South Portland" that could not be captured in their modern versions. Others spoke of shuls and mikvahs, circumcisions and bar mitzvahs, peddlers and pushcarts. Throughout, Yiddish terms were liberally sprinkled, as in the number titled "An Anti-Semantic Song," when the chorus sings,

> You say it's kiggle and I say it's kuggel.
> You say it's Babba and I say it's bubbeh.
> Kiggle   Kuggle
> Babba   Bubbeh
> Let's call the whole thing spitch (speech).[3]

The production powerfully evoked not only the sights, sounds, smells, and tastes of the immigrant Jewish neighborhood, but also nostalgia for a simpler time. As Tanzer explained, her hope was to capture "the spirit of South Portland," because "in the complexity of a mechanistic, automated, impersonal world, we all dream of a return to the simple life of South Portland."[4] To accompany the musical, a replica edition of the community's *Scribe* newspaper from 1920 was printed, with several contemporary pieces added, including Tanzer's "notes from the director," running alongside the lead headline: "Harding Elected President" on the front page. The response to the musical was so enthusiastic that, seven months later, photographic images of the neighborhood were paired with taped interviews conducted during the background research for the show for an exhibit at the JCC titled *Sights and Sounds of Old South Portland.*[5]

In addition to writing and directing the musical, Tanzer became the principal driver of the Portland Jewish oral history project that emerged in the early 1970s. By 1977, the project's corps of volunteers had conducted over two hundred hours of taped interviews. Encouraged by Neveh Shalom's Rabbi Joshua Stampfer (whose passion for western Jewish history led him to write a book on the region's first rabbi),[6] two different organizations formed—the Jewish Oral History and Archive Project and the Jewish Historical Society of Oregon.

With the community still hungry for local history, the Oral History and Archive Project published another replica paper in May 1976, to accompany a new multimedia show titled *Memory Is Survival*. This slideshow used historic photos in combination with the oral history transcripts, and was presented at the JCC auditorium over several consecutive nights. It was accompanied by a photo exhibit titled *Portrait of Our People: Kin and Community* and spawned both a traveling version of the presentation and a series of organizational reunions.[7] The *Memory Is Survival* project covered a broader swath of Oregon Jewish history than had the musical, stretching back to the arrival of the pioneers in the mid-nineteenth century. It included a substantial segment that focused on Old South Portland, drawing a few scenes directly from the musical and talking about the neighborhood as a virtual "shtetl," emphasizing its traditional nature, ethnic stores, ritual practices, and close-knit community.[8]

Whatever Happened to Old South Portland, Memory Is Survival, the oral histories themselves, and published materials such as the commemorative editions of the *Scribe,* all sought to memorialize a community that had passed out of existence. In striving to remember, these projects wove Portland-based reminiscences together with broader American Jewish themes, to create a new, place-based historical memory. The product, the construction of "Old South Portland," served the needs of Jewish Oregonians by directly connecting them to the epic historical theme of East European immigration to New York, and then superimposing that central memory on Portland.

Destroying a Community, Building a History

The wave of nostalgia for historic South Portland in the late 1960s and early 1970s was a direct result of the dispersal of the Jewish community and the relocation of its institutions to more suburban settings. Although many American Jewish communities went through suburbanization at this time, in Portland, the movement was caused not by white flight from the urban center, but by the physical destruction of the old neighborhood resulting from urban renewal. Portlanders voted to create the South Auditorium Urban Renewal District in 1958, ultimately razing fifty-four square blocks. Additional community institutions found themselves in the path of freeway construction or Portland State University's expansion. As discussed in chapter 1, this combination of projects ultimately demolished five of the neighborhood's six synagogues, leading to several mergers and relocations; it also displaced the Jewish Community Center and the Jewish Home for the Aged, providing opportunities to construct new facilities on more expansive campuses in Southwest Portland.

Although most families had moved out of the historic neighborhood well before the urban renewal process began, some vestiges remained in the post-war period. Those still residing in the area by the late 1950s were mostly elderly and of limited means; families of young professionals had relocated farther southwest or to Eastside neighborhoods like Laurelhurst and Irvington. Many Jewish Portlanders, looking back a decade later, recognized that the area had deteriorated, and even agreed that the razing of the neighborhood meant progress for the city. Lillie (Sax) Kugel, interviewed in 1974, explained, "I think it is all for the better. I really do. I wouldn't want to go back and live the way I lived before. I'll tell you that much."[9] Similarly, Lillian Kobin recalled, "Well, of course by that time the whole area had deteriorated to such a point that really I don't think I had too much feeling about it because it wasn't the same place anymore. The same people weren't there, every place had deteriorated and I realized that something had to be done."[10] Besse (Brown) Harris noted that "people . . . have become more affluent and moved to better neighborhoods and are more comfortable financially, economically, materially, emotionally, whatever . . . It's a wonderful feeling. . . . It is very nice to see that they live comfortably."[11]

Despite the deterioration, with nearly all the synagogues and the JCC remaining in South Portland until they were forced to move, families from across the metropolitan area continued to frequent the neighborhood. Many returned to attend synagogue, bring their children to Hebrew school, or visit elderly parents and grandparents; others came to shop at favorite stores, delis, and bakeries specializing in ethnic treats. Rabbi Yonah Geller, who arrived in 1960 to serve Congregation Shaarie Torah, recalled that "everything was in South Portland; Safeway with most of the Jewish products was there. Mosler's Bakery was in South Portland. That was where everyone shopped."[12] These ties made some feel conflicted about the changes. For example, Frances (Schnitzer) Bricker had mixed feelings: "I don't know whether it's a good thing or a bad thing; it's progress."[13] Likewise, Kathryn (Kahn) Blumenfeld felt "mixed emotions. I think it is too bad to see a heritage go, but on the other hand I don't think a ghetto was a good thing."[14] Sadie (Cohen) Geller agreed, "You couldn't let those old buildings stand there. They were just deteriorating and our parents were going, dying and we younger ones naturally were moving away from there, so the old buildings were bare, so when the Urban Renewal came in I thought it was a good thing. Of course, there is that nostalgic feelings of South Portland."

The demolition of the neighborhood triggered an outpouring—and roman-ticizing—of memories; as Tanzer later explained, "There seemed to be a real need in this community . . . to recapture the past and to immerse themselves in this kind of memorabilia and reminiscence."[15] The parallel developments of neighborhood dislocation and nostalgia can be traced through the Jewish

Community Center's newsletter, the *JCC Ace*, as it covered the musical, *Whatever Happened* (performed at the old JCC) and the campaign and planning for the new JCC, which opened two years later. Six months before the show, the *JCC Ace* newsletter featured a story headlined "New Building Plans, Facilities Outlined," on the front page, and contained an insert on cultural and educational programming, alerting the community to an upcoming show: "An original JCC Musical-Variety Show featuring native talent—young and old."[16] Two months later, as the front page introduced the various campaign vice chairmen "already at work for the JCC," an inside page ran a "quiz in reminiscence," designed to attract contributors to the show. Asking questions like "Were you 'shushed' at Shaarie Torah?" and "Can you drive through Urban Renewal and still find where Mosler's Bakery used to be?" The piece urged readers—especially those scoring high on the quiz—to get involved in the coming (not yet named) "Gala salute to old South Portland." "Call immediately and make sure you protect your version of 'good old days' from the version of the same story your friends might tell!" the ad warned.[17] In March 1969, the *ACE* ran a banner headline announcing "Old South Portland March 30, 31, April 1," just above the lead story, "Building Plans at Final Stage."[18] The following November, the *ACE*'s front page proclaimed the plans complete and announced both the start of work on the new JCC site and the opening of the new photo exhibit on South Portland. "Nobody seems to be able to forget 'Old South Portland,'" the article explained, "so in response to countless requests, special showings of the 'Sights and Sounds of Old South Portland' are set for the Jewish Community Center."[19]

The huge effort that went into researching, writing, choreographing, and performing the musical, not to mention the coordination of the reunions and exhibits that accompanied and followed the show, demonstrates the enormous commitment to preserving a historical memory of South Portland. Although the JCC already had an active theater program, it had focused on the performance of existing plays.[20] *Whatever Happened*, with its twenty-three original songs, was an unprecedented undertaking. The success of the musical led the JCC theater group to launch another original show the following year. With the unlikely title *Oy Corvallis*, that musical, about a meeting of matchmakers, premiered at the (old) JCC in the spring of 1970.[21]

Clearly, the flood of nostalgia for South Portland and commitment to preserving its history was closely tied to the physical destruction of the old neighborhood and the relocation of community institutions to other parts of the city. Yet it was also shaped by a broader American—and American Jewish—trend of honoring diversity and ethnic identity in the immediate post-civil rights era. At a time when ethnic festivals and fairs were springing up in cities across the country, books like *World of Our Fathers* were best sellers, *Roots* enthralled television audiences, and *Fiddler on the Roof* dominated box offices, first on Broadway and then in movie theaters. These suggested "a new phase in the cultural politics of American diversity: the coalescence of the ethnic revival."[22]

Within the American Jewish community, the embrace of ethnicity took on even greater significance in the aftermath of the Holocaust. The decimation of Europe's Jews left America the largest and wealthiest Jewish community in the world, a community with a new responsibility for the long-term survival of the Jewish people. Yet, as American Jews embraced their arrival in the middle class, they grappled with the loss of Jewish coherence. Integration into suburban communities came at a price; modern Jewish life seemed lacking in rich religious and cultural resonances, and the move into the suburbs and the assimilation it represented was portrayed by some as "a movement away from honesty and cultural authenticity."[23] In contrast, the East European shtetls and older ethnic neighborhoods where immigrants first settled in the United States came increasingly to be remembered as sites of Jewish authenticity, cloaked with nostalgia. The shtetl, imagined in the musical *Fiddler on the Roof* as Anatevka, became a symbol of authentic Jewish tradition, as "Tevye encapsulated the world of tradition coming to terms with modernization, and in particular Americanization."[24] Similarly reified was the Lower East Side of New York, which became the symbolic neighborhood of origin of all American Jews. Embraced, according to historian Hasia Diner, as "the American Jewish Plymouth Rock,"[25] the Lower East Side came to represent a lost "Jewish authenticity in America . . . a moment in time when undiluted eastern European Jewish culture throbbed in America."[26] Historian Catherine Rottenberg explains that the neighborhood, in retrospect, became sacrosanct,

> suffused with both mystique and nostalgia. By evoking its name, by identifying with it, Jewish Americans can both stake a claim in common Jewish American history and in a dominant Jewish American narrative, one that tells the story of poor immigrants who rose out of the quintessentially Jewish American ghetto and managed to enter mainstream middle class U.S. society. Just as importantly, the neighborhood has come to represent authenticity, a place where Jews could be truly themselves. In the minds of many contemporary U.S. Jews the Lower East Side lays claim to a purer and more authentic Judaism, one that has to a great extent been lost or at least diluted.[27]

The centrality and power of the Lower East Side and the shtetl in American Jewish consciousness in turn shaped the sacralization of "Old South Portland" as a local story of origin and site of authenticity. Elements of Eastern Europe and the Lower East Side were transcribed onto South Portland as the three places blurred in projects like *Whatever Happened* and *Memory Is Survival*. As oral histories were collected to inform community histories, the community histories looped back on themselves to inform the oral histories. Old South Portland became revered (now with capital letters) as the community embraced the neighborhood as historical touchstone, paralleling the process of sacralization of the Lower East Side (also with capital letters).[28] References to pushcarts and comparisons to shtetls popped up, not only in the musical production, but also in history books and exhibits produced during and after the revival. South Portland became the symbol of community memory; as Shirley (Soble) Nudleman put it in the title of her humor column, which ran in the *Jewish Review* in the early 1970s, "We Could Stroll Down Memory Lane, but They Built a Freeway over It."

In the space of about a decade, a new Oregon Jewish history had emerged. Earlier versions centered on the mid-nineteenth-century frontier experience of individual Jewish pioneers playing key political and economic roles in far-flung parts of the state. In 1953, Congregation Beth Israel's celebration of their ninety-fifth anniversary featured "an evening of fun in the Old Western style," with participants asked to come in period costumes and "Victuals: Chuck Wagon Style" served.[29] In contrast, the new history emerging in the late 1960s and early 1970s focused not on pioneers, but on the collective, urban experience of immigrants living in an ethnic community in South Portland.

Oregon Jewish History: Old and New

In 1958, Samuel Suwol, a Portland Jewish lawyer, wrote what is generally considered to be the first history of the Jews of Oregon, an eleven-page pamphlet, titled *Jewish History of Oregon*. Although Suwol was a resident of Portland, had attended Lincoln High School,[30] and was writing while the immigrant neighborhood was declining but still intact, his account was virtually silent on South Portland and its residents. Rather, Suwol's history told a story that focused mostly on nineteenth-century Jewish settlers and emphasized themes of overcoming adversity, inclusion in pioneer society, and civic leadership. Like many pioneer histories, the account championed the achievements of settlers who crossed the plains, fought in the Indian wars, helped to establish towns, and in the process, gained the respect of their fellow pioneers. The bulk of Suwol's account concentrated on individuals who arrived prior to the turn of the century and those who occupied positions of leadership, particularly elected office. Although several South Portland congregations and institutions like Neighborhood House were mentioned, Suwol made no comment on their location; nor did he discuss South Portland as a neighborhood or as a center of Jewish community, past or present.[31]

The year after Suwol published his history, Rabbi Julius Nodel's account of the first hundred years of Congregation Beth Israel was published. Given the German origins of this Reform congregation founded in 1858, one would not expect a strong focus on the South Portland immigrant community of the early twentieth century, and, indeed, there is little discussion of the area or its residents. Yet what is said is revealing, for it demonstrates an understanding of Oregon Jewish history that, like Suwol's, places the experience of the pioneers and their descendants at the center, and the later-arriving East Europeans at the periphery (Sephardim go unmentioned as a community in Nodel's account). Published in 1959, the centennial of Oregon statehood, during a period of renewed celebration of the pioneer and the frontiersman as the iconic Oregonians, Nodel's first chapter was titled "In the Beginning" and opened with an account of the "eight Jewish frontiersmen" who founded Beth Israel in 1858.[32] In contrast to these German immigrant congregational founders, identified so clearly as part of the Oregon pioneer story, Nodel repeatedly characterized the later-arriving East Europeans as outsiders to the community, calling them "Jewish fugitives from East European official and semi-official pogroms," "complete strangers to the community," "unfortunates," and "of a different world."[33] Although he wrote of the mid-twentieth-century descendants of those immigrants who had become part of the Beth Israel community and expressed satisfaction that "snobbery" toward East Europeans "has long since passed out of the Congregation's history,"[34] Nodel was quick to explain the earlier distance between established Jews and the turn-of-the-century newcomers: "Poor and frightened immigrants, arriving in Portland with their few pitiful belongings, tied in bundles or straw cases secured with strings and rope, did not appear like kinsmen of the American Jewish citizens by any stretch of the imagination." Not only were the East Europeans of a different background, but, in Nodel's view, they were "lacking the ruggedness and confidence of the pioneer Jews who had preceded them a half-century earlier."[35]

The theme of foreignness also characterized Nodel's description of the South Portland neighborhood. Referring to it as "Little Russia," Nodel explained that the area was "a voluntary ghetto, so to speak, where the 'new Americans' had the security of being close to many companions who had undergone the same misfortunes and whose mutual understanding required no hasty readjustments under pressure." Showing none of the nostalgia toward South Portland that would be so pervasive just a decade later, Nodel wrote, "Today, a few lonely kosher delicatessen stores, and two synagogues, soon to be abandoned for more modern buildings are all that remain today as markers of this by-gone era."[36]

Suwol's and Nodel's accounts, coming in the late 1950s, after many Jewish residents had left the area and at a time when the neighborhood was being widely characterized as blighted in public discourse, carry none of the fondness of later accounts. Suwol—despite the fact that he must have been quite familiar with the area, given his attendance at Lincoln High—does not even mention it as of significance in the Jewish history of Oregon. Nodel characterizes the area as foreign, impoverished, and ghetto-like. The descriptors that would become so common in the period from 1969 on—"self-contained," "shtetl-like," "family-centered," "warm," "intimate," not to mention the detailed descriptions of holiday rituals, Saturday evening "promenades," and mouth-watering ethnic treats are completely absent in these accounts, just as they were absent from the Portland Development Commission's characterizations of the area as "dilapidated" and "obnoxious." And neither Suwol nor Nodel refers to the area as "South Portland" or "Old South Portland." How could they have done so? The entire historical conception of "Old South Portland" as a warm, supportive, ethnic community was a *product* of urban renewal and its destruction of the neighborhood. And the chief architect of that narrative was Shirley Tanzer.

In 1979, Tanzer reflected on the extensive oral history project that she had initiated and led. Noting that she "came to Oral History" by way of the theater, Tanzer explained that she was drawn to the opportunity "to do an original musical about the 'old neighborhood,' the coming to America, and then to Oregon, the 'settling in,' the realization and/or disappointment with the American Dream. . . .

The production, "Whatever Happened To Old South Portland? which I directed became a tremendous outpouring of community spirit from a community scattered, fragmented, and thought to be gone. The South Portland area epitomized the enormous struggle of all transplanted and immigrant peoples who with tremendous self-determination left all that was familiar and settled in the western part of this country, a place that was puzzling, frightening, challenging and free.

The script for this show was developed and written from verbatim testimony— the experiences that South Portlanders lived through. These interviews told us that from this new found freedom emerged first generation Americans—athletes, educators, lawyers, business men and women. No matter where they went, they retained ties with the old teeming neighborhood (their shtetl) of shared sights, smells and sounds.

Succeeding generations became increasingly well assimilated in this "great American Dream" and when urban renewal and freeways obliterated the "quaint" and dilapidated old structures, the elders wept for a time no longer remembered and a place no longer seen. It was this passionate need to capture the experiences of the immigrant Jews to the American West that spawned The Oregon Jewish Oral History and Archives Project.

There was the realization that this historic show was not the culmination of efforts to preserve local history; rather, it was a beginning. A pioneer history was not the answer to the growth and needs of a contemporary Jewish community. The western Jewish community needed a social history of immigration, family life, institutions and community from a personal and varied perspective. I perceived that what our community needed was a history from the "inside out," that rare perspective of the ethnic's own perception of his experiences.[37]

As Tanzer's reflections make clear, only with the passing of the neighborhood did it become a site for nostalgia—and that nostalgia fed a new historical narrative that provided a usable past for an urban ethnic community, something that the old Oregon Jewish narrative could not provide. Whereas the old pioneer history had served the purpose of claiming a place for Jews in Oregon history, "Old South Portland" spoke to the concerns of an increasingly assimilated community by placing the Oregon Jewish experience in the mainstream of the American Jewish story. Tracing the creation of the show, the oral history project, and subsequent efforts to fashion this new narrative alongside the developments in the community as it responded to renewal allows insight into the linkage between the two. In addition, setting both in the larger context of the emergence of ethnic culture among American Jews more broadly, and the sacralization of the Lower East Side and the East European shtetl in the postwar period in particular, enables us to trace the ways in which this larger national Jewish narrative was transposed onto the Portland experience.

American Jews and the Creation of an Ethnic Past

The centrality of New York to American Jewish identity is difficult to overstate. In popular culture New York and Jewishness are often blurred; to be from New York is to be Jewish, and to be Jewish is to be from New York.[38] In nineteenth-century Oregon, and elsewhere in the West, Jewish stores often advertised "New York" prices or merchandise, and, not infrequently, adopted business names that tied them to the city. Even among contemporary Jews who have no personal or family history in New York, such connections are often assumed or imagined. For example, Hasia Diner, author of *Lower East Side Memories: A Jewish Place in America*, writes that although she grew up in Milwaukee and, so far as she knows, no one in her family "ever set foot on the Lower East Side," she felt its pull, both through the children's book *All of a Kind Family* and through the accounts of her neighbors, whose trips to the Lower East Side "took the form of pilgrimages, journeys to the source of 'real' Jewish culture, where they could learn from the experts, the high priests of Yiddishkeit, about what we in the provinces should be seeing." When she visited the Lower East Side for the first time as an adult in the 1980s, she writes,

> I felt that I had "come home." It was an emotional, intense afternoon in which everything was new but also absolutely familiar. I looked for my parents on Delancey Street, on Essex and Rivington, as they appeared in the black-and-white photographs of our family album. I knew that they had never lived here, but I kept trying to superimpose the pictures that had been taken of them in Venice,

California, and Chicago in the 1930s and 1940s onto the streetscapes of the Lower East Side of the 1980s.[39]

The nostalgic pull of the Lower East Side is just as evident among contemporary Jewish Oregonians. When several dozen members of Salem's Temple Beth Sholom gathered in 2009 for a program connected to a Lower East Side photography exhibit, participants were encouraged to share their family stories and to engage in discussion about the meaning of immigration and Lower East Side experience for their families. The discussion was heartfelt and nostalgic. Members brought in photos and artifacts and shared family stories connecting to these themes. Yet, when surveyed at the end of the session, only about half of the participants indicated that they were actually descended from East European Jews, and only about half of them, roughly a quarter of the group's participants, had ancestors who had actually lived in New York City. Not surprisingly for a western Reconstructionist congregation, there were roughly as many present who were Jews by choice or children of Jews by choice as there were descendants of immigrants who passed through New York. Among those born Jewish, many were from families that had resided in Chicago, Los Angeles, or elsewhere in the Midwest or West. Although lacking real connections to the actual, historic place, the power of the Lower East Side as a Jewish communal memory was palpable. The group repeatedly invoked a shared history that could be traced back through the Lower East Side to a shtetl in Eastern Europe, responding emotionally to common tropes of that story—of grandparents who were peddlers, of immigrants arriving in steerage, of glimpsing the Statue of Liberty, and of hopes for a new "promised land."[40]

That a group of twenty-first-century Jewish Oregonians, whose families arrived in Salem via Chicago, Seattle, Los Angeles, Alaska, and Des Moines as well as New York, and among whom were a number without Jewish ancestry at all, would so powerfully identify with the Lower East Side is suggestive of the power of that story for American Jews. Beginning as early as the 1920s and 1930s, but especially in the period since the 1960s, the Lower East Side emerged as the central story of origin for American Jews. Diner and others have explored the process that she calls the "memorialization of the Lower East Side," arguing that it emerged after the neighborhood's heyday, as part of a larger nostalgia for an Eastern European Jewish world that had been destroyed during World War II. By the 1960s, when many of the last barriers to Jewish integration and inclusion in white middle-class America had fallen, the story of immigrant hardship, of poverty, of struggle, and of alienation provided, in the words of Beth Wenger, "a cultural construct that helped Jews interpret their history and make sense of their experience as Jewish Americans." The Lower East Side evoked "memories of the East European shtetl," with its ethnic foods and Yiddish culture, but also marked the beginnings of American Jewish life.[41]

Yet, as Diner, Wenger, and others point out, the Lower East Side of American Jewish memory was, like all historical memory, reshaped and refashioned to meet contemporary needs. Historian Jenna Weissman Joselit explains, "From their safe and lofty perches, high above Riverside Drive or overlooking Prospect Park, the former sons and daughters of the Lower East Side recast the landscape of their youth, transforming its cluster of dingy, smelly, mean streets into 'picturesque havens of domesticity.'" In the process, she claims, "a slum became a shrine."[42]

In historical memory, the Lower East Side became more uniformly Jewish and East European than was actually the case. It also became more religious. Historian David Kaufman argues that Lower East Side memory culture places the synagogue at the center, despite the "historical view of synagogues as peripheral to the immigrant experience," and historical research demonstrating that "only a fraction" of Lower East Side Jews were "actively engaged" in synagogues.[43] Early on in the creation of this historical memory, Wenger explains,

> the image of Orthodox Jews, bearded men and women with kerchiefs, overtook most representations of the Lower East Side even though Orthodox Jewry had been a minority within the neighborhood's Jewish population. When the *Forward* published its anniversary edition in 1927, one of the articles reported that when the East Side was in its heyday, every neighborhood business remained closed on the Sabbath. But in fact, by the early twentieth century, many Lower East Side stores had already begun doing business on Saturdays.[44]

Indeed, the entire construct of a place called the Lower East Side (with capital letters) emerged *after* the neighborhood's moment had passed. According to Diner, at the time when it was home to its largest Jewish community, the area did not have a fixed name and was instead often referred to as "the Jewish Quarter," "downtown," "the Russian Quarter," "the Hebrew Quarter," "the Jewish east side," and "the ghetto."[45] The point here is not to discredit the collective memory of the Lower East Side, but to understand that the histories that communities construct draw on the past and shape them in response to their present needs. In the latter half of the twentieth century,

> American Jews needed a Lower East Side, a place of origin through which they could represent themselves, and a venue from which to describe the loss of Jewish authenticity in the face of collective, and individual achievement. . . . At the heart of the sanctification of the Lower East Side lies the theme of personal success, bought at the price of Jewish coherence, a price the authors no doubt felt was worth what it got them, but not without a degree of regret.[46]

Many of the same conflicting emotions surround the sacralization of the shtetl as memorialized in *Fiddler on the Roof*. Opening as a Broadway show in 1964 and as an Oscar-winning feature film in 1971, *Fiddler* became an instant success. As studies charted a surge in intermarriage among second- and third-generation, assimilated young people, American Jews publicly worried that "the thorough Jewish sense of belonging in America could eventually lead to the disappearance of the people: annihilation by love, not hate."[47] *Fiddler*'s direct engagement with marital choice and intermarriage was only part of its broader grappling with questions of tradition and change that made it such a symbol of American Jewish identity. *Fiddler* was quickly embraced as a symbol of Jewish authenticity, and its portrayal of the fictional shtetl Anatevka became the iconic image of the shtetl origins of American Jews, a reference point for family and community stories. [48] In recounting his family's 1917 departure from Russia nearly ninety years later in an oral history, Oregonian Nate Director explained, "We had to leave, just like in *Fiddler on the Roof*."[49]

Side by side, the historical memories of shtetl origins, flight from persecution, and immigrant settlement on the Lower East Side were, by the 1960s, the core symbols of American Jewish identity. As Portland's Jews wrestled with their own concerns about communal dispersal, assimilation, and loss of identity, they drew on these symbols in telling their own story, both embracing the broader American Jewish memories embodied in these tropes, and transposing them onto specific, place-based memories of South Portland. What emerged was a story that was both universal and local. As an article in the May 1976 *Historical Scribe* explained, "Old South Portland symbolized all people who have ever ventured into strange new lands. Old South Portland was the first step in the attainment of the American dream. One need never have set foot in Old South Portland to understand what it was all about."[50]

Shtetls and Pushcarts? Anatevka and the Lower East Side Come to Portland

As urban renewal and highway construction razed the area that had been the Jewish immigrant neighborhood, *Whatever Happened to Old South Portland* became the first of several community efforts to memorialize the neighborhood. Written and produced in the era when the iconization of the Lower East Side was at its peak, and when *Fiddler* was in the process of becoming the most familiar representation of the East European immigrant story, *Whatever Happened* drew repeatedly on those tropes, grafting the language of shtetls and pushcarts onto the neighborhood, and in the process creating Old South Portland.

The repeated use of images of pushcarts provides an interesting glimpse of this process of history making. In the opening scene of *Whatever Happened*, Marty Zell returns to Portland after many years' absence and meets cabdriver George Rickles at the airport. Soon, the two realize that they grew up together in South Portland. Zell, envisioning the neighborhood of his childhood, exclaims, "I can hardly wait to see it! The pushcarts . . . the produce wagons . . . the marriage broker."[51] Several scenes later, the "Battle Hymie of South Portland," quoted at the opening of this chapter, is sung, including the line, "Now towers rise and fountains flow, o'er streets where pushcarts rolled."

Despite these repeated references, there is no evidence that pushcarts—well known as a dominant feature in the iconic Lower East Side landscape—were particularly prevalent, or present at all, in South Portland (the same could also be said for marriage brokers—an image likely imported from *Fiddler's* Anatevka, where matchmaking is a central plot point). Turn-of-the-century Portland newspapers do not refer to Jewish pushcarts in South Portland; rather, the vast majority of pushcarts mentioned in the Portland press are in stories from New York.[52] In fact, Portland was one of several western cities to pass ordinances around the turn of the century targeting Chinese peddlers. The result was that, "by 1910 all peddling was prohibited, except for meat, ice, bread, and newspapers."[53] Although it is certainly true that some of Portland's East European Jewish immigrants began their careers as peddlers and junk dealers, the specific image of pushcarts crowding the streets of South Portland appears to have been imported from New York. This is particularly clear in a later *Whatever Happened* scene between Zell and Rickles:

Marty: My father had a grocery store.
George: Everybody had a store. And if they didn't have a store, they had a pushcart.
Marty: And if they couldn't afford a pushcart, they put a sack on their back and collected rags and bottles.
George: My father, may he rest in peace, was wiped out in the stock market crash in '29.
Marty: He made so much money with a pushcart he played the stock market?
George: No, a stockbroker jumped out the window and fell on him![54]

Here, a New York image (and well known punchline)—complete with suicidal stockbroker—is imported wholesale and transposed onto South Portland.

Although Shirley Tanzer and her cowriters based their script on the oral testimony of those who had lived in the neighborhood, it seems that they, and not their informants, introduced pushcarts to the Portland scene. The original interviews for *Whatever Happened,* conducted in the mid-1960s, prior to the show's premier in 1969, have not been transcribed. However, among the approximately 150 oral history transcripts from the Tanzer-led oral history project of the 1970s, there are no informants who place pushcarts in South Portland. Arthur Markewitz, born in Portland in the first decade of the twentieth century, emphasized that "South Portland wasn't particularly a typical eastern ghetto with pushcarts and those things, you know, and a garment industry."[55] Nevertheless, there were interviewers who, presumably influenced by images from New York, believed that pushcarts had been part of the scene, and asked about them specifically. For example, in this 1974 exchange between informant Lillie Kugel and an oral history project interviewer, it is the interviewer who introduces pushcarts to the conversation:

> Kugel: And dad used to peddle. He used to go to different houses and buy clothing and then sell it. But he only did that for about a year.
> Interviewer: With a pushcart?
> Kugel: No. He had a horse and buggy. Then after that he had a little second-hand store down on Third and Everett Street.[56]

The only informants who remembered pushcarts were those like Julius Zell, Marty's father and the chair of the JCC building campaign, who mentioned seeing pushcarts during his sojourn in New York, before coming to Portland.[57] Typically, those who recalled peddling in Portland refer to horse and cart businesses or, in some cases, to beginnings as pack peddlers. For example, Manley Labby recalled that his father "did what a lot of other Jews did when they first came here; he bought a wagon and a horse and went out and sold fruit and later junk."[58] Likewise, Harold Schnitzer recalled in a 1977 interview that the company that grew into Schnitzer Steel began with his father, Sam Schnitzer, peddling in Astoria, "buying old clothes, picking up old rubber boots and all kinds of old junk. . . . He went by foot and he would hire a wagon to pick things up for him."[59] What such accounts make clear is that the pushcarts were a collective memory imported from New York.

Yet, in the wake of *Whatever Happened*, the pushcart became a part of the shared memory of Jewish South Portland and a familiar trope in the telling of local Jewish history. The absence of actual pushcarts in Portland explains why, although there are many photos of Jewish businesses in Portland from the early twentieth century, references to pushcarts are typically accompanied by photographs from New York. Thus, the opening of the 1976 slideshow, *Memory Is Survival*, interspersed slides of "Portland Jew in a downtown scene," with scenes from steerage, Ellis Island, and "pushcarts in New York." Slides of "pushcarts and peddlers," appeared again later in the show, as the East European migration was detailed.[60] Similarly, in *The Jews of Oregon, 1850–1950*, published in 1987, Steven Lowenstein writes about, and provides pictures of, several South Portland businesses, such as Dora Levine's fish shop and Mosler's bakery, and adds that "live chickens . . . as well as fresh fruit, vegetables and other produce were often purchased not in a store but from a

Local historical projects such as *Memory Is Survival* used stock photos of crowded New York streets to suggest a similar scene in South Portland. Courtesy OJMCHE

Although there is no evidence of pushcart peddling among Portland Jews, through projects such as *Whatever Happened to Old South Portland*, pushcarts were incorporated into historical memory. Here a pushcart is displayed as part of an exhibit at the Oregon Jewish Museum in 2005. Courtesy OJMCHE peddler's cart."[61] He does not specifically mention pushcarts, but does provide an image of crowded shopping area on Hester Street in New York to set the scene for his chapter about East European immigrants.[62]

The introduction of pushcarts into community histories likely led to their subsequent entry into family stories, as images from *Whatever Happened* and *Memory Is Survival* came to inform oral histories. For example, Manley Labby explained in his 1975 oral history that his father brought the family to Woodbine, a Jewish agricultural settlement in New Jersey, and then to Portland, taking care to avoid New York because the "little experience he had in that city was not palatable to him." In contrast, a 2004 account by his nephew, Dan Labby, a native of South Portland, claims that the same man (Dan's grandfather, Manly's father) "was one of the pushcart peddlers, you know, on lower Hester Street."[63] Much as the overland journey had become a shorthand way of referencing all it was to be an Oregon pioneer in histories past, pushcarts became by the late twentieth century a symbol of the quintessential Jewish American experience. Direct connections to pushcarts lent authenticity to the Oregon Jewish experience by directly linking it to that narrative.

Pushcarts were not the only way in which the emerging South Portland memory culture drew connections to the New York neighborhood. For example, although the population density was on an entirely different scale, descriptions of crowded streets in Portland's "Jewish" neighborhood also called to mind the Lower East Side. South Portland was largely a community of single-family homes and small apartment buildings—not the larger, crowded tenement buildings of New York. Certainly, during the immigrant period, families often doubled up and houses built for a single family might house multigenerational or extended families and boarders. Yet descriptions of South Portland implicitly exaggerated its crowding and busy street life by using language common in descriptions of the Lower East Side. During the opening shtick between Rickles and Zell in *Whatever Happened*, Rickles claims, "It was like a beehive, the people swarming from early morning to late at night." Later, Zell describes First Street as "teeming with life." [64] Such descriptors subsequently became common in histories of the neighborhood, as did other sorts of direct and indirect references to the Lower East Side. Lowenstein, after describing South Portland's crowded shopping streets in the days leading up to the Sabbath and the strolling and socializing on Saturday nights, urged his readers, "Try to imagine the sounds, the smells, the motion along First Avenue for the several blocks between Grant and Meade Streets."[65] Decades later, in *Stories from Jewish Portland,* Polina Olsen similarly suggested, "Some compare First Street in South Portland with Delancey Street on New York's Lower East Side. The self-contained community had everything Jewish immigrants might need."[66]

Housing density in South Portland was considerably lower than it was in New York. Courtesy OJMCHE

Just as pervasive in these historical representations of South Portland were comparisons to "the shtetl." The chorus of the theme song in *Whatever Happened*, repeated ten times in the show, asks "What has become of Old South Portland? What has happened to my stedt-e le? [*sic*]." Similarly, in *Memory Is Survival*, after a series of reminiscences about South Portland and slides of scenes from *Whatever Happened* with voice-overs drawn from the play's script, a shtetl scene was projected as the narrator said, "The nostalgic affection for Old South Portland is similar to the nostalgic affection for the shtetl. In both, the feeling of community was a precious thing."[67] Interestingly, these references were not vaguely to "a shtetl" but to "THE shtetl" or "MY shtetl," suggesting a specific image. It seems likely that, for many audience members experiencing these shows in the wake of *Fiddler*, which in addition to its Broadway, traveling, and silver screen versions, would be the first community musical performed in the new JCC's auditorium in 1974, Anatevka was the shtetl called to mind. Along with references to shtetls, mentions of *heder* (traditional religious school), *melameds* (*heder* teachers), *shochets* (ritual slaughterers), and other shtetl fixtures also conjured images of *Fiddler*. Although a far greater number of Jewish children in South Portland were educated in the modern and assimilationist-oriented Portland Hebrew School—including the children of orthodox Shaarie Torah congregants—*Whatever*

Happened made several references to learning in *heder*.[68] The song "What did the Heimish Folk Do?" asked about the activities of "The shocket [*sic*] who is ailing; the melamed who is glum; Zohn Cobbler who is wailing, from nailing his thumb?"[69] Certainly, such individuals were present in South Portland early in the century, but the focus on these characters served both the general purpose of evoking nostalgia for a bygone era and of linking Portland to the shtetl. The same was true in later published accounts. Lowenstein's caption for a picture of houses in South Portland reads, "Life in South Portland recreated the closeness and intimacy of the shtetls of Eastern Europe."[70]

References to shtetls also appear in the oral histories—both actual shtetl origins in Eastern Europe and comparisons of the Portland neighborhood to a shtetl. Dora Levine, whose fish store was one of the most frequently mentioned businesses in reminiscences about South Portland, combined references to Eastern Europe and New York when she characterized the neighborhood: "It was like a shtetl village. I'll tell you Saturday night right on the corner where I have my store was like Coney Island. All the people there came alleh [all]."[71] "Shtetl," in such testimony conveyed the self-sufficiency and separateness of the community, the close personal ties among residents, and the profoundly Jewish nature of the place. Gussie Reinhardt, longtime resident of the neighborhood and leader of the fight to save Neighborhood House and Kesser Israel from the wrecking ball, explained, "People chose to live close to each other and it was a wonderful way to live, really, very much as we think of a shtetl because in this small area, anything that anybody needed for good living was available within walking distance."[72]

With, or more often without, the use of the word "shtetl," these ideas were repeatedly invoked in the oral histories. For example, Frieda (Gass) Cohen conveyed all this when she described the South Portland she remembered from the 1910s:

> At that time upper South Portland housed practically every Jewish person in the city. There were very few that lived any place else. It was really a teeming place for the Jews, and what an exciting place. They brought up their children, they educated them, they sent them to Hebrew School. They never had to go out of the neighborhood to do their shopping. All of their Jewish grocery stores were in the area, and two or three kosher meat markets. . . . The children grew up in the neighborhood and more or less stayed in the neighborhood all of the time that they were growing up.[73]

Dan Labby, born in Portland in 1914, recalled store by store the route from his house to his grandmother's house; after naming eight separate businesses in addition to "a series of mom and pop stores as well as junk stores," Labby concluded, "so that whole place was a kind of contained little village."[74] Likewise, Gussie Reinhardt gave popular presentations about the area in later years. Her 1996 talk at the Robison Home was titled "Old South Portland, Memories of a Jewish village in the early 1900s." The notice of the talk read: "For Portlanders, Gussie Reinhardt's talks about the South Portland Jewish neighborhood have the same quality—nostalgia for an era when everyone knew everyone and values were shared along with everything else. . . . The warmth was that of a place where everyone belonged and was cared for."[75]

Like memories of shtetls, many of these accounts painted the neighborhood as overwhelmingly, if not entirely, Jewish. *Memory Is Survival* quoted Diane (Holzman) Nemer reminiscing about how "the whole neighborhood was a Jewish neighborhood, and that's the only kind I knew. On the whole block there might have been two families that were not Jewish, and they lived across the street."[76] Some informants reported that it was "all Jewish," and then remembering Italians and others, corrected themselves and offered the example of Colistro and Halperin's deli, an Italian-Jewish partnership, or of other non-Jewish friends and neighbors. Shirley Tanzer made an effort to tell a more inclusive story—an article in the *JCC Ace* published her request for help in locating "the Italian, Chinese, and Negro families who were raised in South Portland." The story listed several family names and admonished, "If you know the whereabouts of any of these families, please contact them and Shirley!"[77] Despite these efforts, in historical memory, Old South Portland, like the Lower East Side, became more intensely Jewish than the neighborhood had actually been. This was not lost on Joe Colistro, who complained to a reporter, "It is a tragic event in our history that the Jews should choose such a well-produced extravaganza in which to misrepresent the development, growth and subsequent death of Old South Portland." Ironically, Colistro overcorrected when he claimed, "It's a matter of records that Old South Portland was primarily an Italian colony with a light sprinkling of Jews and Irish. Why, they didn't even give credit to the Italian who owned and operated the best delicatessen and bagel parlor in the area—Colistro and Halperin."[78] Actually, the show did mention the deli, although it reversed the two owners' names, calling it "Halperin and Colistro's."

In addition to remembering the neighborhood as more densely Jewish than it actually was, South Portland, like the Lower East Side, was also portrayed as more uniformly religious than was actually the case. Certainly, many of the early twentieth-century immigrants were more traditional in religious outlook and ritual practice than the German Jewish community that preceded them, or than their own descendants. Like their counterparts in other cities, Portland's East European and Sephardic newcomers founded synagogues of their own, enabling them to continue practicing in a form that was familiar. Yet evidence suggests that, in general, those migrants who chose to leave larger cities and venture to smaller and more remote communities like Portland were often those who were more flexible in their practice.[79] Indeed, several of the earliest "Russian" congregations in the city were quite modern in their practice, embracing choirs and English language sermons as early as the 1890s.[80] By the 1920s, upwardly mobile immigrant families had begun shifting their membership from more traditional shuls, like Shaarie Torah, to more liberal congregations like Neveh Zedek and Ahavai Shalom.[81] Despite this, remembrances of South Portland, like those of the Lower East Side, tend to depict an almost uniformly Orthodox practice.

Although many oral histories of Portlanders who grew up in the 1910s, 1920s, and 1930s suggest a range of observance, the historical memory of that period constructed in the 1960s and 1970s highlighted religiosity. Remembering the community as traditionally religious linked South Portland to the memory of the Lower East Side and the shtetl, and imparted an additional layer of authenticity. An example can be found in the historic *Scribe*, published in conjunction with *Memory Is Survival* in the spring of 1976. Its centerspread featured a set of drawings titled "Historic Jewish Portland," depicting Portland's historic synagogues. Neighborhood House and the B'nai B'rith Center (precursor to the JCC), vital but more secular institutions in the immigrant neighborhood, were not pictured.[82]

The emphasis on religiosity also reflected contemporary concern about the waning of religious observance. The historical memory of Jewish South Portland emerged when Jews in Portland, like American Jews nationally, were going through a process of self-examination in the wake of surveys revealing historically low levels of observance. Several Portland congregations had not survived the process of urban renewal, and the number of Orthodox congregations in particular had fallen (particularly if one counts the shift at Shaarie Torah from Orthodox to traditional). Portland's own 1971 survey concluded that there had been "rapid erosion" in the "basis of identity in Jewish religious ritual," and led the Federation to create a series of task forces to address the issue.[83] As Jews locally and nationally assessed these concerns, they looked back nostalgically on the religiosity of the past as part of a lost authenticity. Historian David Kaufman, commenting on the emphasis on the "sacred space of synagogues" in Lower East Side memory, argues that old synagogue buildings attract attention in such remembrances because "their very decrepitude bespeaks a lost culture."[84]

The Birth of Old South Portland

The goal of *Whatever Happened* was to remember the vanished neighborhood. In the process, the show and the projects that followed it *created* Old South Portland. Located immediately south of downtown in a city divided east-west by the Willamette River, the neighborhood, technically, was part of Southwest Portland. At the time of urban renewal, the area was officially known as the

South Auditorium District. Although often informally called South Portland, that did not become the official name of the neighborhood until 2006, when the neighborhood association changed the name from the Corbett, Terwilliger, Lair Hill Neighborhood Association. A 1976 *Oregon Journal* article, looking back at urban renewal as "the death of a neighborhood," explained that "there are those who remember and speak fondly of old 'South Portland,'" the quotation marks suggesting that this name for the area was not in general use.[85] During its heyday, the most heavily Jewish sections of the area were sometimes called "Jewtown," while other nearby clusters were known by some as "Little Italy" and "Little Russia."[86]

Yet "Old South Portland" is used commonly today to refer to the historic Jewish neighborhood. Oral histories conducted early in the twenty-first century are replete with nostalgic references to the neighborhood. "We lived in Old South Portland," Richard Matza explained in a 2013 interview. "Man, that was a great place to live."[87] Arden Shenker, interviewed in 2007, claimed, "People who grew up in Old South Portland have a bond and a tie that is much, much stronger than you find in people growing up in Portland today."[88] And Howard Marcus, whose family moved to South Portland in 1941 when he was ten, remembered,

> South Portland, Old South Portland was a wonderful time, I mean when I mention Mosler's Bakery, going in there and then when they moved up on Fourth Street and it was only like three blocks from my house and stopping in there. Mosler always had thirteen bagels for a dozen. I'll always remember that, he gave thirteen. And every once in a while I'd go in there and he'd give me a cookie or something and I'd get a dozen bagels.[89]

Wendy (Simon) Liebreich recalled weekly visits to the area after Sunday school: "At that time in Old South Portland is where all my family lived. A lot of my aunts and uncles did. And they had delicatessens. We would go over there. They had big pickle barrels and salami. We always got bagels and corned beef and pickles. It was great."[90]

In contrast, when Shirley Tanzer interviewed Dora Levine in 1969, as part of the research for the musical, neither one of them used the term "Old South Portland," despite the fact that their interview focused heavily on the neighborhood.[91] Even in the oral histories conducted in the 1970s, after the musical, there were many references to "South Portland," but few to "Old South Portland."[92] Frieda Cohen called the area "upper south Portland," and used "Old South Portland" only when referring specifically to the musical.[93] In a 1975 interview, Manley Labby, in the midst of a detailed description of the neighborhood, explained, "It is what is known as the Old South Portland," suggesting that the appellation was attached later.[94] Interestingly, although the oral history subjects tended not to use

Shirley Tanzer (right) interviews Dora Levine in 1969 as part of the background research for *Whatever Happened to Old South Portland?* Courtesy OJMCHE

"Old South Portland," the interviewers and transcribers working for the oral history project did so routinely, both in the abstracts they wrote summarizing the interviews and in their questions.[95] When Abe "English" Rosenberg was interviewed by Michele Glazer in 1977, she asked several times about "Old South Portland," although he never referred to the area by that name.[96] Likewise, interviewer Eva Rickles asked Joanna Menashe several times about "Old South Portland," but in her responses, Menashe just referred to "the neighborhood."[97]

These usage patterns strongly suggest that, just as "the Lower East Side" became the official name for the New York neighborhood only as historical memory was constructed, "Old South Portland" was a name made real by the musical and subsequent activities to memorialize the neighborhood, including the interviews themselves. One can actually see the term being coined in the run-up to the show. The December 1968 *JCC Ace* trivia quiz about the neighborhood indicates that it is for a "Gala salute to old South Portland," with only this one mention of South Portland by name, and "old" not capitalized. By January, the casting call was titled "Wanted from Old South Portland," and an accompanying article about the show is headlined "JCC Prepares to Look Back in time to Old Days in South Portland." By February, the show had been named and references to "Old South Portland" were consistently capitalized. "Old South Portland" was again used in the advertisement for the November 1969 photo exhibit, and in the materials surrounding the oral history project. In the 1976 profile of Shirley Tanzer in the *Historical Scribe*, "Old South Portland" is used four times, not including its use in the title of the musical.[98]

Subsequent community histories, like Lowenstein's and Olsen's, also use "Old South Portland," including Lowenstein's use of it in a chapter title, and Olsen's in a book title.[99] In recent years, Olsen has run a popular walking tour of the neighborhood.

Where earlier histories such as Suwol's and Nodel's looked to the pioneers and politicians as the key to understanding the roots of Oregon Jewry, the memorialization of South Portland during the 1960s and 1970s cemented the place of East European immigrants and their children in the community story. By the mid-1970s, the "real Oregonians" in the Jewish community were no longer only those who could trace their families back to the nineteenth-century community founders. The story of immigrant struggle in turn-of-the-century Portland had become a new founding story, with its own resonance as an authentic American story of overcoming adversity and making it in a new land.

Beyond South Portland

Although South Portland was the most visible product of the historical activity triggered by urban renewal, the focus on community roots did not end there. In Tanzer's words, "This historic show [*Whatever Happened*] was not the culmination of efforts to preserve local history: rather, it was a beginning."[100] The Jewish Archive and Oral History project was the most immediate outgrowth. Captivated by the interviews she conducted in preparation for the show, Tanzer discovered the field of oral history during her subsequent studies at Portland State University. As she gained expertise, she not only conducted interviews but also trained cadres of others, both within and outside the Jewish community. By 1973, she had secured the support of the Portland Section of the Council of Jewish Women and an office at the JCC. Working closely with project coordinators Renee Holzman and Susan (Woolach) Marcus, historian Marianne (Lehman) Feldman, and a corps of fifteen women who served as interviewers and transcribers, the project conducted oral histories with over 150 individuals between 1974 and 1978.[101]

As the oral histories proceeded, a separate organization, the Jewish Historical Society of Oregon, took shape. Rabbi Stampfer, a history enthusiast and spiritual leader of Congregation Neveh Shalom, is credited with the idea of forming the society. Stampfer brought to the table a strong sense of the place of Oregon in a broader Jewish and world history. Noting Portland's significance as the second oldest Jewish community in the West and the upcoming American bicentennial, Stampfer worked with organizational leaders Alice (Turtledove) Meyer, Sidney Teiser, and Harold Hirsch to incorporate the Oregon Jewish Historical Society in November 1974, with an aim of collecting, publishing, and exhibiting Oregon Jewish history. The first meeting of the new organization, in January 1975, drew sixty people, and *Memory Is Survival* was one of the group's early projects.[102] By 1977, the Jewish Historical Society and the Oral History and Archive Project, recognizing their parallel missions, merged, and Tanzer was named executive director.

These developments—particularly the ongoing oral history project—led to a broadening of the scope of Oregon Jewish history. Although the impetus for the musical and initial oral histories was the razing of the South Portland neighborhood, the Tanzer-led project aimed to document a wide variety of Oregon Jewish experiences. Oral histories were conducted with descendants of the nineteenth-century pioneers, Jews who had lived in remote areas of the state, and more recent arrivals, particularly wartime refugees. Just as *Whatever Happened* added East European immigrants and their children to a historic cast of characters that had once included only pioneers and politicians, documentation of the lives of more diverse Jewish Oregonians led to the gradual inclusion of their stories in community histories. In this way, Sephardic immigrants and Holocaust survivors, whose distinct stories had not been prominent in the earlier histories, came to be recognized as integral to the Oregon Jewish story.

The evolution can be seen clearly in the case of the Sephardic community. South Portland had been home to a contingent of Sephardim who arrived from the Turkish coast and the Isle of Rhodes beginning in 1909 and founded a congregation, Ahavath Achim, in 1916.[103] By the late 1960s, their descendants were well integrated into the broader Jewish community; Sephardic children grew up attending the Portland Hebrew School or Sunday school at either the Reform, or, more often, the Conservative congregation. Although Ahavath Achim continued as a separate congregation, many second- and third-generation Sephardim had close family ties through marriage to Ashkenazic families. Their assimilation into the broader Jewish community appears to have led to an overlooking of their distinctive historical experience in *Whatever Happened*. The individuals, institutions, and businesses named in the show—as well as the many Yiddish expressions sprinkled throughout the production—were firmly anchored in the East European immigrant experience. No Sephardic businesses or families were mentioned by name. The lone reference was to the disastrous attempt to move the Ahavath Achim synagogue to a new location outside the renewal zone:

> George: Shaarie Torah came down once, came down twice . . .
> Ahavai Shalom came down . . .
> Neveh Zedek came down . . .
> Sephardic Synagogue came down, fell down.
> Marty: Do you suppose there's something anti-Semitic about Urban Renewal?[104]

It is notable in this exchange that congregational names are used for the three Ashkenazic synagogues, but not for Ahavath Achim.

Despite this neglect in the 1969 production, the oral history project that emerged from the show did include a few interviews with Sephardim. Harry Policar, who had long served as athletic director at the JCC and at the B'nai B'rith camp at the Oregon Coast, was probably included because of his professional activities; his Sephardic roots seem somewhat incidental in the interview. However, Eva Rickles's interviews with Ezra and Joya Menashe, and with Joanna (Capeluto) Menashe, both in early 1975, focused heavily on their Sephardic background and detailed the history of this group of Rhodes natives in Portland. The Ezra and Joya Menashe interview, which Rickles continued in a second session the following November, spans more than forty pages, and provides a detailed history of Congregation Ahavath Achim, from its founding through the building's destruction during the move and the building of a new synagogue.[105] Several additional interviews were conducted in the Sephardic community in 1985, including two in Ladino.[106]

The Menashe family interviews likely provided the basis for the increased attention to the Sephardic community in the 1976 slideshow, *Memory Is Survival.* With a series of thirteen slides, *Memory* succinctly told the story of Sephardim in Portland, focusing particularly on the synagogue and quoting Ezra Menashe's account of the traumatic moment when the building was irreparably damaged during an attempt to move it out of the renewal zone.[107] Although the coverage made up less than 10 percent of the presentation (the show included 199 slides), in mentioning Sephardic origins and community history and providing more detail on the congregation and the story of its buildings, it went well beyond that in *Whatever Happened.* Steven Lowenstein's community history, published in 1987, provided similar coverage—including a brief history of the congregation and a few other mentions of the community, but hardly a comprehensive treatment. Such neglect of Sephardic roots, of course, was not unique to Portland. In a review of the field of American Jewish history in 1990, Jonathan Sarna identified the study of Sephardic immigrants and their children as one of the most neglected areas of research.[108] Historian Aviva Ben-Ur notes, "More often than not, Sephardic Jews are simply absent from any sort of portrayal of the American Jewish community."[109] Indeed, Ben-Ur's 2009 monograph claims to be the "first full-length, academic study of non-Ashkenazic Jews in the United States," although she also notes that attention to Sephardic studies in the United States has increased in recent years.[110]

In Portland, the Sephardic story became far better understood and represented in communal memory in the late twentieth and early twenty-first centuries—culminating in the 2014 gala, exhibit, and book commemorating one hundred years of Sephardic community in Portland: *Vida Sefaradi.*[111] Oregon Jewish Museum director Judith Margles noted that the 2014 celebration was "the Sephardic community's *Whatever Happened*," shaping collective memory and evoking a wave of nostalgia much as the earlier musical had done.[112]

Inclusion of the Sephardic community in local Jewish history began about a decade after the musical, fostered by the merged historical society and shepherded in part by Rabbi Stampfer. Stampfer's interest in the diverse histories of world Jewry was key to bringing an exhibit on the Jews of Kaifeng (China) to Portland in 1984, and his visit to that community was well documented in the *Jewish Review*. The following year, Stampfer made his first visit to the community of crypto-Jews in Belmonte, Portugal. During a subsequent visit, he conducted the first open Shabbat service held in Belmonte in five hundred years. His work in Portugal—which included editing an English edition of a history of the Belmonte community, published in Portland by the Institute for Judaic Studies—brought an awareness of the historic Sephardic community to Portland, surely contributing to increased interest in the local community.[113] The Institute for Judaic Studies, yet another organization that Stampfer was instrumental in founding, began as a group focused on introducing Judaic studies to local college campuses. By the mid-1980s, they broadened their mission, establishing a variety of programs, including lectures, study marathons, and conferences designed to bring academic Judaic studies to the broader community. Although these programs ranged widely in terms of topic, including everything from Biblical study and ethics to the modern Middle East and literature, a number of them supported an expanded understanding of Jewish diversity, and of Sephardic history and culture in particular. Their second annual conference, in 1985, was "The Sephardim: A Cultural Journey from Spain to the Pacific Northwest" and featured several nationally known scholars of Sephardic studies.[114]

In 1990, Stampfer's vision led to the founding of the Oregon Jewish Museum (OJM), whose goals included providing "public exposure to the cultural aspects of the many different Jewish communities."[115] Despite its lack of a facility, OJM immediately began to address this goal. Its first exhibit, *Jews of Greece*, a traveling show from the Bay Area's Magnes Museum, opened in 1990 at the Multnomah County Central Library, and brought the Portland Jewish and Greek communities together for a series of events.[116] Interspersed with Jewish-themed art shows, the OJM subsequently brought a series of exhibits focusing on diverse Jewish communities—Sephardic women in Turkey (1993), Jewish women around the world (1996), Jewish life in Germany (1999), the Jews of Kaifeng (2000), the Jews of the former Soviet Union (2000).

Despite—or perhaps because of—the existing Jewish Historical Society, the museum's mission statement, adopted in 1990, said nothing about local history; the mission was "to preserve, research and exhibit art and artifacts of the Jewish people."[117] Margles, a founding museum board member, recalled a sense among the group that Jewish history and art was something that had to be brought from elsewhere to Oregon. She remembered little consciousness of Oregon Jewish history and culture; rather, the group shared a sense that "the only way the community would understand the history of the Jews was to bring it from outside."[118] Still, Rabbi Stampfer, in an interview at the time of the museum's founding, did express ambitions relating to local history: "Ultimately, the Oregon Jewish Museum will collect artifacts from local families and house a permanent exhibit of Oregon Jewish history complementary to the Oregon Historical Society, preserving the history and traditions of Jewish settlers in the Northwest."[119] Although the emphasis on the "Jewish experience in Oregon" would not be formally incorporated into the museum's mission until 1995, when it merged with the Jewish Historical Society of Oregon,[120] attention to local history would come sooner.

In 1992, the museum undertook sponsorship of a major exhibit at the Oregon Historical Society. Curated by Beth Hatefutsoth (the Museum of the Diaspora) in Tel Aviv, *In the Footsteps of Columbus* was a traveling exhibit documenting the history of Jews in America from 1654 to 1880, and Portland would be its only stop in the Pacific Northwest. The show provided the first opportunity for the museum to examine local history—according to Judith Margles, it "opened the possibility of doing local Jewish history."[121] The group—still made up entirely of volunteers—embarked on an ambitious plan to curate a companion show titled *In the Footsteps of Lewis and Clark: Jews in Portland, 1849–1992*. Using the event to launch its program of local collections, the museum sent out a plea: "The Oregon Jewish Museum Needs Your Treasures!" asking donors to lend "artifacts, household goods, legal documents and records, clothing and other textiles, books, photographs or religious items," with an aim toward displaying these in the exhibit and beginning to "build an inventory and catalogue the Judaica and historical collections of Portland and Vancouver area families to be used in upcoming exhibitions to showcase and preserve our local history."[122]

Largely through the efforts of the OJM, both versions of *In the Footsteps* and the accompanying events did much to create local connections to the broader American Jewish historical narrative and highlight a new vision of Oregon Jewish history. With an emphasis on the presence of Jews and Jewish communities at every stage and in every region of American life, the exhibit provided many images of Jews in the West.[123] The locally produced exhibit flyer highlighted these western scenes, playing on the "footsteps" theme by using a trail of footprints to lead the viewer's eye through a series of images representing American Jewish history. Starting with a picture of sailing ships in New York's harbor, the trail led to successive images that moved forward in time and farther west. The final four images, roughly a third of the space on the flyer, were all from the West Coast, two from Los Angeles, one from

San Francisco, and the final shot from Portland. Local efforts to place visual emphasis on the West, as well as the suggestion that the trail of Jewish history led westward and to Portland, provided a view of American Jewish history that was quite at odds with the conventional New York-centric view.

The local connections to the national exhibit were highlighted in a lunchtime lecture series organized by Rabbi Stampfer. The series was headlined by Kenneth Libo, author of the exhibit catalog (best known for his work with Irving Howe on *World of Our Fathers*), who provided an overview. The other four lectures specifically focused on the local connection: Oregon Historical Society director Chet Orloff spoke on "The Jewish Experience in Oregon," writer and OHS staffer Terence O'Donnell discussed "The Place and the Face," Oregon historian E. Kimbark MacColl addressed "Twelve Unique Contributions to Oregon Public Life," and Portland State University professor Craig Wollner spoke on "Jewish Values in the Making of Oregon's Progressive Political Culture." In addition, the OJM organized an event focusing on "Oregon's Jewish Histories of Immigration," featuring Stewart Durkheimer on German immigrants, Jerry Stern on Eastern Europeans, and Dr. Victor Menashe on Sephardim. Finally, Wollner offered a concurrent summer course through Portland State University on Jewish immigration to Oregon.[124]

The inclusion of Menashe's reminiscences on the Sephardic community and the structuring of the session around these three communities suggests far greater appreciation of Sephardic significance to local Jewish history than had been evident in *Memory Is Survival*. Both the immigration lectures and the storyline developed for *In the Footsteps of Lewis and Clark* placed the Sephardic community on par with the Germans and East Europeans as key components of the Jewish community. Interestingly, the narrative about East Europeans in the storyline document relied primarily on the national (i.e., New York) version of the story, with little local elaboration, whereas the history of Sephardic immigration was much more specific to Portland—perhaps because the Sephardic story is not generally well represented in historical materials on Jews in New York. The Oregon-focused exhibit also added coverage of later-arriving refugees from Nazism and World War II, as well as the "ongoing exodus" of Jews from the Soviet Union, Ethiopia, Iraq, Israel, and California who were continuing to arrive in Portland. At a time when there was considerable public anxiety in Oregon about newcomers from the south "Californiaizing" the state, the storyline ended its list of newcomers, tongue in cheek, with "Californian Jews looking for the freedom of a better way of life call Portland home."[125]

The inclusion of Holocaust survivors as part of the local story was largely a product of the 1980s and 1990s. Although unmentioned in *Whatever Happened*—to do so would have been anachronistic given its focus on the prewar neighborhood—survivors and refugees who had escaped just before the war, like the Sephardim, were touched on, but not featured extensively, in *Memory Is Survival*. Yet by the mid-1970s, the Tanzer-led oral history project had started collecting the testimonies of a few Holocaust survivors. In 1983, those testimonies became the seeds of the Oregon Holocaust Resource Center (OHRC), yet another organization founded by Rabbi Stampfer. Directed by Sylvia Frankel, the OHRC embarked on its own oral history project, eventually collecting the testimonies of nearly a hundred Oregon-based survivors.[126] The OHRC made Holocaust education its central mission, establishing a speakers' bureau made up of local survivors as well as bringing in visiting scholars and organizing Holocaust remembrance ceremonies, exhibits, and essay competitions.[127]

For many of these survivors, as for their counterparts across the country, the oral history project and speakers' bureau provided the first opportunity to share their story. Hans Biglajzer, born in Germany in 1926, survived the Lodz Ghetto and Auschwitz. By 1985, Biglajzer was one of several survivors on the OHRC speaker's bureau, but it wasn't until 1990, in an oral history, that he revealed his complete story, explaining, "This is the first time I talked to anybody about this. Nobody ever asked me."[128] A Dutch survivor, Rochella "Chella" Meekcoms was early among the speakers. When interviewed in 1976, she was already a veteran presenter, and felt strongly about providing her testimony: "I do want to talk about it although I can still get upset about it and it hurts me," she explained. "But I feel that it is important and I thought it very important to bring it up to young—to kids that age fifteen, sixteen, fourteen, that age group. It makes a deep impression on them."[129] In Eugene, which began its own Jewish oral history project in 2006, survivors also shared their stories on tape, and in the broader community. As Charlotte Brown explained of her husband, Murray,

> There were not many survivors in Eugene then, so a lot of people came to ask him to speak at the University of Oregon or the university in Corvallis, or they took him to high schools every year to talk about his experience in the camps. At the beginning it was very hard. He really didn't want to do it. It brought back too many memories but then he realized that it should be more out in the open and people should know about it so he went.[130]

The creation of the OHRC, the collection of survivor testimony, and the involvement of many survivors and their families in these efforts helped spark a desire to create a local Holocaust memorial. The idea was first conceived in 1994 and, soon after, the City of Portland identified a site for the memorial in Washington Park, with strong support from Mayor Vera Katz, whose family had fled Nazi Germany in 1933. In 1998, Rabbis Larry Halpern (South Metro Jewish Community) and Ariel Stone-Halpern (Shir Tikvah) accompanied seven local survivors—Eva and Leslie Aigner, Chella and Jake Kryszek, Miriam

Holocaust survivor Jake Kryszek helps to bury soil brought from death camps in Poland as part of the Holocaust Memorial, 2004. Courtesy OJMCHE

Greenstein, Ruth Bolliger, and Al Lewin—as they traveled to Europe to collect dust and ashes from the six Nazi death camps to be buried as part of the memorial. Back in Portland, challenges to the site delayed construction for several years—one of the neighbors explained his objection to living near "a memorial to . . . 'the biggest downer in history.'"[131] After a protracted battle over the site, construction began in 2003, with the memorial dedicated the following year.[132] Both the collection of testimonies of local survivors and efforts to establish a local, public Holocaust memorial had the effect of making the survivors' stories part of Oregon Jewish history. The new focus on survivors was also part of a national trend—from the late 1970s and 1980s on, the collection of survivor testimony was a major focus of Jewish communities nationally.

This new, more expansive vision of Oregon Jewish history, including German and American pioneers, East European and Sephardic immigrants, Holocaust survivors, and increasing numbers of postwar newcomers from elsewhere in the United States, was central to the communal history presented at the OJM. Beginning in 1998, first at its location in the Montgomery Park building, then in a storefront location in the city's historic Chinatown, and, finally, at a new, larger facility in Northwest Portland, the OJM offered a regular cycle of exhibits on local history that helped to flesh out these diverse stories. Thematic exhibits, focusing on local congregations, businesses, experiences in the armed forces, celebrations of holidays, and even vacations at the Oregon Coast routinely included artifacts, photos, and testimonies from a variety of Jewish Oregonians of German, East European, and Sephardic

Oregon Jewish Museum executive director Judith Margles and President Craig Wollner sign the lease for an expanded facility in Northwest Portland, 2009. Courtesy OJMCHE

background, as well as many who came to Oregon not as immigrants but after a number of generations in America. A reinvigorated oral history project, driven in part by these thematic exhibits, continues this day. By 2014, the merged Oregon Jewish Museum and Center for Holocaust Education (OJMCHE) had nearly six hundred interviews in its collection.

As Shirley Tanzer worked on *Whatever Happened* and *Memory Is Survival*, she was conscious of the need to construct a past that would meet the needs of the contemporary community. Hasia Diner explains,

> Historical memory is not falsehood or fabrication. Rather, it functions as the set of stories that a people tell themselves and others, to explain who they are, where they came from, and the places they have been. . . . Although these stories derive their power in part from their mooring in reality, the more they are told, the more fixed they become. They metamorphose from being just pieces of information about the past into memory when, in [Pierre] Nora's words, they become an element in the "lived reality of groups." Ordinary information about the past enters the sacred space of memory when a people need it for their present circumstance and bundle together those pieces of information into a tightly woven tapestry that constitutes their narrative. . . . At the right moment in time, under

the right conditions, ordinary places become transformed into spaces throbbing with meaning.[133]

Rocked by the razing of the historic neighborhood, physical destruction of its key institutions, and the psychological toll of pessimistic reports and persistent worries about the dangers posed by assimilation, the Portland Jewish community was drawn to a story that validated and authenticated their historic experience. By connecting their local history to the iconic Jewish American story of immigration, acculturation, and mobility, *Whatever Happened to Old South Portland* met the community's needs and was warmly embraced as a new foundational story. In the years since, additional threads—those of the Sephardim, the survivors, and other newcomers—have been woven into that story, allowing Jewish Portlanders to give meaning to their past and continue to build a sense of identity. As the community grapples with new social, cultural, and demographic challenges—skyrocketing numbers of unaffiliated twenty-somethings in East Portland, new kinds of diversity in family structures, Jewish identities, and relationships to faith and to community—its history will continue to evolve to speak to these new needs.

CHAPTER THREE

A Woman's Place . . .

"It is impossible to read a newspaper today without finding at least six articles on Women's Lib," Shirley (Soble) Nudelman wrote in her column, "We Could Stroll Down Memory Lane . . . but They Built a Freeway Over It," in November 1971. Nudelman confessed to having mixed feelings about the women's movement. On the one hand, she explained, "I am not the type to picket, burn my underwear, or join the City Club. . . . I have enough trouble thinking of excuses not to go to meetings as it is." On the other, she conceded, "Equal pay for equal work and giving women a job usually considered 'only for men' are projects with which I fully agree." Taking the self-deprecating, humorous approach that made her so popular with readers of the *Jewish Review,* Nudelman recounted the scene that took place when she broached the subject of "working wives" with her husband:

> "What do you think about working wives?" I asked.
> "Wonderful idea," he enthused, "you could start by vacuuming the carpets."
> "It would have to be something where I could start after the children leave in the morning and be finished before they get home." I mused, ignoring the male chauvinism.
> "That would give you time to clean the cupboard," he noted.
> "I'd like something where I could be creative and meet interesting people." I pointed out.
> "How about baking something creative for the Den Mothers who will be here tonight?" uttered the Cub Master of Pack 811.
> "Maybe I could write a book and illustrate it. I wouldn't even have to leave the house that way." I said, already counting my royalties.
> "Speaking of books," he replied, "let me see your checkbook."

After explaining her shortcomings as a housekeeper and hostess, and again distancing herself from women's liberation by insisting, "I'm not looking to be Miss Shirley or addressed as Ms. instead of Mrs.," Nudelman got to the crux of the issue: "Being known for myself does appeal to me."

It never bothered me as a child to be asked my name and then be identified as "Sam and Ida's oldest daughter." When I got married and became "Jerry's wife," I was thrilled. It didn't upset me as a Sub Deb advisor being introduced as "Sandy's sister." Playing cards at a luncheon immediately marked me as "Fagel's granddaughter." In a few short years "Ol' Mom" proudly became "Sheila's mother," "Sharon's mother," "Jeff's mother"—even occasionally "Spunky's mommy."

Now that my name appears at the bottom of this column, people finally identify me just for myself. Only last week, walking into the JCC building, a friend came out with a newcomer to the Portland Jewish community.

"I'd like you to meet Portland's Erma Bombeck," he said, by way of introduction.

At last, my name is right on the tip of everyone's tongue. They've finally discovered the real me. Oy! The price of fame!![1]

Like millions of women across the country in the 1960s and 1970s, Nudelman was feeling the ground shift beneath her feet as established gender roles and expectations were contested. She, like many middle-class housewives who had dedicated themselves to home and children in suburban settings, began to look for something more.

More suburban, more middle class, more educated, with fewer children, and less likely to need to work for wages than American women in general, Jewish women were notably overrepresented among those leading the domestic life critiqued by Betty Friedan in her landmark 1963 book, *The Feminine Mystique*.[2] National trends held true in Oregon: the 1957 community census revealed that (affiliated) Portland Jews were twice as likely to be professionals as the population at large and far more likely to have a college degree.[3] Given their local and national profile, it is not surprising that many American Jewish women responded to Friedan's analysis. Jews were overrepresented in the ranks of the National Organization for Women and other feminist groups, just as they appeared disproportionately in the other liberal/progressive movements of the era. In addition, like Nudelman, many who did not identify explicitly as feminists responded to the movement's critique of gender roles and opted to seek employment or other new activities that expanded their horizons.

The personal and professional shifts in the roles of women in the 1960s and 1970s had an impact well beyond their families, shaping organizational, communal, and religious life. Jewish women's groups broadened their advocacy work to include explicitly feminist causes and shifted their practices to reflect new sensibilities about gender equality. Synagogues, federations, and other community-wide organizations were challenged to revise their notions of gender roles, and began to include (and even welcome) women as equals and even leaders, rather than confining them to separate auxiliaries, women's divisions, and ritual roles. Women who were raised believing that their primary occupation would be as wife and mother at home and—through the programs of women's organizations like Hadassah, congregational sisterhoods, and the Council of Jewish Women—in the community, found their assumptions questioned and challenged, by others and by themselves.

Even the most cursory review demonstrates the dramatic shift in women's roles in Jewish community over the last sixty years. A sample of three editions of the *Jewish Review* over its 1960–2010 run shows the pervasiveness of the shift. In the January 1962 edition, women appeared primarily in segregated "women's pages," which included the "social and personal news," such as wedding, engagement, and birth announcements, as well as notices of club meetings. At a time when the publication focused the bulk of its attention on the Jewish Welfare Federation's annual drive, the pages devoted to the campaign reflect the gender segregation in the community: men were organized into divisions based on occupation (the doctors and lawyers divisions, for example), and men chaired divisions such as "major gifts," while women operated in a separate Women's Division, organized by the region of the city in which they lived. All the women taking leadership roles in the campaign were identified by their husbands' names. Women's Division "Chairman" Mrs. Jack Cohen explained the mission of the Women's Division in maternalist terms: "Women today have a special contribution to offer this large family of ours—in our own city, —in the U.S.A.—and overseas; we create the values for living as a family and as a community." In addition to appearing in reports on the Women's Division, the Council of Jewish Women, and Hadassah, the 1962 *Review* also mentioned women involved in the broader communal organizations that focused on children and families. A story about a Jewish Family and Child Services (JFCS) membership drive listed a female president, Mrs. Alan Rosenberg (Eve), three other female officers, and a female membership drive chairman; only one officer and the executive director of the JFCS were male. News from the synagogues suggested a clear division between men's and women's roles, with sisterhood activities running alongside men's club programs. For some joint activities, such as the Beth Israel annual Men's Club-Sisterhood Dinner, the women planned the menu while the men were in charge of the program.[4]

By the mid-1970s, it was clear that there had already been a substantial shift in gender roles. In a sample edition of the *Jewish Review* from February 1975, community news included several articles about women speakers who were headlining community-wide events. One, a Holocaust survivor, was the keynote speaker for the Federation's Initial Gifts Dinner. "Bar mitzvah" listings had been replaced with "bar and bas mitzvah" notices. Shirley Nudelman's column was a regular feature; in this issue, it recounted her decision to go to work for pay, "after twenty years of 'doing nothing.'" Nudelman explained

Harriet Mesher, Leah Napom, Millie Gold, Ceil Heims, and Lois Maizels attend NCJW Portland Section's Angel Ball in 1968. Women donated clothing to the group's thrift shop to qualify for tickets to the ball. Courtesy OJMCHE

that she was motivated by the desire to be able to say "I didn't get the house clean and let's go out to dinner—I'm tired from work," rather than "I didn't get the house clean and let's go out to dinner—I'm tired from playing tennis (or substitute bridge, mah jong, shopping)." Despite such changes, however, much in organizational life remained gender segregated, including coverage of the Federation's separate Women's Division, a sisterhood lunch featuring wedding planning as the topic, and a Hadassah food fair. An article about the election of a new board at the Robison Home reveals that, while all the officers were male, women were serving on the board.[5]

By the early twenty-first century, the shift in women's roles was profound, reaching virtually every area of community news and events covered by the paper. To be sure, many women's groups, including Hadassah, the National Council of Jewish Women (NCJW), and congregational sisterhoods were still active. Yet what was most notable in the January 2001 edition is the gender integration of most community events and the prominence of women throughout, in terms of both communal and intellectual leadership. A large percentage of community professionals mentioned in the 2001 edition were women, including Oregon Jewish Museum executive director Judith Margles, JCC financial aid director Michelle (Blumenthal) Caplan, former Neveh Shalom co-executive directors Sheri (Golden) Cordova and Sylvia (Schwartz) Pearlman, and Rabbi Ariel Stone-Halpern.[6] An article on the Federation's Super Sunday listed Todd and Felicia Rosenthal as event cochairs, as well as a number of other female campaign officers. Priscilla (Bloom) Kostiner appeared on the masthead as president of the *Review*. In addition, several cultural events featured women speakers, including author Anita Diamont (lecturing at Beth Israel), philosopher Rebecca Goldstein and historian Laina Farhat Holzman (each speaking in the Jewish Writers and Scholars Series), and psychologist Silvia Rimm speaking at a benefit for the Sifray Noam Fund, created in memory of Noam Stampfer. The one feature on a women's organization, Z'havah, a new, younger group within the Women's League (formerly Sisterhood) of Neveh Shalom, focused on leadership training.[7] The shift in women's roles evident in the community press demonstrates the veracity of historian Deborah Lipstadt's argument that "there has been no realm of Jewish life, religious or secular, educational or communal, cultural or political, that has not been affected by a shifting attitude regarding women's roles."[8]

As profound as the impact of changed gender roles has been, historians argue that the tradition of Jewish women's activism in early and mid-twentieth-century America both paved the way and eased the transition. As Hasia Diner, Shira Kohn, and Rachel Kranson explain in *The Jewish Feminine Mystique*, well before the feminist revolution, Jewish communal life provided women with "a launching pad from which to make an impact on the world beyond their homes."[9] Organizations like the NCJW, B'nai B'rith Women (BBW), and Hadassah encouraged engagement both in local communities and in the broader world, promoted education on civic and global issues, and fostered activism, awareness, and social responsibility. They trained women as fundraisers, advocates, lobbyists, and educators. In Paula Hyman's words, congregational sisterhoods "did more than decorate the sanctuary for festivals and pour tea for congregants at Oneg Shabbats."[10] And in her analysis of Hadassah, Shirli Brautbar argues that even in the 1950s, when the consensus on traditional women's roles in America was strongest, this Zionist women's group "took domestic ideology and turned it on its head by portraying motherhood as a political and cultural mandate." As "mothers to the Jewish people," Hadassah women were "impelled to act politically on their children's behalf,"[11] a position quite reminiscent of the 1962 assertion the Portland Federation Women's Division chairman quoted above. The embrace of this maternalist mission, according to historians, did much to buffer the "social revolution" of the American women's movement for American Jewish women. Hasia Diner and Beryl Lieff Benderly explain,

> Rather than a break with the past, the feminist transformation elaborated on themes that have sounded from the beginning. The same drive for achievement, education and a life of meaning, the same pragmatic self-confidence and practical idealism, the same belief in their right and ability to affect the world that animated generation of their foremothers now carried the American Jewish generations of the late twentieth century toward definitions and expressions of their womanhood and their Jewishness at once deeply traditional and strikingly original.[12]

Both the continuities and the changes for Jewish women in Oregon were similar to those of their counterparts in Jewish communities across the country. Yet, Jewish Oregonians were also shaped by the particularities of place and by distinctive factors in local community demographics and development. Beginning in a period of relative conservatism and stability—even stagnation—Jewish Oregon, and particularly Jewish Portland, became in the late twentieth and early twenty-first centuries a community noted for progressivism and innovation, as well as for relative secularism and inclusiveness. As this regional character emerged, it was reinforced by the newcomers it attracted. Just as the combination of regional identity and selective migration affected the dynamics of the local engagement with Zionism and the character of emerging congregations, so too did regional distinctiveness shape the ways in which women and the community grappled with changing gender roles. Although many of the changes experienced by individual women, their families, and communal organizations were parallel to those in other communities, the skewing of Oregon Jewry toward the progressive end of the Jewish spectrum in the 1990s and early 2000s reinforced the emphasis on gender equity and women's spirituality in Oregon Jewish life.

Home, Hearth, and Hadassah

Well before the feminist movement of the 1960s and 1970s, many women struggled privately with gender expectations; indeed, Friedan's book's greatest significance was to name suburban women's "problem that has no name" and make it a subject of public discussion. For the generations of women who came of age earlier, expectations had been clear. As Helen (Rubenstein) Stern, born in 1926, succinctly explained, "We really were programmed to get married."[13] Evelyn (Asher) Maizels, born fifteen years later, agreed: "In those days you went to college to get your MRS degree. You didn't go to get a degree, because women married somebody."[14] Margaret (Selling) Labby, born in 1918, recalled that her parents gave her a typewriter when she graduated from Reed

College—with the implication that she might become a secretary and that "would have been the best I could do." It was, she recalled, "rather symbolic of the times. My brothers—Philip went to medical school, Ben went to medical school and John worked in the business world."[15]

Many accepted these expectations without much question. Toinette (Rosenberg) Menashe explained, "We always took it for granted in our generation; our husband's career came first and it was a given—something not even up for discussion. That's the way it was."[16] Others chafed against them. Elaine Cogan recalled, "In those days, most mothers didn't work outside the home, but I was always doing something." In her case, that "something" included writing a weekly public affairs column for the *Oregon Journal*, hosting a weekly radio show, and actively engaging in civic life through the League of Women Voters and, eventually, professional public affairs and urban planning work.[17] Sylvia (Schnitzer) Davidson, a political activist in Oregon's Democratic Party and a central figure in the Adlai Stevenson and John F. Kennedy presidential campaigns in the state, explained, "I was born a feminist."[18] Similarly, Fanny (Kenin) Friedman mused, "I think I was a woman liberationist when I was a girl,"[19] and Joyce (Margulies) Loeb, born in 1936, recalled telling her parents, "I wish I had not been born a girl. I wish I were a man. Then there would be no question about these kinds of things." Hoping to study architecture at University of California, Berkeley, Loeb recounted that when she visited the department, "They basically patted me on the head and said, 'Look around; there are no women in here.'"[20]

Even for women of a later generation, professional aspirations were frequently questioned. In the late 1960s, when Sylvia (Edelson) Stevens considered studying medicine, her father, a surgeon, explained that "it would be a waste of an education because I was a girl and I would get married and I wouldn't practice and what would be the point of spending all that money on an education?" Instead, Stevens tried nursing, and then returned to home economics and graduated unsure of her direction. By the mid-1970s, after marrying and moving around the country as a military wife, she decided to return to school to study law, hoping to "do something to improve the lives of women and children."[21] Despite struggling with gender discrimination in a field that was still mostly male, Stevens eventually moved from a private firm to a position with the Oregon Bar, and, in 2010, was named executive director of the Oregon State Bar.[22] Ellen Rosenblum, who would serve as federal prosecutor; judge on the district, circuit, and Oregon Court of Appeals; and as attorney general, found few female role models when she began law school in Eugene in 1972. When she became a partner in a Eugene firm in the late 1970s and her partners tried to take her out to celebrate at a country club, she was escorted out of the men's grill.[23]

Although many women coming of age before, or even during, the 1960s did get a college education, as these accounts suggest, their professional horizons were limited by gendered expectations. "Women didn't have many options," Maizels explained. "You could be a teacher; you could be a nurse; you could be a secretary."[24] Those who did work, even in "female" professional fields like social work or education, generally did so only until they married or began to have children. Eve Rosenfeld, a social worker who wanted to remain engaged in the field after getting married and becoming pregnant, sought volunteer opportunities with the Jewish Federation rather than professional employment. As she recounted in a 2004 oral history, "I walked into Jewish Federation. . . . I said, 'I *used* to be a social worker [emphasis added].'" Rosenfeld was soon invited to join the JFCS board, a volunteer position, and played a part in professionalizing the agency. When her youngest child was in school, she began to work for pay again, heading Beth Israel's Sunday school. Several years later, she was hired as congregational affairs director, with responsibility for programming, events, and staffing committees.[25]

Toinette Menashe began to teach while her husband did his residency at Oregon Health Sciences University (OHSU)—"I couldn't be a nurse—didn't want to be a secretary. So teaching seemed to be something I might be able to do." She found that most of her peers stayed home once they had children; working was taken as "a sign that—'Gosh—can't her husband support her?'— that sort of thing. So most of my friends were working—but again, once they had children, that stopped."[26] Lois (Sussman) Shenker, who was happy to stay home with her children, recalled that her father-in-law "didn't want me to work after we were married because it didn't look good that Arden's wife should be working. That was a mindset."[27] Even when a family needed the income, many husbands were reluctant to have their wives work. In a 1975 oral history, Ruth (Meadows) Schnitzer explained,

> My husband is of the old school. In those days, before women became liberated, we did not have children for five years and I did not work. And I should have been [working] because my husband was only making $100 a month when we got married, but that was the way my husband wanted it. . . . He did not want me to work. He wanted me to be home or whatever. . . . But I should have been working. When I see what is doing today, I see I was foolish.[28]

Even many who directly challenged gender expectations often ended up on a traditional path. Helen (Weinberg) Blumenthal, born in 1923, studied in a premed program before working as a riveter and then volunteering for military service during World War II. After the war, she worked as a nurse, and much later earned a certificate in Middle East studies at Portland State University. Years later, she expressed regret that she had not taken advantage of the GI Bill to further her studies when she was younger. But, she explained, "in those days women just helped their husbands through school or . . . stayed home and had children."[29] Madeline (Brill) Nelson studied biochemistry at Stanford and worked in a lab researching polio in the early 1940s, but she continued to work for only a few months after marrying Roscoe Nelson. She recalled, "I got pregnant and that was the end of my work for pay and from then on it was all volunteer."[30]

Of course, some women, either by choice or by necessity, flouted the expectations of the era by working for sustained periods. Bernice (Rosenfield) Gevurtz spent a number of years working, first in the insurance industry in San Francisco, then in Washington, DC, as a legislative assistant, at a New York law firm, and then back at the US Capitol for Senator Jacob Javitz. "I wanted to be in Washington, DC, and be part of the new frontier. The whole thing was very exciting," she recalled. Even after marrying, moving to Texas, and giving birth to her son, she continued to work, first because of her husband's illness, and subsequently, in Portland, after their marriage dissolved.[31] Such exceptional women who pursued traditionally male professional careers were well aware that they were challenging societal norms. Cecille (Sunderland) Beyl, a second-generation female doctor born in New York in 1935, remembered being told that she was "taking the place of a man in the medical school." After moving to Oregon in 1967, she inquired about a position at a clinic and was told the doctor would call her back. She recalled, "One day I was home, and the phone rang. A man's voice said, 'Dr. Sunderland, please,' I said, 'This is Dr. Sunderland.' And he said, 'Oh! They didn't tell me it was a woman. I'll call you back.' Let's see, it's what, forty-two years later? He hasn't called back yet."[32] Beyl began *volunteering* in the pediatric cardiology clinic at OHSU, before being selected for a fellowship there. After completing the fellowship, she practiced pediatric cardiology at OHSU for thirty years.[33]

The many stories of women such as Ruth Schnitzer and Margaret Labby testify to Friedan's "problem that has no name." Schnitzer returned to work in 1956, despite her husband's objections and the fact that she still had children at home. "After twenty years of playing cards and going to luncheons," she explained, "I was sick and tired of my life." Looking back two decades later, Schnitzer expressed great satisfaction with her decision: "I've never been sorry. I have felt that I am a better person for having done that."[34] Also bored at home, Labby decided to return to school for her teaching credential and began a fifteen-year teaching career in 1957. She recalled being openly questioned by a colleague on her first payday. Proud to be earning her own money for the first time, she was jarred when "the math teacher behind me waiting to get his check said something like, 'You shouldn't be earning money. You shouldn't be a teacher. You are taking money from us. Your husband is a doctor.'"[35]

Rosemarie (Frei) Rosenfeld told a similar story. Even early on in her married life, Rosenfeld felt ambivalent about staying at home: "I had a good education in school, but I got married and I couldn't go to work. . . . I said, 'I want more. I want to do something. I want the same education you had. There are a lot of things I want to do.' He [her husband] thought I meant another child, I think [laugh]." Later, in the 1970s, Rosenfeld went back to work against her husband's wishes, after earning a master's degree in social work at PSU. "I felt that I was missing something," she recalled. Her husband still had qualms, saying that "whatever I did between 9:00 and 5:00 was fine as long as he had dinner. And when I graduated he gave me a Cuisinart and a tennis warm-up outfit. You know, the kitchen and tennis [laugh]." Rosenfeld ended up working part time for fifteen years, deriving great satisfaction from "working, having a job, earning money so that I didn't have to charge his birthday presents to him."[36]

Some women raised with traditional views went back to work after losing their husbands through divorce or death. Nina Weinstein, born in 1915, worked in a variety of office jobs before marriage, but then stayed home for the next twenty years. After her husband's passing, she was working part time for a travel agency when a friend helped her to find a position on Bob Straub's gubernatorial campaign. When Straub was elected, he asked her to work in his office at the state capitol: "He waltzed me into the Governor's office and said, 'Now this would be your office. . .' And I looked at that gorgeous walnut paneling and I thought this would not be bad [laughs]. So I did. I went to work there for four years."[37] Evelyn Maizels took a job as a receptionist at Beth Israel after her divorce in the mid-1970s; she later worked for several service agencies, both within and outside of the Jewish community.[38]

Even before it was common for married women and mothers to be employed, to say that they were confined to home and children would be an overstatement. Middle-class American women had extended the "female sphere" over the course of the twentieth century, often through women's clubs, which asserted themselves in a variety of public arenas, particularly those involving the welfare of women, children, and families. Such groups often used maternalist concerns to justify their activity in local and national affairs connected to the education of children, family health, or the urban environment. In Portland, the League of Women Voters was particularly active, and is the secular group most frequently mentioned in the oral histories of Jewish women.[39] Within the Jewish community, there were numerous options for women, including groups active in a variety of social, cultural, philanthropic, Zionist, and civic causes. Several of these—most notably Hadassah and the NCJW—had long histories of pushing the boundaries of gender roles and fostering engagement of women in their local community, national Jewish issues, and the broader

Jewish world. Others had more limited purviews, focusing on specific institutions, such as synagogues, child services, or retirement homes. When traditional gender roles became increasingly contested in the 1960s and 1970s, some of these groups suffered, finding it difficult to compete with the new demands on their members' time. More often, however, women's organizations embraced the shifts, both directly, by incorporating women's liberation goals into their missions, and indirectly, by providing skills and training that women were able to carry into the workforce.

As we have seen, middle-class women in the 1950s and 1960s were often well-educated, but discouraged from pursuing careers. Although some flouted these expectations for economic or personal reasons, a larger number worked within societal expectations, focusing their attention on their roles as wives and mothers. For many of these women, organizational life provided an important outlet. Secular groups such as PTAs and the League of Women Voters (LWV), and Jewish organizations, like synagogue sisterhoods, Hadassah, NCJW, and BBW offered their members opportunities to meet other women for social purposes and to purposefully invest their energy in meaningful activities beyond their homes and families. Carrie (Bromberg) Hervin devoted decades of tremendous energy to Hadassah and LWV and served a term as president of each. She saw their missions as complementary: "The League of Women voters . . . [makes] citizens aware of their responsibility, just as Hadassah makes the Jewish people aware of what their responsibilities are as Jews."[40] Whether enhancing programming at their children's schools, fostering community at their congregations, assisting new immigrants or the disadvantaged in the local community, raising money for institutions at home or in Israel, educating themselves and others about social problems, or advocating for state- or national-level progressive legislation, organizational work provided women with opportunities for meaningful engagement with one another, with their community, and with the world.

In terms of sheer numbers, sisterhoods were probably the Jewish women's organizations that, collectively, claimed the largest number of members. In addition to the various congregational sisterhoods in Portland and around the state, the Robison Home and the Jewish Educational Association (which ran the community-wide Hebrew school in Portland) also had sisterhoods dedicated to their support. Traditionally, sisterhoods functioned essentially as women's auxiliaries (some were called auxiliaries instead of sisterhood); the sisterhood representative (generally the president) was often the only woman on a congregational board. Synagogue kitchens tended to be the primary province of the sisterhood; their members were responsible for providing refreshments at congregational events, managing the kitchen, and supporting kitchen projects through fundraising. They also frequently supplemented Sunday schools through special projects. This range of activities is reflected in the records of the sisterhood (in this case called the Ladies' Auxiliary) at the Sephardic Ahavath Achim congregation during the 1950s and 1960s. These show the group raising money for Sunday school scholarships (the congregation did not have its own school, thus, children attend the schools of the larger congregations) and for kitchen equipment. In addition, the group contributed to broader fundraising efforts including the congregational building campaign, the Federation Women's Division campaign, the purchase of Israel bonds, and the Mothers' March on Polio. In 1968, the auxiliary put on a luncheon to raise money for the Federation's Israel Emergency Fund. Aside from fundraising, the group planned or contributed to the planning of a variety of congregational events, including a Mother's Day dinner, numerous luncheons, and annual picnics, Chanukah parties, and Purim dinners.[41]

Some sisterhoods, particularly those at larger congregations, took on broader service projects. For example, the Beth Israel Sisterhood participated in a national braille project for decades beginning in the 1960s. The sisterhood funded the local Volunteer Braille Service and provided volunteers willing to take on the lengthy training and ongoing work of transcribing textbooks and other materials for blind and limited-sight schoolchildren and adults.[42] In addition, they ran a busy schedule of social, cultural, and educational programs, including teas (often with musical entertainment), book review programs, lectures and workshops on current events, parenting issues, travel and art, and excursions to exhibits and concerts. Regular monthly meetings featured lunch and a program that might include entertainment, an educational lecture, or an arts and crafts activity. Like many sisterhoods, Beth Israel ran the congregational gift shop and kitchen.[43]

Many women devoted huge amounts of time, often to multiple organizations, as "professional volunteers." This term was sometimes used to describe women who made a virtual career of volunteering. A number of women fit this description, some of them engaging in a remarkable array of activities. For example, over a period of volunteering that spanned from the 1940s through the 1990s, Gussie Reinhardt served terms as president of Hadassah, Robison's Sisterhood, the Kesser Israel board, and JFCS; volunteered as a Young Judea leader and as a fundraiser for Israel Bonds, the Jewish National Fund, Federation, and AMIT (an Orthodox Zionist women's organization); served as a Democratic precinct committeewoman; led the fight against urban renewal in Lair Hill; and, as a former professional dancer, was heavily involved in bringing dance events to Portland.[44] Similarly, Lena (Kleinberg) Holzman served as president of Beth Israel's Sisterhood, the NCJW Portland section, the LWV, her local PTA, and the YWCA, in addition to serving on the Portland Art Museum, Portland Symphony, and Red Cross boards. She also headed the Federation's Women's Division campaign no fewer than nine times over the course of a volunteer career that spanned from the 1930s into the 1970s.[45]

Alice Meyer's career as a "professional volunteer" was highlighted by board service and office holding in an array of community organizations including leadership roles with the LWV, Multnomah County Library, and cofounder and first president of the Oregon Jewish Museum.[46]

"Professional volunteer" was also an apt term for professionally trained women who drew on that training as volunteers. For example, Lois Shenker not only volunteered as a Campfire Girls leader, in the Federation campaign, and at the JCC; she also put her professional training in education to work as a volunteer Sunday school teacher at Neveh Shalom.[47] Likewise, Eve Rosenfeld's training and professional experience as a social worker made her a particularly effective member of the JFCS board.

For a younger generation of women, too, volunteer service could amount to a virtual job. Linda (Nemer) Singer, for example, was heavily involved in the resettlement of Russian families. Working with Bernice (Bromberg) Rosencrantz, who organized a JFCS warehouse full of donated furniture and household goods to supply to the newcomers, Singer's job was "to go in and bring the sheets and the dishes and the *tchotchkes* to make it a home," and then to greet the family. In this way, Singer worked with "dozens and dozens" of families. This volunteer work, in turn, led to her "career" as a volunteer on the Women's Division board of the Federation, where she eventually served as campaign chair and division president. All this was in addition to her service on the Robison Home Board, the Portland Jewish Academy board, and participation on several Federation missions to the former Soviet Union.[48]

An array of donor luncheons, newsletter tributes, and other such programs endeavored to honor these devoted volunteers, but many felt that this work was undervalued in comparison to paid work—although this often remained unarticulated until later. As early as the mid-1950s, despite her activity in the community, Ruth Schnitzer reported feeling like "a parasite" because she was not working for pay.[49] For many more women, such as Lois Shenker, it was not until the 1970s that they began to feel awkward about identifying themselves as housewives when asked what they did. Lois was doing "lots of stuff" in the community, but reported a feeling of not "fulfilling my destiny."[50] Even in organizations that relied almost entirely on volunteers and that frequently honored their efforts, women's volunteer work was sometimes devalued. For example, in 1962, Hadassah held a "Tribute to Achievement" at a donor luncheon to recognize "Portland citizens who have achieved recognition in various endeavors that may be correlated with the scope of Hadassah's work in America and Israel." Interestingly, despite the fact that the setting was a lunch intended to honor women as volunteers and donors, all but one of the honorees recognized as part of the "Tribute to Achievement" program were men, and all were honored for accomplishments directly related to their paid work.[51]

Still, in a world where gender expectations limited options, women's organizations provided a vital outlet. Women like Ruth Schnitzer, who wanted to work outside the home, turned to Hadassah when those ambitions were stymied—in her words, "He [her husband] wanted me to be home. . . . So I became active in Hadassah." In addition to serving as an officer in that group, Schnitzer also became involved in the Federation's Women's Division and in "B'nai B'rith" (presumably BBW).[52] Women found tremendous camaraderie in these organizations. Shirley Nudelman, who felt confined by gender expectations of the day, found a key social outlet in women's organizations: "We met our friends, that's where we met them and we knew people would come, they would join these groups and that's how you would meet them."[53] At meetings and through newsletters, members celebrated one another's milestone events—anniversaries, new homes, house guests, new grandchildren, and so on—reinforcing social bonds.[54]

Yet these organizations involved far more than fashion shows, tea parties, and luncheons. Women's organizations appealed to potential members by emphasizing the importance of their work, both to the community and to the broader Jewish world. A commitment to service was central to the mission of NCJW's Portland section, which had dedicated itself to direct service through Neighborhood House since the turn of the century. By the 1960s, the women of the Portland section had shifted their attention from the house to a series of local and national advocacy campaigns including civil rights, juvenile justice reform, and school integration.[55] Likewise, BBW members were reminded that their efforts provided critical support for "the ADL [Anti-Defamation League] Program (the fight against bigotry and discrimination); our BBYO [B'nai B'rith Youth Organization] program (helping our youth to become better citizens and leaders); [and] our Philanthropy Program"[56] Hadassah consistently conveyed the urgency of its mission to the very survival of Israel; in a 1974 bulletin, members were told, "We must get involved if we are to help Israel survive in a hostile world and also help restore a sense of purpose to our troubled American Jewish community—and the only way to get involved is to belong to Hadassah—the Women's Zionist Organization of America."[57] As historian Shirli Brautbar's analysis makes clear, even an activity as seemingly frivolous as a fashion show had a deeper purpose, as Hadassah women used "beauty-focused culture such as fashion shows, shopping trips, and cosmetic sales as platforms for education and political activism."[58] When Portland Hadassah asked, "Can it be Paris? Or Milan? No!! It is Hadassah's Gala Dinner and Fashion Show," it was not only advertising a fashion show, but also recognizing donors to its critical programs in Israel and educating members and guests about those programs. Donors had the honor of modeling gowns created by students in a Hadassah-supported vocational school in Jerusalem, and the dinner featured a "charming guest speaker," Mrs. Nathan D. Perlman,

Dorothy Kornberg, Sylvia Nemer, Joyce Dolgenow, Betty Rosenfeld, and
Claire Puziss serve as models and fashion coordinators at an Hadassah luncheon
and fashion show, 1950s. Courtesy OJMCHE

national chair of Hadassah Medical Organization, discussing "the new 25 million dollar Hadassah-Hebrew University Medical Center."[59]

In addition to emphasizing service and impact, women's organizations
made appeals to the intellect of members. Hadassah advertised its regional
conference in 1965 by asking women, "How would you like to spend three
wonderful days being entertained, stimulated, inspired, and informed?"[60]
Such conferences, and even the regular monthly meetings, offered women the
opportunity to discuss issues of national and regional importance; the 1965
Hadassah conference would, according to President Helen Blumenthal, provide an opportunity to talk about national programs as well as "the problems

which are unique to us, particularly that of Arab students and propaganda in our colleges, universities and high schools."[61] Local chapters of Hadassah encouraged their members to keep up with the news on the Middle East by subscribing to publications like the *Near East Report*.[62] The organization also touted its American Affairs program, explaining that, through it, Hadassah members "are kept informed on vital domestic issues and on international developments affecting the struggle for freedom and democracy. This program is designed to help equip Hadassah members to act intelligently, as individual American citizens, on community, state and national problems."[63] Hadassah newsletters reported the positions of political candidates on Middle East issues, and explained United Nations resolutions relevant to Israel. In addition, although Hadassah's main focus was Israel, meetings sometimes featured local issues; in May 1966, for example, Paul Meyers's presentation to the group was titled "Is It Time for Change at City Hall?"[64]

Likewise, BBW and NCJW published legislative updates on issues of concern, sponsored panels on local ballot measures, and urged members to vote. B'nai B'rith Women were encouraged to mentor B'nai B'rith Girls as they "get out and encourage people to vote." The BBW newsletter explained, "It is time for BBGs to discuss racial problems that are facing our community and our nation."[65] The Salem BBW chapter participated actively in "Dolls for Democracy," a program featuring dolls in the likeness of diverse American historical figures to teach tolerance to public schoolchildren. These organizations also frequently shared communiques from their national organizations, urging participation in local emergency meetings in response to anti-Semitic outbursts in America and abroad, and in support of Israel.[66]

Beyond women's organizations such as BBW, Hadassah, NCJW, and the sisterhoods, women's availability and willingness enabled broader communal agencies and organizations to do considerable work on tight budgets. "I know when I was involved, volunteers did just about everything," Rosemarie Rosenfeld recalled of the Federation. "There was hardly anyone in the office. . . . We didn't have a lot of professionals. Now things are done by professionals and the things that are done by volunteers are less meaningful."[67] When Alvin Rackner arrived in Portland to head the JFCS in 1966, he was the only full-time social worker. Two part-time, female social workers and a secretary filled out the staff;[68] but much work was done by volunteers, and, as we have seen, a number of women served on the board. In addition, women played a key role in raising funds for the agency, as when a homemaker service was started with an $18,000 grant from the NCJW section.[69] Whether in the more traditional endeavors such as sisterhoods' coordination of refreshments and decorations for teas, luncheons, or balls, or in broader community efforts to ease the transition of immigrant families or raise funds for Israel, women's volunteer labor was critical.

THE WOMEN'S SIDE . . .

Campaign leaders of the Special Gifts Division for the women's side met at a kick-off luncheon March 18th to honor the 12 colonels who will head the Special Gifts program. Mrs. Gilbert Schnitzer, co-chairman of Special Gifts, was hostess for the event. From left to right are, standing, Mrs. Louis Gold, co-chairman, Mrs. Gilbert Schnitzer, Mrs. Harold Heldfond, and seated, Mrs. Morris Schnitzer, Mrs. Dan Zell and Mrs. Marvin Schwartz.

Other guests who attended the March 18th Special Gifts luncheon were, left to right, Mrs. S. J. Zidell, Mrs. Jack Cohen, Mrs. Jack Olds and Mrs. Harold Schnitzer, who is Chairman of the entire Women's Division.

The Women's Division of Federation was featured in separate stories in the community press. Courtesy OJMCHE

Even as they enthusiastically performed these roles, gender expectations constrained their efforts. This was particularly true in cases where financial contribution was a primary means of involvement. In an era when supporting Israel and Jews in need around the world had become absolutely central to Jewish identity and the Federation's annual campaign was the pivot around which communal organizations turned, many women had no financial resources of their own. Bank accounts and credit cards were kept in husbands' names since married women were not eligible to get credit cards or hold bank accounts independently until the 1960s. Many women received allowances from their husbands, from which they were expected to manage household and personal expenses. Nudelman's quip in her 1971 column about her husband looking over her checkbook was likely one to which many women could relate.

Accounts of women's efforts to make donations in their own names to the Federation or other communal organizations bring out the poignant challenges these women faced when called on to contribute to communal causes. In the wake of the Yom Kippur War of 1973, Hadassah regional president Reta Kahn joined national leaders in urging women to contribute. "You are to start HADASSAH FUNDRAISING FOR EMEGENCY NEEDS," the women were instructed. "Your first act is to CLEAR ALL TREASURIES and send National at once all monies you are holding for projects [emphasis in original]." The notice reminded Hadassah women of their responsibility not to "stand by while Israeli school children are being murdered, three million isolated Jews in the Soviet Union helplessly watch their precious Jewish heritage being snuffed out, or Soviet arms, missiles, planes and pilots are being sent to the surrounding Arab countries."[70] Certainly, Hadassah women, like their counterparts in sisterhoods and other groups, frequently organized events designed to raise money for such campaigns. Yet many also wanted to be able to make individual donations, and these donations were frequently listed by name in organizational newsletters, or, in the case of the Federation, in the *Jewish Review.*

The challenge of making such a donation without an independent source of income had long been a subject of discussion among women. A September 1957 BBW newsletter pragmatically addressed the issue as the organization's donor event approached. Since the women had "four months in which to earn or save the $15.00 which is the donor pledge for 1958–59," the newsletter compiled a list of "many novel ways in which your donor pledged might be earned," including babysitting; making candy, baked goods, clothing, or crafts for sale; organizing block bingo games; and selling magazine subscriptions or cosmetics. The newsletter also encouraged members to send suggestions for additional ways to earn money, offered the women the opportunity to sell ads for the donor book as a way of earning credit, and advertised the availability of B'nai B'rith banks, into which they could deposit spare change as a means of saving.[71] Jeanne (Mittleman) Newmark, active in Hadassah, NCJW, and the Federation's Women's Division, recalled the challenges of raising money from women:

> We thought, at that time, to raise $360 a year was amazing. We felt so proud of ourselves. I remember how some of my dearest friends chose how to earn this money so that it would be "their" money that they were giving. I remember one of my dearest friends chose not to have her hair done that week. Someone else would collect coupons and the money that she saved from coupons would be put aside. There were ways that, even though we weren't working and were on limited amounts of money, it was important to us.[72]

Meryl (Rosenfeld) Haber, daughter of Rosemarie Rosenfeld, recalled how important it was to her mother to make a donation to the Women's Division in her own name: "She wanted to give her own money to Federation when they asked for money in the Women's Division, so she wanted to get a job so she could earn her own money to do that."[73] Donation listings in the Federation's annual report show that, although the number of volunteers in the women's division far exceeded that in the men's division, the women were only able to raise a small portion of the total raised by the men; in 1967, the women raised $33,987, compared to the men's $251,781. In the individual listings, it was not unusual for wives to be credited with a donation of five, ten, or twenty dollars, while their husbands gave substantially more.[74]

Women's dependence on their husbands was not limited to the financial aspect of participation. For example, when there was a proposal in the mid-1950s to change the regular BBW meeting night, one objection was that, if they did not meet on the same night as their husbands, many women would lack a ride to the meeting. In addition, by sharing a meeting night with the men, the women's group was able to defray the cost of refreshments.[75] A 1965 Hadassah program titled "Marriage, Hadassah Style or Love Me, Love Hadassah" featured a panel of Hadassah husbands; the intent was to educate husbands to support their wives' involvement, with the implication that it was difficult for a woman to participate without her husband's blessing.[76]

In organizations and institutions that served men as well as women, or in settings where men and women came together on boards or in event planning, many women felt frustrated by their implied—or openly stated—subordinate role. Synagogues and communal groups like the Federation and the JCC had few, if any, women on their boards. At the Robison Home, women served on the sisterhood, which was, until 1955, an auxiliary of the Men's Board. After 1955, Robison's Sisterhood became autonomous; only later did the main governing board for the home change its name from Men's Board to Home Board.[77] As Linda (Popick) Veltman put it, "In those days, organizations were run by men. There were sisterhoods. There were ladies organizations. But they were, for the most part, not power organizations."[78] Eve Rosenfeld, who served as JFCS representative to the Federation board in the 1950s, recalls, "I was female and I was young and they sort of tolerated me very nicely, in a nice way. But I don't think that anything I ever said made any difference."[79] Even as late as 1969, when the *Jewish Review* profiled Renee Holzman, then serving on the Jewish Welfare Association board, the article focused on her appearance. Headlined "Pretty Blond Active in Jewish Community," the article noted her age (32) and her weight (100 pounds), and observed that she "lends a touch of beauty to the board of directors of the Jewish Welfare Association."[80]

Shifting Ground, at Home and in the Community

Although the discussion of women's rights in the United States has a long history, and a Presidential Commission on the Status of Women chaired by Eleanor Roosevelt had begun its work in 1961, the eruption of a broad public discussion of gender roles in the 1960s and 1970s is generally traced to the publication of Friedan's *The Feminine Mystique* in 1963. In Portland, the book quickly attracted attention in the Jewish community. It is notable that the first mention of Betty Friedan in the *Oregonian* came in an article about an upcoming forum at the JCC. On Sunday, April 28, 1963, the *Oregonian* ran two separate articles relating to the book—a review on the editorial page and an article previewing the forum, the first in a series of JCC adult education fora focusing on "vital controversial issues, relevant to our world today." The JCC's panel included "a woman educator, a housewife [Mrs. Hershel (Shirley) Tanzer], an anthropologist, and a physician." The *Oregonian's* placement of the story said much about the context that Friedan's book was confronting: a feature in the "Women's" section, the article was sandwiched between the bridge column and engagement announcements, and bordered by several ads

directed at women, including one for a "finishing and modeling school," headlined "a woman's greatest asset . . . her appearance."[81]

As the national discussion of gender roles got under way, many Jewish women's organizations quickly embraced the new sensibilities. In the 1960s and 1970s, young women who had received a Jewish education comparable to that of their male counterparts were often in precisely the places that were "most quickly penetrated by feminist ideas: the American university and the civil rights and anti-Vietnam movements." As these women began to apply their feminist analysis to Jewish life, they challenged communal practices, roles, and traditions, dramatically changing the face of American Jewry.[82]

The National Council of Jewish Women was particularly warm to the sentiments of the emerging movement. According to NCJW historian Faith Rogow, "For nearly eighty years [prior to Friedan] the Council built itself on the need for women to act both in and outside of the home."[83] According to Portlander Linda Veltman, the NCJW was the one local women's organiza-
tion "that had real empowerment" even early on.[84] In September 1968, the Portland section held a two-day "School for Community Action" to address the changing roles of women, with sessions on topics including "Women and Employment, Women and Education, Birth Control and Family Planning, Stages of a Woman's Life, and the Male View of the Woman's Role in the Family."[85] Two years later, the Portland section bulletin urged its members to attend a Women's Equality Conference, noting that "as Council members interested in social movements and change, it is important that we become as aware of the inequalities towards ourselves (women) as the other lack of social needs throughout society."[86] In 1971, the section was a cosponsor of Women's Equality Day, a demonstration aimed at making "women more aware of their rights as individuals."[87] Both nationally and locally, the NCJW consistently took strong positions in favor of equal pay, the Equal Rights Amendment, and abortion rights. In a 1973 letter to the Oregon State Senate Judiciary Committee, the Portland section urged a vote in favor of ratification of the ERA, explaining that "our national organization has supported equal rights for women since 1923."[88] Three years later, past section president Sharon (Rosenblum) Tarlow explained some of the ways in which feminist sensibilities pushed the NCJW agenda forward:

> Now in 1976, we are again faced with changing times—new life styles, working women and new legislation granting women some rights that men have enjoyed for years. . . . We must continue to share our resources with those who need us, but we must also share in the decision of how those resources are used. We must keep our Jewish homes strong, while taking a more active role in synagogue cer-
> emonies. We must be concerned mothers, wives and daughters and extend that concern to those less fortunate than ourselves. As Jews and as Americans, we have an obligation to become INVOLVED–participating advocates in all strata

NCJW members prepare to march in the pro choice Mobilize for
Women's Lives March in 1989. Courtesy OJMCHE

of our community, our nation and the world. . . . Take our traditions, mix them
with NCJW Resolutions, add a bit of the world of our homes plus some volunteer activities and our world and ourselves will grow and be strong—ready for the
changes ahead.[89]

The Portland section's State Public Affairs Committee regularly lobbied,
trained lobbyists, and organized coalitions on issues including abortion rights
and, later, gay rights.

The National Council of Jewish Women was not alone among these groups
in identifying with the women's movement. The Oregon chapter of Brandeis
Women, an organization supporting Brandeis University, ran a 1972 discussion series featuring professional women speaking on "how they made it in
the business world," and a discussion with Eleanor Myers, Women's Equal
Employment Opportunity Director for the Oregon Bureau of Labor.[90] A year
later, the regional Hadassah bulletin touted itself as "an excellent example of
feminine leadership and determination in our modern society" and admonished women to "prepare and work" for "equal standing with men."[91] Like
the NCJW, Hadassah endorsed the Equal Rights Amendment. Moreover,
Hadassah repeatedly articulated its pioneering role as an influential wom-
en's organization operating in an international arena. For example, a 1983
invitation to a membership tea pointed out that, as members of a successful
women's organization that had long engaged in advocacy at both the local and
national level, "Hadassah women have been feminists by today's standards

for over 70 years."[92] A 1977 *Jewish Review* article profiling the various Jewish women's clubs in Portland began by emphatically distancing these groups from traditional stereotypes of female club activity: "Jewish women have always been doers. No teacups, pink and blue bootie chatter social clubs for them. Jewish women's clubs serve a purpose, have a responsibility for a cause, or causes. And they accomplish the goals through hard work, fund raising and volunteer efforts."[93]

Rose (Von Flue) Rustin's experience vividly demonstrates the role that women's organizations could play in drawing newcomers into the life of the community, developing female leadership, and cultivating Jewish identity. Growing up in Silverton in a fundamentalist Christian family that did not support her receiving even a high school education, Rustin hungered for more. Moving to Portland in the 1950s with a high school degree earned through a correspondence course, Rustin worked in several medical offices, ultimately finding employment with Dr. Arnold Rustin. Soon she came to know Arnold's wife, Jean, who had long been active in NCJW and had served as chapter president. The two women became close. Rose admired Jean's worldliness and broad interests, and Jean quickly took Rose under her wing, introducing her to theater, music, and volunteer work. In 1971, shortly after Rose left Rustin's employment to attend nursing school, Jean passed away. Rose maintained her friendship with Arnold, and eventually it blossomed into romance. Once they had married, Arnold called Joan Liebrich, then president of the NCJW section, explaining to her, "Rose needs Jewish people because she doesn't have her own people anymore" (although she had not yet converted to Judaism, she had left the church she had grown up with and was estranged from her family). Arnold knew, according to Rose, "that this would be a good group of women and a good place for me to establish Jewish relationships." Rose found herself "absolutely awed by these women." She recalled that she wanted "to be a part of what they were doing and tried to become worthy of their friendship because I saw them as such educated, smart, capable women. I wanted to be like that. And, and it happened. They, they let me in, so to speak. And I began volunteering and the more I did, the more I liked it, and the more I pushed myself."

Within a short time, Rose was an active NCJW volunteer, representing that organization to a broader Women in Community Service group, first at the local and then at the national level. Not long after, she was elected president of the Portland section, winning that office even before her conversion to Judaism was complete. Ultimately, Rustin not only served as section president, but also was elected to the national board of NCJW. She worked as a "trouble shooter, training, leadership-development person" for the western region of the organization. She also completed an undergraduate degree and celebrated not just a conversion, but also a bat mitzvah at Congregation Beth

Israel, where she was elected congregational president in 1994, the second woman to hold that office.[94]

Even as these groups took strong stances on women's issues and transformed the lives of individuals like Rustin, women's organizations and many of their members were reluctant to explicitly call themselves feminists, and many questioned what they saw as "radical feminism."[95] When NCJW president Esther Landa visited Portland to urge support for the Equal Rights Amendment in 1977, she suggested that the ratification process would have been easier if "radical feminists hadn't gone so far off the main track and alienated so many women." Landa argued that radicals had alienated housewives and volunteers, and urged council members to embrace all women.[96] Amy (Cezer) Tanne, the 1979 incoming Portland section president, worried that "the women's movement . . . made some people feel that *volunteerism* is not a valid occupation. I'd like to see more people realize that they can be fulfilled by giving their time."[97] Even as they shifted roles in their households, communities, and the workforce, some women hesitated to fully embrace the feminist movement. Despite such ambivalence, even among organizations that might, on their face, seem most traditional, sensibilities *did* change. The Robison Jewish Home Sisterhood commemorated its sixtieth anniversary in 1988, emphasizing "Sisterhood has come a long way . . . and in many ways its development mirrors changes in American women during the same period." Underscoring their autonomy, the anniversary book noted that women now served together with men on the "Home Board"—the main governing body of the home—and, they warned, one calls Sisterhood "the Home's 'auxiliary' at one's very great peril."[98]

For women who had earlier embraced staying home with their children, the changing times led to reevaluation. Lois Shenker recalled, "By the time of the feminist movement, Betty Friedan and all that, my kids were in school full time. And then I sort of had to justify what I was doing. . . . It really came from within. I just felt that I was a bright, capable person, I should be doing something worthwhile with my time."[99] In returning to work, women such as Shenker were able to draw not only on their professional training (in this case in education), but also on years of practical experience as volunteers. Shortly after Shenker returned to work for pay as a kindergarten teacher at the JCC, she found herself appointed director of the program.[100] Likewise, Sharon Tarlow's transition from a "volunteer executive" position as Portland NCJW president to "salaried professional" was profiled in an *Oregon Journal* article: "There are some people, even volunteers, who might have said that all she had to recommend herself was 21 years of volunteer work. Mrs. Tarlow didn't look at it that way. She had 21 years of work experience, a lot of it at the management level."[101] And prior to taking on professional executive roles, first at the area office of the American Jewish Committee and then at the Federation,

Laurie (David) Rogoway served in a volunteer capacity on the board of the Portland NCJW section, BBW, JFCS, and Federation, as well as chairing the Federation's Community Relations Committee and Soviet Jewry Task Force.[102] Evelyn Maizels, who worked her way from a receptionist to executive director level positions, explained,

> All of my experiences came from volunteering. I learned all of these things by being a volunteer. I did a lot of volunteering over the years. I was the volunteer coordinator at Mental Health Services West. I did all of the events for Israel Bonds. I put them all together and I started a Women's Division. So when it came time to find a job from Mental Health Services West I saw an ad in the paper and I knew who the executive director was. I said, "Boy, if that person could do it, I could do it." I answered the ad and I got the job.[103]

Similar stories appeared in a 1976 *Jewish Review* article by LaNita (Pearson) Anderson, profiling twenty-one women in the community "who have done volunteer work . . . shifting their goals to a more personalized form of fulfillment in a job, a business of their own, or in a return to college for an undergraduate or graduate degree." Many of these women had returned to school after years of volunteer work in the Federation, NCJW, congregations, JFCS, and other communal organizations; many of them would become prominent leaders in the Federation and other communal organizations in the decades that followed. Among those profiled in the article was Bernice (Kaplan) Feibleman; after an extensive "career" as a volunteer with Temple Sisterhood, the Robison Home, JFCS, and the LWV, Feibleman went back to school for her master's degree in 1966. By 1976, she was employed at Portland State University, where she did vocational counseling and testing, helping other women with their transition back into the workforce. Feibleman succinctly explained the role that women's volunteer experience could play in this transition:

> I've always felt that proportionately Jewish women did more volunteer work per capita than the general population. Making the transition back to school, or for job re-entry, may be an easier step for them [than for other women]. They've already established a participation outside of the home and been involved with those outside of their immediate circle of friends. They don't have as many of the traditional suburbia problems we hear [about].[104]

It is interesting that, although many Jewish women gained both experience and confidence as volunteers in communal institutions, these same institutions often had a difficult time adjusting to shifting expectations and needs of their volunteers. Women expressed frustration with communal organizations that still seemed to want to utilize them in traditional ways. As one unnamed woman told Anderson, "Our roles are changing so quickly, we're evolving so rapidly that the community, particularly the synagogues, don't know how to use us effectively. We are not being trained for administrative positions, or as president [*sic*]." Another informant for the same article complained that women were seldom on boards, and that those who were often were treated a "token." She explained, "We are not really listened to as policy makers. In fact, we really aren't part of the actual decision-making process." It would be incumbent on the community and its institutions, the article emphasized, to "adjust to this changing role of women."[105]

As women turned their volunteer experience into marketable skills and entered the workforce, the organizations that been such an important outlet for them also had to adjust to increasing constraints on members' time. As early as the 1950s, one of the Hadassah groups had a meeting schedule designed for the "business and professional" woman, recognizing that daytime meetings on weekdays were not possible for working women. Even with that option, women such as Ruth Schnitzer, who returned to work in the 1950s, found that she no longer had time in her schedule for volunteer activities. Rosemarie Rosenfeld explained in a 2004 interview,

> I remember distinctly being at a Sisterhood meeting when one of the women who had stopped going to meetings and had started working (she was a real estate salesperson). She talked about this. How it had just released her from all of these things and she was earning money and the next thing I knew she was divorced, of course. But she had just achieved this freedom and she was having a great time. I know a number of my contemporaries whose consciousness was raised (that was the term). Then women's groups lost a lot of their impetus getting women to come to meetings.[106]

As more women returned to work in the 1970s and 1980s, adjusting meeting schedules became just one of the ways that organizations tried to keep women engaged. In the 1950s and 1960s, Beth Israel Sisterhood held most of its regular events, including the various lecture series and board and monthly membership meetings, on weekdays, either in the morning or at lunchtime. For stay-at-home mothers, these meetings (where babysitting was often provided) were convenient. In the 1970s, to accommodate the greater number of working women, the sisterhood offered additional meeting times; members could choose to attend "circle" meetings while their children attended Shabbat school on Saturday mornings, on a weekday evening, or the traditional lunchtime meeting on Thursdays. The weekday evening meetings included a sherry hour, dinner, and a program.[107] Even with these options, the sisterhood found it difficult to draw young, working women. Realizing that they might not want to take additional time away from husbands and children, the sisterhood reached out with invitations to "our younger married women who work away from their homes," inviting them and their husbands to Friday night potlucks and family barbeques. By 1978, a new Sisterhood Young Working Women's Group had coalesced at Beth Israel.[108] Addressing the same issue, a 1989 Hadassah piece on "Career and Working Women" suggested reaching out by emphasizing the "benefits of belonging to Hadassah for career women," ensuring meeting times were convenient for working women, and developing programs designed specifically to appeal to their concerns.[109] A more elaborate piece the same year further examined the impact of shifting work patterns on Hadassah:

> For women and women's groups, this time we are living in is a period of transition. At one point in our lives we were homemakers staying home with children, looking up new recipes, volunteering our time at Thrift shops, schools, hospitals and so on. Now, at every age level there are women in the workforce using their "homemaking skills" to manage a career and a home for their families.
>
> The desires to volunteer are still with us, but the new demands on our lives lead us to make choices about our priorities and add to the stresses in our lives. Perhaps volunteer jobs will be handled differently than they were in previous years. Perhaps our events need to be adjusted to the other demands in our lives....
>
> At all levels, from the presidents to the officers, from the committees to the membership, tolerance and acceptance of the demands on our lives has to be accepted....
>
> In these times of transition we all contribute whatever we can in time, effort and money. Please recognize that what is offered has been made in good faith and with an awareness of the time limitations we all have in our busy lives.[110]

These challenges were central to the NCJW decision in 2000 to sell Neighborhood House. Early in the century, the councilwomen staffed dozens of classes and clubs, ran health clinics, and assisted individuals and families through their work at Neighborhood House. By 2000, as section president Sarah Wetherson explained,

> Women no longer have the time—or the desire—to volunteer full time. Selling our building is an acknowledgement of that reality and also enables us to place more of our volunteer efforts into the service and advocacy that directly changes people's lives.... In concrete terms, it also means that we will have a sizable endowment that allows us to have a voice on the Board of the Oregon Jewish Community Foundation. We will be able to help set policy for that body, adding an important voice for women and children to an organization that handles millions of dollars for human services and the arts in the community.... I feel a collective weight lifted off our Section's shoulders with the sale of the building. I feel that we have opened ourselves to the opportunities that lie ahead of us. If we could make this historic change, what other ways can we re-vision ourselves for the future?[111]

Shifting gender expectations led to changes not only in women's groups, but in the broader community, as the organizations that had long been controlled by men began accepting and even welcoming women as leaders and equals. The Robison's shift from Men's Board to Home Board, with women serving in the same capacity as men, was typical of the shift within many community organizations. The entry of women into leadership positions of all kinds in the Jewish community is evident in organizational histories and in the stories of individual women leaders. After decades of volunteer and board service, for example, Laurie Rogoway was hired as the first area director of the American Jewish Committee, one of the oldest and most influential national Jewish advocacy organizations, beginning in 1978. In 1984, she became assistant director of the Jewish Federation of Portland, with responsibility for the Community Relations Committee, the Women's Division, and Super Sunday. The same 1984 edition of the *Review* that featured a story on Rogoway's Federation appointment also ran a detailed interview with Eve Rosenfeld, then serving as chairperson of the Federation's allocation committee, and a profile of Min (Mudrick) Zidell and Elaine (Jaffe) Weil, the newly named copresidents of the *Review*. Longtime editor LaNita Anderson wrote all three stories.[112] Emily (Georges) Gottfried played a leadership role both as a volunteer and as a paid executive in a long list of communal organizations in the 1980s, 1990s, and early 2000s, including holding several positions that, decades earlier, would have been unattainable for a woman. She served as cantor at the South Metro Jewish Community (a Reform congregation), director of the Oregon chapter of the American Jewish Committee, and then as executive director of the independent Oregon Area Jewish Committee. Her community relations work led to her position as chair of the interreligious Action Network of Washington County, her involvement in the Coalition against Hate Crimes, her role as convener of the Oregon Faith Roundtable Against Hunger, and her service on the Portland Human Rights Coalition, among other commitments.[113]

A similar change was afoot in the synagogues. Increasing numbers of women began to serve, and hold offices, on congregational boards. In 1967, Min Zidell became the first woman to serve on Neveh Shalom's board; Carolyn Weinstein was the congregation's first female executive director, serving from 1978 to 1980; and Elaine Cogan was its first female president, elected in 1978. Cogan recalled feeling some trepidation about possible resistance, particularly among older members, but recalled, "to my delight, I found them very supportive. The women especially expressed their gladness that the men had finally 'done the right thing.'"[114] Even in those congregations on the more traditional end of the spectrum, women rose to leadership positions. Gussie Reinhardt, whose father had been the long-serving president of Kesser Israel, joined that Orthodox congregation's board and served as "chairman of the board under President Barry Brown" from 1966–1975.[115] In 1994, Renee Ferrera was elected the first woman president of the traditional Sephardic congregation, Ahavath Achim, only five years after women were granted full membership in the congregation.[116] In 1999, Linda Singer—a veteran community volunteer who had served as president of the Women's Division of the Federation and on the boards of the Robison Home, the Portland Jewish Academy, and the Federation allocation committee, in addition to her previous service on the Shaarie Torah board—was elected the first woman president of Shaarie Torah.[117]

The story of women's changing roles at the Federation, and of the Women's Division within the Federation, illustrates the shift and demonstrates that, for many women, this was not simply an issue of inclusion, but one of empowerment. As the central fundraising entity for Jewish Portland, supporting both local constituent agencies and the communal contribution to the Jewish National Fund (and frequently to supplemental Israel Emergency Funds), the Federation was the most powerful communal organization, and its officers, executive, and committees frequently served as spokespeople for the community. Not surprisingly, given the gender roles of the time, the Federation functioned at midcentury as a largely male enterprise—officers were overwhelmingly male, as were the hired executive directors. The Men's Division, organized into groupings based on profession and giving category, raised the lion's share of communal funds. The Women's Division functioned largely as an auxiliary. Although women worked hard through the division to get financial commitments from their peers, these gifts were generally small and amounted to a relatively small proportion of the total funds raised. In the late 1960s, the Women's Division raised less than 12 percent of the regular campaign total; only three of twenty-four Federation board members were women. All the Federation officers and all the presidents of the constituent agencies were male.[118]

By the mid-1970s, the Federation's structure began to shift. Although separate men's and women's divisions still operated, there were also combined categories, and women began to appear in the overall Federation leadership rather than exclusively in the Women's Division. For example, in 1975, Susan Marcus was one of two Federation vice presidents, and Marge Cohn served as secretary—and both of them were listed with these names rather than by their husbands' names, which had been the norm earlier. The following year, while Elaine Weil headed up the Women's Division, Charlotte Schwartz cochaired the Business and Professional Division with a male partner.[119] Women like Madelle (Rotenberg) Rosenfeld and Dale (Tobin) Oller benefited from leadership training through the Federation, enabling them to assume responsibility for the recently established Young Women's Division.[120]

Not only were women beginning to participate in overall Federation leadership, but they were now able to give more substantial amounts in their own names than had been true a decade earlier. The 1976 Salute to the American

Jewish Women donor event honoring all the past chairwomen of the Women's Division required a $180 minimum commitment. By the 1978 campaign, there was a separate category for women who pledged between $365 and $1000.[121]

As women became increasingly able to give and grew more integrated into the general Federation campaign, during the 1970s, the Women's Division began to fade away. Although occasionally mentioned in press coverage of the campaigns of the late 1970s, the Women's Division was not featured as a parallel campaign, with separate press devoted to its leaders and events as had been the case in the past. Now the campaign focused on divisions delineated by giving levels, and women played important roles in both the general campaign and the allocations process.[122] By 1984, when the *Review* ran a piece on the founding of a *new* Women's Division, the paper reported that the previous incarnation of that group had been disbanded eight years earlier (a puzzling claim, as the division is mentioned occasionally in late 1970s press coverage).[123]

In any event, the reconstituted Women's Division that emerged in 1984 was a new kind of women's organization and represented a new style of Federation engagement with women. Although fundraising was still a central goal, the group had broader ambitions in terms of engaging and empowering women in ways strikingly different from the old women's auxiliary model. The new division, chaired by Abby Rothschild, focused on outreach and education in addition to its campaign work. Rothschild and Priscilla Kostiner spearheaded the reestablishment of the Women's Division after attending a national United Jewish Appeal Young Leadership meeting in 1981. With a primary focus on younger women, the new group was well attuned to the needs of working women; Susan Abravanel, one of the cochairs of the group's education and programming committee, worked as the cultural arts director at the MJCC and was herself the mother of a young child. In describing their group, leaders voiced concern that women's talents be properly utilized in the community and stressed the importance of outreach to the new generation of women to assess their Jewish needs. Explicitly using a language of "consciousness raising," Abravanel described meetings as active discussions with "lots of sharing of personal struggles."[124]

An October 1984 conference on "The Emerging Jewish Woman" was one outcome of these discussions. A joint effort by the (new) Women's Division, the local American Jewish Committee, and the NCJW Portland Section, the conference was, according to coorganizer Laurie Rogoway, "the first step in an effort to address issues of women and power in the Jewish community."[125] Attended by approximately three hundred (mostly women), the conference featured a cluster of workshops on "community issues" and another on "spiritual issues."[126] The community portion of the conference was keynoted by Betty Friedan herself. An array of workshops on community issues enticed participants with titles such as "Does the Old Boy Network Shut out Women?" "Women and Power," and "The Jewish Superwoman." These workshops encouraged critique of existing power structures in the Jewish community and offered strategies for addressing inequities. In addition, they encouraged women to question assumptions and think creatively about new ways of connecting. A workshop titled "Alone and Making the Jewish Connection," asked "Why does everything in the community seem planned or defined in terms of couples?" Another, "The Jewish Lesbian" asked whether the Jewish community could "fulfill/accept the needs of lesbians," and encouraged participants to consider the similarities between homophobia and anti Semitism. Workshops were led by local women from across the spectrum of ages and backgrounds, including octogenarian and longtime volunteer Gussie Reinhardt; art gallery founder, philanthropist, and real estate executive Arlene Schnitzer; Reed professors Gail Berkeley (Sherman) and Leila Berner; lawyer and activist Emily Simon; political activist Sara Cogan, and many others. A session titled "Feminism for Jewish Men," was led by David Marcus, an attorney who had served on the Federation's executive committee.[127]

The Women's Division would go on to play a key role in connecting women to one another and in helping them to define their place in the community. In 1994, it launched an annual event called Connections. Billed as a "mega event" aiming to bring together multiple generations of women, it was open to women who had pledged $125 or more to the campaign. Through themes such as social justice, the idea of the Connections events was to "introduce many women to the work" of the Federation, to encourage them to give independently, and to show them that "when women work together they can make a difference in the lives of others."[128] As at the 1994 conference, women's empowerment was a recurrent refrain; an article describing the keynote at the Connections event claimed "the power women wield as individuals and together was a recurring theme through the evening."[129] Within two years, the annual Connections event was being billed as the "largest gathering of Jewish women in Portland history."[130] With a focus more on programming than on fundraising, the event, by then called the Women's Day of Jewish Learning, was turned over to the MJCC.

Although fundraising was only one part of the new Women's Division, it did have a significant impact on women's independent giving, and women's leadership in the division led to increased power and influence of women within the Federation as a whole. In 1993, chair Bev (Salmenson) Getreu reported that the Women's Division had raised $547,000 for the Federation campaign, including fifty-three "Lions," women who had given $5,000–$9,999, and ten "Rubies" who had given $10,000 or more. In contrast to earlier days, women's pledges made up a significant portion of Federation revenues (nearly 40 percent in 1993). As the Women's Division celebrated these successes, women played a greatly expanded role in overall Federation leadership. It became common for women not only to chair the women's division, but also to hold offices in the overall campaign, including serving as campaign chair or cochair, and as Federation president. In 1994, Liz (McBride) Menashe became the first woman to serve in that office; in 1999, Priscilla Kostiner—who had chaired the 1996 campaign—was elected Federation president.

Women had come to talk about their participation and the Women's Division in feminist terms of empowerment. They were repeatedly urged to give in their own names, not only because this increased the total number of donors that the Federation could claim, but also to exert their influence as women in the community. As Priscilla Kostiner explained, "Women deserve to make a gift that responds to her own concerns, which may differ from her spouse's." In addition, she emphasized, "Money means influence. The more women give in our own names, the more credibility we have as policy makers."[131]

Although many of the Federation's efforts to cultivate women as leaders and to reach out to them through targeted programming, such as the Connections event, continued into the twenty-first century, the gendered divisions within the Federation were again eliminated in 2004. By that year, what had once been "divisions" focused on fundraising had become "affinity groups" that sought to bring people together in the community through common interests, in the process "underscoring something else they have in common, their Jewish roots." Solomon's Legacy, a group for attorneys, met four or five times a year to eat lunch, mingle, and "get together on issues of mutual interest." A group made up of doctors and others in the health care fields made up the Maimonides Society. In 2004, the Young Adult Division was established, combining the Young Leadership (men's) and Young Women's groups. This young adult group would still play a role in campaign and leadership development, as well as providing programs aimed at different segments of the young adult community—women, singles, couples, and families with young children.[132] Beyond the Federation, women such as Arlene Schnitzer and Renee Holzman played central decision-making roles in their families' foundations, the Harold and Arlene Schnitzer CARE Foundation and the Holzman Foundation, both of which give extensively to local Jewish causes as well as to the arts, education, and other areas. Renee Holzman, for example, did much of the day-to-day work of the Holzman Foundation from its inception in 1990, conducting most of the research, reviewing grant proposals, and making recommendations to the family, which then decides together on causes.[133]

Looking back in later years, many women expressed appreciation for the expansion of their personal, professional, and communal opportunities. Yet some balanced that with recognition of a loss as the entry of women into the workforce led to a curtailment of women's organizational work. Shirley Nudelman bemoaned the fact that "because so many women are working now, they don't have the kind of friendships we got from Hadassah and from Council, from City of Hope, even from sisterhoods of the synagogues."[134] Similarly, Helen Blumenthal lamented that "women's lib and the greater freedom that women have today" had led to declining volunteerism, with a negative impact on the community.[135] Some younger women also regretted these organizational shifts. Meryl Haber enjoyed the hands-on, personal nature of her NCJW volunteer work serving lunch to seniors at the JCC so much that she stuck with it for twenty-one years. She also served on a number of boards and committees, in NCJW, at Beth Israel, and in community organizations like Oregon Museum of Science and Industry (OMSI). "I liked working on these projects because they were local hands-on things," she explained. When, in the 1990s, Council shifted more toward advocacy, she found this focus less appealing, and opted instead to devote her energy to local politics as Neighborhood Association president.[136]

Synagogues: Women on the Board, Women on the Bimah

Changes in gender norms and the feminist movement not only transformed the lives of individual women and the life of the community, but also transformed American Jewish practice. As historian Judith Hauptman argues, "Jewish feminism has made American Judaism . . . drastically different from that of the 1960s," as women became "fully integrated into the religious life of the community."[137] Reconstructionist Judaism pioneered gender equality; well before the 1960s, movement founder Mordechai Kaplan made reform of women's roles a key priority in the movement's broader rethinking of Judaism.[138] Responses to demands for full inclusion of women in prayer services and access to religious rights (and rites) previously reserved for men varied across the spectrum of three major movements. The Reform movement generally accepted (and in some cases embraced) the change as a full expression of their long-standing egalitarian ideology; Conservative congregations more gradually accommodated change as they balanced tradition with the demands of the modern world; and Orthodox congregations were more resistant to feminist demands.

The challenges to traditional gender roles in synagogue ritual were a direct outgrowth of the feminist movement. Jewish women were prominent in the movement, and, particularly in the early 1970s, they began to apply the feminist critique of gender roles in society directly to synagogue practice. Betty Friedan herself intoned in a 1970 speech, "Down through the generations in history my ancestors prayed, 'I thank Thee, Lord, I was not created a woman . . . . From this day forward, I trust women all over the world will be able to say, 'I thank Thee, Lord, I *was* created a woman."[139] Likewise, Letty Pogrebin, the founding editor of *Ms.* magazine, vividly recalled being alienated at fifteen when she was not counted for the *minyan* that gathered in 1955 for her mother's *shiva*.[140] Like many of her contemporaries, Pogrebin received essentially the same religious education as her male peers, and was frustrated by the prohibitions on her participation. Ezrat Nashim, formed in 1972 to advocate for gender equality within the Conservative movement, was only one manifestation of this application of a feminist analysis to Jewish religious practices. With their consciousness raised through participation in the women's movement, Jews began drawing on feminist theory to analyze traditional texts, applying the Exodus story of liberation to their situation as women. Women began to hold feminist Seders, to claim Rosh Hodesh (the celebration of the new month) as a feminist celebration, to create new rituals for women's life events, and to initiate changes in liturgy.[141]

These developments clearly had a significant impact in Oregon, both in terms of practice at individual congregations and in broader community discussion. Perhaps the best example of this is in the 1984 Emerging Jewish Woman conference. Along with the workshops focusing on women's empowerment within the community (discussed above), a parallel series of nine workshops addressed issues of women's spirituality. The keynote for the spirituality thread of the conference was presented by Rabbi Laurie Geller, "one of the first women to be ordained as a rabbi." Geller characterized the male image of God as "clearly idolatrous," comparing "thinking about God as male" to "thinking about God as a golden calf." Geller challenged attendees to develop new rituals for women and to incorporate "images of God as female" into the liturgy. "Theology until now has been a male experience," she explained, calling on women to "listen to our own experience and value it."[142]

The conference's spirituality sessions included "Eve and Lilith: Biblical concepts of Jewish Women," "Beyond 'G-d the Father,'" "Female Life Cycle Ceremonies," "Jewish Women in the Clergy," "Feminism and Jewish Liturgy," and "Jewish and Feminist." Like the community workshops, these were led by local women of diverse backgrounds, including professionals, scholars, and "career volunteers." The workshops directly took on issues of gender in Jewish ritual; for example, the "Jewish and Feminist" workshop promised to explore "the difficulties women have in participating fully in Jewish religious life," examine "laws and customs that are anti-female," and to discuss "suggestions for bringing about change." That workshop was led by Barbara (Weinberg) Schwartz, a public school teacher, principal of Shaarie Torah Sunday school, and cochair of the Women's Minyan. Even workshops with more traditional-sounding topics like "Creating a Jewish Home" and "Be Fruitful and Multiply: Women's Religious Role" directly engaged feminist analysis of traditional life and the challenges of modern gender roles; "Creating a Jewish Home" raised questions about the challenges for single parents. "Be Fruitful and Multiply," led by Rebbitzen Goldie Stampfer, aimed to go beyond the "traditional model" of women's roles to "define valid alternative religious roles beyond and outside of child-bearing." The workshop also promised to address the question of matriarchy/patriarchy in the Jewish family.[143]

As events such as the Emerging Women Conference make clear, Jews in Oregon were engaging in the national discussion of women's roles in community and in the sanctuary. To a large degree, the spectrum of responses in Oregon reflected national Jewish trends. However, the increasingly progressive bent of the Oregon Jewish community, particularly in the 1990s and early twenty-first century, skewed the response toward more acceptance and embrace of change. As an influx of Jews to the area spurred the creation of new congregations clustered at the liberal, and more inclusive, end of the Jewish spectrum, Oregon Jewish spiritual life increasingly reflected the growing progressive sensibilities of Oregonians.[144]

There were also practical considerations driving these trends. Outside of Portland, in small cities and towns where single synagogues or informal gatherings served all comers, inclusive policies were critical to maintaining viable congregations in communities made up disproportionately of interfaith families. Whether they formally affiliated with national movements or not, these congregations drew on Reconstructionist, Reform, and other liberal branches of Judaism as they defined policies that enabled women's full participation, recognized patrilineal descent, and accepted non-Orthodox conversions to allow full inclusion of congregants of diverse backgrounds—and to ensure they reached the required *minyan* for a Torah service.[145] Commitment to inclusiveness was a key factor driving the decisions of Beth Israel in Eugene and Beth Sholom in Salem to affiliate as Reconstructionist congregations in the 1990s. In Salem, the affiliation came early in the decade, as the community moved to hire a rabbi after years of operating as an independent congregation. After a period of study, the community voted to affiliate with Reconstructionism, in large part because of its "big tent" approach. Once affiliated, the congregation's adoption of the Reconstructionist liturgy, with its inclusive and gender-neutral language, tended to reinforce these sensibilities. In Eugene, the decision—in this case to switch from Conservative to Reconstructionist—was more contentious. Although the vast majority of Beth Israel's members were drawn to the gender equality and progressive politics of Reconstructionism, a faction resisted and ultimately split away to form the smaller, Orthodox congregation, Ahavas Torah.[146]

Yet the establishment of a new Orthodox congregation in Eugene was an exception to the general shift away from orthodoxy and toward more progressive congregations.[147] Along with the toll that urban renewal took on Portland congregations, it is clear that shifting gender roles were key to this shift. For example, the demand for women's inclusion was a critical factor pushing the largest of the traditional congregations, Shaarie Torah, from Orthodox to "traditional" to Conservative over the course of the late twentieth and early twenty-first centuries. Prior to merging with Shaarie Torah in the 1980s, Tifereth Israel also gradually moved away from strict orthodoxy; an article on the merger explained that the congregation had "gradually become more Conservative."[148] Though Ahavath Achim continued to identify itself as "traditional," it liberalized both its membership and seating policies with regard to women in the 1990s (the congregation offers both family seating and gender specific seating). By 2010, only one of the four original Orthodox congregations, Kesser Israel, remained Orthodox. Although it was joined in 2007 by Beit Yosef, a small, Orthodox Sephardic synagogue, and the Chabad synagogue Bais Menachem, both located across the street from the MJCC, the proportion of Orthodox among Oregon's Jewish population had shrunk well below the national average.[149]

As the portion of Jewish Oregonians who identified as Orthodox or traditional shrank, sensibilities about gender norms would be a key factor in the proliferation of Reconstructionist, Renewal, and post-denominational congregations in Portland and across the state. Havurah Shalom, founded in 1978 as a less formal alternative to the Reform Beth Israel, was emphatically egalitarian and attracted large numbers of young families; it quickly surpassed Shaarie Torah in size, becoming the third largest congregation in the Portland area. Commitment to gender equity was also the key factor in the establishment of the short-lived Egalitarian Shul at the turn of the twenty-first century. As Dina (Goldberg) Feuer, longtime Hebrew teacher in Portland, explained, that congregation grew out of the frustration of a few women at Kesser, who wanted to participate more fully in services. The group formed a new shul that "was egalitarian, but we wanted it still Orthodox, that is, we wanted it religious enough that the Orthodox would still come."[150] During the period from 1990 to 2010, as new congregations were founded in the Portland area, the number associated with movements committed to gender equality, often with female leadership, is striking. In addition to the Egalitarian Shul (2001), these include P'nai Or (Renewal, 1991); Beit Haverim/South Metro Jewish Community (Reform, 1992); Kol Shalom (Humanistic, 1993) led by Jane Goldhamer; Kol Ami/South Washington (Reform, 1998), led by Rabbi Elizabeth Dunsker; and Shir Tikvah (Reform, 2002) led by Rabbi Ariel Stone.[151] Beyond Portland, Salem's Temple Beth Shalom brought Rabbi Carol Harris-Shapiro to lead the congregation in 1991; Jean Zimmerman, then studying to become a Jewish Renewal rabbi, was serving in the early 2000s as spiritual leader of the small Klamath Falls congregation.[152]

In the state's two largest congregations, Beth Israel (Reform) and Neveh Shalom (Conservative), the shift to gender equality went relatively smoothly. Both congregations had well-educated and growing memberships at midcentury; and both had energetic rabbis who came early in the period (in 1953 and

Among the growing number of female clergy in Oregon were Cantor Judith Schiff (right) and Rabbi Kim Stoloff (left) of Congregation Beth Israel, pictured here with Rabbi Emanuel Rose, 2001. Courtesy OJMCHE

1960, respectively), stayed for decades, and were open-minded and dynamic. Both had strong sisterhoods and a tradition of active women's engagement in congregational affairs. Both would, by the final decades of the twentieth century, bring female clergy—Cantor Judith Schiff (Beth Israel, 1980), and associate Rabbis Ariel Stone-Halpern (Beth Israel, in 1995) and Shoshana Dworsky (Neveh Shalom, in 2002). Rabbi Stone-Halpern would go on to lead Shir Tikvah in 2002.[153]

In the Reform movement, theoretical gender equality was not a new idea; "pronouncements of commitment to women's equality" went back to the early days of the movement.[154] However, it was not until the modern women's movement that changing expectations prompted real action in terms of women's inclusion and leadership in ritual. As early as 1922, the Central Conference of American Rabbis (the Reform movement's national rabbinical body) passed a resolution affirming that women "could not justly be denied the privilege of ordination." Still, prevailing gender norms held sway; a female Reform rabbi was not ordained until 1972.[155] Beth Israel's Judith Schiff was among the first generation of Reform cantors. She had just completed her training at Hebrew Union College when her husband, composer David Schiff, was hired to teach in the Music Department at Reed College. After an audition with Rabbi Rose, Schiff was hired as the congregation's first cantor, and served until her retirement in 2012.[156]

In the Conservative movement, which strives to balance tradition and modernity, the national discussion was more heated. The evolution of bat mitzvah in the Conservative movement is an interesting case. According to historian Jonathan Sarna, one-third of Conservative congregations were performing bat mitzvah ceremonies by 1948, just over half were doing so by the early 1950s, and the rite had become "ubiquitous" by the 1960s and 1970s.[157] Yet, even as bat mitzvah became increasingly common, the question of what the bat mitzvah would consist of remained thorny for decades. In contrast to bar mitzvah ceremonies, which were generally held on Saturday mornings and included reading from the Torah scroll as the central rite, the bat mitzvah was often held during the Friday night service, which does not include a Torah reading. This allowed congregations to skirt the issue of actually calling women/girls up to the Torah, a rite traditionally reserved for men. Thus, Conservative congregations wrestled with the bat mitzvah ceremony as part of a larger set of questions about women's roles in services: Would women be counted in the *minyan*? Would they don the *tallit* (prayer shawl) and *tefillin* (phylacteries) traditionally worn by men? Would they be called to recite the blessings over the Torah and read from the scroll? And if girls would perform these rites at their bat mitzvah ceremonies, shouldn't they then be able to do so as adult members of the congregation?[158]

In 1972, Ezrat Nashim, the "first contemporary Jewish feminist group to concern itself with religious and secular issues,"[159] began to call on Conservative Judaism to endorse full female participation, by counting women in the *minyan*, enabling them to take other traditionally male ritual roles, and opening the rabbinate to women. Conservative constituencies, mostly middle class, well educated, and, by 1972, attuned to issues of discrimination, were receptive. In addition, the Conservative rabbinate had explicitly embraced the principle of change in response to modern life; for example, in the 1950s, the movement had demonstrated its willingness to accommodate members' needs by permitting driving to synagogue on the Sabbath, opening family pews, and welcoming girls equally in camps and schools. The demands by women like those in Ezrat Nashim came from a generation of women "who had learned about Judaism in Conservative circles," many of whom then went on to "become acquainted with feminism on the college campus." Their agenda, according to historian Judith Hauptman was "was accepted earlier and changes occurred more rapidly than might have been expected." By 1973, the movement had voted to allow women to be counted in the *minyan* and to be called to the Torah; individual rabbis and congregations were able to determine the degree to which they would adopt these changes. The question of the ordination of Conservative rabbis, however, was considerably more contested. It took a decade of debate before the Jewish Theological Seminary approved the admission of female rabbinical students in 1983, and in 1985, the first female conservative rabbi was ordained.[160]

Under Rabbi Stampfer's leadership, Ahavai Shalom, and then the merged congregation, Neveh Shalom, placed itself on the liberal end of the Conservative spectrum on these issues, although it was by no means an outlier. Stampfer arrived at Ahavai Shalom already supportive of inclusion

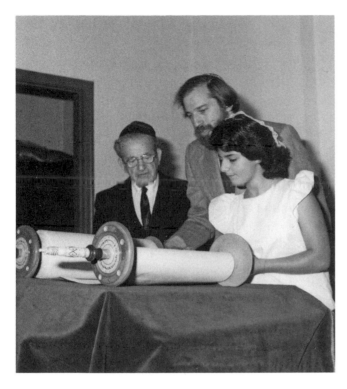

By the 1980s, it had become common for girls to read from the Torah on their bat mitzvah services at many congregations. Here, Miriam Aschkenasy celebrates her bat mitzvah at Salem's Temple Beth Sholom in 1984. Courtesy OJMCHE

of women—the first bat mitzvah at Ahavai Shalom was celebrated by Linda Potter in October 1953, just a few months after the rabbi's arrival and with his strong support.[161] Interestingly, this was three years before Karen Sue Shulkoff would have the first bat mitzvah at Beth Israel; there was a strong tradition of confirmation ceremonies rather than bar/bat mitzvah in the Reform movement.[162] Although there was controversy surrounding the bat mitzvah ceremony in many parts of the country, it appears that "the integration of this ceremony into the Oregon Jewish religious landscape occurred with little objection."[163]

Goldie Stampfer remembered the process of change at Neveh Shalom as a gradual one; first girls had Friday night bat mitzvahs, later, they were called to the Torah. "It was so gradual, it was like ice melting," she recalled.[164] In 1973, the very year that the movement voted to allow the practice, Neveh Shalom president Al Feves communicated to the membership "the fact that women and men share equal religious rights in our congregation." By 1976, the congregation had decided that young women "were to be taught the use of *tallit* and *tefillin* and to have the option of using them." In addition, the congregation instituted the practice of calling the mothers of b'nai mitzvah to the Torah and using a wedding liturgy that reflected the equality of the partners.[165]

Not all the changes regarding women's roles were matters of ritual. For example, Goldie Stampfer remembered a woman asking her husband whether it was permissible to wear a pants suit to services. Rabbi Stampfer replied, "It depends on how you wear it. For myself, I would much rather have you come in a pants suit than stay home."[166] Although there were a few older members who resisted ritual change—Goldie remembered one man walking out when the Stampfer's oldest daughter, Nehamah, led part of the Saturday morning service—the vast majority embraced it. Indeed, a friend of the man who left chided him on his return, saying, "You big, dumb fool. Why did you go out? You don't know what you missed."[167] Longtime member Milton Horenstein was pleased with Rabbi Stampfer's leadership on this issue, explaining, "I feel very strongly about it. I think if a woman like my daughter-in-law, Dorice, could read Torah, and she can read with the best of them, why is she not allowed to do so?" In 1986, when Neveh Shalom hired Linda Shivers as its first female cantor, it became one of the first Conservative congregations nationally to do so. Horenstein recalled that some of the older men objected but "they got used to it, and she's wonderful."[168]

Although it was not the only issue driving the evolution of Congregation Shaarie Torah from Orthodox to traditional to Conservative, the role of women at that synagogue was, without a doubt, central to that process. Looking back on his long career at Shaarie Torah for a 2005 documentary, Rabbi Geller characterized the feminist movement as "one of the most powerful movements that I can conceive of."[169]

Questions about the place of women at Shaarie Torah long predated the feminist movement of the 1960s and 1970s. Until the end of World War II, men and women sat separately in the sanctuary, as they did at Orthodox congregations across the nation; in this case, women were in the balcony. As Nate Director recounted in the congregation's centennial anniversary book,

> When the young men and women came home from the service in World War II and returned to Shaarie Torah, the rabbi's two children still sat with him downstairs, except they were now grown women. After a while Millie Director decided a change was needed. She and several of the young ladies—like Diane Nemer, Frieda Cohen, Ruth Erlich, Shirley Mesher, Thelma Cohen, Fanny Rosenfeld, and other Mothers' Club members—decided that if it was good enough for Rabbi Fain's daughters, it was good enough for them.
>
> So one by one they came down and sat with their husbands. None of the old-timers walked out. This was the beginning of mixed seating and the beginning of our traditional synagogue.[170]

When the congregation (now merged with Orthodox congregation Linath Hazedek) built its new synagogue in Northwest Portland in the 1960s, it offered separate male and female sections, as well as mixed family seating. Shaarie Torah's policy of allowing mixed seating led to its emerging identity as a "traditional" rather than an Orthodox congregation. This terminology was inconsistent—it would continue to be referred to as "Orthodox" or "modern Orthodox" by some for many years.[171]

A letter in the congregational files sheds light on just how strongly many Orthodox Jews felt about the seating issue. When Mark Schnitzer wrote as president of Shaarie Torah to his counterparts in Seattle for advice regarding a *shochet* (kosher butcher) over whom the community was divided, the rabbis in Seattle refused to rule in the matter. Rabbi Baruch Shapiro of Congregation Machzikay Hadath in Seattle explained the refusal: "Why? Because of a very clear fact, the fact that those synagogues where men and women sit together without a *mechitzah* [divider] are considered by the great rabbinical authorities from this generation and also from the great scholars of previous generations . . . not Kosher synagogues." The rabbi continued,

> Therefore, my friend Mr. Schnitzer, think about it yourself. How can we, the rabbis in Seattle, consider the matter since the new *Shochet* will be *Dovening* [worshiping] in this kind of synagogue? What you should do is this: declare a resolution that the men and women from this day forward will sit separately as is the case in all the fine traditional synagogues. Your synagogue should have done this long ago, and even more so now. Your Shaarie Torah synagogue is not only a synagogue in Portland, but for the entire state of Oregon. Therefore, she must be without a doubt Kosher according to the law, so that a Rabbi, a religious Jew, a *Shochet*, should be able to enter her to pray.[172]

Separate seating, of course, was not the only thorny issue for Shaarie Torah. With women sitting together with men, further questions about their role in the service had to be answered. Interestingly, Rabbi Geller, an Orthodox rabbi who began his long tenure at the congregation in 1960, had struggled with this question even before his arrival. In correspondence from 1955, when he was serving a congregation in Texas, Rabbi Geller exchanged ideas with Rabbi Israel Klavan of the (Orthodox) Rabbinical Council of America on the question of how to conduct a bat mitzvah without violating traditional Jewish law. The proposed ceremony centered on candle lighting on a Friday night, since that rite was traditionally performed by women. The key, Klavan explained, was to make it part of "a Friday evening forum (not a service)."[173] At Shaarie Torah, under Geller's guidance, bat mitzvah went well beyond this candle lighting ceremony. As early as 1971, girls at Shaarie Torah were able to celebrate Friday night bat mitzvah ceremonies that included leading part of the service and reading Hebrew Torah portions, although not from the actual Torah scroll (the Torah is not removed from the ark on Friday evenings).[174]

Responding to the demands of women who had both the education and the desire to participate more fully in religious services, Shaarie Torah began holding a monthly "all women's service" by 1985. An article in the *Review* explained that the congregation was "one of only about a dozen traditional or orthodox synagogues in the country to allow this, according to Rabbi Yonah Geller."[175] The Women's Tefillah (prayer) group, which included women from various congregations as well as some who were unaffiliated, had actually started the year before, not coincidentally, the same year as the "Emerging Jewish Woman" conference. Beginning with a Rosh Hodesh (new month) service, the group met for the first year in private homes before the service moved into the synagogue. By 1996, as the Women's Tefillah group celebrated its bat mitzvah year (twelve), a congregational Future Focus group was at work envisioning what was to come for Shaarie Torah. Surveys and meetings revealed that women wanted more opportunities for religious participation, "within the bounds of Traditional Judaism." By 1997, the congregation moved forward with a plan suggested by Rabbi Geller for a "split level" bimah; the lower level enabled women to be called up to the bimah, while the upper level was "reserved for the reading of the Torah and for participation by the rabbi and the cantor. All other parts of the service and all participation by men and women occur at the lower bimah." The following year, Shaarie Torah held its first Saturday morning bat mitzvah. Naomi Kotkins conducted the service and read from the Haftorah from the lower bimah (as would a bar mitzvah). Geller explained, "It is the hope of the congregation that Saturday morning bat mitzvoth will become a standard procedure in the future. The lower bimah was built with this in mind." Assistant Rabbi Baruch Melman noted that girls wishing to also read from the Torah could do so at the Women's Tefillah service.[176] "You couldn't have a Bat Mitzvah like Kesser Israel has where the girl just gets up and makes a talk," explained Geller, "That wouldn't fly [at Shaarie Torah]."[177]

Many congregants felt that continued evolution in women's roles was essential, and that declining membership made the situation urgent. During the first decade of the twenty-first century, the membership shrank, and those who remained were largely elderly. Rabbi Arthur Zuckerman, who came to Shaarie Torah in 2007 (Rabbi Geller retired in 2000), saw a contradiction—although they identified themselves as "traditional," very few of the members were keeping kosher or strictly observing the Sabbath. Given that, he agreed with the many congregants who saw full inclusion of women as a way to attract younger families. As Zuckerman recounted it, "I went to the board and I said, 'Let me get it straight. You're not counting women? Why?. . . There's no reason that you can't count women.'"[178] Even with all the steps the congregation had taken toward gender equity, it was clear to Zuckerman that continued restrictions made it difficult to attract young families and frustrated members who wished to remain at the congregation but longed for further changes. Some had even opted to hold their daughters' bat mitzvahs off-site, so that the entire family could take part as the bat mitzvah girl read from the Torah.[179] Longtime member Milt Carl explained in 2005, "We have to change. We have to have the participation of women in our synagogue or otherwise our synagogue is going to fail."[180] In this, Carl echoed the observation of Milton Horenstein of Neveh Shalom, who observed that "we make a *minyan* just about every morning [at Neveh Shalom]. And why? Because we count women."[181] Shaarie Torah did ultimately follow the same path; all remaining restrictions on women's participation fell away when Shaarie Torah voted to join the Conservative movement in 2013. In 2014, the congregation hired Rabbi Joshua Rose, the son of Beth Israel's Emanuel Rose and a graduate of Hebrew Union College-Jewish Institute of Religion, the Reform seminary.

Not Your Mother's Community...

Looking back in 2005, Lorraine Rose, wife of Beth Israel's Rabbi Emanuel Rose, reported that when she opted to go back to work, after their youngest child turned six, it "absolutely opened a whole world to me." Yet she worried about "how the congregation would handle that."[182] Several decades later, Rabbi Rose's successor, Michael Cahana, came to Beth Israel as part of a working couple. His wife, Ida Rae Cahana, had a cantorial and singing career that included appearances on Broadway and in Carnegie Hall, cantorial teaching and coaching at both Hebrew Union College and the Jewish Theological Seminary in New York, a position as senior cantor of Manhattan's Central Synagogue, and several recording accomplishments. Comparing their experience to that of the previous generation, Rabbi Cahana (the son of a rabbi) explained,

> The era is so different. My children know two professional parents which is just not the reality that I grew up in. My mother was extraordinarily accomplished as an artist and had a career and an experience of her own but it was in many ways secondary to her career as a rabbi's wife. That is not an insult in any way. That was the reality. That is what it meant to be a rabbi's wife in her time. And she was not a typical rabbi's wife by any means, by virtue of her having this extraordinary career (which was not popular in many circles). She broke that mold, which I admire greatly. My children have this experience of a woman who is extraordinarily accomplished and credentialed and successful in her own right and has nothing to do with her husband's accomplishments. That is wonderful. That is a great world and a great example for daughters to have. That you can have two accomplished professionals who absolutely respect each other's accomplishments and *kvel* [take pride] in each other's successes and enable each other's successes without competition or anything along those lines. Hopefully we have created a good model for our kids.[183]

In 2012, Ida Rae Cahana was installed by Beth Israel as senior cantor.[184] And the Cahanas are not the only such couple. Rabbi Ariel Stone (formerly

Stone-Halpern) served at Congregation Beth Israel from 1995–2001, and became Congregation Shir Tikvah's spiritual leader in 2003; her (now former) husband Rabbi Larry Halpern led Congregation Beit Haverim (formerly the South Metro Jewish Congregation) from 1997 until his retirement in 2006. And, since 1990, rabbinical couple Gary Schoenberg and Laurie Rutenberg have brought an innovative brand of spiritual and egalitarian Jewish outreach to the Portland area through Gesher.[185]

Such couples' experiences and relationships with their communities speak volumes about the ways in which shifts in understandings of and expectations about gender have influenced individuals, families, community institutions and religious ritual in the Jewish community. Certainly, these changes are largely a reflection of broader shifts in American society, and are evident throughout the American Jewish community. Yet the widespread embrace of a progressive Oregon identity has shaped Jewish life in the state. A survey of congregational websites, for example, reveals that words like "egalitarian" and "inclusive" abound. Such terms point not only to a generally progressive attitude toward gender, but also to an array of progressive commitments increasingly associated with Oregon.

CHAPTER FOUR

Looking Outward
Minority Consciousness and Civic Engagement

On May 5, 1964, the Community Relations Committee of the Jewish Welfare Federation of Portland published a statement calling for the desegregation of Portland public schools. Endorsed by the Federation and by twelve member organizations including three congregations, the Oregon Board of Rabbis, and local chapters of Hadassah, the National Council of Jewish Women, B'nai B'rith, the American Jewish Congress, the American Jewish Committee, and the Jewish Labor Committee, the statement publicly declared that the vast majority of the Jewish community was unified on this controversial civic issue:

> Experience and history demonstrate the limited educational results when children are educated in separate groups because of race, color or creed. In our judgment the public schools cannot fulfill their purpose of educating our children, if some are denied equal quality of education.
>
> We deem it of the utmost importance that programs of compensatory education and enrichment be accompanied by prompt steps to end de facto segregation.
>
> We earnestly hope that the committee on Race and Education will develop and recommend procedures which will end de facto school segregation in Portland.[1]

Support for desegregation of public schools was broad among northern white liberals in this period, and it is well established that, by the 1960s, Jews were the most liberal white ethnic group in America. Yet, beyond those generalities, the 1964 statement reveals much about the specific ways in which Jewish civic engagement played out in Portland. First, it demonstrates the distance that the community had traveled from just two decades earlier, when Jewish individuals and organizations refrained from making public statements on volatile local racial issues. Second, the statement's wording makes clear that the organized Jewish community was positioning itself to the left of the mainstream liberal community in Portland. Taken together, this suggests that, much like Jews in other parts of the country, Jewish Oregonians felt increasingly accepted, established, confident, and secure by the 1960s, fostering their outspokenness on controversial issues such as race relations. However, the very privilege that allowed them that security was one that chafed; despite their comfortable position, individual Jews and the community as a whole drew on their collective historic experience of discrimination to maintain an outsider identity and distance themselves from white privilege.

These shifts, toward greater and more outspoken engagement in racial discourse and toward more liberal positions, reflect changes within the Jewish community and in the broader community. During the second half of the twentieth century, community leadership passed from a business-dominated older cohort to younger professionals, particularly to lawyers. Stung by professional exclusions that lingered through the 1950s, possessing skills that made them valuable players in civic affairs, and guided by national organizations like the Anti-Defamation League of B'nai B'rith (ADL), these men were key players driving Jewish civic engagement in this era. They were joined by women, who, while still largely confined to traditional roles in the 1950s and 1960s, engaged in civic affairs through voluntary organizations, including the National Council of Jewish Women (NCJW), congregational sisterhoods and service organizations, and secular organizations such as the League of Women Voters (LWV). These men and women came into leadership positions at precisely the time when Oregon was experiencing a shift to a more progressive ethos. Although meeting resistance in several quarters, the new generation of college-educated Jewish men and women were well positioned to play an important role in liberal politics and civic organizations. At the same time, their personal experience with exclusions and prejudice at midcentury and their consciousness of historic and recent anti-Semitism—especially the Holocaust—weighed against their privilege, perpetuating their identification with nonwhites and other "outsiders."

By the middle of the twentieth century, the Portland Jewish community, like its counterparts nationwide,[2] had articulated a strong commitment to civil rights and to fighting prejudice. The community newspaper, *The Scribe*, took a consistent stance against discrimination from its beginnings in the 1920s through the 1940s. In Portland, as elsewhere in the country, Jews understood that fighting anti-Semitism was part of a larger fight against prejudice; individual rabbis and many Jewish organizations and congregations spoke out in favor of civil rights and civil liberties. Growing anti-Semitism in the same period stoked insecurities and tempered communal engagement, particularly where controversial local issues were concerned. This helps to explain why Oregon Jews blasted racist behavior in the South and in urban communities in the East and Midwest, but remained silent on local issues such as alien land laws targeting Asian immigrants and the removal and incarceration of Oregon's Japanese

American population during World War II.[3] That the Jewish community of Portland was able to speak out in a unified voice on local school segregation in the 1960s is a testament to their increased level of confidence and security.

The shift started in the immediate postwar years as the idea that racism was poisonous became widely accepted in American society, evidenced by the 1946 report of the President's Commission on Civil Rights, the public reaction to Gunnar Myrdal's *American Dilemma* (1944), and, later, by Supreme Court decisions such as *Brown v. Board of Education* (1954). Although open racial prejudice and discriminatory policies were still widespread, intellectual, civic, and religious leaders increasingly questioned them, framing them as contrary to America's core principles. The national shift was reflected in Portland, a city with traditionally Southern attitudes on race. In the late 1940s, African Americans who had come to the city to work in the shipyards during the war were openly urged by civic leaders to return from whence they came. By the 1950s, however, influential Oregonians began to advocate a more tolerant approach, including adoption of laws to guarantee minority access to housing, employment, and public accommodations. Although discriminatory practices continued for decades afterward and efforts to enact civil rights protections on the state and local levels were hotly contested, prominent groups like the (all male) Portland City Club and the LWV embraced a progressive racial stance, urging the passage of public accommodation laws and an end to discriminatory hiring and real estate practices.[4] Encouraged by national Jewish organizations, local Jews were part of this progressive vanguard. Organizations like Neighborhood House and the Jewish Community Center (JCC) stepped forward to offer housing to African American families displaced by the 1948 Vanport flood; Jewish volunteers were also involved in efforts to desegregate the workforces of the downtown department stores in the 1940s and 1950s.[5]

In 1952, after purchasing a larger building in their northeast neighborhood, Congregation Tifereth Israel found itself in the midst of a racial controversy when they sold their synagogue to an African American church. At a time when the African American population in the area was expanding rapidly, neighborhood whites mobilized to "defend" the neighborhood. Nearly one hundred residents signed petitions urging the congregation not to go through with the sale, fearing it would encourage more African Americans to move into the area. With support from ADL director David Robinson and an interracial coalition of fifty organizations, the synagogue's members rallied, voting unanimously to move forward with the sale and condemning racially motivated efforts to stop it. The ordeal was a trying time for the congregation; Irene Balk, whose husband Hy was serving as president, recalled getting disturbing phone calls and having to "fend off people who were vehemently objecting to the idea."[6] The stance soon became a point of pride in the congregation, which published an account of the incident titled *Portland 1952: One Ethnic Group Supporting Another.*[7] The synagogue remained in its new building in the same neighborhood until merging with Shaarie Torah in 1986.

The Tifereth Israel incident is just one example of the Jewish community beginning to overcome its earlier reluctance to speak out on local racial issues. By the 1960s, many individual organizations, and the Jewish community as a whole, developed track records of supporting local civil rights causes. Many in the community embraced postwar, liberal attitudes on race embodied in civic organizations like the City Club and the LWV. The 1964 decision of so many Jewish organizations to issue a public statement on school desegregation, and the efforts of the Federation to coordinate the community response, are evidence of that shift.

The 1964 statement is also significant because it suggests that the Jewish community was not simply joining the emerging liberal view in Portland but, to some extent, going beyond. Schools in cities like Portland were segregated not by law, but as an outgrowth of long-standing housing discrimination and real estate practices that pushed African American families into the Albina section of the city's Northeast. Schools reflected the racial segregation of the neighborhoods they served. After the *Brown v. Board of Education* ruling, as in many other school districts outside of the South, African Americans in Portland began to challenge this type of de facto segregation in their local schools. In 1961, the NAACP selected Portland as one of ten western cities in which to challenge de facto segregation, and the local chapter began its campaign the following spring.[8] Portland Public School officials and board members vigorously refuted the segregation charge, claiming that the issue was neighborhood demographics rather than school segregation. After a period of hostility in which a board member "invoked the language of southern segregationists by labeling the NAACP an outside agitator, 'coming in to stir things up,'" the NAACP shifted tactics, launching a campaign to educate the district on the reality of segregation in the Rose City and calling for an independent citizens' committee to investigate the question. District leaders resisted all charges of segregation, arguing—with the support of the *Oregonian* and other local press—that the real issue was housing discrimination, and pledging to resist any plan that would remove children from their neighborhoods rather than focusing on the "root cause" of the problem. District officials, with the support of a segment of the African American community opposed to busing, challenged the NAACP's focus on school desegregation, instead urging investments in disadvantaged schools to address "social and cultural deprivation." A "cultural awakening project" soon emerged, focusing on various enhancements in the district's poorest schools rather than on addressing attendance patterns.

Yet the NAACP persisted, and by 1963 it was operating as part of a new, broader coalition called the Portland Citizen's Committee on Racial Imbalance in the Public Schools (PCCRIPS). The group continued to urge a study of "the social, cultural, and psychological effects of racial imbalance," in Portland, believing there was "evidence of educational inequality so overwhelming that the board would have no choice but to desegregate its schools."[9] By this time, the coalition included the Urban League, an organization with many white liberals among its members. At a contentious school board meeting in May, PCCRIPS formally requested the study, and the board, still defensive and voicing hostility to the plan, agreed. The Committee on Race and Education started its work that summer, led by Circuit Court Judge Herbert Schwab, a former school board member, future chief judge of the Oregon Court of Appeals, and a member of the Jewish community.[10]

The May 1964 statement of the Portland Jewish organizations—issued while the Schwab committee was still at work—referred back to the controversy over the commissioning of the study, noting that the Federation's Community Relations Committee (CRC) "publicly endorsed the request of the Portland Citizens Committee on Racial Imbalance in the Schools [sic] for the establishment of a Committee on Race and Education," due primarily to their concern about "the existence of de facto segregation in the Portland public schools."[11] The statement emphatically put the Jewish leadership on the side of the PCCRIPS and the NAACP at a time when the school board, much of the press, and even many leading liberals were focusing on "cultural deprivation" as the core problem, rather than segregation. As historian Stuart McElderry explains, "Although individuals and organizations continued to speak out against de facto segregation in the press, the bulk of Portland's liberal coalition supported efforts to improve the educational opportunities of poor students, black and white."[12] By continuing to emphasize desegregation and specifically urging the Schwab committee to go beyond educational enhancement by providing for "integration of Negro and white children on the classroom level," the organized Jewish community was positioning itself to the left of many liberal groups.

In addition, the Jewish community's endorsement of the notion that segregation was key to the problem in Portland public schools—and the implication that the solution would necessitate some change in school assignments—distinguished the Portland community from Jewish communities elsewhere. The 1964 statement went beyond what was advocated by several national Jewish groups at the time. The National Community Relations Advisory Committee (NCRAC) was adamant in its emphasis on the preservation of neighborhood schools.[13] Nevertheless, its Portland affiliate, the CRC, was the group that coordinated the strong statement on desegregation. Historian Marc Dollinger notes that, although northern Jews generally supported the *Brown* decision to eliminate de jure segregation in the South, demands for school desegregation in northern cities seemed to place two of their key goals in conflict with one another: "Pluralism demanded integration while Jewish mobility demanded the best public schools." Facing this perceived conflict, "they held firm in their support for neighborhood schools and against mandatory integration," in the northern cities in which they lived.[14] Moreover, Jewish economic mobility gave many members of the community access to new housing and better schools in the suburbs, including neighborhoods inaccessible to nonwhites. In many northern cities, as conflicts over school desegregation heated up and racial tensions increased more generally—particularly in the form of riots in the mid- to late 1960s—despite their liberal inclinations on the school desegregation issue, large numbers of Jews joined other whites in moving to the suburbs.[15]

The Portland community's position is particularly striking because it came at a time when Jewish children in the metro area were overwhelmingly enrolled in Portland public schools. Even after the urban renewal that razed the Old South Portland neighborhood, the vast majority of Jews in the Portland metropolitan area—and thus, the overwhelming majority of Jewish Oregonians—still lived within city limits. A 1960–1961 Portland Hebrew School roster showed that over one-third of enrolled students resided in the Northeast section of the city—relatively close to the Albina neighborhood that was home to Portland's several majority African American schools. Although far more of the Jewish children from Northeast Portland attended schools like Laurelhurst, which were overwhelmingly white, a number went to Irvington and a few to Sabin, schools with substantial and growing African American populations.[16] Any plan involving boundary changes or busing would likely impact them; depending on the scope of the plan, it could also involve those in the other sections of the city.

Of course, Portland's racial composition was quite different from that of cities elsewhere in the country experiencing white flight in response to school desegregation. Even in the postwar era, Portland had only a small African American population; in 1960, the city was still 94 percent white.[17] Certainly, these demographics made the potential consequences of even a vigorous desegregation campaign less dramatic for Jews and other white Portlanders than was the case in Detroit, Chicago, Boston, or New York. At the same time, Jewish residential concentration was shifting westward. By the late 1960s, after urban renewal and the emergence of an institutional cluster around the JCC in Southwest Portland, the percentage of Jews residing in North and Northeast Portland—where the overwhelming majority of African Americans lived—shrank rapidly.[18] Still, in remaining in Portland proper, keeping their children in Portland public schools, and issuing a unified statement on desegregation, the city's organized Jewish community seems to have been bucking the national trend.

Fully describing the conflict over school segregation in Portland could fill its own chapter; Portland continued to struggle with the issue for decades to come, and Jewish Oregonians continued to weigh in, much as they had in 1964. Separately and collectively, congregations and other Jewish organizations published statements in their newsletters, voted on position statements, and spoke out on issues of civil rights at the school district, city, and state level. Additionally, individual Jews provided leadership on commissions and in elective office as their community tackled these thorny issues. In 1970, the CRC weighed in on Portland Public Schools' "Plan for the Seventies," emphasizing the need for "extension of integration of students of different races, economic strata and background," and calling to extend the plan to integrate middle schools to apply also the lower grades.[19] A decade after Herbert Schwab led the 1964–1965 Committee on Race and Education, Jewish lawyer and school board member Jonathan Newman was the central figure in the debate over desegregation in the 1970s. The Newman Plan (1977) was an assertive desegregation proposal that called for busing to limit the minority population in each school to its "overall district representation."[20] The central involvement of Jewish organizations and individuals and the positions they took on these issues were emblematic of the community's engagement in civic affairs in this period, demonstrating its security and confidence, as well as its members' commitment to maintaining their identity as (former) outsiders with a special understanding of prejudice.

Breaking Remaining Barriers, Standing Up for Others

In the 1930s and early 1940s, the organized Jewish community did not hesitate to publicly proclaim its belief in equal rights and its opposition to prejudicial attitudes and discrimination. Statements to this effect were major themes in the *Scribe*, frequently featured in congregational sermons and newsletters, and stated as priorities of organizations such as the B'nai B'rith and the Council of Jewish Women. The general subject of racial prejudice and specific outrages, such as the Scottsboro Boys' case in Alabama in the 1930s, generated much comment within the local Jewish community, as it did nationally. However, controversial cases closer to home were another matter—at a time when Jewish Oregonians were experiencing social and professional exclusions, few were prepared to take an unpopular stand on a contested local issue. For example, in a 1932 case that became known as the "Oregon Scottsboro case," Theodore Jordan, an African American, was accused and convicted of a Southern Oregon murder in a trial rife with prejudice. Even as the case attracted much regional attention and generated protest from civil liberties and civil rights groups up and down the West Coast, the

Oregon Jewish community remained silent.[21] Similarly, the community opted not to publicly speak out against the removal and incarceration of Japanese Americans during World War II.[22] And well into the 1940s, despite the strong communal condemnation of racial prejudice in the abstract or in other parts of the country, major Oregon Jewish firms, such as department stores Meier and Frank and Lipman, Wolfe, and Company followed local patterns of employment discrimination, fearing that if they hired African Americans for sales floor positions, they would lose business and/or that white employees would refuse to work alongside black coworkers. It was not until the mid-1940s that these firms succumbed to pressure by civil rights activists and agreed to hire African Americans to work the sales floor or in manufacturing (as opposed to housekeeping and janitorial positions).[23]

Although Jewish organizations and the community as a whole tended to keep silent on local racial matters, among the activists pressuring employers—and urging legislative action on the city and state level—were a number of members of the Jewish community. Individuals such as businessman Harry Gevurtz worked through interfaith groups including the National Conference of Christians and Jews and the local Committee on Principles and Practices to press coreligionists such as Harold Wendel, president of department store Lipman and Wolfe, to hire African American sales staff.[24] Similarly, Elinor (Cohn) Shank worked with fellow activists through the LWV and professional women's clubs to facilitate intergroup relations, both when she lived in Coos Bay in the 1940s, and in the 1950s after her return to Portland. In fact, Shank earned her real estate license in 1960 specifically because she "thought it might be possible to facilitate housing purchases by nonwhites," in the wake of the state-level fair housing legislation passed the year before.[25] In 1955, three of the four men appointed to establish a formal ACLU chapter in Oregon were members of the Jewish community: attorney Paul Meyer and academics Judah Bierman and Maure Goldschmidt. Bierman served as the new affiliate's first president, alongside fellow community members Jonathan Newman (secretary) and Mike Katz (treasurer); the group subsequently participated in efforts to enact state-level civil rights measures.[26] As these developments suggest, a coalition of liberal civil rights groups had begun to gain strength in Portland in the 1940s and 1950s, as organizations like the NAACP and the newly founded Portland Urban League found allies in prominent white organizations such as the City Club. Interracial coalitions embraced a liberal analysis, casting the "race problem" as one rooted in white prejudice and integration as the goal. Activists worked on issues including jobs and housing, using education and persuasion to convince white employers to hire African Americans and white homeowners to accept them as neighbors.[27]

Although the growing coalition of activists included individuals from a variety of professional backgrounds, at its core was a cadre of Jewish lawyers who became central figures in attacking Oregon's historic racism, and whose leadership helped shift the organized Jewish community toward the kind of direct involvement on civil rights issues evident in the school desegregation battles of the 1960s. Radical historian Michael Munk has called Irvin Goodman—who coordinated the defense in the "Oregon Scottsboro Case" and drafted Portland's antidiscrimination measure in 1950—"Portland's most celebrated radical attorney."[28] Along with Goodman, Munk also recognizes Gus Solomon, Leo Levinson, Reuben Lenske, Gerald Robinson, and Charles W. Robison as Jewish lawyers active in defending the civil liberties of radicals and minorities in the 1930s and 1940s.[29] Gus Solomon and Harry Kenin, also Jewish Portland attorneys, were among the state's earliest members of an informal ACLU group that operated beginning in the 1930s. Kenin, who served on the Portland school board (1932–1942) and in the state senate (1938–1942) was "the first to introduce strong civil rights legislation to Oregon." Gerald Robinson, who later served as Urban League president, was involved in drafting the legislation.[30] David Robinson not only served as the longtime director of the Oregon ADL, but also served terms as president of the Urban League and the City Club, was founding chair of the Mayor's Commission on Human Rights, and chair of the state Labor Bureau's Civil Rights Division.[31] In the 1950s, these established, liberal Jewish attorneys were joined by younger Oregonians and new arrivals, including several who brought with them civil rights and civil liberties commitments and experience. Among them were Paul Meyer, Richard Neuberger, Hans Linde, Jonathan Newman, Don Willner, Herbert Schwab, and Sid Lezak. When a formal chapter of the Oregon ACLU was established in 1955, many of these men served on the organizing committee and/or as founding officers.[32] This group would be prominent in Oregon's civil rights efforts, in the emergence of a viable, liberal state Democratic Party, and in shifting the Jewish community toward more vocal engagement in volatile local issues.

The national prominence of Jews in the civil rights movement has long been linked to a "minority consciousness" born out of personal and historic experiences of discrimination. Among the emerging group in Oregon at midcentury, such experiences were quite immediate. Whether they were native Oregonians returning home after completing their professional training or newcomers to the area, these Jewish professionals struggled to find employment well into the 1950s and even, in some cases, the early 1960s. Accountant Henry Blauer interviewed at several firms when he arrived in Portland in the late 1940s. Despite strong credentials, he was not hired. He realized that "if you went to City College and your name was Blauer [you were] clearly of a certain religious persuasion" and therefore unlikely to find work at one of the non-Jewish firms in Portland. There was also discrimination against Jewish medical doctors. Several informants mention quotas in medical schools; a few, including George Bodner, explained that they opted to go into dentistry or ophthalmology because of medical school restrictions that limited the number of Jews per class in the 1940s and 1950s.[33] Robert Lintin, who completed a residency at the Mayo Clinic, became the first Jewish doctor in Eugene in the mid-1950s; he discovered later that there had been opposition within the medical community to his setting up a practice.[34] Richard "Dick" Littman, who identified himself as one of the first openly Jewish faculty members at the University of Oregon, confirmed Lintin's account, citing a "rumor" that "the Lane County Medical Association had characteristically turned down Jewish doctors," into the early 1960s.[35]

The challenges for lawyers have been particularly well documented. When Morris Galen arrived in Portland as a newly minted lawyer in 1950, he was told by other Jewish attorneys, "You are going to find that you are wasting your time. No firms in Portland hire Jews."[36] That would soon change, largely through the efforts of Gus Solomon. Raised in Portland, Solomon studied law at Stanford and Columbia, returning to his hometown in 1929. Pervasive discrimination at the established Portland law firms stymied his efforts to get hired, and ultimately he opened an independent practice, sharing office space for a time with fellow liberal Jewish lawyers Irvin Goodman and Leo Levinson, taking a variety of civil liberties cases, and serving as cooperating volunteer attorney for the ACLU prior to the establishment of a formal Portland chapter in 1955.[37] His own frustrating job search inspired him to assist young Jewish lawyers once he was in a position to do so. When he was named by President Truman in 1949 to the federal bench, he was in such a position. Soon, he played a role in placing attorneys Ossie Georges and Paul Meyer at King, Miller.[38] Similarly, Leon Gabinet recalled that when he came to Oregon as a young attorney in the mid-1950s, Judge Solomon "really wanted to see to it that Jewish kids had entrée to the law firms here. He made it his life's work." Thus, Judge Solomon played a role in Gabinet's securing a position at Hart, Spencer: "They were the top firm in the state and that seemed to be the momentous occasion, when they hired a Jew, then it sort of opened the door for a lot of others. Everybody then felt that they had to do it."[39] And when firms remained reluctant, Solomon, as chief judge of the US District Court for Oregon (1958–1971), did not hesitate to provide a push. Picking up the phone in his chambers at the federal courthouse, he called hiring partners directly, identified himself, and informed them that he was sending over a well-qualified candidate. "Subtle, he was not," recalled Meyer Eisenberg, who was clerking at the Oregon Supreme Court in 1959 when Judge Solomon sent him to see the senior partner of one of the remaining firms.[40] Like Judge Solomon, many Jewish professionals of this generation had internalized the slights they experienced and committed themselves to fighting all forms of prejudice wherever they could. Joy Alkalay recalled that, when she interviewed for a position as secretary in David Robinson's office, he told her, "We don't tolerate any discrimination in this office. If I find out that you have discriminated against someone you won't be working here anymore."[41]

Even after they were admitted to previously closed firms, in a professional world where social contacts were critical to doing business, exclusive clubs were an additional barrier. Hart, Spencer, for example, held meetings at the Arlington Club and annual firm dinners at Waverly Country Club, neither of which admitted Jews—"It was uncomfortable for me," Gabinet recalled years later.[42] Solomon, along with fellow lawyers Hy Samuels and Moe Tonkon, led the fight to break down barriers to membership at the Multnomah Athletic Club (MAC), Arlington, the University Club, and Waverly. Although Jews were among MAC's charter members, and some of these families continued to hold memberships, the club restricted new entries sometime in the 1920s.[43] It became the first to give way when MAC recruited Judge Solomon in 1958. Judge Solomon kept at the other clubs in a determined campaign, combining techniques that included education (sending materials on integration of clubs to board members) and boycott (refusing to attend meetings at these clubs, urging others to do the same, and even convincing entertainers not to perform there). In 1965, Judge Solomon tried to convince Vice President Hubert Humphrey's staff that he should not attend an event at Waverly; when that tactic failed, he enlisted national Jewish organizations and major campaign contributors to complain in Washington, DC. He succeeded in getting the event moved to a private home. Numerous oral histories testify to these barriers to club memberships, and to the role of lawyer Moe Tonkon, widely recognized as the first Jew accepted at the University Club (1966), Arlington (1967), and Waverly (1972).[44] Even after the initial barriers fell, Jews still faced difficulties; some believed that the clubs continued to limit Jewish membership through quotas or a separate screening by a "Jewish committee."[45] These suspicions were confirmed decades later by Robert Liberty, whose father, Bob Liberty, was elected president of the MAC in 1969. When the elder Liberty went to the club manager to check on the long-delayed application of his friend Roger Meyer, the manager revealed to him that there was a separate process for Jews, with lists kept of those who had been approved in advance for membership by a prominent member of the Jewish community, sometimes called "the king of the Jews." This separate screening process was ended by Liberty—when told of his decision the club manager reportedly tore up the list, saying, "Thank God. I've been waiting years for this moment." Meyer, and a number of other Jews whose admission had been delayed, were soon admitted to the club.[46]

Both direct experiences of prejudice and the connections developed through professional and social affiliations fed the broader involvement of these men in civil rights and civil liberties causes. Henry Blauer, while quickly moving into leadership positions in Jewish groups including the JCC and Congregation Beth Israel's board, also joined the Tri-County Community Council and the ACLU.[47] Many of these men were active in B'nai B'rith, a fraternal organization that in an earlier generation had fostered connections among Jewish merchants and their employees. As early as the 1930s, its membership began to shift toward professionals, especially lawyers.[48] By the 1950s, professional groups, such as doctors, accountants, and attorneys, took turns hosting events for the lodge. A "Lawyers Night" held on April 24, 1957, for example, included free cocktails, dinner, and "special entertainment." According to the invitation, of 120 lodge members at that time, fifty four were attorneys.[49] Events such as Lawyers Night were critical to building professional ties, particularly at a time when the club restrictions were still in place. At the same time, organizations like the B'nai B'rith and its ADL provided resources and programming relating to its central mission of fighting prejudice and vigilantly tracking anti-Semitic activity. These helped to draw many of those involved in local lodges like Portland's into civil rights work and reinforced their minority consciousness with a consistent message that the fight against anti-Semitism was part of a broader fight against prejudice in all its forms.

Efforts of groups like the B'nai B'rith were greatly reinforced through congregational involvement. Reform rabbis were early to embrace a progressive social agenda, and this was particularly true at Beth Israel, whose religious leadership had included such luminaries as Rabbi Stephen Wise.[50] Over the course of the first half of the twentieth century Wise and his successors, Rabbis Jonah Wise and Henry Berkowitz consistently preached a social justice message and engaged in the fight against prejudice.[51] From his first sermons and congregational missives in 1950, Rabbi Julius Nodel followed suit. In the face of an effort to overturn the recently passed Portland antidiscrimination ordinance, in the fall of 1950 Nodel featured the issue in a sermon and appeared as a speaker at a community rally in Library Hall.[52] His successor, Rabbi Emanuel Rose, not only spoke out on civil rights in his sermons and newsletter messages beginning in the first weeks of his tenure, but was also appointed to serve as one of six members of the Oregon Advisory Committee to the US Civil Rights Commission in 1962.[53] Rose regularly brought the progress of the Reform Movement's social action efforts to his congregation's attention, sharing the Central Conference of American Rabbis' messages on race relations and calling on members to be "in the forefront" of the "war upon inequality."[54] In the summer of 1963, the *Beth Israel Bulletin* printed an excerpt from President Kennedy's speech to Congress in support of the Civil Rights Act, and then ran a full page "letter from the Rabbi," calling congregants' attention to the coming March on Washington:

Dear Friends:

There is no current issue more consistently challenging to the American moral conscience than the problem of civil rights.

We should realize that secular and religious organizations are spearheading nationwide attempts to encourage mass national support of the absolute and immediate need for guaranteeing not special favors, but the basic inherent right of equal opportunity.

This Wednesday, people of all creeds and racial backgrounds, organizations and institutions in mass numbers, including our own Union of American Hebrew Congregations and the Central Conference of American Rabbis will be together on an historic day in our nation's capital. Were funds available, I, too, would be there along with so many others.

We pray that all violence will be avoided. Perhaps the march in and of itself will accomplish little legislatively, but it will be a potent national denunciation of racism as well as an affirmation of the dignity of man never before expressed by so many in the *same* place at the *same* time.

We are in Washington, D.C. in spirit on this 28th day of August, 1963.

Emanuel Rose, Rabbi[55]

Five years later, after racial disturbances in Albina in the wake of the Martin Luther King Jr. assassination, Rose was the leader of a group of clergy who pressured Mayor Terry Schrunk to make a "forceful statement" on race relations at Portland's memorial service for Dr. King; Rose "stressed that opportunities were needed to educate a white community who failed to even recognize that problems ever existed."[56]

Along with these rabbis, the leadership of men such as David Robinson and Harry Gevurtz served to link the community—and particularly the Beth Israel congregation—to the fight against prejudice and discrimination, as both served in leadership capacities in Portland's civil rights community while serving terms as congregational president of Beth Israel in the 1950s. When Robinson's election as temple president was announced in the congregational newsletter, he was identified not only as the regional ADL leader, but also by his Urban League and Fair Employment Practices Committee positions.[57] By highlighting the role of its spiritual and lay leaders in the city's civil rights coalition and embracing those activities as an expression of Reform Judaism, the congregation explicitly made civil rights a communal cause. By the early 1960s, with Rabbi Rose's encouragement, a Social Action Committee emerged to coordinate congregational involvement in a variety of progressive causes, including civil rights. Although many Beth Israel members were more conservative in their personal politics, the leadership of Rabbi Rose and of members including Robinson, Schwab, and Newman on citywide civil rights initiatives was embraced and affirmed by the congregation. For example, in 1965, the Beth Israel board of trustees approved a resolution congratulating Herbert

Schwab and his Committee on Race and Education on their report and urging that it "be immediately implemented by concerted and continuous effort to obtain a well-integrated community in both human and educational opportunities."[58] The broader Jewish community similarly affirmed these activities by selecting many of these same men for leadership roles in the Federation and other community-wide organizations. For example, at the time when the Federation's CRC was coordinating community support for the school desegregation measures, Hershel Tanzer and Jonathan Newman were both officers on the Federation board.[59]

Beth Israel was the congregation most associated with these activities, but other Portland congregations and their spiritual leaders also embraced the civil rights agenda. Congregation Tifereth Israel's stance in defense of its building sale became a point of pride for that congregation. Neveh Shalom held programs such as a forum on "Interracial Problems in Portland," featuring local civil rights activist and minister T. X. Graham, speaking after services on a Friday night during the school segregation controversy.[60] At the traditional congregation, Shaarie Torah, Rabbi Geller was outspoken in his support for civil rights. In a 1963 sermon, Rabbi Geller looked to Moses to define when it is appropriate to interfere in the affairs of others, arguing, "We must be in the forefront in the battle for social justice on every level." Referencing Mississippi, he continued,

> Clear thinking men will not sit on the sidelines and pretend the situation does not exist, but will plunge into the fracas and take a stand in behalf of the underprivileged and the wronged.... Segregation in schools, discrimination in employment, intolerance in housing and other forms of subtle bigotry are not things to be overlooked for they affect the very heart of America. Of course, we find those who advocate the hush-hush policy of speaking softly, but they are those who are afraid. Moses-like, we too must take a stand and make our influence felt.[61]

A year later, he expressed strong support for the long-delayed federal Civil Rights Act in a sermon, arguing that "the most serious problem faced by this nation in a long while is that of civil rights. . . . The law must come first and then be followed by morality."[62]

Overlapping messages coming from fraternal, religious, and secular organizations worked together to foster engagement of Jewish Oregonians in efforts to fight discriminatory practices at the city, state, and federal levels. Personal experiences as professionals who had faced employment and social restrictions were reinforced by the leadership of individuals prominent in city and statewide civil rights efforts, and fed by the resources developed at the national level by organizations such as the B'nai B'rith, at a time when "civil rights became a central religious issue for American Jews."[63] Jewish organizations with long-standing interest in progressive causes were joined

in their antiprejudice work in the 1950s and 1960s by groups that had historically been more focused on internal communal matters, as civil rights became
a prominent issue embraced not only by the Reform congregation and the
NCJW section, but by numerous more traditional synagogues and groups
like the B'nai B'rith. Although Neighborhood House's recruitment of director
Archie Goldman, a man with strong civil rights credentials, in the late 1940s
was consistent with the NCJW's long-standing commitment to intergroup
work, the JCC's 1953 decision to hire director William "Bill" Gordon, who
honed his commitment to fighting prejudice and discrimination while working in the South, reflected its interest in expanding in this direction.[64]

Beyond Persuasion: Legislating for Change

In the 1940s, civil rights coalitions in Portland focused on efforts to educate
and persuade, such as when men like Harry Gevurtz met personally with
department store owners and managers to convince them to hire African
Americans. By 1950, both local and national activists felt the moment had
finally come to enact legal change to ensure "equal access to jobs, homes,
places of public accommodation and education."[65] Legislative efforts in Salem
to pass a civil rights bill guaranteeing equal access to public accommodation
went back decades, repeatedly failing. Although a fair employment law was
enacted in 1949, it was not until 1953 that the legislature finally approved the
Oregon Civil Rights Act. After the defeat of a state-level public accommodations law in 1945, the civil rights coalition in Portland went to work on a city
ordinance. A sustained campaign and study by a mayor's committee led to the
unanimous passage of the ordinance by the Portland City Council in February
1950. However, in just over a month, opponents gathered sufficient signatures
for a referendum on the measure. In November 1950, Portland voters overturned the civil rights ordinance by a vote of 76,000 to 61,000.[66]

The efforts to pass city- and state-level civil rights measures were supported
by a broad coalition of progressive groups that included civic groups such as
the City Club and the LWV, civil rights groups including the Urban League
and the NAACP, and religious groups, among them individual congregations
and coalitions such as the National Conference of Christians and Jews and
the Portland Council of Churches. By any measure, Jews—who made up only
about one half of 1 percent of the state's population, and well under 2 percent
in Portland—were conspicuous in these efforts. And the prominence of these
individuals inspired and fueled broader communal engagement.

Oregon's 1949 Fair Employment Practices Act, the sixth such state-level
law in the country, was introduced by state Senator Richard Neuberger, who
played a key role in shepherding the bill to victory. Nationally, both the ADL
and the Urban League were engaged in the fight to expand Fair Employment

Richard and Maurine Neuberger were the first married couple to serve together in the Oregon legislature, he in the senate, she in the house, 1950. Courtesy OJMCHE

Practices legislation, which, of course, targeted practices that discriminated against Jews as well as other minorities. Therefore, it was natural that, as director of the ADL and president of the Urban League from 1949 to 1951, David Robinson was selected to chair the state-appointed advisory commission on fair employment practices that investigated and championed the bill. Hershel Tanzer, a recent Reed graduate and future Federation leader, was tasked by the ADL with "organizing public support for the legislative passage of the Fair Employment Practices Act." This entailed lobbying in Salem and travel throughout the state; Tanzer traveled to Southern Oregon and talked to fraternal groups like Kiwanis Clubs as he campaigned for the bill. Jacob "Jake" Tanzer, Hershel's younger brother, recalled following his brother's efforts and going as a teenager to Salem with his parents to watch as Senator Neuberger championed the bill in the senate; the experience made a big impression on him.[67] Just over a decade later, Jake Tanzer, by then a young lawyer, served as a marshal at the March on Washington and a Justice Department lawyer investigating the murder of civil rights workers in Mississippi.[68]

Subsequent civil rights legislation at the state level was, similarly, strongly influenced by progressive Jews. Sid Lezak arrived in Portland as a freshly minted University of Chicago lawyer and quickly became involved, serving on the NAACP legal redress committee. According to his account, Oregon's 1953 public accommodations law originated at David Robinson's house: "something … that I am proud of is that in David Robinson's basement … a group of us met to draft Oregon's first Public Accommodations Law which ultimately passed the legislature."[69] Likewise, Paul Meyer recounts that he, Jonathan Newman, and John Buttler (not Jewish) drafted the ACLU's proposed version of a fair housing act for Oregon (although it was the NAACP's version that ultimately moved forward and was passed by the legislature in 1957).[70] Representative Don Willner, another member of the Jewish community, was a key sponsor both of the housing bill and of a measure to extend public accommodations protections to "semi-public establishments" including barber shops, trailer parks, and campgrounds.[71] Rabbi Rose and University of Oregon law professor Hans Linde served as two of the six members of the state-level advisory committee to the US Civil Rights Commission in 1962.[72]

Not surprisingly, given both the professional and fraternal links it fostered, the Portland B'nai B'rith lodge, earlier focused more strictly on Jewish affairs, became increasingly engaged in local civil rights efforts in this period. Regular ADL updates appeared in the group's newsletters, and articles suggested a particularly keen interest in state-level civil rights measures. In the same April 1957 edition that announced "Lawyer's Night," the main news item was titled, "ADL and B'nai B'rith Support Oregon Civil Rights Measures." Explaining that "Portland Lodge 65 and its hard-hitting Anti-Defamation League are in the forefront of activities in support of two important pieces of civil rights legislation before the Oregon lawmakers in Salem," the piece outlined the two measures sponsored by Willner, noted the lodge's history of backing similar recent measures, and urged continued support for these efforts as part of the "upward climb towards making Oregon and the nation a better and more secure place in which to live."[73] Two years later, Ben Padrow, a Portland State University speech professor, chaired a lodge committee that worked to prepare statements in support of state measures further expanding civil rights.[74] In the fall of 1961, Padrow, then the newly elected lodge president, laid out his priorities for the coming year, including a human relations conference with participation from local school districts, universities, and the state, to address "education for better human relations." He also aimed to use the lodge as a "forum" for controversial discussions, and as a vehicle for supporting the "fight for stronger civil rights legislation."[75] The lodge not only honored prominent civil rights activists like Robinson and Padrow by electing them to its highest office, but also recognized both Jewish and non-Jewish achievement in this area with its annual Brotherhood Award. In 1961, the award went to Robinson; the following year, it went to Oregon's labor commissioner, Norman Nilson (not Jewish), for his "pioneering survey of migrant labor conditions in Oregon in 1958."[76]

In addition to being professional colleagues and comrades in organizations such as the ACLU, B'nai B'rith, and the Democratic Party (especially its young leadership group) many of the core group of Jewish civil rights activists had close personal ties. Newcomers Jonathan Newman, Paul Meyer, and Don Willner all had attended New York's Fieldston School, established by the Ethical Cultural Society, and moved to Oregon in the early 1950s after completing law school—Newman and Meyer at Yale, and Willner at Harvard. In Oregon, they joined a growing network of Jewish young professionals, several of whom had been classmates at Reed College, active in the same constellation of liberal groups.[77] These circles intersected with that of Richard "Dick" and Maurine (Brown) Neuberger, who were both Democrats serving in the early 1950s in the state legislature, he in the senate, she in the house.[78] Meyer, Newman, and economist Mike Katz all served as close advisers to Dick Neuberger during his successful 1954 US Senate race, a victory considered a key event in the Democratic surge after years of Republican domination in the state.[79] Hans Linde, another young lawyer, fresh off a US Supreme Court clerkship and a stint as legal adviser to the US delegation to the UN, served as Neuberger's chief legislative assistant in Washington.

During the same period, many of the same Jewish attorneys were involved in the Lawyers Committee of Young Democrats, which fought to open voter registration and fend off challenges to voters at the polls.[80] Also active in the Democratic Party was Sylvia (Schnitzer Nemer) Davidson, a former WAVE and Reed College graduate who was central to the efforts to reinvigorate the Democratic Party in Oregon in the 1950s, working on several key congressional and presidential campaigns.[81] For a state with such a tiny Jewish population, their presence in the Democratic surge was striking. As Leon Gabinet recalled, "We met all these people like the Young Democrats and lo and behold, they were all Jews my age."[82]

Also notable is the large number of this group who would serve in public office, particularly in the state's judiciary. Herbert Schwab, who had served on the Portland school board from 1950–1959 and chaired the board-appointed committee investigating segregation in the schools in 1963 and 1964, became the first chief judge of Oregon's Court of Appeals in 1969. Jacob Tanzer joined him on that court in 1973, and later moved up to Oregon's Supreme Court in 1980, where he served with Associate Justice Hans Linde, appointed in 1977.[83] Both Schwab and Tanzer left the Court of Appeals just before Jonathan Newman joined that court in 1983. Sid Lezak, became the longest-serving US Attorney in the country, serving under five presidents from 1961 to 1982; he balanced his duty to enforce the law with his personal stance as an opponent of the Vietnam War by sending young men refusing induction to a diversion program or to community service, rather than to prison. Years later, Lezak would support the admission of one of those men, Robert Wollheim, to the state bar; and in 1998, Wollheim was appointed to the Oregon Court of Appeals.[84] Two additional Oregon Court of Appeals judges, Rick Haselton and Ellen Rosenblum, also had connections with Lezak: Haselton clerked for Lezak while a law student, and Rosenblum was a young partner in a Eugene law firm when Lezak invited her to help open a branch of the US Attorney's office in Eugene. Haselton joined the court in 1994, becoming the first Orthodox Jews to serve in Oregon's judiciary. He became chief judge in 2012.[85] Ellen Rosenblum served ten years as a federal prosecutor. She was appointed by Governor Neil Goldschmidt to the bench as a Multnomah District Court judge in 1989. She was subsequently appointed to county circuit court, and then to the Oregon Court of Appeals. In 2012, she was elected attorney general for Oregon, the first Jew and first woman to hold the position.[86]

Other political leaders who emerged from this group of Jewish activists included Don Willner. After his service in the Oregon House, Willner was elected to the state senate, where he served for a decade, beginning in 1963. Speech professor Ben Padrow, who had championed the civil rights bills in his role as B'nai B'rith lodge president, became chair of the Multnomah County Democratic Central Committee in 1964, and was elected to the Multnomah County Commission in 1970.[87] He developed a career as a political consultant, most famously running the successful mayoral campaign of maverick outsider Bud Clark. Neil Goldschmidt, after graduating from the University of Oregon in 1963, served as an intern for Senator Maurine Neuberger (who was elected to her husband's seat after his death from cancer in 1960), and became the West Coast coordinator for fund-raising and recruitment of students for work in Mississippi on voter registration during Freedom Summer in 1964. After completing law school and returning to Oregon, he, as discussed in chapter 1, began a political career, serving as city commissioner, mayor, US Secretary of Transportation, and Oregon governor, before his exit from politics over his fear of the revelation of his sexual abuse of a teenage girl during his term as mayor.[88]

Among these individuals there was a broad range in terms of degree of engagement in the Jewish community. Several were deeply involved.

Jonathan Newman, son of the well-known San Francisco and New York rabbi, Louis Newman, was a leader at Congregation Beth Israel and served a term as Federation president.[89] Neil Goldschmidt grew up at Temple Beth Israel in Eugene, and, in Portland, became an active member of Congregation Beth Israel. Willner, on the other hand, was only minimally involved with Jewish organizations and was married to a non-Jew; yet he did serve as president of the Institute for Judaic Studies. Paul Meyer's upbringing was so secular-leftist that he joked that his marriage to Alice (Turtledove) Meyer, a Reform Jew, was "an intermarriage."[90] Nevertheless, he served on the board of Congregation Beth Israel in the 1960s, and was particularly active in its Social Action Committee. Although the most common congregational affiliation among this group was with Beth Israel, there was representation from a range of synagogues. Padrow was a member of the small Orthodox congregation Kesser Israel.

Whether or not they identified as religious, the connections between their activism on issues like civil rights and their cultural heritage as Jews was often a point they made quite clear. Elden Rosenthal, who came to Portland as a young attorney in 1972 and became involved with the ACLU in 1975, was very explicit in tracing his attraction—and that of other Jewish lawyers—to civil rights cases to this heritage:

> I would say in American culture there has historically been something that has sensitized Jewish men and women to civil liberties issues. . . . When your father or your grandfather was the victim of a pogrom, or a holocaust, it's much easier for a young man or woman to understand that it can happen here . . . and if you grow up in a culture where the Holocaust is something that's discussed in the first person around the dinner table . . . by the time I was a very young man, it was just engrained in me how important it was for everybody to understand civil rights and protect them. My mother's family, they were victims of pogroms in Russia, and my grandfather was, according to the family history, snuck out of Russia in a wagon to come to America. And my dad's family, most of them, were killed in Germany. . . . So, I would say that those cultural influences would have been the primary reasons that being a civil-rights lawyer seemed so important to me. . . .
>
> You know, being Jewish up until relatively recently meant that you were an outsider; it meant that you did suffer discrimination, and so again it's much easier to see how important these laws and the Bill of Rights are when you're in a minority group.[91]

Similarly, in an essay about his experience in Mississippi in the aftermath of the Freedom Summer murders, Jake Tanzer, who considered himself "totally non-religious," rooted his interest in social justice in Jewish tradition: "I was deeply moved at age ten when we learned of the horrors of the Holocaust. It meant that there was something special about being Jewish that required vigilance." He continued,

When I was taught at home, at Sunday School, and at Passover Seders of the historical oppression of Jews, there was always an important subscript: that the oppression of any people or race or religion even in America was as immoral and dangerous as what had happened to the Jews of Europe and of ancient Egypt. I began to be aware of discrimination against Negroes, as they were then called, even in Portland, but especially in the Jim Crow South. I was taught that the vigilance was a duty, particularly for Jews, that extended to all people.[92]

The analogy between the Jewish experience in Egypt and the African American experience in the United States was particularly vivid for Tanzer during his work for the Justice Department in Mississippi in 1964. Interviewing witnesses as he investigated the murders of civil rights workers Andrew Goodman, James Chaney, and Michael Schwerner, Tanzer had the opportunity to meet a 105-year-old African American who was born a slave. Tanzer reflected, "To us, slavery was ancient history, like the Jews in Egypt, but to the Southern blacks of that era, the memories and lore of slavery remained a living part of their culture."[93]

Minority consciousness also shaped Jack L. Schwartz, who began representing Native American tribes as a young lawyer in the mid-1970s. A 1985 *Jewish Review* profile of him noted that he had become "the first white man ever to be adopted by the [Celilo-Wyam] tribe," in recognition of his efforts to preserve Native rights. In explaining his dedication to this cause, Schwartz noted similarities between the trials of Native Americans and the story of his grandparents, who had been pushed out of Russia by anti-Semitism: "the Indians have as little clout as the Russian Jews of the 19th century shtetl did.... If I were living 50 or 60 years ago, I'd be doing the same work, only my clients would be Jewish." After exploring the connections between his professional work and his ethnic background, he noted, "The handful of other lawyers in the country who work with Indians are also Jewish."[94] And lawyer Larry Kleinman drew parallels between his work, representing PCUN (Pineros y Campesinos Unidos del Noroeste), a Latino farmworkers union based in Woodburn, and his "immigrant grandmother protesting for tenant rights." As he explained, "Many of us—Jews—are not very far removed from our immigrant roots.... More than anything, growing up in the '60s as a Jew in America, it was impressed on me the importance of the civil rights movement and movements for justice."[95] Perhaps similar sensibilities informed Don Willner, who also served the Latino farmworker community both as a lawyer and as state senator. Willner, who represented the short-lived Colegio Cesar Chavez in Mount Angel and championed efforts to create better conditions for migrant laborers, recalled picking up Cesar Chavez in 1971 at the Portland airport for a rally at the capitol in Salem. "We get down there, there's a crowd of people there. An Anglo involved in working on the program—has no idea who [Cesar Chavez] was, and says, 'Hey fella, would you pass out these sandwiches?' Cesar Chavez takes the sandwiches, passes them out to people in the group, then goes up to the steps of the state capitol and makes the keynote address."[96]

It is telling that men like Tanzer, Schwartz, and Kleinman, all of whom began their professional careers in the 1960s and 1970s, referenced *historic* Jewish experiences rather than personal encounters with anti-Semitism to explain their engagement in civil rights. Unlike those who entered the professions in earlier decades, they did not personally face barriers in finding employment in Portland.[97] Although communal memory was also cited by the older generation, Jews coming of age in the 1960s and beyond had to rely more exclusively on historical examples to invoke minority status.

At the same time, their increasing distance from personal experiences of anti-Semitism helped Jews to shake off earlier insecurities about speaking out.[98] As they became accepted and secure members of the white middle class—and particularly as the black-Jewish alliance became unstable in the late 1960s—the invoking of historical memory served as a reminder of communal obligations. Historical memory of discrimination, both recent and far removed, was an important way for Jews to mark themselves out as something other than "just white" and, in particular, to distance themselves from what would later become known as white privilege.[99] Even as they inevitably benefited from employment and housing practices that advantaged whites, the continued minority consciousness of Jews helped them, in the words of historian Eric Goldstein, "to avoid the stinging realization that they, too, were now part of the white elite," since "seeing themselves as part of an oppressive white majority was like seeing themselves as *goyim* (non-Jews)."[100] As Camille Debreczeny points out in her examination of Portland-area Council of Jewish Women activity in this period, invoking historic memories of anti-Semitism, whether in the form of the Holocaust, experiences of older generations, or the Biblical exodus recounted in annual Passover Seders, "served to reinforce a Jewish minority sensibility in a way that tacitly avoided Jewish culpability in white oppression, in spite of their relative integration into whiteness by this period."[101] Whether advocating school desegregation in the 1960s and 1970s, tackling racial bias in the court system in the 1980s, welcoming Southeast Asian refugees in the 1970s and 1980s, or speaking out against hate crimes in the 1990s, NCJW members tended to frame their activity in terms of "minority solidarity," despite their undisputed acceptance by this time as whites. As Debreczeny points out, "the rhetoric used by Council to discuss race and racism frequently reflected the challenges of reconciling a long history of exploitation and oppression with a current state of ever-increasing acceptance and privilege."[102]

Unlike their male peers, Jewish women did not need to rely solely on historic experiences of discrimination to understand the impact of prejudice; men controlled communal organizations, and those groups that were most influential in the broader civic arena, such as City Club, were exclusively male. Additionally, married women's dependence on their husbands in an era when they had limited employment opportunities and were not even able to hold credit cards or bank accounts in their own names reduced their ability to make their own political and charitable contributions.

For many Jewish women the LWV, along with groups like the NCJW, became an important route into civic affairs. According to historian Jennifer Stevens, Portland's LWV was essential to bringing women into the public arena in the 1950s and 1960s, pushing at gender boundaries by taking up "important urban environmental work that was not directly related to domestic issues or their role as public housekeepers." Stevens makes the case that the LWV played a critical role in shaping Portland's new urbanism and the shift from traditional raze-and-build development to a more thoughtful, progressive approach. Through studies of urban issues that were thorough and professional, and through their subsequent lobbying efforts, the LWV had a major impact on regional- and state-level planning, contributing to developments including the creation of urban growth boundaries and a Portland metropolitan regional government.[103] And, like the City Club, the LWV was open to Jewish participation and leadership.

Participation in the LWV provided a springboard into public affairs for many Jewish women. As Margaret Labby explained, the League provided "basic training on how to get involved."[104] In 1952, Labby was appointed to the board of directors of the league, where she served with Barbara Schwab, who was elected first vice president that year.[105] Alice Meyer was active in the LWV for several decades beginning in the early 1960s. She worked on projects ranging from local candidate fairs to statewide membership drives and served on the state LWV board.[106] Elinor Shank, as we have seen, was involved with the LWV both at the Coast and in Portland and participated in a LWV study of integrated housing in Portland that helped to feed civil rights efforts to challenge continued segregation.[107] Elaine Cogan, who became an important voice on urban planning and civic engagement, gained early experience through the LWV and served as that organization's president. Through the league, she became involved in the Model Cities program, which aimed to promote citizen engagement; this work would lead to her appointment to the Portland Development Commission, which she later chaired.[108]

Although the LWV provided entrée into civic affairs for women and had a significant impact on Portland's development, it was no substitute for full inclusion. Politically active women including Elaine Cogan, Mildred Schwab, and Vera Katz were all involved (along with many non-Jewish female leaders) in protests that led to gender integration of the City Club in the early 1970s, just as each of them assumed a public position—Cogan on the Portland Development Commission, Schwab as city commissioner, and Katz as a

Vera Katz during her term as Speaker of the House for the Oregon Legislature, 1985–1990. In 1992, she was elected to the first of three terms as Portland's mayor. Courtesy OJMCHE

member of the state legislature. After the City Club voted down two proposals to admit women in 1971, a group of politically engaged women, who met socially in a group they called the "Wednesday Winos," changed their name to Politically Oriented Women and "descended on the club." Despite weekly protests, the proposal to admit women still failed to win the two-thirds vote needed to change the policy. They did, however, succeed in convincing a number of men to drop their memberships in protest. Even City Club president Sid Lezak resigned over the issue. Finally, in 1973, on the fourth vote, the club approved the admission of women.[109]

The City Club protests were critical, according to historians Tara Watson and Melody Rose, to the 1973 surge in female activism in Oregon, when a "bipartisan group of female legislators" worked with allies to pass eleven "explicitly feminist bills into law" in addition to ratifying the Equal Rights Amendment.[110] One of these activists was Vera Katz, who as a freshman legislator that term authored a bill that "ended discrimination based on gender or marital status when applying for credit or in public places." Even decades later, Katz considered this bill—which would ensure women in Oregon the right to open bank accounts and credit cards in their own names—one of her greatest legislative accomplishments.[111]

Beyond Portland: Minority Consciousness

Although Jewish Oregonians shared similarly liberal sensibilities in other parts of the state, the web of overlapping congregational, fraternal, professional, and civic ties among Jewish activists was largely a Portland phenomenon. Very few Oregon cities had a sufficient Jewish population to support even a small congregation or B'nai B'rith lodge, much less the thick networks developed in Portland. Those Jews who emerged as activists in the smaller communities did so largely via secular groups, as did Elinor Shank in the 1940s and early 1950s in Coos Bay, through her involvement in the LWV. Even from her remote post on the Oregon Coast, Shank was connected with Jewish currents in Portland, where she had grown up. She was involved in the ADL through B'nai B'rith Women, attended regional conventions, and arranged to bring David Robinson and Bill Berry of the Urban League to Coos Bay for a professional women's club conference on intergroup relations. She recalled, "I was standing at the door and I noticed that my neighbors on both sides were peeking behind the shades. The Shanks had a black man [Berry] walking into their home. It was an event, you know."[112]

In Eugene, there was enough of a Jewish presence to create a small-scale network within civil rights circles by the early 1960s. When psychologist Martin Acker arrived in 1961, he involved himself in starting the local chapter of the Congress of Racial Equality (CORE). Although only minimally affiliated with the Beth Israel, then the only congregation in Eugene, Acker nevertheless saw his civil rights activities as rooted in "Jewish morality." He recalled finding Jewish community through this work: "The people involved with me in the civil rights movement, the faculty people involved with me, were Jewish for the most part."[113] Acker's experiences were echoed by Richard Littman, also involved in the formation of CORE in Eugene. Littman, too, traced his civil rights involvement to his sense of otherness: "It's not quite as distinctive as being black, but everybody knows you're Jewish. . . . There are all kinds of little signals that are really very clear that you belong to a distinctive category, and sometimes those things are very good. And sometimes they're not." Littman, too, found Jewish community in Eugene among fellow University of Oregon faculty members and in the movement: "I think that the members of the Jewish community that we knew tended to be concerned about civil liberties in general."[114]

In Eugene, and to an even greater extent in smaller communities, even when they did not experience outright anti-Semitism, Jews continued to have a strong sense of outsider consciousness. Living in Independence for a year in the late 1940s, Merritt Linn told his classmates that his family could not afford a Christmas tree, preferring that they think he was poor to revealing that he was Jewish; his family was chagrinned when a helpful neighbor delivered a tree to their door. He felt "very, very aware of being Jewish there," and recounted that his sister claimed that, growing up as a Jew in Monmouth, Independence, and Salem in the late 1940s and early 1950s, she "felt like a Martian."[115] In such communities, mutual support and fellowship in the face of minority consciousness was often key to affiliation. After moving to Independence, and then Monmouth from Chicago in the late 1940s, Merritt's mother, Dina (Schaffer) Linn craved contact with Jews and went to great lengths to find them:

> One day I saw in the Monmouth newspaper that a man by the name of Kaplan, a doctor Kaplan was going to be a professor at the Monmouth College and my cousin was visiting with me and she said, "Let's go visit him. It's a Jewish family," and I said: "Oh I'm so shy," and she said, "We're going to do it." So we knocked [on her door] and her name was Sally Kaplan. We walked in. There were crosses all over the house. She was Catholic and we did become good friends, and she, she was lovely to me. . . . [Later] I wrote a letter to B'nai B'rith, Salem, Oregon [without a street address], and it was the mailman [who delivered it]. The town was so small, [the mailman knew who all the Jews were]. Salem was small. And so the mailman knew to take it to a Jewish person, to Dr. Harry Brown whom he contacted. . . . I wanted my children to go to Sunday school and then a very wonderful woman, I [had] never met her, sent me a letter. A party was being held in Salem, it was a shower and she invited me to it.

Once her family moved to Salem, which had a small Jewish community and a recently built synagogue, Linn became heavily involved with fundraising for the local community and for Israel, and joined B'nai B'rith Women. "I was friends with every family," she recalled of this period in Salem. "It was just a beautiful time in my life."[116]

Even in the final decades of the twentieth century, there were many areas of the state where Jews were so few in number that many residents had never had any contact with the community. Don Zadoff, living in Eugene in the 1970s, would travel to smaller towns like Junction City, "to go to a church and tell them what a Jew was." He continued,

> It was very novel to me because here I was brought up with that background [in New Jersey] where everybody knew, but out here there weren't that many Jews and there weren't Jews in the small communities—you know, they weren't a presence in the small communities—but I did go out several times just to lecture on things like that. I also did lectures in town here; again explaining to whatever the community was that I was lecturing to about what a Jew was and what we thought and so forth.[117]

As late as the 1990s and even into the twenty-first century, Jewish families in cities like Salem, where there were rarely more than a handful of Jewish children in any one public school, continued to feel excluded by overtly Christian

Members of Temple Beth Sholom, joined by other Salem residents, move their Torah scrolls to their new building during the "Torah Trek" in September 2006. Courtesy *Statesman Journal Media*

content in December music programs. In Ashland in 1999, theater professionals worked with Jewish teens to create a play based on their experiences. Funded by a grant from the Jewish Federation of Greater Portland, the play, *Lech Lecha—The Journey* made clear, as the *Jewish Review* put it in a headline, that "Growing Up Jewish in Oregon Outback No Piece of Cake."[118]

Sometimes, the experiences were more dramatic. Alvin Rackner, director of Jewish Family Services in Portland, recalled that a Jewish family from Grants Pass approached them for aid in the 1960s—they had been refused welfare in that city and reported that "people had made anti-Semitic comments to them while they applied for it."[119] Likewise, the *Jewish Review* ran a story in 1996 headlined, "Hate Campaign Drives Jewish Family from Oregon," reporting on a Jewish family in rural Jackson County that had suffered multiple attacks, including having swastikas drawn on their property.[120] In Salem, fear of anti-Semitism kept Temple Beth Sholom from publishing a directory well into the 1970s. A Jewish doctor joining a Salem-area practice in the early 1990s was shocked when, during his first, probationary year, one of the senior partners stated at a meeting that the group needn't hire a Jewish candidate since "we've already got one Jew." In the early 1990s, a mother's effort to open a discussion about the overwhelmingly Christian repertoire of the music program at her children's Salem elementary school resulted in several veiled threats and a raucous meeting at which another parent suggested that she should go back to where she came from.[121] By the early 2000s, however, a more welcoming attitude was palpable: in 2006, when Salem's Congregation Beth Sholom moved its Torah scrolls from its original building to a new, larger synagogue building five miles away, their "Torah Trek" was greeted with enthusiasm all along the route; neighbors and church groups joined the welcoming celebration.

Communal Embrace

Even as Jews in smaller communities continued to struggle with minority status, the Portland community's confidence was reflected in its willingness to assert itself on local racial issues, a sharp contrast to earlier years, when individual activists, but not communal organizations, had entered the fray. The transformation that began in the 1950s had fully taken hold by the 1960s, as suggested by the school desegregation controversy. By then, not only was the number of activists larger, but Jewish communal organizations—and the community as a whole—were increasingly willing to take public positions on divisive issues. With even the most exclusive social and professional circles opening to Jews, their confidence in asserting themselves as defenders of minority rights grew. Although they still grounded their liberal sensibilities in a minority consciousness born of historical experience, their confidence, ironically, reflected their own growing distance from that experience.

By the early 1960s, even groups whose focus was not on domestic affairs had embraced the notion that it was the obligation of Jews to publicly stand for civil rights. A good example can be found in Hadassah, the leading Zionist women's organization. The central mission of Hadassah was to support Israel, both through philanthropic human service projects in Israel and through advocacy at home. The bulk of their local programming and newsletter was tightly focused on such projects; meetings and events often included educational components about Israel, speakers who had recently returned from visits there, reports on the situation in the Middle East, and pitches for particular projects. Yet in November of 1963, the group devoted a lengthy piece in the newsletter to civil rights. "Hadassah Members Urged to Voice Support of Civil Rights Bill," ran the headline of the article, written by Mrs. Victor [Toinette] Menashe. Framing the plea as part of Hadassah's consistent efforts to keep its members informed, and noting that President Kennedy had asked for cooperation in "mobilizing public opinion in favor of the bill," Menashe's piece emphasized that individual action could help end "now and for all time . . . racial discrimination and segregation." The core of Menashe's case stated,

The demands of the negro [*sic*] population of America are simply those already encompassed in the fourteenth amendment of the Constitution and the Bill of Rights. Unfortunately, these are often denied them. What negroes do want, specifically, are homes not slums, jobs suitable to their capabilities, and equal education to make possible the homes and jobs. The obligation to meet these demands is embodied in the Administration's Civil Rights Bill, which is said to be the most comprehensive Civil Rights Bill ever to receive serious consideration from the Congress of the United States. The Bill stresses fair and equal voting rights, freedom from discrimination in places of public accommodation and business establishments, school desegregation and equal employment opportunities. . . .

Every single one of us is of the most vital and unique importance in a democracy—that what each of us does, or fails to do, might well affect the tide of history. We, of Hadassah, feel it is our obligation and responsibility to study the issues, to arrive at considered judgements, and then to act upon our findings with intelligence and vigor.[122]

In the months that followed, Portland's Hadassah chapter published several additional calls for support for the bill, and sponsored related programming to educate their members on the issue.

The transition from a more distant, general form of advocacy to specific, local engagement can be traced in the *Jewish Review* in the early 1960s as the newly founded paper began to define its role under the editorship of Ben Padrow.[123] In the first years of the decade, despite the role of individual activists and communal leaders in civic affairs, the *Review* tended to focus on national rather than local stories when it came to race relations. The March 1960 issue carried a wire service story noting that several Jewish women's organizations had joined the National Organization of Women for Equality, a group dedicated to combating school segregation.[124] In July, the paper printed a piece by nationally known civil rights advocate Harry Golden, urging American Jews to fight "for the rights of the Mexican wetback for instance; for the end of racial segregation in the South, and for the Negro and the Puerto Rican in the North with their terrible housing and employment problems of discrimination."[125] Similar stories ran throughout the early 1960s, as in 1962 when the paper printed a wire service story reporting President Kennedy's call for action on civil rights.[126] Later the same year, it published another Golden column, this time on the injury sustained by Pennsylvania Rabbi Levine during the Freedom Rides in the South, as well as printing several stories about international efforts to stop racism.[127] Despite the frequency of such national stories, the *Review* did not provide coverage of growing racial tensions in Portland; although it ran numerous civil rights stories printed from the Jewish wire services from its inception in 1959, there are very few examples of local civil rights/race relations stories in the extant copies of the paper in the first few years.[128]

Not surprisingly, the paper increased both news and editorial attention to the broader civil rights movement during the early to mid-1960s, roughly coinciding with the peak of the movement, as the nation's attention was riveted on the Birmingham Movement and the March on Washington in 1963, Freedom Summer and the passage of the Civil Rights Act in 1964, and the Selma marches and passage of the Voting Rights Act in 1965. In June 1963, the *Review* published an article about San Francisco's Freedom March (with no apparent Jewish connection) and a lead editorial asserting that Jews should be "ashamed" of racism in the United States and particularly in the Jewish community:

> We of the Jewish community are particularly pained over the situation in the areas of disturbance in the South, for we have a long memory. Even in this the twentieth century we still remember that we had once been in bondage in Egypt and our hearts go out to the underprivileged, the humiliated, the deprived. Our own struggle for equal rights has never been a purely selfish one—and this is borne out by history though some of our Negro friends fighting for liberation may not be aware of it.
>
> Racism is the dirtiest word in the human lexicon, barring none. As long ago as in the days of the lyricist of the Song of Songs the beauty of the piece was compelled to sing out that she was black but comely because she had been tanned by the sun. Evidently people in those days too had to justify their color.
>
> We are ashamed of racism wherever it crops up. We are doubly humiliated when it raises its ugly head in a Jewish environment—such as denial of swimming pool facilities in New Jersey by Jewish owners to a Negro family of the Jewish faith. We are not unmindful of the strains behind the black-white struggle that is bleeding our country. But as Jews we can hold but one position—that we are all children of one creation and that we all share a common destiny. There are threads stronger than skin that hold men together.
>
> In this faith alone is there hope for survival in this our rapidly changing world.[129]

Such pieces reflected broader trends, as national Jewish organizations embraced northern liberal attitudes toward the civil rights struggle. The *Review* conveyed this activity to its readers, featuring stories such as one in 1963 that focused on a discussion of "changing Jewish community needs" at a national Council of Jewish Federations meeting in Florida that included "the role of federations in relation to the civil rights crisis." Another story the same week reported on the National Community Relations Advisory Council's statement on human rights, calling for civil rights legislation.[130]

Yet, as it continued this national coverage, the *Review* slowly began to include greater attention to the local issues. The first local civil rights story came in October 1961, when the *Review* reported on an Oregon B'nai B'rith/ADL-initiated conference on Human Relations Education, focusing on topics including minority children in the classroom.[131] By 1963, the paper was reporting on the local school segregation issue. By 1964, not surprisingly—given that the *Review* was an arm of the Portland Jewish Federation, whose Community Relations Committee coordinated the joint statement on school desegregation—the coverage morphed into direct advocacy, and the statement appeared in the paper's editorial section. Additional local stories in this period focused on the Portland NCJW section-sponsored panel on civil rights, titled "Is Portland Meeting the Challenge?" and a JCC adult education forum on "The Status of the Negro in Our Community," intended to focus on "such vital concerns affecting the Negro citizens of our community as employment, housing, public accommodations and education."[132]

As these stories suggest, local coverage was driven by Jewish communal engagement directly in these issues. The *Review* informed readers that the B'nai B'rith Youth Organization's regional convention had included speakers from the NAACP.[133] In May 1964, the *Review* conveyed an ADL message asking supporters of the civil rights bill to "act quickly" to contact their representatives, in addition to the coverage of the joint statement condemning the segregation of children in school. In May 1965 the *Review* reported that the Temple Beth Israel Brotherhood, Conservative Neveh Shalom, and Orthodox Shaarie Torah were jointly sponsoring a talk by Rabbi Gumbiner about his experiences in the civil rights march from Selma to Montgomery.[134]

Both nationally and locally, the NCJW pioneered such engagement. Since opening Neighborhood House early in the century, the group had been emphatic about welcoming all; the fact that the first graduate of Neighborhood House's sewing school was African American was a point of pride mentioned in Neighborhood House, NCJW, and individual oral histories. As many middle-class Jewish families moved out of the South Portland neighborhood in the 1930s and 1940s, and as fewer Jews needed the kinds of social services that Neighborhood House had provided for immigrants, the clientele at the house became increasingly diverse. Faced with a decision about whether to remain a center focused on neighborhood needs or to relocate to better enact a Jewish mission, the women made a conscious decision to embrace the neighborhood mission; by the 1940s, Jews were a small minority of those served at the house and "intergroup work" and race relations became central, leading to the selection of social worker Arthur "Archie" Goldman as director in 1947. In 1954, the Portland NCJW turned over day-to-day management of the house to a community-based social service agency, to which they leased the building for one dollar per year.[135]

Although NCJW had removed itself from the direct provision of services at Neighborhood House, it did not withdraw from engagement on controversial local issues. In 1963 they became involved in the Portland Women's Committee on Civil Rights; "Portland Section members have a genuine responsibility to participate" in this group, its newsletter admonished. By the next year, NCJW had become a "permanent member" of the group.[136] NCJW continued its involvement in local and national civil rights issues, and specifically in the school segregation issue, over the course of the decade, and into the 1970s. In 1969, when a member of the Portland Citizens' Committee for School Integration visited a NCJW section meeting asking for support on a petition to integrate the schools, the section signed on.[137] A 1970 letter endorsing the school district's Plan for the Seventies noted, "We would be remiss not to state that we abhor the climate that permits de facto segregation to continue."[138] In the late 1970s, the Portland's NCJW was the only Jewish organization among thirty-eight groups that formed the Community Coalition for School Integration, which produced a detailed report and recommendations for extending desegregation while avoiding imposing a disproportionate burden of that action (such as busing) on African American students.[139] Even as other Jewish organizations expressed concerns about the possibility of quotas, or racial maximums and minimums, the Portland NCJW—like its national office—continued to embrace affirmative action.[140]

Portland NCJW members went beyond issuing statements and created projects that provided opportunities for hands-on engagement. Acting in accordance with a national initiative involving the new Head Start program, Portland section women stepped up to volunteer for a preschool program for disadvantaged children run through the Portland JCC. Headed by Helen Gordon, longtime leader of the JCC preschool and the wife of JCC director Bill Gordon, the program aimed to expand the center's existing preschool, to "take in 40 or 50 children from the Albina District," for a program that would "also involve the parents of the culturally deprived children." This went beyond the national NCJW's eight-week project, allowing the Portland women to extend their involvement for the full year.[141] Ultimately, the preschool partnership continued through the end of the decade, alongside several other volunteer efforts in the community, including additional early childhood education initiatives. Engagement with groups such as the Albina Child Development Center, in turn, led to more intergroup work, as when Portland section women were invited to use the Albina Art Center for future meetings, or when section president Jean Rustin "poured at the Founders' Day Tea of the National Council of Negro Women," at the Albina Art Center in December 1969.[142]

These notices make clear that council women continued their work on civil rights and race relations even after many other Jewish organizations began to turn their attention elsewhere. By the late 1960s, many white liberals, including many Jews, had become alienated by black nationalism and black power movements. Across the country, the combination of the radicalization of the civil rights movement and the 1967 Six-Day War crisis led Jewish organizations to turn inward, toward specifically Jewish issues, a trend widely noted

NCJW Portland section president Jean Rustin, with a group of children at the Iris Day Court Head Start program in Albina, 1971. Courtesy OJMCHE

by historians of American Jewry.[143] In addition, affirmative action drove a wedge between Jewish and African American organizations, as many Jews, recalling the quotas that limited their numbers in elite universities earlier in the century, opposed any affirmative action plans that suggested quotas. As the Federation's Community Relations Committee (CRC) explained in a 1970 statement supporting further desegregation of public schools, "As a minority group which has experienced discriminatory quotas, we question fixed percentage limitations for any racial, ethnic, or cultural group."[144]

The pressures within the Jewish community to shift focus can be seen in a "special consultation meeting" that the Portland NCJW section held in 1969 with a representative from the national office about "the future of Council in the next decade." Section women were presented with challenges almost entirely revolving around the issue of perpetuating Jewish identity in the face of full integration, and asked, "How can the Portland section bring Jewish content into its activities?"[145] Yet, even as they embraced a number of more Jewishly-focused projects, ranging from supporting the Oregon Jewish oral history project to helping to settle arriving Soviet Jews, the Portland NCJW women remained dedicated to intergroup work, presumably because they perceived this work to be an expression of the Jewish identity and values they were seeking to perpetuate. In 1969, for example, the group endorsed the petition of the Portland Citizens' Committee for School Integration, a group concerned that the school enhancement and voluntary transfer programs enacted in the wake of the Schwab report were ineffective.[146] The same year, section president Jean Rustin participated with other NCJW leaders from across the nation in the Pearl Willen Institute for Urban Crisis program in Baltimore, which aimed to facilitate an immersive experience in the "black ghetto." On her return, she implored her section sisters, "we must each get involved in inner city problems." She continued,

> There is a tremendous resource material available in Portland. We need not do this on our own. We need to educate ourselves first before charging into the community. We must investigate our own feelings and learn our own prejudices. We need to reach our own members and start on the Community Action School. We need a good name for the project. . . . We need groups of people in task forces to quietly go out to discover how community agencies work . . . police, garbage collection, welfare and then hold a one day institute.[147]

Rustin's emphasis on the need for education and self-examination in understanding the racial problems of the day was reflected in the group's ongoing responses to the school segregation issue. Their 1970 statement emphasized, "We cannot achieve successful integration in our schools or in general society until the majority understands and shares a mutual respect with the minorities."[148] From 1977 to 1989, the section partnered with other groups to offer Green Circle training, an antiracism education program, to public schools.[149]

The same message carried through their work on juvenile justice well into the 1980s. Juvenile justice was a cause the Portland section initially embraced through volunteer work at the Multnomah County Juvenile Home in the late 1950s. In the 1960s and 1970s, the NCJW group sponsored a range of programs for the Juvenile Home residents, ranging from swimming at the Neighborhood House pool to dental care and summer camp scholarships. In 1981, long after many Jewish organizations had turned inward, the women of the council initiated a Juvenile Court Monitor program, which began with a sixteen-month study of the Multnomah County juvenile court, focusing on the issue of overrepresentation of minority youth in the system. The final report, *Defining Justice for Children*, found that minority children were disproportionately charged and sentenced with detention, even when controlling for factors like poverty. Echoing Rustin's statement on the importance of self-examination of one's racial attitudes, the report admonished "all Multnomah County Juvenile Court personnel" to "examine their attitudes about racial and ethnic minorities and develop procedures to guard against discrimination."[150]

Along with the NCJW section, Congregation Beth Israel's Social Action Committee (SAC) also remained engaged well after many white liberals had turned their attention elsewhere. The SAC was rooted in a long tradition of service and civic engagement, both at the Beth Israel and in the Reform movement more broadly. In 1960, the Reform movement (Union of American Hebrew Congregations) purchased a building in Washington, DC, as a center for the Social Action Movement of Reform Judaism. Back in Portland, the Beth Israel *Bulletin* hailed the news as "the fulfillment of a dream of the late Roscoe C. Nelson [a Beth Israel member], who declared in a 1929 address to the UAHC in San Francisco that there is no subject 'more vitally Jewish than that of Social Justice.'"[151] The following year, the SAC was formed at the temple and began exploring a range of subjects for study, including divorce, family planning, and the social problems of migrant laborers. In the fall of 1961, with Roscoe Nelson (the son of Roscoe C. Nelson) chairing, the SAC sprang into action.[152]

Although the committee initially chose to focus on divorce as a societal problem, particularly in terms of its relationship to juvenile crime, the committee's attention soon shifted toward race relations, as this issue captured the attention of the city and the country. When the school desegregation issue came to the fore, it was the SAC that considered, approved, and passed on to the congregational board recommendations to endorse the various desegregation plans.[153] At times, SAC chafed against a more circumspect board, as they pressed for authority to take independent action and the board tried to rein them in. When the congregational board suggested that SAC's name be changed to "Social Action Study Group," the committee pushed back, refusing the name change and unanimously passing a resolution that SAC "be empowered to take action on the basis of proper study in areas of local concern to the congregation.[154] The following year, board member Harold Hirsch wrote a letter questioning the SAC's activity in endorsing a specific ballot measure on educational funding. Hirsch asked whether this crossed the line from "social action" into "political action." The committee again pushed back, arguing that "if it took no such stands it could take no really meaningful action."[155] Interestingly, by the following fall, Hirsch had become a member of SAC.

Like the local NCJW Section, Beth Israel's SAC was notable for its continued engagement in issues of race relations. Even in the late 1960s, after many Jewish organizations began to focus on specifically Jewish issues, the SAC kept Portland race relations at the top of its agenda. In 1967–1968, for example, they focused heavily on planning a conference on local racial issues. In preparation, the committee brought in activist Reverend Paul Schulze to provide "background on the urban situation in Portland." Schulze noted rising "black consciousness," and emphasized that "the white community can no longer plan what we are going to do for the Negro, it must be total involvement of the population. . . . *They* must have the assurance that *they* will have something to do with their destiny [emphasis in original]." The February 1968 conference opened with a Friday night sermon by a national leader of the Reform Movement's social action initiative, who provided an overview of the "urban situation." The balance of the weekend included workshops on topics such as "Understanding Black Revolution," "Model City—What It Is and Is Not," "Power Balance," and "Handicaps of the Present Political Strategy." [156] Later that spring, when Rabbi Rose shared with SAC a letter he had received from congregant Bruce Blank in support of the findings of the Kerner Commission Report on urban riots, the committee moved to have a summary of the letter printed in the *Bulletin*, along with an appeal to members to write to their congressmen. [157] In 1970, SAC placed both the latest school desegregation plan and police practices at the top of their agenda. [158] Although other issues ranging from neighborhood concerns to the settling of Soviet Jews to advocacy on Israel gradually took more of the committee's attention, race relations in the city remained a consistent concern. Advocacy and education efforts around racial issues continued to be part of the SAC's agenda well into the 1980s, when a black-Jewish dialogue emerged as a major initiative. [159]

Like the NCJW section, SAC members felt that their efforts should not end with education about the issues; rather, they strove to put their ideas into action. In the wake of the 1968 conference, while some SAC members hoped to direct the group toward specifically Jewish issues, locally and nationally, the majority "favored aiming our energies specifically toward the problems of Negroes in our community." [160] The committee had already begun investigating the possibility of direct action—including investing congregational funds in housing for African Americans—a suggestion that had come out of the February workshop. [161] In a similar vein, SAC became involved in an American Jewish Congress effort to connect "hard-core unemployed" with potential employers, by generating a list of congregants willing to employ candidates screened through the Urban League. [162] This effort originated in the decision by the Portland chapter of the American Jewish Congress to respond to the Martin Luther King Jr. assassination with a campaign to encourage "Jewish employers . . . who wish to make concrete their support for the principles for which Martin Luther King lived and died," to do so "by hiring Negroes and other members of racial minorities." [163]

The Social Action Committee's involvement in this initiative continued into the 1970s. In 1972, the committee's efforts led to Beth Israel's endorsement of Project Equality, "an interfaith program to encourage affirmative action for equal employment by ourselves and those with whom we do business." As

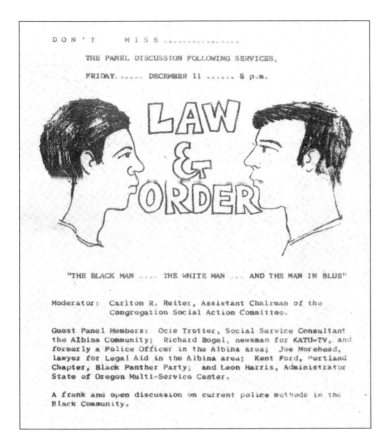

Flyer from a Congregation Beth Israel Social Action Committee program addressing the troubled relationship between Portland police and the African American community, circa 1980. Courtesy OJMCHE

part of that commitment, the congregation sent a letter to members and to its suppliers, asking them to sign on to the effort to commit to open job opportunities to minorities.[164] Similarly, SAC urged congregants to buy stock in the Freedom Bank, "Oregon's first and only Black bank," which provided opportunity through the extension of credit to African Americans.[165]

For the NCJW section and Beth Israel's SAC, such commitments on local racial issues were part of a larger portfolio of civic activities. Along with their attention to racial bias in schools and courts, the section either ran or contributed to the running of dozens of programs, ranging from adult literacy tutoring to summer programs for low-income youth, and aided a wide variety of agencies with missions that ranged from sheltering domestic abuse victims and providing services for teen parents, to offering job training to women, youth, and former inmates.[166] Likewise, SAC worked on a number of causes, including advocating for public school funding measures; monitoring the protest of migrant workers being led by Cesar Chavez; cooperating with the temple's sisterhood in encouraging volunteers to help at the Albina Child Care Center; engaging in the issues facing the synagogue's immediate neighborhood; contributing from their SAC fund to food kitchens, literacy programs and women's shelters; and addressing youth issues like drugs, changing sexual mores, and amnesty for draft resisters.[167]

In the late 1970s, as an influx of Southeast Asian refugees arrived in Portland, both groups stepped up to provide aid. The NCJW section was pleased to lease Neighborhood House to the Indo-Chinese Cultural Center, seeing the development as a return of the facility to its original mission of aiding immigrants. "Wonderful news abounds!" read the letter to members, "This happy turn of events will open up exciting opportunities and volunteer efforts by Portland Section members as the needs of the 'Boat People' are great."[168] Likewise, SAC took up the cause of the Southeast Asian refugees, emphasizing the urgency of their plight and "the very real concern of us as Jews who have also experienced another kind of holocaust."[169] The committee spearheaded Beth Israel's adoption of several refugee families in 1979. Similarly, the *Jewish Review* spotlighted the so-called Boat People, and related their plight directly to Jewish historic experience. "Jews have a special obligation to try and save victims of the new Holocaust," the *Review* article explained, "This has been a constant refrain within the Portland Jewish community since the plight of the Indo-Chinese Boat People became public knowledge. So many see the similarities between extermination of Jews in the face of world apathy 40 years ago and the plight of the Boat People today."[170] Later in the same edition, the *Review* reprinted a *New York Times* article about the plight of the Jewish refugees aboard the *St. Louis*, under the headline, "The Boat People of the Past." An article in 1981 celebrated the "adoption" of a large Vietnamese family that had been aided by the Rogue Valley Jewish community.[171] In the mid-1980s, the paper featured similar stories about local Jewish involvement in the sanctuary movement, aimed at sheltering Central American refugees and preventing their deportation.[172]

Although the response to Southeast Asian refugees was very much in line with the activities of the NCJW section and the Beth Israel Social Action Committee, by the late 1970s locally based social action was no longer the central focus of the organized Jewish community that it had been just a few years earlier. Coverage in the *Jewish Review* demonstrates that, after surging in the early 1960s and peaking around the time of the communal discussions of local school segregation, these activities began to wane as the Jewish community, like its national counterparts, increasingly looked "inward," to more specifically Jewish issues, particularly support for Israel and for Soviet Jewry. There were certainly exceptions, as with the response to the Southeast Asian refugees; yet much of the attention of the *Review*, its parent organization the Federation, and even the CRC, the Federation arm most focused on intergroup relations, turned inward, beginning in 1967 in the wake of the Six-Day War. The Federation's 1971 census found that 75 percent of Portland's affiliated Jews agreed with the statement that "Jews, as Jews should speak out on social and political issues of the day."[173] Yet in the 1970s and 1980s, the social and political issues that garnered the most attention from local Jewish communal organizations trended away from the urban social issues that had been so central in the 1960s.

Despite the fact that CRC priorities in the mid-1980s included work "to promote equality of opportunity without regard to race, religion, ancestry or gender," along with support for Israel and Soviet Jews, a review of their materials in this period makes clear that the emphasis was overwhelmingly on the specifically Jewish issues.[174] Even much of their intergroup work at home was focused on coalition building in support of Israel and Soviet Jewry, and a survey of the community press and the records of many local Jewish organizations demonstrates that far more energy, money, and time were focused on settling Soviet Jewish families in the local community and supporting Israel than on community relations or civil rights. This shift was accompanied by the focus in the early 1970s on the celebration of ethnic identity through community projects like *Whatever Happened to Old South Portland,* the initiation of the Jewish oral history project, and the creation of historical exhibits. The same concerns about ethnic and religious assimilation that prompted these activities also fed efforts to build up local Jewish social, cultural, and educational institutions and programming at the expanded Mittleman Jewish Community Center.

Jewish organizations nationally and locally—particularly those like the ADL that had long focused on anti-Semitism and prejudice in all its forms—continued to monitor prejudice and played a leading role when issues arose locally. Certainly the most prominent such incident in Portland was the 1988 murder of Mulugeta Seraw. Seraw, an Ethiopian student, was beaten to death in front of his Southeast Portland apartment by three members of "white pride" groups, the East Side White Pride and the White Aryan Resistance. Ultimately, not only were the three assailants tried, but Seraw's family, represented by the Southern Poverty Law Center (SPLC) and the ADL, succeeded in winning a civil suit against Tom and John Metzger, the father and son leaders of the White Aryan Resistance, for inciting the murder. Elden Rosenthal, one of the founding members of Congregation Havurah Shalom, worked with the SPLC's Morris Dees on the case, which presented an important opportunity to apply the strategy, used by Dees against the Ku Klux Klan in the South, of holding hate groups responsible for the acts they inspired. When Dees came to Portland to meet with a group of lawyers who might work with him, Rosenthal told him, "I've been waiting my whole career for this case." "I knew when he described this case," he explained in an oral history, "that this was the whole reason why I'd become a lawyer." The incident served to awaken community members to the growing threat of white supremacist groups in the region, and Jewish organizations became centrally involved in local coalitions responding to hate groups. According to Rosenthal, the case "provided a lot of emotion and impetus in our community to examine our attitudes toward our minority population."[175]

As Rosenthal's wording suggests, while there were concerns about attacks by white supremacist groups on Jews—and, in fact, there were several incidents in this era, including one in which neo-Nazis fired on Temple Beth Israel in Eugene in 1994, as well as a series of lectures by Holocaust denier David Irving in Portland—the responses to hate groups were, to a large degree, focused on defending other racial and ethnic minorities in the state. As Susan Abravanel, chair of the Federation's CRC, emphasized in a 1993 interview, rather than having a narrow focus on anti-Semitism and Israel, the CRC—and the Jewish community—was "passionately concerned" about a wide range of social, economic, and other issues. "Through their historical struggles Jews have learned that as long as one group's rights are at risk, so are, potentially, the rights of all groups."[176]

As right-wing extremism and hate crimes became an increasing concern in the Pacific Northwest during the 1990s, the American Jewish Committee spearheaded the 1997 creation of the Coalition Against Hate Crimes.[177] When, in the wake of the September 11 attacks in 2001, Muslims and other Middle Easterners became the target of hate crimes and of government surveillance under the Patriot Act, lawyer Emily Simon (another Havurah Shalom member) helped to enlist twenty-five Jewish, Portland-area lawyers to provide pro bono representation to Arab and Muslim locals, and worked with the ACLU as it trained local lawyers to represent clients coming under FBI scrutiny.[178] Simon was also a central figure in a Muslim-Jewish dialogue group that began meeting in early 2003 and involved rabbis Daniel Isaak (Neveh Shalom) and Joey Wolf (Havurah Shalom), as well as Reed scholar Steven Wasserstrom and the CRC's Susan Abravanel. Elden Rosenthal, too, played an important role in these efforts, and also represented Brandon Mayfield, a Muslim Portland-area attorney who was falsely accused in the 2004 Madrid train bombings. Mayfield succeeded not only in winning damages and an apology from the federal government, but the judge also declared parts of the Patriot Act unconstitutional; that ruling, however, was later overturned.[179]

Gay rights was the civil rights issue that most captured the community's attention in the 1990s and early 2000s. Oregon became an early battleground state in this area thanks largely to the efforts of the Oregon Citizens' Alliance (OCA), a group that repeatedly put measures to restrict gay rights on the Oregon ballot. Echoing their role in the civil rights era, Jewish Oregonians, as individuals and as an organized community, became prominent among the anti-OCA forces. Particularly notable was activist and philanthropist Sanford Director. Widely known as "Portland's gay mayor," Director was able to use his connections to marshal political and philanthropic support for organizations such as the Cascade AIDS project, Esther's Pantry, and the Right to Privacy Political Action Committee. In addition, he—and "his drag alter ego," Sandra Dee—coordinated numerous drag performances through the Imperial Sovereign Rose Court and other organizations, raising tens of thousands of dollars for "gay-friendly charities when the need was greatest," during the AIDS crisis.[180]

Although a coalition of gay rights activists had tried to win protection through the state legislature in the 1970s—including a measure sponsored by then Representative Vera Katz, which won approval in the house but not the senate—it was Governor Neil Goldschmidt who was responsible for the first state-level measure protecting gays and lesbians from employment discrimination. In 1987, Goldschmidt signed an executive order banning discrimination in the state's executive branch based on sexual orientation. In response, the OCA proposed a 1988 ballot measure that would overturn Goldschmidt's order and prohibit any future state officials from requiring "non-discrimination against state employees based on sexual orientation." The measure passed by more than a 5 percent margin, although it was later overturned in the state Court of Appeals. Between 1992 and 2004, Oregonians voted on an additional four anti–gay rights ballot measures, including Measure 9 (1992), which aimed to add an amendment to the Oregon Constitution that labeled homosexuality, along with "pedophilia, sadism and masochism," as "abnormal, wrong, unnatural and perverse." Measure 9, and an additional attempted ballot measure in 1994, would have prevented gays from receiving "special rights" by forbidding state and local governments in Oregon from passing protective laws. Both of these measures were defeated, as was another Measure 9 in 2000 that would have prohibited teaching about homosexuality in public schools. Finally, in 2004, voters passed Measure 36, which constitutionally defined marriage as between "one man and one woman." This constitutional amendment prohibited gay marriage in the state until it was overturned in federal court in 2014.[181]

The repeated appearance of these measures on the state ballot and the vitriolic campaigns that they inspired made gay rights a central issue in Oregon. Voting was split sharply along geographic lines, with the urban progressive areas consistently voting against these measures. Jewish communities, concentrated in the anti-OCA strongholds, even more confident and accepted than they had been in the 1960s and proud of a heritage of civil rights support, quickly jumped into the fray. Beginning in 1992, the Jewish community provided a strong and unified voice supporting gay rights in the public arena. For example, in the 1992 *Oregon Voter's Pamphlet,* the local American Jewish Committee, NCJW, Federation, ADL, and New Jewish Agenda were all—along with a variety of other progressive groups—signatories to anti-Measure 9 statements. In addition, twenty Jewish community representatives came together to form a political action committee (PAC) to oppose Measure 9. Calling itself the Jewish Committee of People of Faith Against Bigotry, the PAC published a statement in the pamphlet, invoking the Holocaust with the words "Never Again," and quoting Elie Wiesel. Their piece also included an excerpt from Rabbi Stampfer's statement in the Neveh Shalom newsletter, calling the measure "one more example of the intolerance that is all too rampant in our society which does not tolerate norms and views that are different from the position of the self-appointed guardians of morals in our society."[182] In addition to these efforts, individuals such as Steven Wasserstrom, professor of religion at Reed College, submitted anti–Measure 9 letters to the editor of the *Review*, and the paper covered the issue extensively, as well as publishing feature articles positively profiling gay and lesbian individuals and welcoming policies.[183] At an October rally that drew 10,000 to Pioneer Courthouse Square to say "no on 9," former Governor Neil Goldschmidt was the opening speaker. Standing next to his mother on the podium, Goldschmidt, "told rally goers about growing up Jewish in Eugene when the community there comprised only about fifty families. He said that despite his minority status, he always felt a strong sense of acceptance throughout the broader community. That is why, he said, Measure 9 seems to him to be especially foreign to the traditions of Oregon." Other Jewish voices were prominent among the rally's speakers, including Rabbi Rose, who gave the event's concluding remarks.[184] Rose emerged as a prominent voice in this fight, frequently linking his position on gay rights to Jewish values. While participating in a 1993 panel in anticipation of another OCA initiative that would emerge in 1994, he explained, "Because of our own history of oppression . . . when we see attempts to limit the rights of others, we rear up in defense as if we were attacked." Rose went on to draw on his recent trip to the new Holocaust Museum in Washington, DC, linking the OCA's proposed measures to Nazi antigay policies.[185]

The Jewish response to that 1994 OCA ballot measure was equally strong. Rabbi Rose and Rabbi Laurie Rutenberg of Gesher were speakers at the big "No on 13" rally in October, and the *Jewish Review* published several opinion pieces, including one by editor Paul Haist and another by the CRC director Robert Horenstein, clearly framing the issue as one of tolerance versus intolerance. Horenstein's op-ed piece is an indication of the stepped-up role of the Federation's CRC in the 1994 campaign. Rather than Jewish groups coming together to form a PAC as they had in 1992, the CRC itself took on the coordinating role for the 1994 campaign, bringing together eighteen different Jewish organizations, including all the major Portland-area congregations and the Oregon Board of Rabbis, to endorse an argument in opposition in the *Voter's Pamphlet*. The statement, coauthored by Horenstein and CRC chair Susan Abravanel, was succinct:

Rabbi Joey Wolf and his family attend Havurah's gay pride service, 1992. Courtesy OJMCHE

We oppose discrimination and stand firm in our support for the equal rights of all people.

We oppose the OCA's Ballot Measure 13, just as we opposed the OCA's Ballot Measure 9 in 1992. Language changes aside, Measure 13 is the same as Measure 9; the effects would be identical.

We urge you to vote "NO" on 13.

In addition to the eighteen organizational signatories, the names of twenty-three individual sponsors, including a number of Federation and congregational leaders, and rabbis Isaak (Neveh Shalom), Rose (Beth Israel), Wolf (Havurah Shalom), Geller (Shaarie Torah), Schoenberg (Gesher) and Rutenberg (Gesher) also appeared.[186] Interestingly, Rabbi Geller had publicly disagreed with the Reform movement's 1990 decision to allow ordination of openly gay rabbis, arguing that homosexuality was "immoral" and a "sexual deviation," in a heated exchange of letters in the *Review* in 1990.[187] Despite this, he took a clear position against the OCA ballot measures, and when the OCA brought in an Orthodox rabbi from New York in 1992 to speak in support of Measure 9, Geller criticized him, commenting, "I don't think he represents anybody but himself." Geller explained that, although he saw homosexuality as morally wrong, he opposed Measure 9 "as a denying of civil rights and privileges to members of society. . . . Once you deny rights to one group, you can deny them to another group."[188]

The debates in Oregon on these issues and the Jewish community's strong stance in favor of gay rights likely influenced Ron Wyden's early position in favor of same-sex marriage. Wyden, the son of Jews who had fled Nazi Germany, was a sitting US congressman running in a 1995 special election for the Senate seat vacated by Bob Packwood when he first publicly stated his position on the issue. According to his chief of staff, Josh Kardon, an interviewer asked an unexpected question about gay marriage, something the campaign had not yet discussed. Wyden responded that gays and lesbians should have the right to marry, just as anyone else did. Wyden took this position at a time when it was politically risky. Public opinion nationally and in Oregon was strongly opposed to gay marriage, as evidenced by the congressional passage of the Defense of Marriage Act (DOMA) in 1996, and Oregon voters' approval of Measure 36, banning gay marriage, in 2004. In taking this position, Wyden, who won the election and assumed his Senate seat in February 1996, became the first US senator to publicly support gay marriage. During his freshman year in the Senate, he made a floor speech against DOMA and was one of only fourteen members of the Senate to vote against that bill.[189]

The Jewish community again spoke with one voice on ballot Measure 36, the 2004 state constitutional amendment that limited marriage to heterosexual couples. Clearly, the various branches of Judaism and their local representatives held a range of views on whether rabbis should perform same-sex marriages. When Multnomah County began issuing marriage licenses to same-sex couples in March 2004, several rabbis were among the many clergy who conducted marriage ceremonies, while others rejected them as against Jewish law.[190] Still, the community united in opposing the proposed amendment "on a church-state basis," with CRC approving a resolution against the measure and a number of rabbis, including Rabbi Maurice Harris of Eugene's Beth Israel, playing a central role.[191] The Oregon Area Jewish Committee, the CRC, and the Oregon Board of Rabbis filed an amicus brief in federal court supporting the legal challenge to Oregon's ban on same-sex marriage.[192] Misha Isaak, son of Neveh Shalom Rabbi Daniel Isaak, was one of the three lead attorneys in that 2014 case.[193]

In the so-called post–civil rights era, many Jews and other white liberals began to think of racism as a relic of the past. This may have been particularly so in Portland, where the arrival of large numbers of newcomers to a city that they perceived as pervasively progressive made it easy to forget about (or never learn of) Oregon's historic racism. As Oregon—and especially

Members of P'nai Or participate in Portland's gay pride parade, 2010. Courtesy OJMCHE

Portland—became known as a bastion of liberalism in the final decades of the twentieth century, Jewish Oregonians became less distinctive. Whereas an earlier generation's identification with racial outsiders based on historic and personal experiences of anti-Semitism had driven the community into the liberal vanguard in the 1950s and 1960s, by the 1990s and early 2000s, the (at least theoretical) embrace of diversity, multiculturalism, and progressive values among middle-class white Portlanders was so pervasive that the Jewish community's sensibilities were increasingly mainstream.

As the rights of members of the LGBTQ community became a central public issue in Oregon, Jews joined—and in some cases led—the emerging progressive camp supporting those rights. The fights at the state level helped to open many synagogues and other communal organizations to the gay community and make a welcoming posture a high priority, often by making links to the historic Jewish commitment to civil rights and fighting prejudice in its various forms.[194] Clearly, as they had in the 1960s, many Jewish Oregonians at the turn of the twenty-first century continued to see this activity as aligned with their Jewish values. Indeed, in the extensive Portland Jewish population survey conducted in 2009, a plurality of respondents—fully 39.8 percent—believed that "promotion of civil rights and tolerance" should be *the* "highest priority" for the organized Jewish community.[195]

CHAPTER FIVE

Looking Inward

Oregonians and the Jewish World

> We instantly set about to complete the last-minute preparations of taping up the windows. In the midst of this work, at 1 p.m., we heard the first shells land and immediately entered our shelter. This was the beginning of 48 hours of almost constant bombardment.
>
> —Rabbi Joshua Stampfer, "Diary of an Israelite"
> *Oregonian*, August 20, 1967

> About 2 weeks ago the United States Embassy, along with other embassies here, advised their citizens to leave the country. Why did we stay? On the first day of the war, when two Jordanian fighter planes flew overhead, pursued by three Israeli fighter planes, we wondered why—I did some more wondering when we spent the first night of the war sleeping in an air raid shelter.
>
> —Rabbi Emanuel Rose, "A Report from Israel"
> *Oregonian*, June 18, 1967

From June 5 to June 10, 1967, the eyes of the world were on the Middle East, as Israel launched a preemptive strike against Egypt, which had been massing its army on the border for several weeks. Responding to what was largely perceived as an existential threat—Egypt's president Gamal Abdel Nasser stated that "the destruction of the State of Israel" was the war's aim—Israel destroyed the Egyptian air force and pushed into the Gaza Strip and the Sinai with ground forces. When Jordan and Syria joined in the attack on Israel, the country improbably defeated its much larger neighbors. In only six days it took control of territory in the Sinai, the Gaza Strip, the Golan Heights, and the West Bank, reuniting Jerusalem under Israeli rule. The war and the quick victory brought American Jewish passion for Israel to new heights. Like their coreligionists around the world, American Jews experienced an intense wave of pride and relief, as Israel again emerged as a powerful symbol of Jewish rebirth and survival.

Although situated seven thousand miles from the conflict, Jewish Oregonians had an additional, personal connection to events in Israel. By

Rabbi Stampfer with Israeli President Zalman Shazar in 1967. Courtesy OJMCHE

coincidence, the rabbis of Oregon's two largest congregations were in Israel in June 1967. Rabbi Emanuel Rose, who arrived in Israel in April 1967, and Rabbi Joshua Stampfer, who had been there since the previous October, were both on extended sabbaticals with their families, with a total of eight children between them. As the rabbis of congregations Beth Israel and Neveh Shalom, respectively, the two men served synagogues whose combined memberships included the majority of all affiliated Jews in Oregon. In addition, both rabbis were well-known public figures, frequently speaking in the community, and active in interfaith affairs and civic events.[1] To congregants, Jews in the region more generally, and many others in the broader community, they were familiar figures or even friends, who drew Oregonians into the faraway events through their personal accounts. In their letters home, reprinted in synagogue bulletins, in letters sent to congregants, and in features published in the *Oregonian*, the rabbis went beyond the headlines, conveying the mood of the country, explaining the practical realities of life in a war zone, and, ultimately, describing the elation and historic significance of the victory and reunification of Jerusalem.

The rabbis' firsthand accounts gave Jewish Oregonians a direct link to an event widely seen by historians of American Jewry as pivotal, not only in the history of the Jewish state but in American Jewish identity. The intensity of the Six-Day War and the miraculous victory elevated Israel to the very center of American Jewish civic religion; for decades afterward American Jews were unified in their support for Israel, seeing the Jewish state as central to their own identity as Jews. Coming at a time when the civil rights coalition of the earlier 1960s was breaking up, the Six-Day War is considered a key factor in the American Jewish community's turn inward. Although community leaders emphasized universal goals and interfaith alliances in the two decades following World War II, the embrace of ethnicity in the late 1960s combined with alienation from former allies as the civil rights movement radicalized. This led to a shift in focus toward internal, Jewish affairs, both at home and abroad. Unified, proud, and committed to their role in supporting Israel, American Jews in the wake of the Six-Day War embarked on a program of what historians have called "mobilization," dedicating themselves to support of the Jewish state through advocacy and fundraising, a mission that drove the agenda of communal organizations for decades afterward.

At the same time, in bringing the West Bank, the Sinai, Gaza, and the Golan Heights under Israeli occupation, the 1967 war sowed the seeds for later controversy and division among Jews in Israel and across the United States. Within twenty years, as Israel's image morphed from scrappy David overcoming the united Arab Goliath in 1967 to powerful occupier suppressing stone-throwing children during the Intifada of the late 1980s, unanimity began to break down. The election of right-wing Israeli governments with expansive territorial visions led to increasing criticism from American liberals, and to division and conflict within the Jewish community. With the more traditional and most embedded members of the American Jewish community tending to take a harder pro-Israel line, mainstream Jewish organizations generally followed suit. In response, those more open to negotiations and territorial compromise—often from the less Orthodox and more liberal segments of the community—began to challenge mainstream organizations, resulting in a more fragmented community profile.

Both communal demographics and the increasingly progressive political profile of the state combined to shape the responses of Jewish Oregonians. Like their counterparts elsewhere, Oregon's Jewish communities turned inward in the years following the 1967 War, focusing increasingly on specifically Jewish issues, including Israel and Soviet Jewry, as well as on the expansion of communal programming. As the American Jewish consensus on Israel started to fragment in the late 1980s, the communal discussion in Oregon reflected the local underrepresentation of the Orthodox and most embedded segments of the community—those who tended to take a harder line on the peace process. In addition, Oregon as a whole, and particularly the Portland area where the vast majority of Jewish Oregonians lived, emerged as a bastion of progressivism in the late twentieth century. Reflecting that ethos, the region's Jews tended to be relatively conciliatory in their views of Middle East politics. Beginning in the late 1980s, Jewish attitudes toward Israel were fragmenting in Oregon, with publicly aired divisions. Rabbis Rose and Stampfer, who expressed such similar impressions and emotions when they wrote from Israel about the Six-Day War, came to represent quite different camps in the communal dispute.

The Six-Day War: The View From Oregon

As Jewish Oregonians followed the increasingly tense situation in the Middle East in the spring of 1967 and reflected on it in the months that followed, through the accounts of the two rabbis they were able to gain a personal view of events. Beth Israel congregants experienced the buildup to war through the eyes of Rabbi Rose, who sent a missive to his congregation on May 24 (it was received at the temple a week later, and then sent out to the membership). Writing from Tel Aviv, Rose was well aware that "war could well break out literally any minute," and described the way that people and vehicles were vanishing from the normally crowded streets of Tel Aviv as reservists were called up to Israel's "citizen army." He wrote that taxis were disappearing as their drivers reported for service, and that buses became "infrequent . . . for a fantastic number of them were removed from the streets for conversion into mass army ambulances."[2]

Both rabbis provided the *Oregonian,* as well as their congregational bulletins and personal correspondents, with accounts of war preparations and life under fire. Stampfer's "Diary"—published in full later in the summer in the *Oregonian*'s Sunday magazine section—described the family readying their bomb shelter, filling sandbags, and stocking medical supplies. The rabbi also went through training to participate in a Hebrew University firefighting unit. In letters later published in Neveh Shalom's *Chronicle,* Stampfer's wife, Goldie, and their teenage son, Noam, also wrote of the war preparations. Noam described the ways that he, his brothers Meir and Shaul, and their high school friends were able to make contributions to preparation efforts when he wrote from Jerusalem on May 26:

> Yesterday Meir and I joined a group of high school kids to put up posters indicating public shelters around Jerusalem. Shaul is taking a course in First Aid for the civil Defense Service. One kid in my class has worked daily from 3:30 to 10:00 pm delivering telegrams for the post office, taking the place of a man who was mobilized. By next week nearly all the high school kids will be doing some sort of voluntary work.[3]

As the family anticipated the war, Rabbi Stampfer reported "a strange sense of unreality about the whole business. . . . We came to accept the tension of Arab threats as part of a normal way of life."[4] Despite the tension, all three Stampfers emphasized in their letters home their commitment to remain in Israel. Goldie ended a letter penned on May 23 or 24 with the words, "Much more I had wanted to write before but mainly—we're staying here as scheduled. Calm, but concerned. Love, Goldie"[5] Rabbi Stampfer echoed his wife in a May 25 letter to congregants, "We are determined to stay here and do everything we can to help," and encouraged them to participate, writing, "We hope that in every way—through public statements, financial support, etc., you will play your role in this struggle for freedom."[6]

Both rabbis also shared with hometown readers their families' experiences under fire. *Oregonian* reporter Stan Federman spoke with Rabbi Rose via "transatlantic cable telephone" after the second day of fighting, reporting that the family—including three daughters ages five, three, and two—was sleeping in a bomb shelter in a blacked-out Tel Aviv.[7] Explaining his family's decision to stay in Israel in a letter written on June 8 (and published in the *Oregonian* ten days later), Rose emphasized that "while we have been in severe danger of air and artillery attack at times, my family could always go home. The citizens of Israel have nowhere else to go." Ultimately they felt, according to the rabbi, "there was no choice for us."[8] The situation of the Jerusalem-based Stampfer family, where fighting was far heavier, was even more precarious. When the war began, Rabbi Stampfer raced in his car to Nehama's school (the youngest child, Elana, attended a kindergarten near their apartment). The boys ran home, bringing the news that "a large shell had landed in the high school, but fortunately no one was injured." Rabbi Stampfer described "forty-eight hours of almost constant bombardment," at the start of the war. On the first night,

> it sounded as though the world was coming to an end. . . . Every few moments, the skies were lighted with bright flares and with the flash of artillery fire. Our children were frightened as we tried to comfort them by saying that noise doesn't hurt. Our 10-year-old (daughter) Nehama responded, "I'm not afraid of the noise, just what goes with it."[9]

The two rabbis provided an intimate window into events, and their messages reinforced the major themes in most American Jewish sources. Rose repeatedly marveled at Israel's "citizen army," able to triumph because soldiers were "fighting for their very being" and had "a deep love of the land." He also emphasized the unity of Israelis in supporting the army, describing citizens lined up in the streets to give blood and volunteering to do the work of those called up for service: "Kids deliver the mail and pour sand bags; older people give blood and make bandages—if you are an Israeli you are in the war."[10] Both rabbis reported the exhilaration of the victory at war's end, with Stampfer describing the "unbelievable wave of joy" as Israelis "realized that for the first time in 2,000 years, the Jewish dream of a free Jerusalem was fulfilled."[11]

Central to the rabbis' accounts was their joy at the reunification of Jerusalem under Israeli rule. Rose recounted hearing the radio broadcast of the victory in Jerusalem, when the Israeli prime minister, defense minister, and army chief of staff arrived at the Western Wall and "the soldiers who had just conquered the city leaned against the wall of the Temple and cried."[12] Stampfer, in a letter written on June 10 and published a week later in the

Oregonian, shared his experience as "one of the first civilians" to enter the Old City. He noted evidence of the shelling, damage to streets and shops, and bodies "still being carried on stretchers," and described the scene at the Western Wall: "We stood there and marveled at the sight that greeted our eyes. Here stood the great wall resting on massive rectangular rocks that date back to the First Century. In front of the wall a vast crowd was gathered. Most of them were soldiers still carrying the sub-machine guns slung over their shoulders but with prayer books in their hand." Soon, Stampfer wrote, Israeli president Zalman Shazar arrived on the scene:

> For the first time in 2,000 years, the head of a Jewish state had come to worship on the Temple Mount. He ran to the wall and kissed it with tears running down his face. He recited a Psalm of Thanksgiving to which everyone responded with a heartfelt Amen.
>
> Then the Scroll of the Law was open and read just as it is done on a holiday. The reading was punctuated with scattered rifle fire as snipers were still trying to do their deadly work.[13]

A few days later, Stampfer again joined the throngs at the wall for the festival of Shavuot, reporting, "The lower stones of the wall were completely covered by the mass of worshippers that was pressed against it. Everyone fought to approach it for at least a fleeting moment to press his lips against the worn reminders of the people's ancient glory. At intervals along the way, arks containing scrolls of law were already standing and 20 simultaneous services were in progress."[14]

Both rabbis exulted in Israel's victory, and conveyed their hope for future peace and for recognition and security for the Jewish state. "I am glad I am here in these historic hours," Rose wrote.

> I rejoice over the Israeli victories against those leaders who refuse to accept the existence of Israel. I have felt the anxiety of possible bombing; I have run to the shelters with my wife and children hoping that we would be safe. I have seen the destruction of war and I feel more strongly than ever before that the most urgent need of all nations is disarmament. The world must destroy not people but the weapons of all nations.[15]

Stampfer similarly noted that "despite the jubilant tone that prevails here in wake of the military victories, the prayer for peace is in everyone's heart . . . but the prayer is also for a peace that will be lasting, based on the recognition by all of Israel's neighbors of its right to live in security."[16]

That Oregonians were able to read firsthand accounts by rabbis whom knew, in many cases personally, made a pivotal event for the American Jewish community even more immediate. It is difficult to overstate the significance of the Six-Day War for American Jewish identity. As historian Hasia Diner explains, "The war, its prelude and aftermath, shook American Jews deeply. Wherever they congregated they talked about the crisis, speculating on what it would mean if the Arab armies actually did what they had promised and destroyed the Jewish state and annihilated the Jews living there."[17] Coming scarcely two decades after the end of World War II, the crisis sparked deep fears of a new Holocaust. "Will God permit our people to perish? Will there be another Auschwitz, another Dachau, another Treblinka?" asked theologian Rabbi Abraham Joshua Heschel.[18] As the symbol of Jewish survival and rebirth after the Holocaust, "the prospect of Israel's destruction seemed unbearable." Such an outcome would represent, according to historian Melvin Urofsky, Hitler's final victory.[19] This sense of crisis led American Jews to raise $240 million for Israel in 1967, in addition to buying nearly $200 million in Israel bonds.[20]

In the aftermath of World War II, the American Jewish community took the lead in providing for Jews worldwide, raising the funds to aid survivors, to settle them in Palestine, to build the Jewish state, and to absorb additional refugees from North Africa and the Middle East in the wake of Israeli independence. Major fundraising campaigns were coordinated through the federation system, in which regional federations—a Jewish version of the United Way—could raise money locally under one umbrella, and then allocate funds to a combination of local, national, and international Jewish organizations and institutions. In the 1950s and early 1960s, the United Jewish Appeal (UJA) raised $60 to $75 million dollars per year to aid Jews outside the United States, and about two-thirds of those funds went to Israel. In addition to fundraising, American Jews established an apparatus for advocacy; the American-Israel Public Affairs Committee (AIPAC) and the Conference of Presidents of Major American Jewish Organizations both took shape in this period, aiming to build support for Israel in Washington and lobby on her behalf.[21]

In the Portland area, the Jewish Welfare Federation had a well-organized campaign, dominating the headlines of the *Jewish Review* (one of its community subsidiaries) with accounts of the activities of its various divisions made up of groups of male professionals, and a "Women's Division." In the "Special Campaign Issue" in March 1967, a few months before the outbreak of war, the *Review* reported that pledges were up by 15 percent over the previous year, and played up the friendly competition among accountants, attorneys, physicians, and dentists, as well as the other divisions. Rosters of cochairs and hostesses for various campaign events and pictures of black-tie dinners filled much of the front page of this and many other issues. Yael Dayan, daughter of Moshe Dayan, the Israeli general and defense minister who would, three months later, lead his troops in victory, addressed the Women's Division lunch at Temple Beth Israel. Soon after, Rabbi Herbert Friedman warned donors at a dinner at the Benson Hotel not to

> become complacent about our role in Israel. . . . We must make doubly sure that Israel will always be there as a refuge for Jews everywhere, and at any time. Our weapon for survival of Israel is money. When you can buy history you are buying the greatest thing in the world. What greater heritage can we leave our children than the stability of a country we can call our own?[22]

The local and national fundraising and advocacy networks that had been put in place in the decades following World War II enabled Jewish communities to quickly step up in the crisis in 1967. Even before the war's outbreak in early June, Hershel Tanzer, president of Portland's Federation, published a message on the *Review*'s front page, asking readers to come forward with financial support and advocacy.[23] The local community quickly did just that, giving, as the *Review* reported later, "as it has never given before to help the people of Israel meet their health and social welfare needs during the greatest crisis which the Jewish state has ever faced." The Federation received donations large and small, some with touching personal notes. "I am fourteen years old and old enough to know what is going on in Israel," read one. "Enclosed in this letter is five dollars I earned berry picking to go toward helping Israel."[24] The sense of urgency, and the "presumption that every Jewish person should feel an obligation to give,"[25] lingered in the aftermath of the Six-Day War as Israel coped with a flood of refugees from North Africa and the Middle East, as well as the continuing threat of war. In the years after 1967, the Federation continued to run a two-pronged campaign, the regular campaign (roughly half of which went overseas, mostly to Israel) and a separate Emergency Fund, devoted entirely to Israel. A 1970 campaign ad, under the headline "The Next War," explained,

> That is the violent voice of determined hatred. The voice of promised Arab attack. The voice of warning that Israel will still have to fight for peace. And this is the voice Israel hears 24 hours a day while she waits and guards against the next war. To keep this guard demands all her energy, all her resources, all her money and all her strong citizens. Which leaves little or nothing for other vital needs. . . .
>
> These human needs have historically been met by people who care. Now as the screams for the next war drown out the call for help, you, through the United Jewish Appeal, must try to hear the call. And you must answer.[26]

Six years later, the surprise attack that started the 1973 Yom Kippur War demonstrated that such warnings were not hyperbole.

Beyond inspiring support for Israel, the Six-Day War played a key role in reorienting the American Jewish community, shaping priorities and identities. The war bolstered Jewish confidence and self-image as Israel miraculously emerged as the victorious underdog, feeding a renewed ethnic pride.

Tourism and immigration to Israel surged. The Six-Day War came to represent a watershed in American Jewish history; in its wake, Israel came to occupy the center of what it meant to be an American Jew. Hasia Diner explains, "the victory in the Middle East seemed to have unleashed among American Jewry a new kind of assertiveness about themselves and their connection to the little country that stood up to its powerful neighbors."[27] Susan Abravanel, prominent in Portland's Federation, and a local and national leader in organizations including the Jewish Council for Public Affairs and the American Jewish Committee, recalled the impact of the Six-Day War in an opinion piece written in 1998, when both she and the state of Israel were celebrating their fiftieth birthdays. She recalled her long-standing sense of connection with the Jewish state, but noted that the relationship was "one that I rarely shared with non-Jewish friends. After the Holocaust, there was a sense that we had to be careful, not to draw too much attention to 'things Jewish.'" She was deeply moved by the war: "Israel's and my 19th year, the year of Israel's stunning victory . . . whose significance would change me forever. Suddenly, our secret was out. The whole world rejoiced along with us. It was okay to be Jewish and the more closely related to Israel the better."[28]

Along with this sense of pride, the events of 1967 altered American Jewish communal priorities. The war, according to historian Marc Dollinger, "taught Jews the limits of accommodationism . . . [which] pushed them toward a more isolationist approach to American pluralism." As they saw many of their former allies from the civil rights movement gravitate toward the Palestinian cause, they found that, "despite forty years of political activism, Jews could not rely on support from their historic allies."[29] Jonathan Sarna claims that the war "jolted the American Jewish community" from its earlier focus on universalism and ushered in a new, more inward orientation. Although this shift was already under way, product, in part, of the fragmentation of the liberal consensus in the mid- to late 1960s and the broader societal shifting from "the politics of consensus" to the "politics of identity," the 1967 War and its aftermath intensified the trend, placing Jewish priorities—not only Israel but also the fate of Jews in the Soviet Union and local concerns like education—at the forefront of the Jewish agenda.[30]

These national shifts were evident on the ground in Oregon. Alice (Fried) Mandler, a longtime volunteer at Neveh Shalom, noted the increased engagement that followed the war: "We all became very, very proud and we walked with our head very high up on the streets." The war, she explained, "pushed the Jewish people to more education, to more educational programs, more reading about Israel, to be more interested in our background, our ancestors."[31]Arden Shenker, Portland community leader and cochair of the Federation's Attorney's Division in 1967, saw a similar impact:

The fact of Israel and its peril and its dire need was enough of a testament to change the views of American Jews generally and certainly in Portland. Giving had to be substantially increased. The campaign trebled in that one year. And I think Jewish consciousness more than trebled in that same time. People became concerned about Jewish education, Jewish communal organizations. I was the president of the Jewish Educational Association. . . . The enrollment of the Jewish Educational Association at the time, at the Portland Hebrew School, more than doubled. We also substantially upgraded the quality of the teaching and the curriculum. I became active in Congregation Neveh Shalom. I was the Vice President of the congregation and worked with Rabbi Stampfer in the development of what became the Institute for Judaic Studies. I became involved in the University of Judaism, which is now called American Jewish University, and I was the Pacific Northwest Coordinator of both programming and fundraising. That was true in Portland generally; the fact of giving and fundraising was a mirror of the general Jewish consciousness that was so substantially increased at that time. We were very much engaged in what is called in Hebrew "Haskalah," which is public affairs awareness. We were constantly cranking out statements for consumption by the Jewish community and for the general community to maintain support for Israel. Support for Israel in the general community was very high. You didn't need to turn-around the viewpoint at that time. You needed simply for it to continue its support.[32]

The broad support for Israel noted by Shenker was reflected in local programming, the community press, and communal surveys. In 1971, the Federation's study of Portland Jewry had revealed many discouraging trends, leading to much hand wringing about the fate of a community that was declining in numbers, dispersing, disinterested, lacking in Jewish knowledge, and losing its "common core of religious belief and identity."[33] But there was one bright spot in the survey: Israel. Fully 95 percent of respondents expressed a high level of interest in the Jewish state, and that interest cut across age cohorts and movement affiliation. Even nonaffiliated Jews were "hardly very different from the others."[34] And respondents were willing to act on this interest: nearly all highly approved of raising money to support Israel (96 percent); 90 percent favored bond drives; and, even among the nonaffiliated, similar majorities expressed interest in visiting and approved of political advocacy for Israel. When asked about the "importance of Israel to the Jewish people," strong majorities—ranging from 75 percent of the nonaffiliated to 81 percent of the Reform—said it was "very important"; well over 90 percent saw it as either moderately or very important; fewer than 5 percent saw it as "moderately unimportant," and no respondents at all considered it "totally unimportant."[35]

This strong interest in and identification with Israel was nurtured in the *Review*, which extensively covered Israel and American Jewish campaigns to support the country. Feature stories about missions of local leaders to Israel served—much as the accounts of the two rabbis had—to make links to Israel more personal. For example, in the fall following the war, the *Review* provided detailed coverage of the participation of seven Portlanders in a UJA Study Mission to Israel. A full-page invitation to the annual meeting of the Federation, which was headlined by a report on the mission, appeared on the front page of the November edition, which also featured a report by Federation President Hershel Tanzer. Tanzer's account not only described meetings with Israeli leaders including Prime Minister Levi Eshkol, Defense Minister Moshe Dayan, Foreign Minister Abba Eban, and Chief of Defense Itzhak Rabin, but also conveyed the emotion of visiting the newly reunified Jerusalem. "If I live to be a thousand years old, I shall never forget today. I could never convey what has happened to me by words," wrote Tanzer of the experience. Abba Eban's hour-long remarks on the reunification were followed by a two-minute standing ovation; "Julius Zell got his autograph," added a star-struck Tanzer. Throughout the mission, participants witnessed the aftermath of battles in the physical remains of bombed military vehicles, in awe-inspiring visits to air force bases, in a new agricultural settlement in the Golan, and at the airport, where the group "stood and watched with tears in their eyes" as two hundred refugees arrived as immigrants to Israel. Throughout the mission, Israeli officials conveyed the message that, now more than ever, Israel's future depended on "the Jews of the free world, particularly the American Jews."[36]

As was typical in the American Jewish press in this period, Palestinians (generally referred to as "Arabs" until the early 1970s) were often portrayed less as a newly occupied people than as potential beneficiaries of the war. Tanzer described refugees in Gaza with a mix of orientalist romanticism and pity; the market there "thronged with an Arabian nights crowd," while veiled women balanced jars on their heads and men smoked water pipes. The condition of the "ragged children" was clearly attributable in Tanzer's account to Egypt, under whose occupation the refugees had "fester[ed] in conditions that are indescribable" since 1948.[37] Similarly, when Rabbi Yonah Geller of Portland's Shaarie Torah journeyed to Israel in 1970, he reported,

> Jerusalem in particular is undergoing vast expansion programs in which both Jew and Arab will benefit. The old dilapidated sections are being demolished and new buildings erected on the spot. Perhaps this accounts for so little friction between Jew and Arab in that city since the Arabs also are receiving better homes, better medical services, and a higher standard of living. It should be noted that Arabs are employed in all kinds of projects, with the exception of those involving security.[38]

This message became even more emphatic in the years that followed, as a stronger Palestinian movement coalesced and its message began to stir sympathy, particularly on the American left. A 1976 advertisement by the

Anti-Defamation League of B'nai B'rith asked readers, "Guess what country has increased the average life span of its Arab population by 18 years: Israel," and contrasted "what the Israelis have done for the Arabs living in Israel" with Arab nations holding "their own citizens" in "unbelievable squalor." It concluded, "These Palestinians live in camps only because the Arab states cheated them out of their own independence, by taking away their land in 1948."[39] In 1975, when the United Nations General Assembly passed a resolution that equated Zionism with racism, the organized Jewish community in Oregon, and across the country, condemned the vote as anti-Semitic. At its November annual meeting, Portland's Federation voted to condemn the United Nations vote, and shared with attendees supportive messages from the Ecumenical Ministries of Oregon and similar groups.[40] Morris "Moe" Stein, executive director of Portland's Federation explained,

> Never did Zionism visualize nor advocate the displacement of others. And somehow or another, the world is ready to lay the burden of the Arab refugees on Israel rather than on the real culprits, the Arab governments, who refused to help resolve the tragedy in constructive ways. The Arab strategy is clear. It is to isolate Israel from the rest of the world, to make her a non-country. And after she is a non-country for a while, then she can be eliminated and disappear, and who will care? And who will be most instrumental in making certain that this chilling and terrible strategy will be thwarted? You and I, the Jews of America and of the free world. We must continue to remind our governments and the people of the world that Israel, and the Jewish people, have the right and must be guaranteed the right, to survive and flourish.[41]

Such messages, according to historian Theodore Sasson, are typical of the "mobilization" period, when American Jews embraced an idealized vision of Israel. At a time when only about a third of American Jews—and a considerably smaller percentage of Jewish Oregonians[42]—had visited Israel, and far fewer read Hebrew or had access to Israeli news publications, understanding of Israel was mediated by rabbis and Federation leaders, often through press outlets like the *Jewish Review,* which the Federation controlled and operated as an arm of the fundraising enterprise. Earlier in the twentieth century, there had been much communal conflict between pro- and anti-Zionists, as well as among Zionists of various political stripes. In contrast, during the mobilization period, which reached its high mark in the wake of the Six-Day War, there was a tremendous degree of unity on Israel among American Jews. The American-Israel Public Affairs Committee, the UJA, and local federations promoted "unconditional support" for Israel, and portrayed Israel as a democratic bastion of progressivism and enlightenment. American Jews embraced a vision of a Jewish state so reverential that political scientist Daniel Elazar dubbed it "Israelolatry." Israel not only embodied the "survival and rebirth of the Jewish people after the Holocaust," but also the finest of Jewish American democratic values. [43] This is visible in Portland Federation executive director Morris Stein's recounting of Prime Minister Golda Meir's remarks to a 1971 mission to Israel: "After dinner, our Golda speaks to us. . . . She talks about what Israel means to the Jewish people. She talks about the importance of Israel being a country of social justice." [44] Given the idealized image of Israel, criticism of Israel or Zionism, as in the United Nations vote in 1975, could only be understood, according to American Jewish leaders, as anti-Semitism. In the face of such attacks, American Jews' role was to stand together with Israel. As Federation president Arden Shenker explained at the 1976 Israel Bonds meeting in Portland, "The slogan of the Portland Jewish Welfare Federation Campaign, on behalf of the United Jewish Appeal, is more than a slogan. 'We Are One,' is a symbol of solidarity. Tonight we demonstrate that solidarity. We build together." [45]

The key role for American Jews in this building project was financial support. Also critical was advocacy. In a practice begun earlier and continuing into the twenty-first century, national groups like AIPAC and the National Jewish Community Relations Advisory Council, a coordinating body of local Community Relations Councils and federations, regularly sent out briefings and alerts to mobilize local activists to advocacy. Although far from the nation's capital, supporters in Oregon had a role to play. The files of Arden Shenker are filled with such missives. "Now is an important time to deluge our government friends," a memo from November 1988 reads, "Utilizing American Jewish influence molders for carrying our message might also be considered." [46] Likewise, the *Review* regularly reported on the positions of elected officials and candidates on matters of concern to the Jewish community—particularly their positions on Israel. Moe Stein, who served as the Federation executive director for a decade beginning in 1967, recalled the close relations cultivated with elected officials by Federation leadership:

> We really did quite well because the relationship between members of the Jewish community and the political leadership was super. Clay Meyers [*sic*] was State Secretary at that time, and he went to every bar and bat mitzvah in town and probably every Jewish wedding. They knew him. [Governor] Tom McCall was a delight. It was easy to arrange appointments with Tom McCall. I used to take the Israeli Consul General to meet with him. That was marvelous. [Congresswoman] Edith Green might have been a little bit less accessible but she was certainly accessible. [Congressman] Les AuCoin . . . these were people that folks like Arden Shenker or Jim Meyer could just pick up the phone and talk to.

When Bob Packwood won an unexpected victory over US Senator Wayne Morse in 1968, Stein recalled, longtime community leader and attorney Moe Tonkon arranged for Federation and CRC leadership to meet with him. Although Tonkon worried "that we had been too tough on Packwood," Stein was delighted in Packwood's unexpectedly strong, pro-Israel stance, exclaiming, "Packwood just came out gung-ho for Israel. He just amazed us."[47] Because Federation and the *Review* were nonprofits and could not advocate for particular candidates without compromising their tax status, Stein explained to readers during the 1976 political campaign, the *Review* would provide statements of the major candidate on Israel and other issues concerning Jews, and simply urge readers to vote with these in mind.[48] When specific issues flared—as when the Carter administration proposed sale of war planes to Egypt and Saudi Arabia—Senators Mark Hatfield and Packwood were asked for responses, which were printed in the *Review*.[49] When the Federation published an annual report in the mid-1980s listing the responsibilities of the Community Relations Committee—a group that had earlier focused much of its energy on relations between Jews and other groups locally—its mission to "communicate Israel's positions and needs to the public and government" was the first item on the list.[50] To that end, community members were invited to seminars designed to help them respond more effectively to critics. For example, in 1984, AIPAC held a statewide conference, sponsored by the American Jewish Committee, the ADL, Hadassah, and the CRC, aimed at training community members for advocacy.[51] A similar seminar in 1986 featured Senator Carl Levin of Michigan and was cosponsored by AIPAC and the CRC. Participants were to be trained in advocacy on a variety of "Jewish issues" including briefings on how to respond to "the campaign to discredit Israel."[52]

Although fundraising for and coverage of Israel was certainly not a new trend in the Jewish press, the singularity of the focus was unprecedented. Where the *Review* had once routinely run local and national stories, as well as opinion pieces, focusing broadly on minority rights and specifically on the civil rights movement, such pieces became far less evident after the 1967 War, replaced by an almost exclusive focus on the Jewish world that reflected both local organizational orientations and national Jewish trends.[53]

Turning Inward: Beyond Israel

The inward turn toward specifically Jewish issues following the Six-Day War in 1967 was evident in local activities. In the decade before the war, the pages of the *Review,* of organizational newsletters, and even of rabbis' sermons and missives reflected extensive engagement in the local community. In contrast to the early part of the century, when the Jewish community focused on serving their own through programs at Neighborhood House and Federation-supported charities, volunteer activity increasingly focused on non-Jewish Portlanders in the 1950s and especially in the early to mid-1960s. The engagement of so many community organizations in the public debate over school desegregation and the provision of preschool education to disadvantaged, mostly minority children, were emblematic of that period. In the late 1960s and early 1970s however, there was a shift toward internally focused service programs that set the tone for subsequent decades. By far, the biggest emphasis was on aid to Soviet Jews.

As we have seen, organizations such as the Portland section of the NCJW and Congregation Beth Israel's Social Action Committee (SAC) remained active in an array of programs serving the general community, even after the 1967 War. Yet even for those groups, a shift toward activities focusing on specifically Jewish issues and causes is clear. It is even more apparent in the *Review*, both in its selection of national and international wire service stories and in the local programming reflected in its pages. The increased ethnic pride associated with the Six-Day War and great concern about fading Jewish identity raised in the 1971 survey combined to foster programming that was more Jewish in focus. This emphasis was evident in the embrace of local Jewish history that resulted in *Whatever Happened to Old South Portland* (1969), the subsequent oral history project (early-mid 1970s), and the proliferation of organizations such as the Oregon Jewish Historical Society (1976), Institute for Judaic Studies (1983), the Oregon Holocaust Resource Center (1983), and the Oregon Jewish Museum (1990). Not coincidentally, the same period saw the expansion and rearticulation of the community Hebrew school program as well as the 1986 creation—after over a decade of discussion—of the Portland Jewish Academy day school, the first nondenominational Jewish day school to operate in Oregon.[54] All these developments suggest a desire to counter assimilation and speak to the embrace of ethnic identity.

However, after Israel-related activities, the greatest portion of communal activism and philanthropy focused on Soviet Jewry. The plight of Jews under the Soviet regime was not a new issue in the late 1960s, but it was dramatically invigorated after the Six-Day War. Most critically, Jewish confidence generated by the war affected Soviet Jews directly, leading to a "cultural and political awakening" and a surge in emigration requests.[55] Driven by their new confidence and assertiveness, and by the displaced energies of liberals who felt alienated by the radicalization of the civil rights movement in the late 1960s, American Jews took up the cause. A historian of the movement explains: "As the civil rights struggle petered out and the nonviolent era of student activism drew to a close, the Soviet Jewry movement emerged. With its peaceful tactics, it satisfied the needs of those who could not subscribe to the student militancy of the late sixties."[56] Charles "Charlie" Schiffman, who arrived in Portland in 1987 to begin his twenty-three-year tenure as director of Portland's Federation, aptly described the connection that many young Jews drew between the two causes. As a college student in Memphis, he was assigned to report on the 1968 Poor People's March on Washington as it passed through town soon after Martin Luther King Jr.'s assassination. Schiffman recalled, "At that point, I started to realize this incredible struggle that was going on and to become sensitive to it. And then later on, in a sort of parallel sense, I became sensitive to what I think is the other great civil rights struggle, and that is the struggle to free the Jews of the Soviet Union. That too was a massive worldwide thing that transpired."[57] Soviet Jewry provided a cause that satisfied the desire to focus on the needs of fellow Jews in an age when most American Jews had arrived in the middle class and had little need for assistance, according to historian Marc Dollinger.[58] The issue provided a national communal focus that, along with Israel, became what Sarna has called a "centerpiece" of "religious action programming." Soon, American Jews were recognizing Soviet Jewish struggles in their Passover Seders with a "matzah of hope," "twinning" American youth with Soviet counterparts for b'nai mitzvah ceremonies, holding marches, and traveling on missions to the Soviet Union to meet with "refuseniks" (Soviet Jews who had risked their livelihoods by applying for exit visas and had been denied). Such programming was "deeply empowering," and embraced enthusiastically by American Jews who were "sensitized to their failings during the Holocaust era, schooled by the sixties in political activism, and deftly exploiting Cold War politics."[59]

Prior to 1967, there had been some local attention to the plight of Soviet Jewry, but it was not the central issue it would become later. On April 24, 1964, the community participated in a Statewide Sabbath of Protest on the issue, and secured a statement by Governor Mark Hatfield condemning Soviet anti-Semitism.[60] The following week, the same Community Relations Council communique that included the joint statement in support of the desegregation of Portland Public Schools also listed Soviet anti-Semitism as one of three "on-going concerns." Portland was working "in association with hundreds of other communities" and with national groups to address this problem through advocacy work and to raise awareness in the local community. Yet, in contrast to the local schools issue, which the CRC had researched for ten months and to which they devoted considerably more space in the column, no specific action or project was recommended.[61] Other mentions of Soviet Jewry in this period generally came in the form of wire service stories reprinted in the *Review* or in advertisements or statements by national Jewish groups to raise awareness. For example, in advance of Passover in 1966, the paper ran a story explaining how to incorporate a "matzoh [*sic*] of oppression" into the Seder to raise awareness of the issue. The following fall, the paper ran a piece titled "A Declaration of Rights for Soviet Jewry."[62]

Congregation Beth Israel's weekly bulletin in early 1965 gives a sense of the degree of community attention to issues that were "internal" (specifically Jewish) versus those that were "external" (involving the broader community and intergroup relations). Naturally, the bulletin's primary purpose was to convey congregational news, listing weekly events, donations to various funds, information about youth groups and sisterhood and brotherhood activities, and so on. Still, quite regularly, there were notices pertaining to broader societal events allowing insight into congregational focus and priorities. In the first newsletter of 1965, the only notice in the bulletin that was not some sort of congregational business was an item titled "Defenders," consisting of a quote from parenting expert Agnes Benedict about the importance of speaking up against prejudice. The following week's bulletin ran a resolution, passed by the SAC and approved by the board, endorsing the Schwab Plan for addressing segregation in Portland public schools and urging immediate implementation. Two weeks later, the first mention of Soviet Jews appeared for that year—a note that, instead of a sermon that week, a film on the issue, *The Price of Silence*, would be shown. In February and March, congregants heard sermons that included "Viet Nam: Political or Moral?" "You and the Negro," and "The Shocking Waste of Soviet and U.S. Space Efforts." Late in April, the bulletin announced the temple brotherhood would be addressed by Rabbi Gumbiner of Berkeley, who would "relate his experience during the recent Civil Rights March from Selma to Montgomery."[63] As this run of announcements suggests, Soviet Jewry was just one of a number of social issues on the congregation's radar, but was overshadowed by race relations. Certainly, it was not a primary focus of the congregation.

Likewise, the temple's SAC concentrated most on civil rights and "urban affairs" up through the late 1960s. Not until a June 1968 meeting did evidence of pressure to shift the group's gaze inward appear in the minutes. At that meeting, as the SAC discussed its agenda for the coming year, a faction tried to shift the group's focus toward "Jewish issues," both at home and abroad.[64] The majority, however, voted to maintain the focus on "urban issues" for the 1968–1969 program year. The first specific mention of Soviet Jews in the records of the SAC came in September 1969, when Rabbi Rose suggested the group take up the issue. Even so, the SAC maintained its course, focusing heavily on plans to address Portland school segregation (now through a plan called Portland Schools for the Seventies) and articulating a new statement of purpose reiterating its outward-looking, social justice orientation:

> The purpose of the Social Action Committee is to foster conditions conducive to creative Jewish living in a free society; conditions of democratic pluralism assuring freedom of religious belief, of thought and of expression; conditions in which all are accorded equal opportunity, equal rights and equal justice; in which groups may freely cultivate their distinctive group values while entering fully into the general life of the society, with mutual acceptance and regard for difference....
>
> Accordingly, the Social Action Committee works for equality of opportunity, without regard to race, religion, ancestry or origin; freedom of thought, opinion,

expression and association; freedom of religion and maintenance of separation of church and state; and amicable relationships among ethnic, racial, national, religious, and other groups.[65]

Later that year, however, the inward turn occurring in Jewish groups across the country came to the fore in the SAC. In the summer of 1970, the group reorganized into two subcommittees. The first dealt with "the problems of the Jewish community, internationally, nationally, and locally," and the second with "the problems of the black and other minority communities in Portland which appear, from time to time, to require attention and action by the committee."[66] By early 1971, the Jewish Affairs subcommittee honed in on Soviet Jewry as its main focus, urging "some action that would indicate concern about Soviet Jewry" as a major priority; it participated in an April rally on this issue, and then another in October.[67] In this, they joined the Community Relations Committee, the American Jewish Committee, and other national groups and their local affiliates in prioritizing the issue. Refuseniks were of particular concern. Denied exit visas, refuseniks languished in the Soviet Union, under surveillance and with little means of support. American Jews and Israel advocated for their release, with communities sometimes "adopting" particular refuseniks as "prisoners of conscience." In addition, supporters—including Rabbi Joshua and Goldie Stampfer, and Dr. Victor and Toinette Menashe of Portland—traveled on clandestine missions to meet with refuseniks, smuggling Jewish books and ritual items into the country for them.[68]

Along with missions, advocacy efforts, and media campaigns, rallies in support of Soviet Jewry became increasingly common tactics for raising public awareness in the 1970s. In May 1970, Shaul Stampfer, Rabbi Stampfer's oldest son, then nearly twenty-two years old, organized a rally for Soviet Jewry in Portland's Park Blocks; the protest drew one hundred participants and received front-page coverage in the *Jewish Review.*[69] When a Soviet-American trade conference was held at the Hilton Hotel in Portland in the fall of 1972, the Federation helped to organize a rally to bring attention to the plight of Soviet Jews.[70] Federation leaders also approached public officials such as Governor Tom McCall, and organizations like the Portland Council of Churches, to sign statements circulated by national advocacy groups demanding that any economic cooperation between the United States and the Soviet Union be tied to the latter, rescinding "severe restrictions placed upon Jewish citizens of the USSR."[71] The *Review* covered such developments prominently. In May 1971, the front page featured a photo of an interfaith service, in which the Portland Council of Churches expressed the support of "the Christian Community for the plight of Soviet Jews."[72] Similar programming and advocacy continued through the 1980s. Even as the Soviet Union opened up under Mikhail Gorbachev, Jewish groups, locally and nationally, worked to keep up the pressure. The Community Relations Community took the lead role in Oregon,

Shaul Stampfer speaking at Portland's first rally for Soviet Jewry, 1970.
Courtesy OJMCHE

doing advocacy work with the state's elected officials, providing information to Jewish and other groups locally, releasing statements to the media, and organizing protests. When the group held a major rally for Soviet Jewry in December 1987, Governor Neil Goldschmidt presented a proclamation calling on President Reagan to take action on the issue.[73]

As advocacy and public awareness efforts continued in the 1970s and 1980s, a third, much more hands-on, philanthropic effort took shape: Jewish Oregonians stepped up to sponsor Soviet Jewish refugees wishing to resettle in the state. As the post-1967 wave of Soviet Jewish migration began, migrants left the USSR, officially bound for Israel. Soviet authorities granted exit visas only to those who had received invitations from relatives there and many had to wait months or years for the visas. Those who were permitted to leave traveled to Vienna or Rome, where they received entrance papers for Israel and groups such as Hebrew Immigrant Aid Society (HIAS) made arrangements for their onward migration. However, on arrival in Western Europe, some of these migrants declared their desire to go not to Israel, but to the United

States. By 1976, facing mounting pressure from the American Jewish community, HIAS began providing support to those migrants who wished to resettle in the United States, increasing dramatically the number able to do so. By the early 1980s, about 200,000 Soviet Jews had arrived in the United States.[74] Soviet authorities soon shut down emigration, but the doors opened again as the country began to liberalize under Mikhail Gorbachev; in this later wave of migration, which continued through the 1990s after the breakup of the Soviet Union, emigrants were able to travel directly to the United States. During the 1990s, according to an article in the *Jewish Review*, approximately one million Soviet Jews migrated to Israel and 300,000 to the United States, including 243 families (some of them multigenerational families, including more than one household) destined for Portland.[75]

Although the migration to Oregon represented only a tiny portion of the total, given the small size of Oregon's Jewish community it was, proportionately, a relatively large influx. Both the local resettlement program and fundraising to aid Soviet immigrants to Israel became central to community campaigns and to the agenda of Federation committees that had earlier focused more on local community relations. The Federation's 1987 annual report listed Israel advocacy and support, and support of Soviet Jews "and other oppressed Jewish communities" as first among the CRC's goals, which also included promotion of equality, freedom of speech and association, freedom of religion, separation of church and state, and "amicable relations among racial and ethnic groups."[76]

As Soviet refugees arrived in America, Jewish communities around the country stepped up to sponsor them. In Oregon, several groups took up the project of aiding local resettlement. Again, the Federation, which had earlier met the challenge of post–World War II resettlement of Holocaust survivors through its constituent agency, the Oregon Service for New Americans, was central to the project. That group used its own caseworkers and worked with the Council of Jewish Women to assist newcomers in obtaining housing, jobs and other assistance. When Soviet Jews began to arrive in the early 1970s, these processes were reactivated, with the Federation coordinating the resettlement plans through the Jewish Family and Child Services (JFCS), and the women of the council, along with other community groups, providing volunteers to assist with outreach, hospitality, and provision of goods. As a story in the secular press reported, "Portland is one of several U.S. cities with highly organized plans to help absorb Jewish persons leaving the Soviet Union during recent relaxing of visa policies."[77]

By September 1976, JFCS reported that it was resettling a Soviet émigré family each month, most of them drawn to Portland through family connections or because of a match with job prospects in the area.[78] Nine months later, the Federation increased its allocation for resettlement from $56,897 to just over $70,000.[79] A 1978 *Oregonian* article reported that 148 Soviet Jews had been settled in the Rose City since 1973, more per capita than had been settled in any other American city. Jewish Family and Child Services counselor Nina Conheim explained, "Different Jewish communities have different priorities, and Portland's community has chosen Russian resettlement as its priority. The people in Portland are accepting their responsibility to their fellow Jews."[80]

The Russian influx quickly became JFCS's largest project. Executive Director Alvin Rackner recalled that when he was recruited to that position in 1966, he was the agency's first full-time social worker (there were also two part-time social workers). As the JFCS took on Russian resettlement, it added positions, and soon had three people working full time on the project, led by Carol (Kane) Chestler who directed the program. At its peak, the community was receiving one or two families per month; as Rackner emphasized, "that is a lot for a small Jewish community."[81] Federation campaigns during the peak periods frequently featured the immigrants' needs. For example, a 1988 ad for a Federation fundraiser warned: "The Russians Are Coming! The Russians Are Coming! Wrong! They Are Here! and more are on the way."[82] The following year, Federation's "Passage to Freedom" campaign ad featured pictures of Rabbis Geller (Shaarie Torah), Wolf (Havurah Shalom), Kinberg (Beth Israel-Eugene), Rose (Beth Israel-Portland), Stampfer (Neveh Shalom), and Wilhelm (Chabad) with the caption "We Are Working to Help Resettle Soviet Jews Here in Portland. . . . Will you help too?"[83] By 1990, the peak year of the migration, the Federation set a goal of raising $1,500,000 for "Operation Exodus" (a massive resettlement program), one-third for local efforts and the remainder for projects in Israel.[84] Even the tiny Southern Oregon Jewish community stepped up to participate: a fundraiser at Temple Emek Shalom in Ashland drew two hundred participants and raised $48,800 for Operation Exodus, nearly double their goal of $25,000.[85]

Russian resettlement posed a number of challenges for local organizers. Families left everything behind, and had to be supplied not only with apartments, but also with all the furnishings. They needed work, and their opportunities were limited by poor English skills and by educational and licensing requirements mandating retraining and recertification to enter their previous professions. During the peak periods of immigration, first in the mid- to late-1970s, and again after the collapse of the Soviet Union, pleas for donations of household goods and notices listing new arrivals' employment qualifications were posted regularly in the *Review* and in organizational and congregational newsletters. Beyond such practical needs, many also required help in adjusting to American expectations. A 1974 *Oregon Journal* feature on the newly arrived Dubinsky family explained, "In Russia one was assigned a job and kept on doing it. Some of their Portland friends are impressed with

A group of Soviet Jews arrives at the Portland airport, 1991. Courtesy OJMCHE

their work ethic, but say the newcomers don't understand it's possible to start at the bottom and work up."[86] The immigrants' social adjustment was aided by a combination of JFCS counselors and social workers, and a network of community volunteers. By 1981, JFCS had published a 130-page bilingual guidebook for Russian immigrants by Tanya Lifshitz, which explained American life, treating topics as diverse as using public transportation, the need to purchase health insurance, how to write a check, and how to buy groceries. The guide warned newcomers unfamiliar with free markets about advertisements and product placements that would tempt them to buy things they didn't need; and explained that, in America, "the responsibility for finding a job lies with the individual, not the government, nor the educational institution from which one graduates."[87]

Those who worked with the Russians found much satisfaction in the task, drawing parallels with early twentieth-century efforts to aid East European immigrants, often by the same organizations. A 1993 NCJW publication titled "Moments in History, NCJW and Immigration," explained, "Today, when

NCJW sections resettle Soviet Jews, they are continuing the work begun in 1903. In those earlier years, unlike 1992, it was not so important to know whether immigrants were fleeing a political or an economic peril. What we did know was that they needed help. And they, of course, were our parents, our grandparents and our great grandparents!"[88] An unnamed Portland council woman recounted, after helping to welcome a new Russian family,

> I entered the apartment with dinner in my arms and there, standing with their coats still on, was the family. At that moment all I could see were my grandparents arriving seventy years ago to the United States from Russia, bringing with them my future. There before me in almost the same attire, looking joyous, tired, bewildered and oh so brave, a Jewish family coming to a new world, 1974, with the same hope of preserving their heritage. At that moment a wave of unexpected emotion came over me. My eyes filled with tears as I reached out to my people.[89]

The assumption expressed by this volunteer, that these Russian immigrants were motivated by the promise of religious freedom and the opportunity to reconnect with their heritage was not always realistic. Distanced from Jewish tradition during decades of Soviet rule, many newcomers were not practicing Jews and—not unlike many of their predecessors at the turn of the century—were motivated more by socioeconomic opportunities than by religion. Yet some community members, concerned about fading American Jewish identities, saw the newcomers as a possible source of renewal. As historian Hasia Diner explains, "American Jews, primarily through the federations and the other social-service agencies, took on the project of 'Judaizing' the immigrants, who did not necessarily want to go through this process."[90] For this reason, Portland organizers made an effort to settle Russian families in the Southwest neighborhoods near the JCC (which offered the arriving families a year of free membership), Congregation Neveh Shalom sponsored a cultural club for Russians, various congregations hosted services designed to welcome the newcomers, and the enrollment of the first Russian student in the Hillel day school merited an article in the *Review*.[91] The secular press also featured stories emphasizing the religious freedom angle; for example, a 1976 *Oregonian* piece focused on the recently arrived Vishnevetsky-Galperin families and their celebration of Chanukah, under the headline "Glow of Chanukah Special for Family."[92]

Yet, as the community worked to ease the transition of the immigrants, it became clear—as a *Register-Guard* article pointed out—that many came "not to practice Judaism but simply to escape prejudice suffered because of it."[93] Carol Chestler, the 1978–1984 JFCS Russian resettlement coordinator, explained in an interview years later that Jewish Oregonians romanticized the "religious freedom" motive, which she called the "myth we wanted to believe."[94] Similarly, Alvin Rackner recalled that "people wanted to see that they were coming here for religious reasons. Well, that was sometimes the case but more likely it was the result of anti-Semitism whether you were religious or not. And also they came for economic opportunity, which is the reason why our parents and grandparents moved here."[95] Certainly, some did become involved in the Jewish community or more interested in religion. For example, Yulia Libov, who arrived as a child in 1991, credited Federation and community support, not only for her successful adjustment to America, but also for helping connect her with her Jewish heritage; she would be the first Soviet refugee to celebrate a bat mitzvah at Congregation Neveh Shalom.[96] Although JFCS resettlement caseworker Sharon (Stern) Singer noted that many Russian families "become very involved in Portland synagogues and the Jewish community,"[97] most—like many other Jewish newcomers to Oregon in the final decades of the twentieth century—had a largely secular outlook.

The relationship of Russian newcomers to Judaism was not the only controversy surrounding the migration. In the same 1975 issue of the *Review* that reported the JCC was helping Russian families to adjust was a reprint of a story from *Moment Magazine,* exploring contradictions inherent in a migration that had begun as a movement to bring Jews to Israel, but ended up settling many in the United States. Here, *Moment* editor Leonard Fein explained that "the miracle of Jewish resurgence in the Soviet Union was supposed to be about Israel and Jewishness, not about the United States and upward mobility." Zionists worried that, when émigrés opted for the United States over Israel, they "suggest that Israel is not all we say it is." Ultimately, however, Fein made the case that the newcomers were making the same choices that American Jews had already made, and that it would be unfair to judge them for that choice. Interestingly, the *Review's* publisher prefaced this piece with a note explaining its relevance to the Portland community because it "suggests answers to the questions which many have raised."[98] According to JFCS director Alvin Rackner, these concerns were discussed not just in the broader community, but also within the Federation. Given the centrality of supporting Israel to the Federation's mission, it is not surprising that some argued "we ought to encourage them to go to Israel and refuse to have them come to Portland." Rackner felt it was not the JFCS's place to "carry out a political agenda"; rather, their purpose was to provide services to those in need. His position, that "we didn't make those kinds of choices for people and we didn't manipulate people into their choices," was supported by the JFCS board and, ultimately, by the Federation, which continued to raise funds for Soviet resettlement both in Israel and in Oregon.

The robust responses to fundraising campaigns suggest that despite reservations some held about their choice of destination, the community enthusiastically took up the cause of Soviet Jewry. Along with the Federation's efforts, a number of congregations and other organizations stepped up to welcome the newcomers and help socialize them, encouraged by messages that not only framed this as an opportunity to help coreligionists, but also as a significant moment in Jewish history, a "New Exodus." An article in the 1989 Passover issue of the *Review* explained the migration in just this way, referring to the Russian refugees as "the modern Israelites" who were part of a "transformation from slavery to freedom."[99] That fall, Portland Jews were urged to "Come Celebrate and Meet the Faces of Freedom! Join us in welcoming the new Soviet Jewish members of our community during their first Simchat Torah Celebration in Freedom!"[100]

Beyond the work of the Federation, congregations, and other organizations on behalf of Soviet Jewry, a few individual Oregonians stand out in their devotion to the cause. In addition to the Stampfers and Menashes, who made risky, clandestine journeys to meet with refuseniks, Jerry and Helen Stern were particularly notable in their efforts, inspired by the experience of Jerry's parents, who had emigrated from Russia in the early twentieth century. In 1989, the Sterns traveled to the Soviet Union, visiting with émigrés who were preparing for their journey; a feature in the *Review* explained, "Stern's father came to the U.S. from Russia when he was 14. Jerry Stern says that, if it were not for the help of agencies in New York City, his father would have been totally destitute."[101] The Sterns's trip to Russia was the culmination of an effort to reunite with long-lost relatives in the central Russian town of Saratov. After meeting thirty-seven relatives during their 1989 trip, the Sterns brought many of them to Portland during the 1990s. As Stern explained in a 2009 oral history, "My father did everything in the world he could to try to help his parents, and his brothers and his sisters and nieces and nephews who were stranded in the Soviet Union. Anyhow, I felt that, with them being gone that it was my duty to try to find them. Not a duty; I wanted to do it. So I searched in any way I possibly could." In addition to sponsoring his own relatives' migration to Portland, the Sterns single-handedly funded a "freedom flight," and challenged the Portland community to match their effort by sponsoring seats on a second flight for 250 Jews, at $1000 a seat. In February 1992, as Sterns's freedom flyers arrived to begin their new lives in Israel, they were met by three generations of the Stern family.[102]

Debating Israel: Accommodating Dissent

The campaign for Soviet Jewry was only one of a number of "internal" issues in the 1970s and 1980s that drew the community together. The celebration of local history, the reinvigoration of programming, and the opening of expanded communal facilities like the Mittleman Jewish Community Center and the Portland Jewish Academy all suggested that Jewish life in Oregon—particularly in Portland—was reenergizing. The protracted efforts that went into merging the Jewish Educational Association (afternoon Hebrew school) and Hillel (traditional day school) to form the new Portland Jewish Academy (nondenominational day school) on the campus of the MJCC helped to foster a sense of common purpose in the community. Along with this, of course, fundraising and advocacy for Israel remained central to community identity and unity. In the late 1980s, however, unity on Israel would be challenged.

The "mobilization model" of the relationship with Israel was premised on the belief that American Jewry's role was to provide uncritical support, "taking the lead from Jerusalem."[103] Fundraising and advocacy was not focused on specific policy positions, but on leaving those decisions to Israelis and their government. Historian Sasson notes, "The willingness of American Jews to provide blanket support for Israeli policies reflected their devotion to Israel as a cause, their tendency to idealize the state and its leadership, and their great remove from the political conflicts that, by the mid-1970s, increasingly divided Israelis."[104] Ironically, then, the devotion and commitment was, in part, a product of distance—American Jews fervently supported Israel, yet their view of the state was often romanticized and symbolic "rather than personalized and experiential."[105] In the American Jewish community, this unified support for Israel lasted until the mid- to late 1980s, when, in the wake of the Palestinian Intifada, idealized visions of Israel began to be replaced with more realistic understandings.

Public discussion of Israel among Jewish Oregonians reflected national patterns. In the decade after the Six-Day War, it is difficult to find *any* communal sources that question or critique Israel. Consensus was so strong that those with doubts were reluctant to express them publicly. Although the *Review* made an effort to "reflect the richly diverse attitudes and opinions of Portland's Jewish community" by encouraging readers' letters and beginning a regular "question of the month" feature to solicit reader opinions, correspondents were hesitant to share critical views on Israel.[106] For example, in the summer of 1977, the paper printed eight reader responses to the question, "What do you think about the Israeli settlements on the West Bank?" All eight supported settlement, with several making analogies to the American West, arguing that there was no need to return conquered territories. The most nuanced response was that of Judy (Freeman) Kahn, who pointed out that "there are two peoples involved here who have had the same land continuously as their home," and expressed concern that although "Jews have always been the conscience of the world . . . we may be getting like the rest of the world." Still, Kahn affirmed that "we have every right to the spoils of war, we won the land fairly, and historically we can claim it." The editor noted that "there were viewpoints given in this random survey which were not in favor of Israel establishing territories on the West Bank," but that "these persons would not allow their names to be used."[107]

Over the next decade, Jewish Oregonians started to transition from "mobilization" to what Sasson calls an "engagement" model, characterized by more realistic and diverse views of Israel and its problems, and more selective advocacy and fundraising through targeted political and philanthropic campaigns, rather than solely through the umbrella, mainstream groups that long dominated American Jewish communal organization.[108] Unlike the summer of 1977 letter writers who preferred not to have their critical views of Israel appear under their names, increasing numbers of community members—including key leaders—took sides on specific matters of Israeli policy, rather than simply supporting government positions. As they did so, advocates of the consensus model pushed back, reiterating their support for Israel and emphasizing the need for solidarity, particularly in "public." Although well aware of the paper's role as the voice of Federation, *Review* editors began asserting their commitment to covering the range of opinions in the community. They repeatedly published calls to readers to share their views and welcomed dissent. Indeed, examination of local sources suggests that the transition from mobilization to engagement began relatively early in Oregon and that local leadership more quickly came to terms with, and even embraced, community debate than was the case nationally.[109]

On the pages of the *Review*, the first clear questioning of consensus came in October 1977, in direct response to the summer's "question of the month" responses and the editor's statement that those with critical views did not want their names used. Reader Stanley Loeb expressed concern about this reluctance to openly share contrary views, explaining that "by and large there are a few major differences between Israeli policy and segments of American Jewish opinion. But where there are differences, they should be freely addressed." Loeb directly took up the issue of settlement, arguing against annexation of the occupied territories and noting that the majority of the inhabitants of the West Bank were not Jewish, "have not enjoyed the principle of self-determination," and were "entitled to political representation in a government of [their] own choosing."[110] Aside from Loeb's letter, however, there was little hint of dissent during the next several years, as both news coverage and opinion pieces remained in sync with official Israeli policy. For example, it was not until Israel moved into negotiations with Egypt that a discussion of what "Israel should give up for peace" took place.[111] When Israel and Egypt signed the Camp David peace accords requiring Israel to withdraw from the Sinai, the paper paired reports on the withdrawal with a feature series on Judaism and Islam, reminding readers of a history of coexistence and commonalities.

Concurrently, the paper continued in its advocacy role, mobilizing communal response to counter criticism of Israel appearing in the local, secular media, as in the case of a 1982 documentary titled *Holy Land, Bloody Ground*, that aired on KGW-TV, the local NBC affiliate. In addition to a critical news article about the show, the *Review* printed scathing letters from Arden Shenker (chair of the CRC), Laurie Rogoway (director of the local affiliate of the American Jewish Committee), David Roberts (executive director of the Federation), and Rabbi Stampfer.[112] All emphasized the importance of calling out the media for biased reporting on Israel; as the Israeli *shaliach* (official government representative), Zeev Kozansky explained, "Considering the biased information people are provided in the American media, I feel it is even more important to have someone balance this with facts from the other side."[113] Kozansky's assertion that it was incumbent on American Jews to become more informed (via the correct sources) to better support Israel was a frequent refrain. A *Review* piece on the subject effectively laid out the expectations of this consensus period:

> It's important, but it's not enough for Portland Jews to financially support Israel. They also should keep aware of current affairs, visit Israel, support those politicians who endorse Israel's positions and pray for the homeland according to a group of Portland Jews interviewed recently by the *Review*. Shenker said that Jews should become more involved in Portland Jewish activities because this, too, will indirectly benefit Israel. Reading Jewish publications such as the *Near East Report*, the weekly newsletter published by AIPAC, the only lobbyist group for Israel in the U.S. is one of the best ways of supporting the country, according to Gussie Reinhardt. She is a long time worker for Hadassah, Kesser Israel, the National Council for Jewish Women, and American Mizrachi Women . . . Any threats to Israel should not go unchallenged by Portland Jews since that country represents the rights of Jews everywhere to live and survive in a free world, said Harold Pollin, vice president of the Federation.[114]

During this period, Kozansky frequently contributed opinion pieces, explaining Israel's official position and calling out critical portrayals as biased. Such portrayals were consistently framed as coming from outside the Jewish community; the duty of the community was to respond to them with a unified voice.

Although the local Jewish community was mobilized behind the Federation's efforts to raise funds and embraced Israel as central to Jewish identity, their engagement was—as Sasson's analysis suggests was typical of the period—more celebratory and philanthropic than analytical. For example, at the 1981 Israel Expo at the MJCC, participants could visit re-created Israeli markets, dancing, food stands, a scale model of Masada, and replicas of the Jaffa Gate, Chagall windows, and even a Western Wall where they could pray and leave notes. Similar events invited community members to "celebrate the Israeli way" at a Purim Ball, or to "visit the [Jewish Community] Center for a small taste of Sukkot in Israel."[115] These events evoked the sounds, sights, tastes, and smells of Israel, but provided few opportunities to explore or debate the specifics of Israeli politics or policies. The lack of critical engagement was evident in the pages of the *Review*, which provided its readers substantial coverage of national, international, and Israeli politics, but seemed to provoke little debate in the community on these, or any, topics. *Review* board chairperson Harry Turtledove expressed his frustration with community quiescence in 1982, calling the "virtual absence of any expression of opinion, in the form of letters from the paper's recipients" the most "glaring deficiency" of the paper.[116] This situation soon changed. Just a few years later, communal debate over Israel became so heated that the CRC felt the need to develop a "Civil Discourse Guide."[117]

Nationally, historians have traced the first internal challenges to the post-1967 American Jewish consensus on Israel to Breira,[118] a group founded in 1973 to challenge Israeli nonrecognition of the Palestine Liberation Organization (PLO) and, implicitly, the American Jewish establishment that supported that position. When it began a vocal campaign in 1976, publishing advertisements in publications such as the *New York Times*, Breira's positions provoked a severe backlash that played out in the secular and Jewish press and led to demands to fire Breira supporters from Jewish organizations, to exclude the group from communal coalitions, and to stigmatize them as pariahs. After tremendous pressure from mainstream groups, Breira dissolved within a year. By criticizing both Israel and the American Jewish establishment, in the words of historian Jack Wertheimer, groups like Breira were "breaking the taboo." Wertheimer used that phrase as the title for his 1996 article on the topic, and opened the piece by quoting the Passover allegory of the "wicked child," suggesting just how far outside the pale such questioning was.[119] In that passage, the child demonstrates through his question that he is outside of the community and is therefore branded "wicked." The story concludes that because of this, had he been among the Jews in Egypt, he would not have been redeemed.

Despite the taboo, a series of events soon led to increased questioning of the consensus view among American Jews. Although there had been a high level of support for Israel in 1982 when the war in Lebanon began, the complicity of Israel in the massacre of Palestinians at Sabra and Shatilla (by Christian Phalangists), the controversy over the arrest of American Jew Jonathan Pollard for spying for Israel, the attempts of the hard line Likud government to pass restrictive "who is a Jew" legislation, the Intifada (Palestinian uprising), and the eventual negotiations with the PLO were all topics that led to increasing debate over Israeli policy among American Jews. Jewish establishment organizations like the ADL, AIPAC, the national Council of Federations, and the American Jewish Committee maintained their practice of supporting official Israeli policy, yet the emergence and increasing prominence of dissenting groups including the New Jewish Agenda, American Friends of Peace Now, and, later, the New Israel Fund and J Street were indicative of a new willingness to challenge both Israeli policy and the American Jewish establishment.[120] Although these groups also faced widespread criticism, they fared better than had Breira. New Jewish Agenda (NJA), founded in 1980, emphasized the connection between Jewish values and social activism, taking strong positions on a variety of domestic and international issues, including supporting gay rights, feminism, and the environment, and advocating for the underprivileged and disenfranchised, both at home and abroad. The group called for mutual recognition among Israel, its Arab neighbors, and the PLO, as well as for Palestinian "national self-determination, including the right to the establishment . . . of an independent and viable Palestinian state in the West Bank and Gaza."[121] Although NJA, like Breira, was denounced for its outspokenness on internal Israeli issues, it succeeded in gaining admission to Jewish councils and federations in some cities by the mid-1980s, including Los Angeles in 1984. In other cities, such as Washington, DC, the group was excluded after bitter debates.

With these challenges came a national discussion of communal dissent and the role of the Jewish newspapers—most of which, like the *Review*, were either published or supported by their local federations—in giving voice to that dissent. This discussion was reflected in the *Review*'s December 1983 reporting on the annual meeting of the General Assembly of the Council of Jewish Federations. Coverage focused heavily on dealing with internal communal controversy, particularly a session titled "Reconciling Diversity with Unity—Creative Management of Different Viewpoint in the Jewish Community: A Federation Responsibility." *Review* editor LaNita Anderson paired her report on this session with one on the concurrent meeting of the American Jewish Press Association, emphasizing the spectrum of opinion on the topic. Some editors believed letters and opinion pieces deemed divisive ought not to be printed in the communal press, while others felt the open airing of differences was vital to both communal health and the viability of newspapers. Examples were given of community newspapers that had refused to cover communal controversies or to print ads of organizations like the New Jewish Agenda. Tellingly, Anderson's article presented the spectrum of opinion on these topics, but provided more space to those advocating openness, and the *Review*'s coverage actively invited discussion. An insert posed a series of real cases discussed at the meeting of editors—including questions of running ads for groups like NJA and providing news coverage of communal scandals or dissent—and challenged readers: "Be an editor or member of a community paper board and decide how you would have dealt with these actual issues that came up around the country."[122]

As Harry Turtledove's comments the year before suggest, there was already a push within the *Review* board toward making the paper a venue for communal debate on controversial issues. Since the 1976 appointment of an editorial board, the paper had defined itself as a "community newspaper rather than a house organ," although the board was still appointed and its business records were still kept by the Federation. In the summer of 1984, the publication moved toward legal independence, consolidating all operations and business records at a separate office. Although the *Review* continued to receive major financial support from the Federation, it became an independent "community-owned publication."[123] When Elaine Cogan assumed the editorship in September 1985, she announced, "Not only will the *Review* be a communicator of news, it will also be a forum for diverse opinion and commentary." Two years later, when Marc Lowenthal took the position, he emphasized in his first editorial the "challenge of trying to be even-handed in Portland's diverse Jewish community." The following year, he wrote that he was willing to disagree with specific Israeli policies, while continuing to emphasize his support for Israel.[124] The *Review*'s—and the broader community's—openness to diverse views would soon be tested.

The first sign in Portland of what would become a sustained communal conflict over Israel came in 1984, when the *Review* ran an article on the establishment of a local chapter of New Jewish Agenda. The lengthy February 1984 article provides a glimpse into NJA's reception in Portland. Reporter Donna Schatz presented an overview of NJA's origins and goals, interviewing several local activists and reporting that approximately fifty people attended the group's regular Portland meetings. She noted the diversity of the chapter in terms of age and background, and quoted members' descriptions of NJA's goals and character. Schatz also interviewed several of NJA's detractors, including Celia (Wicks) Ettinger, a former Jewish Education Association director and Hadassah activist, who soon became a central figure in Jewish communal debates over Israel. Ettinger expressed grave concern about NJA's criticisms of Israel, arguing, "There's no shortage of people ready to pounce on Israel. Why should Jews add to it?" Confirming the consensus stance of leaving policy decisions to the Israeli government, Ettinger was particularly critical of NJA's position on peace negotiations and the need for Israel to withdraw from the occupied territories; she called it "the height of arrogance" for American Jews to "preach to the Jews of Israel. . . . It's their heads on the line."[125] Cindy Saltzman, chair of the Israel Committee, formed to advocate for and promote Israel and Aliyah (immigration to Israel), was even more direct. After attending an NJA meeting to "check [it] out," she was asked whether she considered NJA progressive; she responded, "If progressive means intelligent, no, they're not progressive. My overall feeling from the workshop was that the people were naïve and misguided. They neither had their facts straight nor had the desire to learn."[126]

With the growth of groups like NJA in Portland, [127] the communal quiescence that had troubled Turtledove soon became a distant memory.

Expressions of dissenting views grew increasingly common, and the pages of the *Review* became a site for vigorous, even rancorous debate. Given its long-standing roots in and continued financial support from the Federation, it may have been expected that the *Review* would tilt heavily toward a consensus position, yet the paper's editors were repeatedly taken to task by champions of the consensus view who felt that the *Review* was tipping dangerously to the left. Rabbi Yonah Geller expressed this opinion on several occasions. Writing in April 1986, he charged,

> It is obvious that the *Portland Jewish Review* is totally under new editorship, and that it no longer reflects the conservatism of this Jewish community. I, for one, am not sure that the new trend in which emphasis has been placed on the far-out left such as the New Jewish Agenda . . . truly represents the sentiments or the feelings of the majority of this Jewish community. While it may well be stated that the paper should represent every facet of the community, this does not imply that those on the periphery should be given such strong recognition. A center position is most desirable. The New Jewish Agenda represents a very small percentage of our Jewish community. These misguided idealists are reminiscent of the liberals of the '60s. . . . However, when they apply their criterion to Israel, it becomes downright dangerous. . . . In order to achieve peace in Israel, you must be able to negotiate with Arabs in good faith. There must be a united opinion and a united agreement in which all parties can agree. . . . If, as has been suggested, by these misguided liberals, Israel were to reduce the size and effectiveness of her armed forces, she would be jeopardizing the life and safety of every Jew living there. . . . Let it be clearly understood that Israel's very existence is dependent upon her military strength.[128]

Geller's critique touched off a wave of letters. Several expressed satisfaction with the paper's coverage, and, in a few cases, went on to rebuke Geller for, in Rose (Kagan) Leopold's words, the "inflexibility of his mind and spirit, the hardening of his heart." Others agreed with Geller. For example, Helen (Weinberg) Blumenthal suggested that the paper change its name to "Voice of the New Jewish Agenda."[129]

This controversy was followed in the fall by heated discussion of an Israeli proposal to identify converts to Judaism on their Israeli identity cards—a move understood as an effort to delegitimize conversions conducted by the non-Orthodox movements to which the vast majority of American Jews belonged. The aborted measure was so disturbing to American Jews that it caused a widespread rethinking of the mobilization model; indeed, because the measure carried such great weight for American Jewish identity, even the leaders of the Federation and other mainstream groups were openly critical. In Portland, a number of letter writers, including Federation president Harold Pollin and Beth Israel Rabbi Emanuel Rose, suggested that the Federation, and American Jews more broadly, exert influence "to counteract any religious repression by any group toward others." Rabbi Stampfer went further, suggesting that American giving through the United Jewish Appeal should be used for specific education, health, and other projects without being turned over to "a government that continues to practice discrimination against Reform and Conservative Jewry. . . . I would be very pleased if Portland Jewry, which has long enjoyed a reputation for progressive and humanitarian leadership should assume a national leadership role in this vital issue." As Pollin explained, the Portland Federation agreed to try to exert its influence on the issue, but stopped short of Stampfer's proposal, deciding that it was inappropriate "to divert Federation funds from the established channels of distribution of Israel at this time. . . . The Federation stands with Israel, even though it sometimes acts in ways we may not agree with."[130] Two years later, when Prime Minister Yitzhak Shamir formed a coalition with religious parties favoring revisions to the Law of Return that would limit automatic citizenship to Jews born of a Jewish mother or converted by Orthodox authorities, Portland Federation officials again joined in protesting the proposal.[131]

The Intifada, which began in December 1987, put the Middle East conflict—and particularly the Israeli occupation of the West Bank and Gaza—on the front pages of newspapers around the world and provoked much soul searching about the nature of the occupation and the role of American Jews as supporters of Israel. In the first edition after the outbreak (January 1988), the *Review* surveyed community leaders, trying to "represent the diversity of views from right to left" on the crisis and its underlying causes. In addition, in order to get a "the full spectrum of Jewish public opinion," editors again invited readers to respond. Over the coming months, community leaders and members aired their views in the paper, at community fora, and at a variety of other venues, advocating everything from a two-state solution to permanent annexation of the territories, some standing firmly behind Israel and others condemning its tactics as brutal. In the process, the long-standing practice of supporting Israel without getting involved in policy disputes was called into question. As Rabbi Rose explained, "I think that one of the mistakes that the world Jewish community has made in the past has been its essential unwillingness to be critical of Israel when Israel is deserving of criticism." Rabbi Bruce Diamond of Salem went even further. Criticizing what he termed the "11th Commandment for the organized American Jewish community . . . Though Shalt Not Publicly Criticize the State of Israel,'" Diamond argued that "silence is concurrence" and that, rather than being morally complicit with Israel's response to the Intifada, American Jews should call out "Prime Minister Shamir and his Likud thugs," who were "posing a greater threat to the Jewish state than Yasser Arafat and his ilk." After being taken to task for this comment in a letter from Seattle Cantor Zvi Slotki in March, Diamond walked back his comments in April, saying that Shamir, in fact, was not worse than Arafat.[132] Emotions flared not only in the letters to the editor, but also in fora such as that sponsored by the CRC in early June 1988, at the MJCC. There, Arden Shenker, then the chair of the Israel Task Force of the National Jewish Community Relations Advisory Council, emphasized, "What is at stake today in Israel is its survival," a view that New Jewish Agenda activist Stew Albert claimed was outdated, given Israel's military strength and nuclear capabilities. Rather, Albert warned, what was at stake was Israel's "spiritual survival." "For Israel to fulfill its destiny," he cautioned, "it cannot be an occupying power."[133]

It was during this period—in the months after the start of the Intifada—that an unlikely spokesperson for a two-state solution emerged: Rabbi Joshua Stampfer of Congregation Neveh Shalom. Stampfer had impeccable credentials as a supporter of Israel. Born in Palestine, the grandson of a Zionist pioneer on one side and the Chief Rabbi of Jerusalem on the other, Stampfer had deep ties to the Zionist project and the Jewish state. Although he had been raised in the United States, the family kept in close contact and, in 1929, spent a year in Palestine. During that sojourn, eight-year-old Joshua was directly touched by the struggle over the land: just weeks after visiting relatives in Hebron, he learned that they were among the sixty-seven Jews killed in anti-Jewish riots in the city. During 1947 and 1948, Stampfer, by then a married rabbinical student, spent another year in the Holy Land. He was there to hear news of the United Nations vote in favor of the partition of Palestine that led to creation of a Jewish state. He was there to see Golda Meyerson (later Golda Meir) address the crowds in the streets, warning of the fight to come. He suspended his studies and joined the Haganah (Jewish defense force) in the War of Independence, returning to the states because of his wife's difficult pregnancy just before independence was declared. And, as we have seen, his 1966–1967 sabbatical year placed him back in Israel during the Six-Day War.[134] By the late 1980s, Stampfer had taken three sabbaticals from Neveh Shalom, spending each in Israel. He had led numerous congregational tours to Israel, as well as several for Christian clergy and for Portland State University students, and considered his efforts "to bring my people closer to the land of Israel and to devote myself to its welfare," one of the "guiding principles" of his rabbinate.[135] Until early 1988, he had embraced the consensus Jewish position that it was unthinkable for Israel to negotiate with the PLO. Even among those in the Jewish community who were critical of the Israeli response to the Intifada, at that time, to call for the establishment of a Palestinian state as part of a two-state solution was to step well outside the mainstream and place oneself on the fringe of American Jewish politics. Yet it was at this moment that Stampfer embraced the two-state solution and became its leading spokesperson in the Oregon Jewish community.

Although Stampfer remained firmly in the consensus camp until the late 1980s, the path that led him to break ranks began decades earlier. Just two years after Portland State University established its Middle East Studies Center in 1959, the rabbi had joined the faculty as a professor of Hebrew. Soon, he developed a friendly relationship with Nouri al Khalady, a Syrian native who taught Arabic in the program. Through the friendship, Stampfer developed greater awareness of prejudices within the Jewish community:

> I experienced a great deal of unwelcome criticism from many Jewish Zionists in the community who could not accept the fact that I was teaching in an academic program along with Arabs or Arab sympathizers. I was appalled by the chauvinism and narrow-mindedness of many in our Jewish community who simply could not accept the notion that there were two sides to the questions that faced us in the Middle East. The level of racism, in regard to Arabs, was very similar to attitudes toward blacks by so many in the white community. The teaching experience was probably the beginning of my search for understanding and compromise between Jews and Arabs.[136]

The seeds planted in the early 1960s took several decades to mature. In January 1988, about a month after the start of the Intifada, Stampfer was invited by a friend to meet with Quaker peace activist Ron Young. The meeting intrigued him enough to accept an invitation to an interfaith meeting of Muslims, Jews, and Christians on the Middle East conflict in Washington, DC. There, the rabbi was struck by "the opportunity to hear Palestinians speak about their anguish, their sufferings, and their aspirations . . . [and] the chance to sit and talk with them, one to one." Through this experience, Stampfer realized that the views of Palestinians as terrorists, so widespread in the American Jewish community, were a product of demonization. Experiencing an "epiphany," Stampfer announced his "conversion" on the issue to his congregation in February 1988, explaining that "the Palestinian cause . . . was a just one," and that "the Jewish community at home and abroad . . . had to begin paying serious attention to the aspirations and goals of the Palestinians." Stampfer's sermon was so far beyond the normal range of discourse within the community that his congregation received it with a shocked silence.[137] His call for Palestinian self-determination and a two-state solution was covered by the *Oregonian* in an article titled "Portland Rabbi Calls for Independent Palestinian State." Later in the same year, the paper ran a profile of the rabbi headlined "Joshua Stampfer: A Man of Moral Courage."[138]

Soon, Stampfer formed a Portland chapter of the Inter-Religious Committee for Peace in the Middle East, organized a Witnesses for Middle East Peace interfaith fact-finding trip to Israel and the occupied territories, and become a vocal speaker in support of a two-state solution. His activities were widely covered, not only in his congregation's newsletter and the *Review*, but also in the *Oregonian*, which reported on the February 1989 mission to Israel in a five-part series.[139] Other Oregon rabbis, such as Eugene's Myron

Kinberg, who also joined the Witnesses trip, and groups like New Jewish Agenda, had earlier called for direct negotiations with the Palestinians; yet they were considered radicals, outside the mainstream of the Jewish community.[140] As a long-standing Conservative rabbi of the state's largest congregation, Stampfer's embrace of this position was unprecedented. He was widely invited to speak at interfaith gatherings, regional colleges and universities, and events such as the inaugural meeting of Portland State University's Friends of Israel for a Palestinian State.[141] His stance on the issue was debated vigorously within the Portland Jewish community. A rival group, Oregonians for Israel, formed in 1989 under the leadership of Celia Ettinger, "long considered one of the community's leading voices in supporting current Israeli policies." That group dedicated itself to "supporting the democratically elected government of Israel, free of external political and economic pressure."[142] Rabbis Rose and Geller signed on as honorary cochairmen of the new organization.

Interestingly, it was Beth Israel's Rabbi Rose who became Stampfer's most prominent opponent on the issue. Rose was widely known in the community for his social justice activism. He had been outspoken in support of civil rights in Portland, played a key role in encouraging his congregation's Social Action Committee, and was an early and vocal critic of the Vietnam War. Rose was no hard-liner on the Palestinian issue—like Stampfer, he had attended the January 1988 meeting with Ron Young, and in his public statements about the Intifada he had been critical of Israel "not living up to its ethical standards." Yet Rose felt that his colleague had gone too far: "To champion a PLO state crosses a line I think I shouldn't, as an American citizen, cross. . . It is a line [Stampfer] shouldn't cross." Stampfer was, according to Rose, playing "into the hands of Israel's most prominent detractors."[143]

Not long after Stampfer's return from the Witnesses for Middle East Peace mission in February 1989, Rabbi Rose joined Arden Shenker and MJCC executive director Fred Rothstein in attending an Israeli government–sponsored "Solidarity Conference" in Jerusalem. Rose, in a clear reference to Stampfer's widely covered advocacy efforts, explained that he was motivated by deep concern "over the simplistic solutions to the conflicts in the Middle East which have been fostered in this community."[144] Soon, the two were openly feuding. When they faced each other in a March debate at Portland's World Affairs Council, Rose predicted that the Intifada would subside and "some form of self-government" would be extended to Palestinians; Stampfer quipped "I was tempted to add at the end of that prophecy, 'then the Messiah will come.'" In return, Rose took Stampfer to task for his stance, stating, "No one has the right to dictate to Israel whom the country should speak to. That's a process Israel has a right to go through."[145] As Havurah Shalom's Rabbi Joey Wolf emphasized the importance of hearing diverse opinions, claiming that "harmony . . . requires more than one voice," Rabbi Yonah Geller countered that the attention to critics of Israel was creating a distorted perception of Jewish public opinion, which was "in support of Israel, against a Palestinian state."[146] The *Oregonian* reported that the disagreement among the state's three most prominent rabbis, Stampfer, Rose, and Geller, was "unprecedented," especially given that the longtime colleagues had "previously worked to present a united front on many issues, including the Arab-Israeli conflict."[147]

By October 1989, the debate had grown so vigorous that the Portland CRC felt compelled to issue a "Civil Discourse Guide." Concerned that the community was becoming polarized, and shaped by parallel discussions on the national level within National Jewish Community Relations Advisory Committee (resulting in a set of "Guidelines for Participating in Jewish Community Events and Decision Making"),[148] the CRC emphasized the need for "cooperative discussion": "It is the position of the CRC that ongoing dialogue conducted among sincere parties on subjects of Jewish importance is a communal obligation and responsibility."[149] The Federation also presented a "position paper" on Israel, stating:

> The Jewish Federation of Portland supports Israel and its people in their desire for a secure and peaceful future.
>
> We recognize that a number of Portland Jewish groups share these aims but may follow widely diverse paths toward achieving their goals.
>
> In order to maintain its position as a consensus organization capable of mobilizing support for vital needs from the entire Jewish community, Federation is, and will remain, independent of all such organizations.
>
> Individuals, including members of our board, may express their personal views. These expressions, however, are opinions of the individuals involved and should not be construed as reflecting Federation's positions. To the extent that the Federation Board adopts positions on issues, they will be identified as such.
>
> Guidelines for civil discourse have been established by the Community Relations Committee and distributed to all local Jewish organizations. The Federation encourages all organizations to abide by them.[150]

The Federation's official neutrality was a far cry from its traditional role as the key umbrella organization for consensus mobilization and advocacy.

As the new guidelines were rolled out in the *Review*, the New Jewish Agenda and Oregonians for Israel staked out their positions with full-page ads. Oregonians for Israel's ad in the November issue read, "Negotiations Not Capitulations, Peace Not Suicide. Yes Mr. Shamir, We Stand With You!" New Jewish Agenda countered the following month with, "2 Years Of The Intifada: Dayanu! Let 1990 Be The Year When Negotiations Begin."[151] By January, a local chapter of Americans for Peace Now had formed, taking out its own full-page ad, listing local members and inviting others to join.[152]

Despite the Federation's official recognition of "widely diverse paths" and its efforts to keep the peace, activists in these organizations often felt that

Oregonians for Israel and New Jewish Agenda ran dueling ads in *The Jewish Review* in late 1989. Courtesy OJMCHE

there was little tolerance for their position. Paul Meyer, founding president of Portland's Americans for Peace Now chapter, recalled that the Federation characterized the group as "extreme."

> We were treated very disrespectfully in the conventional Jewish community. I remember that we wanted to hold a community-wide public debate, sponsored by the Community Relations Committee, and we wanted to speak directly with the board of the Jewish Federation to explain what we thought the critical issues were for our community and for Israel. Well, we were given a brief opportunity to speak to the Community Relations Committee (mostly younger people) but we weren't permitted speak to the Board itself.[153]

As Meyer's account suggests, those Jewish Oregonians who advocated negotiations toward a two-state solution in the late 1980s and early 1990s, like their counterparts nationally, often felt they were fighting an uphill battle against a long-standing American Jewish consensus that stood firmly against proposals to engage with the PLO. Yet it is clear that, in Oregon, those critiquing consensus positions were actually relatively well received. The combination of a growing Jewish community that identified strongly with the emerging progressive sensibility of the state and the leadership of long-standing, respected rabbis from large congregations—first Stampfer and

Kinberg, then Wolf—shaped this reception. Indeed, as suggested by Geller's 1986 allegation that the *Review*'s editors had embraced a pro-NJA bias, advocates of the consensus view felt increasingly beleaguered in Oregon, particularly in the pages of the community newspaper, which actively encouraged the public airing of diverse views on Israel, featured positive stories on groups like NJA, published their advertisements (often signed by dozens of prominent community members), and began including features like the 1991 "Voices for Peace," in which the views of activists, including a number from the left, were showcased.[154]

In the wake of the 1992 election of Israeli prime minister Yitzhak Rabin, those who stuck to the long-established consensus view would feel increasingly marginalized. As the Rabin government moved into direct talks with the Palestinians, the long-standing commitment of mainstream groups to respect Israel's right to make her own decision suddenly placed those opposing negotiations with the PLO, territorial compromise, and an eventual two-state solution in a difficult position, and mainstream groups had to shift their stance to reflect the new reality. Not only activists in groups like Peace Now and the New Jewish Agenda, but mainstream leaders like Shenker agreed that Rabin's election vindicated "those in the U.S. Jewish community who spoke out against Israeli settlement policy over the objection of other Jewish groups."[155] Stampfer, in particular, felt vindicated, writing,

> I strongly opposed Shamir's policies because I felt that they were disastrous for Israel. Many of the self-appointed patriots of Israel in Portland sharply criticized me for speaking out. They insisted that only Israelis in Israel have the right to speak out.
>
> Well, Israelis have clearly spoken in the voting booth. They have rejected a government that was more concerned with land than with human beings, a government that failed to respond to the fundamental principle of Zionism, the ingathering of the exiles.[156]

"Everyone who loves Israel has the right and duty to speak out on behalf of what he or she believes is best for Israel," Stampfer concluded, comparing his activities to those of Vietnam War protestors. Protest "didn't make me a traitor ... but a true patriot of Israel."

Meanwhile, a newly formed chapter of Oregonians for a Safe Israel tried to balance their commitment to the elected government of Israel with their conviction that its negotiations were endangering the state. Running ads encouraging readers to support Israeli settlements and protesting at the 1993 community celebration of the "handshake anniversary" (the handshake between Rabin and Arafat) that talks with Arafat would lead to "suicide" rather than peace, the group continued to stake out a conservative position on the peace process.[157]

Certainly, the election of Rabin did not end the Middle East conflict or the debate in Oregon and elsewhere about the best path forward. Jewish Oregonians who had opposed direct negotiations remained suspicious of Arafat and the peace process laid out in 1993 in Oslo; some continued to publicly vilify Stampfer, branding him as "sanctimonious," and accusing him of encouraging "the enemies of the Jewish people."[158] Both locally and nationally, some seemed to negate their former commitment to supporting official Israeli policy by speaking directly *against* the government's decision to directly engage with the PLO. Yet, as historian Wertheimer asks, "How could the American Jewish community refuse to grant legitimacy to a group that had members serving in the cabinet of Yitzhak Rabin?" That year, Americans for Peace Now was admitted into the Conference of Presidents of Major American Jewish Organizations.[159]

Similar reversals and debates continued throughout the 1990s and well into the twenty-first century in the wake of the assassination of Prime Minister Rabin and the unraveling of the Oslo process. A second Intifada, new waves of terrorist bombings in Israel, a new Lebanon War, and a protracted Gaza conflict all shifted Israeli politics back to the right, and major American Jewish organizations followed suit, supporting the governments of Ariel Sharon and Benjamin Netanyahu as they had Rabin's. Yet, nationally and locally, the shift toward open, and usually, but not always, respectful, debate had been made. As *Review* editors affirmed after publishing yet another round of vitriolic letters in August and September 1992, "It is the view of the editorial administration of this paper that differences of opinion among an educated, thoughtful and concerned community are an inescapable fact of life and are a required part of a healthy process in which a consensus evolves continually, which, while it may not be shared by all, establishes a community's broad identity at a given moment."[160]

In the process, the center had shifted leftward, in the direction of territorial compromise and a two-state solution. Even in the face of a new wave of terrorism, the momentum locally seemed to be on the left—despite the shift back to the right in Israel, and in mainstream advocacy organizations. Speaking in his capacity as director of the Federation's CRC, Robert Horenstein's commentaries in the mid-1990s took a strong position in support of continued engagement with Arafat and the PLO, even in the face of a spate of bombings. In the run-up to the May 1996 Israeli election, Horenstein argued against the conservative Likud Party in a column featuring imagined dialoguess with his (presumably fictional) straw man, Cousin Marty.[161] Likewise, *Review* editor Paul Haist, who started his twenty-year tenure in 1992, framed the Likud/Netanyahu victory in that election in a decidedly negative light. Haist's coverage focused on the reassurance by local leaders, including Rabbi Rose and Federation executive vice president Schiffman, that, although Israelis had voted "for security," they were still "committed to peace." In an opinion piece titled "Election Post-Mortem: Where Do We Go from Here?" Horenstein urged continued work toward peace and expressed hope for a national unity government, which would bring the defeated Labor Party, and its commitment to a two-state solution, back into the coalition. Portlanders from organizations like Oregonians for a Safe Israel, who were pleased with the Likud victory, were not well represented in local coverage, but several penned a letter congratulating Netanyahu and expressing gratitude that Israelis had elected him over "Prime Minister Shimon Peres and his left-wing, Arab-supporting coalition government." They reminded the "Jewish leadership in Portland" of their obligation to "support the democratically elected Israeli government of Netanyahu as staunchly as it did that of Peres,"[162] suggesting their strong perception that local Jewish leadership had embraced the kinds of strategies that had been at the margins in the late 1980s.

Coverage seems to bear out that perception. Horenstein, in his "Inside Community Relations" column, used his position as a Federation professional to publicly critique Israel's move toward a more orthodox position on conversions, a position that was problematic because it did not recognize conversions performed by non-Orthodox rabbis. Horenstein urged the community to voice dissent in "productive" ways, while continuing their commitment to supporting Israel and the Federation.[163] In the spring of 1997, the Federation published a formal call for Israel to "end the religious monopoly of the State (Chief) Rabbinate" on conversions. Although this was certainly an issue that provoked much criticism from many in the American Jewish community, Rabbi Rose commended the Portland Federation for its leadership, noting, "I think it is the first federation to make such a direct statement."[164]

The following year, seven of Portland's eleven congregational rabbis, along with a number of community leaders, signed an ad titled "Break the Silence," calling for negotiations with Palestinians toward a two-state solution.[165] The ad, which led to a new round of recriminations in the *Review*, again suggests that the Portland Jewish community had shifted to the left. Similarly, when Americans for a Safe Israel held a rally against territorial compromise in July 2000, only the rabbis from the more traditional/Orthodox congregations participated, and the event drew a "crowd" of only forty participants.[166] And when, in the spring of 2002, in the face of both the Second Intifada and a surge of bombings in Israel proper, *Review* editor Paul Haist invited eight Portland-area senior rabbis and Charlie Schiffman to respond to a series of questions about events in Israel, the vast majority of them advocated territorial concessions, despite the fact that the Israeli government at the time, led by Prime Minister Ariel Sharon, had not yet committed to such concessions. As the headline explained, "Most—Not All—Agree Some Settlements Will Have to Go." Haist wrote that, in response to a question about "whether

Israel should abandon its West Bank and Gaza settlements or make other very significant reductions in the interests of peace," six of the nine local rabbis "were unequivocal in their view that the settlements are problematic and that getting out—in varying degrees—is an indispensable key to peace. Two others fell as strongly in the opposite camp, while a third strongly sympathized with the minority view, but finally acceded, grudgingly and only in part, to majority opinion."[167] The six in the majority included the rabbis of the community's largest congregations: Neveh Shalom, Beth Israel, and Havurah Shalom. As the *Review* ran their responses in a series over several editions, the community was rankled by local controversy, as some Jews joined an April pro-Palestinian demonstration at Pioneer Courthouse Square, and others, including Havurah Shalom Rabbi Joey Wolf, attended an Israel solidarity rally at the MJCC with a banner advocating withdrawal from the territories.[168] Rabbi Wolf's assertion that, in his use of military force in the territories, Prime Minister Sharon had acted "like the Gestapo," touched off a particularly vitriolic exchange of letters that continued for several weeks. In a June 15 editorial titled "Clearing the Air," Paul Haist responded to the controversy by emphatically affirming the paper's commitment to airing diverse views.

Among the rabbis expressing more dovish, proterritorial compromise views was Rabbi Daniel Isaak, who succeeded Rabbi Stampfer at the pulpit of Neveh Shalom after the latter's retirement in 1993. For example, in the 2002 series, Isaak joined Rabbis Rose, Stampfer, and Wolf in applauding the courage of Israeli reservists who refused to serve in the Occupied Territories for moral reasons. Stampfer compared the reservists to conscientious objectors during the Vietnam War, and Wolf exclaimed, "Bravo. We support you and can only imagine the horror you have been forced to confront as you encounter the innocent victims of oppression and despair caught in the middle." Using more measured language, Isaak "saluted their courage," adding, "I also salute the fact that the Israeli government has not taken action against them."[169] Later in the same series, Isaak joined those colleagues who saw the settlements as an obstacle to peace.[170] A year later, Rabbi Isaak, along with a number of nationally known figures and local colleagues Stampfer, Wolf, Husbands-Hankin, and others, was a signatory to advertisements calling "to bring the settlers home to Israel."[171] In addition, Rabbis Isaak and Wolf, along with lawyers Emily Simon and Elden Rosenthal and the CRC's Susan Abravanel, became involved in a Jewish-Arab dialogue group that began meeting in this era to discuss both issues arising for Arabs and Muslims in the wake of the Patriot Act and Middle East issues more broadly.[172]

The repeated embrace of community debate about Israel in the pages of the *Review* and the willingness of local rabbis and other communal leaders to question Israeli policy and advocate direct negotiations were signs of a relatively early and strong embrace of the engagement model in Portland. Also characteristic of that model was a shift in philanthropic engagement with Israel. In contrast to the mobilization period, when fundraising for Israel was centrally coordinated by federations and allocated through the United Jewish Appeal, under the engagement model, American Jews exercised more discretion by donating funds to specific, single purpose organizations that aligned with their politics and concerns. This shift included the vast expansion of "American Friends" organizations, such as American Friends of Peace Now or American Friends of Hebrew University, which collect donations directly for their Israeli counterparts. In addition, groups like the New Israel Fund were established to support an array of progressive causes in Israel, including a strong human rights agenda. Although these shifts became characteristic of American Jewish engagement with Israel at the turn of the twenty-first century, Portland began to move in this direction slightly ahead of the pack. As early as 1986, Rabbi Stampfer had suggested the possibilities of channeling aid directly to social services and other programs, rather than through the Israeli government. Not until 1998 did Portland's Federation establish the Oregon-Israel Fund, which dispersed funds directly to community-chosen causes in Israel. Yet this local initiative preceded the 1999 national move to begin to give federations a more direct role in making decisions about the allocation of funds in Israel.[173]

Given the profile of the community, it is not surprising that Jewish Oregonians were slightly ahead of the curve. Concentrated in the Portland area, with its largest non-Portland outpost in Eugene, the Jewish community of the state reflected its decidedly progressive context. Cathryn Priebe's study of Portland community attitudes on Israel suggests that the progressive environment in the Rose City provided a space in which critical perspectives on Israel could develop.[174] In addition, national studies make clear that Orthodox Jews—of whom there are relatively few in Oregon—are far more likely to be hawkish on Israel, while Reconstructionist, secular, and "post-denominational" Jews—precisely those groups that are overrepresented in Oregon—are disproportionately on the left with regard to Israel.[175]

A number of national studies have tied the breakdown in community consensus to a distancing of American Jews from Israel, emphasizing that surveys suggest diminishing support for the Jewish state.[176] Theodore Sasson, arguing directly against this "distancing" thesis, claims that the issue is not of diminished connection to Israel, but of more personalized and diversified engagement expressed through targeted giving, focused advocacy for specific positions within Israeli politics, and expanded virtual and real-life personal connections. Although comparisons of local to national attitudes are made difficult by the mismatches in survey questions, Sasson's interpretation seems a compelling way to frame Jewish Oregonians' engagement with Israel. Clearly, the Oregon Jewish community would be a prime candidate for

Portlanders rally in support of Israel at Pioneer Courthouse Square in downtown Portland, July 26, 2006. Courtesy OJMCHE

Members of J Street protest in Portland, 2011. Courtesy OJMCHE

"distancing"—Jews in Oregon are far more likely than their national counterparts to identify as secular, to opt not to affiliate with a congregation, and, when they do affiliate, to tend to choose synagogues other than Orthodox or Conservative. They are, like Jews in the West more broadly, more likely to intermarry. All these factors—along with the relative strength of a critical communal voice on Israeli politics—would suggest that this would be a community susceptible to distancing.

Yet the philanthropic data and public opinion surveys do not suggest any evidence of exaggerated distancing among Oregon Jews at the turn of the twenty-first century. The percentage of Portland's Federation funds allocated to the major umbrella fundraising group for Israel and other overseas Jewish aid, the UJA/UJC,[177] decreased over time, from approximately 45 percent in 1990–1991 to approximately 42 percent in 2004–2005. Yet those decreases are *less* dramatic than was the case elsewhere. The national combined allocation of the federations to United Israel Appeal (the portion of overseas aid going to Israel) fell from 47 percent to 23 percent in the same period. Portland's allocation fell less precipitously than was the case nationally, and the community maintained a relatively high level of support for overseas Jewry, including Israel.[178] Likewise, in the 2009 Portland survey, almost 36 percent of Portland-area Jewish households felt "strongly" (19.4 percent) or "fairly strongly" (16.4 percent) connected to Israel, compared to 30 percent of the 2014 national Pew survey of Jewish attitudes, which found 30 percent "very attached." Among those in the Portland survey who were classified as "highly involved" in the community, the overwhelming majority (72 percent) felt connected to Israel, and only 8 percent unconnected. Despite the national concern that distancing would negatively impact fundraising for Israel, nearly two-thirds of all Portland Jewish households surveyed in 2009 (58 percent) would like to see financial support for Israel by American Jews increase or stay the same; among those from affiliated households, this figure rose to 71 percent. In comparison, in the 2000 National Jewish Population Survey, just over 50 percent of respondents strongly agreed that Israel needs the financial support of American Jews.[179]

In the wake of the Six-Day War, American Jews turned inward, focusing on more specifically Jewish causes and issues and embracing a strong consensus around supporting Israel and Soviet Jewry. Even as consensus on Israeli politics diminished in the late 1980s, Israel remained central to American Jewish identities. As American Jews shifted from mobilization to engagement, romanticized understandings of Israel were replaced with more nuanced, complex, and realistic relationships, feeding more direct connection with specific policies, ideologies, and causes in Israel.

Although Jewish Oregonians' engagement in "internal" and "external" issues during the second half of the twentieth century followed general national patterns, there were some variations. Beginning the era during a period of relative insecurity and communal stability (or, as some saw it, stagnation), Jewish Oregonians tended to be somewhat restrained on issues of civil rights and social justice, embracing these causes in the abstract, but somewhat hesitant to take a public, communal stance locally. As they regained their footing in the 1960s, and emerged increasingly confident about their ethnic identity in the 1970s and beyond, local engagement in both secular civic issues at home and in the Jewish world converged with national trends. However, beginning in the 1980s, as Oregon, and particularly Portland, began to grow rapidly and become identified as a progressive center, Jewish Oregonians reflected this new context. As the community shifted from "mobilization" to "engagement" and the long-standing consensus on Israel was challenged, Jewish Oregonians seemed to experience the transition in exaggerated form. And, although the community's relatively secular, liberal, and even "post-denominational" profile in the 1990s and beyond would suggest great vulnerability to "distancing," there is little evidence of such a trend. Instead, they innovated new ways of embracing Jewish identity on Northwest terms, invigorating the community as it moved into the twenty-first century. Jewish Oregonians in the 1990s and early 2000s would not only hold diverse views on Israel and the Middle East, but would act out their Jewish identities in a variety of ways that reflected an Oregon ethos.

CHAPTER SIX

The *Jewish* Oregon Story

Today, rosh chodesh Elul and erev Shabbat, we celebrated the dedication
of our mikveh [*sic*] with our rabbis and friends! It's a beautiful morning in late
summer, the sun is shining, the water is clear and warm and we blow the
shofar to awaken us to return.

—Dedication of Mayan Miriam (Miriam's Well),
Eugene, Oregon, August 29, 2003[1]

Eugene, Oregon, seems an unlikely place for a mikvah (Jewish ritual bath).
A city known for its hippie vibe, embrace of the offbeat, and left-wing politics is not where one would expect to find an institution most associated with
Orthodox Judaism and, in particular, with the laws of ritual purity pertaining
to marital relations. Immersion in the mikvah denotes purification; it marks
conversion to Judaism and a woman's monthly transition back from impurity (*niddah*) to a pure state in which marital relations are permitted. In traditional practice, men also may visit the mikvah as a purification ritual prior
to the Sabbath.

Yet Mayan Miriam is a very Oregon institution. Built in the spirit of sustainability, local sourcing, and "do-it-yourself" so embraced by early twenty-first-century Oregonians, it offers the mikvah experience with an egalitarian,
welcoming, environmentalist, and even feminist ethos. Situated in the backyard of Libby and Joseph Bottero, the mikvah is built in the spiral shape of a
shell as a reminder of "our roots in the ancient sea, and of our kinship with all
life . . . [and] because of the spiral's symbolic cosmic connections to life: from
the DNA in our cells to the ocean waters from which we evolved to the vast
galaxies of the universe."[2] The spiral-shaped tub and the adjacent *bor* (reservoir), which fills with the plentiful Oregon rainwater falling on the roof of the
locally made yurt housing the mikvah, is "organic looking."[3] Its windows face
the four cardinal directions, and it is infused with natural light from the dome

Mayan Miriam mikvah sits in a yurt in the backyard of the home of Libby and Joseph Bottero. Credit: Libby Bottero

overhead. Although great care was taken to ensure that the mikvah conformed to all the strict *halachic* requirements, neither its owners nor the rituals performed within are strictly traditional.

Libby Bottero first immersed in a mikvah when she converted to Judaism in the late 1960s, just before marrying her first husband and bearing their child. The marriage was short-lived, but her connections with Judaism and with the ritual of the mikvah were not. She found that first experience "transformative," and made a point of visiting the local mikvah wherever she traveled for many years afterward. Although it would be over four decades before Mayan Miriam took shape, she recalls, "I always had this dream to build a mikvah where anyone could come."[4]

In 1968, after visiting a variety of synagogues to explore different streams of Jewish life, Libby and her young son moved into the House of Love and Prayer in San Francisco. Founded by Rabbi Shlomo Carlebach, who would later become a major figure in the Jewish Renewal movement, the House of Love and Prayer was known as a "Jewish hippie commune," which was, in Libby's words, "both *Shomer Shabbat* [Sabbath observing] and a source of certain mind-altering substances."[5] There she met Rabbi Zalman Schachter-Shalomi, the founder of Renewal Judaism, and Aryeh Hirschfield, who became a major figure in Eugene Jewish life in the 1970s and early 1980s. After his ordination, Rabbi Hirschfield served Renewal congregations in Ashland (Havurah Shir

Hadash, 1985–1995) and Portland (P'nai Or, 1996–2009).[6] It was during her time at the House of Love and Prayer that Libby began regular visits to the mikvah in San Francisco's Mission District.

After moving from San Francisco to Corvallis, Libby met and married her second husband, Joseph Bottero, also a convert to Judaism, and became involved in the community, first at Beit Am in Corvallis, and then at Temple Beth Israel in Eugene. Relocating to Eugene, the Botteros began thinking seriously about building a mikvah. For women such as Libby, who found deep meaning in the monthly ritual of immersion, the only options at the time were to drive the four-hour round-trip to the mikvah in Portland, or to immerse in a natural body of water, such as the Willamette River. For much of the year, the latter was an uncomfortable and unsafe option.

The Botteros first established a natural pond mikvah in their Eugene backyard, but soon began talking about building a more lasting structure. Inspiration came from Rabbis Carlebach, Schachter-Shalomi, and Myron Kinberg of Eugene's Temple Beth Israel, as well as from *The Jewish Catalog*, a 1960s-era popular guide that "encourage[d] ordinary Jews to be empowered with the knowledge to do *mitzvoth*," such as hanging a mezuzah or building a sukkah.[7] When it became clear that Beth Israel was not going to incorporate a mikvah in its plan for a new synagogue building in the early years of the twenty-first century, the Botteros moved toward fulfilling their long-held dream.

While taking care to fulfill all the specifications for a kosher mikvah, they were also committed to making the mikvah experience welcoming to all and available for diverse, often nontraditional, ceremonies. Along with conversions, monthly, and prenuptial immersions, Mayan Miriam has been the site of a variety of life cycle and healing rituals: marking a clean start after a divorce or a miscarriage, ritual cleansing before or after cancer treatments, and many others. The mikvah has been used, as is tradition, by brides to be and also by same and opposite-gender couples immersing together in advance of their vows. It has been the site of women's Rosh Hodesh (new month) ceremonies and women's *minyanim* (prayer groups). Although not a large pool, it has hosted a rather crowded group immersion by a local women's *minyan*. In 2015, the mikvah was the site of a ceremony to mark the conversion of twin boys carried by a surrogate mother from Oregon for a gay Israeli couple (because the surrogate mother was not Jewish, an immersion ceremony preceded the baby boys' bris). Libby Bottero recalls that the two Israeli men, each of whom was biological father to one of the twins, "wrote the most beautiful, deeply moving essay in Hebrew and English, explaining the names, what it meant to them to be fathers. . . . We were all in tears and hugging. . . . It was so deeply meaningful to them and to us who were witnesses."[8]

The mikvah in Eugene is an apt symbol of twenty-first-century Judaism in Oregon. Set amid the trees, the mikvah in the yurt speaks to embrace of place

Dedication of the Mayan Miriam mikvah in Eugene, August 29, 2003. Seated from
left are Shonna Husbands-Hankin, Rabbi Maurice Harris, Rabbi Yitzhak Husbands-
Hankin, Ari Royce (age one), Libby Bottero, Aviva Perlo, and Aviva Spiegel (and baby).
Credit: Libby Bottero

and commitment to stewardship—a commitment readily visible in the proliferation of environmental and sustainability projects that became so common
among Jewish Oregonians in this period. The do-it-yourself nature of the
project and welcoming of diverse expressions and participants are characteristic of the creative, hands-on outreach efforts embraced by Oregon congregations, federations, and new, independent Jewish organizations. The emphasis on personal spirituality in the various life cycle and healing rituals at the
mikvah resonates with the exploration and individual religious experiences
characteristic of the Northwest. All these elements are particularly embodied
in trans- and post-denominational expressions of Judaism that have so prolif-
erated in Oregon since the 1990s, suggesting a strong embrace of sensibilities
that came to be associated with the state as part of the "Oregon Story" of the
1970s and beyond.

In the late twentieth century, Oregon, and especially Portland, developed a
distinctive identity as a trendy, progressive, quirky, green center. Although
popularized in the early twenty-first century as "Portlandia" through the
eponymous television show, elements of this identity extend beyond the city

limits and decades back in time. The environmental sensibility and emphasis on thoughtful development originating in the Governor McCall and Mayor Goldschmidt era, the emergence of an innovative arts and cultural scene, and even the association with the counterculture and, later, hipster culture, drew large numbers of young professionals and other creative, well-educated migrants. Portland became known for its emphasis on light rail and bikes over cars, its neighborhood-based decision making, its extensive network of parks and food carts, and its embrace of sustainability, creativity, and the unconventional. Such sensibilities are expressed by taglines such as "a city where young people go to retire," and bumper stickers admonishing, "Keep Portland Weird."[9]

At times, the reputation overshadows the reality. Despite perceptions of Oregon (and the Northwest more broadly) as a progressive center, there are countervailing forces. The environmentalism so championed by progressive Oregonians was strongly challenged in timber country—most vividly when preservation of the endangered spotted owl pitted environmentalists against logging communities. Similar conflicts between development and preservation have played out around issues of water use, dams, and salmon. On the social front, the Oregon Citizen's Alliance became one of the most prominent anti–gay rights groups in the country—and succeeded in getting several measures on the statewide ballot. A similar group, the Oregon Defense of Marriage Coalition, sponsored a successful measure prohibiting gay marriage in 2004.[10] In addition, despite much theoretical welcoming of diversity, Oregon remains far whiter than its neighbors to the north and south, a legacy of racial exclusions and discriminatory practices that lasted well into the twentieth century. In his recent history of the state, David Peterson del Mar characterizes Oregon as polarized, based largely on geography: well-educated creatives in Portland, Eugene, Ashland, Corvallis, Bend, and other pockets along the coast and in the Willamette Valley embraced the "good life" growing out of the Oregon Story, while in more rural areas in the south and east, "many Oregonians felt excluded from or hostile to the new Oregon."[11]

The Oregon Story and the more recent emergence of Portlandia are closely entwined with the recent history of the state's Jewish community, which is, not coincidentally, overwhelmingly concentrated in precisely those centers that most exemplify the state's progressive reputation. The engagement of Jews in local and statewide progressive movements in the postwar period positioned the community and its leadership to be responsive to—and active in—the development of the state's modern character. Higher than average educational levels and liberal politics meant that Jews were overrepresented in the particular cohorts of migrants attracted to the state in these decades. Whether natives or newcomers, Jewish Oregonians gravitated to those cities most associated with progressive values. They have been contributors to the modern Oregon Story, and their institutions and identities have, in turn, been shaped by that story. From bumper stickers proclaiming, "Keep Portland Meshugah" to the Eugene mikvah in a yurt, Jewish Oregonians have embraced local sensibilities about individual expression, spirituality, the environment, and inclusion that make up what might be called the Jewish Oregon Story.

New Jews, New Identities

As discussed in chapter 1, after years of stagnation, the number of Jews in Oregon began to grow in the 1970s and 1980s, and that growth accelerated at the turn of the century. In the 1990s and early 2000s, the population increased several times over, outpacing the general population growth of the region.[12] Many chose Oregon for its vibrancy and values—the embrace of an environmental ethos, a commitment to an inclusive community, and an affinity for what Oregonians like to call "weirdness." Yet, as sociologists Goldstein and Goldstein have emphasized, these Jewish migrants were not representative of the larger communities from which they came. Jewish migrants to the West tended to be more secular in orientation, younger, less likely to be in-married, and less "embedded" in their Jewish communities of origin than those who remained behind.[13] Not surprisingly, many of these migrants opted not to become involved in the Jewish community after relocating to Oregon. Those who did seek Jewish connections often did so in ways that reflected the particularities of the region and those drawn to it. The result was a changing Jewish landscape in Oregon in the 1990s and early 2000s. As lifelong Portlander Joyce Loeb observed in 2008,

> There is the explosion of different congregations as people have come here from all different parts of the country. They have brought a richness with them. . . . I think Portland was a very insular place and change was not something that was necessarily welcomed. It was hard to see certain things change and new ideas come in. Although there was always a group of people who were accepting of the change and maybe eager for it. But I think it was a lot of the new people who came in who brought that change. And then, of course, as their ideas didn't quite mesh with what was already here, new organizations were started.[14]

Evidence of the impact of migration can be found in the synagogue affiliation rates, which have been affected by both migration and context. Nationally, communities that experience high levels of in-migration often lag in affiliation rates; this is especially the case when migrants are young, as many young families delay joining a congregation until their children are ready to begin religious school. The secular orientation of Jewish migrants to the Northwest magnifies the pattern, as does the broader religious landscape of the Northwest—low levels of church attendance among the general population tend to reduce the pressure on newcomers of all faiths to join a synagogue or church.[15] That Oregon's synagogue affiliation rates are among the lowest in the country is a reflection of both selective migration and the generally low religious affiliation rates of the region.

Nationally, the 2013 Pew Research Center *Portrait of Jewish Americans* found that 22 percent of Jews "describe themselves as having no religion." These are individuals "with direct Jewish ancestry or upbringing, who consider themselves Jewish, yet describe themselves as atheist, agnostic, or having no particular religion."[16] These "Jews of no religion," are overrepresented in the West—home to 23 percent of all Jews, only 20 percent of "Jews by religion" reside in the West, compared to 31 percent of "Jews of no religion."[17] In the 2009 survey of Portland-area Jews, only 33 percent described themselves as religious Jews, while nearly half (46 percent) considered themselves cultural Jews; about a fifth (21 percent) reported they were either "non-practicing Jews or Jews by birth only."[18] The unusually high numbers of secular and nonpracticing Jews made Jewish Oregonians particularly difficult to count—the numbers reported from the 2009 survey were the subject of much controversy and were revised downward in 2011.[19] Regardless of which survey numbers one believes or how one defines Jewish identity, it is clear that the growing population of Jewish Oregonians is more diverse in spiritual, cultural, and communal preferences than ever before.

The high proportion of secularly oriented Jews creates particular outreach challenges. Jewish Community Centers have long been central to efforts to reach cultural and secular Jews not engaged through congregations. In Portland, as early as 1943, a JCC document articulating the "Major Objectives of the JCC," pointed out that "a larger percentage of the non-affiliated Jews in our community are members of the Center," which served as "a physical expression of the Jewish environment," and "a place where the Jew, be he Orthodox, Reform, Conservative, Yiddishest [*sic*], Hebraist, or Secularist, may engage in activities which, because of their sectarian nature, are not provided for in public institutions." Supporters believed the JCC could "stimulate participation in Jewish community life."[20] The 1971 population survey, with its warnings about the threat to communal survival posed by low growth rates, the out-migration of young adults, geographic dispersal, lack of knowledge and interest in Jewish history and culture, and the waning of ritual practice spurred renewed attention to the potential role of the JCC, especially since the new building provided room for expanded activities and was seen as the potential anchor for a new Jewish residential center.[21]

By the 1980s, just such a center had emerged in Southwest Portland. In addition to the new day school, the JCC—renamed the Mittleman Jewish Community Center or MJCC—would soon expand its early-childhood education program. Nearby, Chabad, which began operations in Portland in 1984, also opened a preschool. Soon it, like the MJCC, would offer an array of camps, educational programs (including its own day school), and other outreach activities. Nearby, Cedar Sinai Park housed a senior complex, including the Robison Jewish Home and the Rose Schnitzer Manor. The hope that such a clustering would result in the emergence of a "Jewish neighborhood," or at least a concentrated settlement, also bore fruit. By the mid-1970s, roughly half of the metro area's Jews lived in Southwest; up from a third a decade earlier. In addition, settlement in that area has continued to be highly correlated with "high involvement" in the community—so much so that when the Orthodox congregation Kesser Israel finally left its old building in the historic South Portland neighborhood for a new location near the MJCC in 2008, the *Jewish Review* proclaimed that the congregation would now be "back in the heart of Jewish Portland."[22] When a 2011 "Demographic and Opportunity Study" by the Jewish Federation of Greater Portland divided the community into three segments—"high involvement," "moderate involvement," and "low level of involvement," based on factors such as organizational affiliation, membership in a congregation and/or the JCC, and participation in Federation campaigns, the highly involved were heavily concentrated in Southwest Portland: 50 percent reported living in that area, with no more than 10 percent residing in any other single region of the metro area. The Southwest also was home to the plurality (30 percent) of moderately involved Jews and 20 percent of the low-involvement group.[23]

Clearly, the residential strategy had worked in terms of attracting potential high-involvement Jews and fostering those tendencies. However, it did not hold up as well in the final decades of the twentieth century in terms of encouraging concentrated settlement of the region's Jewish community. Able to engage fully in secular society in a way that their predecessors could not, Jews dispersed across the metropolitan area in the 1990s and early 2000s. Exercise-conscious young professionals had many health club options available to them beyond the MJCC, and many were drawn by the charm of older Eastside neighborhoods as Portland's new urbanism took hold. The most recent data demonstrate that, despite the apparent success of efforts to create a Jewish "neighborhood" or geographic center in the 1970s and 1980s and the continued tendency for those most attached to community to reside there, the influx of the 1990s and 2010s was far less centered. The 2009 survey found only 36 percent of the metro area's Jewish households in Southwest Portland (including the southwest suburbs), down from nearly 50 percent in 1971. Population on Portland's Eastside totaled 54 percent, up from 47 percent in 1971, with the greatest growth in the areas farthest from the MJCC.

Table 2: Residential Distribution

	Southwest (including suburbs)	Northwest	Southeast	Near Northeast/ North	Far Eastside & Clackamas, Clark Cos., WA/Other
1971 JWF Survey*	49%	5%	10%	14%	23%
2009 Jewish Households**	9823 (36%)	2856 (11%)	3472 (13%)	1979 (7%)	9205 (34%)

*The 1971 survey used a sampling method to ensure that the geographic spread of those surveyed was representative of the known Jewish community. To determine geographic sampling proportions, they used the zip codes of households known either by virtue of congregation or JCC membership or Federation donations, not the actual count—therefore, only the percentages appear here. Thus, the percentage figures here were predetermined based on a population of Federation donors—by definition, this favors areas of the metro area where Jews were more likely to affiliate.

**For the 2009 survey, geographic divisions within Multnomah County are based on neighborhood associations; here the figures are reported for the Southwest Neighborhood, Southeast Uplift Neighborhood Coalition, Neighbors West/Northwest, North Portland Neighborhood Services and Northeast Coalitions only. The final two, North Portland (NPNS) and Northeast (NECN) have been combined to reach the Northeast/North figure. The other areas—Central Northwest Neighbors (CNN), East Portland Neighborhood Office (EPNO) and "all other far eastern zip codes" are listed in the final column, along with the total for Clackamas and Clark (WA) counties. I have included the Washington County suburbs with the figures for Southwest, so this includes the heavily populated Beaverton area, adjacent to Southwest Portland.

Furthermore, although there were more than twice as many "high-involvement" as "low-involvement" Jews in Southwest, the numbers were reversed in Southeast, with three times as many "low-involvement" Jews as high.

A parallel trend in the final decades of the twentieth century was a surge in interfaith marriages. The falling of remaining barriers to full inclusion led not only to residential dispersal, but also to soaring intermarriage rates. Whereas the 1971 survey found an intermarriage rate of only 5 percent in the Portland Jewish community (a rate lower than the national rate), in 2009 nearly two-thirds of respondents (61 percent) reported having an immediate family member who was married to a non-Jew, compared to the national figure of 42 percent.[24] Although direct comparisons are difficult because of variations in methodology and wording of questions, these figures make clear that, as in the West more broadly, the rate of interfaith marriages among Jews in the area is higher than the national average. The 2000 National Jewish Population Survey found an intermarriage rate of 41 percent in the West, significantly higher than the national rate of 31 percent, and well above any other region of the country.[25] Increases in interfaith marriages are a natural outgrowth of greater inclusion and acceptance in the broader society and the corresponding decrease in exclusively Jewish social clubs for teens and young adults. Migration patterns that bring less embedded Jews to the West also contribute to high interfaith marriage rates, as does the overall low percentage of Jews in the region. Ultimately, geographic and demographic patterns are mutually reinforcing: surveys show that interfaith couples are less likely to raise their children as Jews and more likely to fall into the "low-involvement" group; this makes them less likely to prioritize proximity to Jewish institutions as they make their residential choices.

Congregations recognized these demographic challenges early, and demonstrated flexibility as they reached out to changing constituencies. The Reform and Reconstructionist movements' recognition of patrilineal descent attracted congregations with growing numbers of interfaith couples. A welcoming posture toward interfaith couples and recognition of patrilineal descent were key factors in the decision of Salem's Temple Beth Sholom to become the first congregation in Oregon to affiliate with the Reconstructionist movement in 1990. When the South Metro Jewish Community hired Rabbi Larry Halpern in 1997 and began to expand programming, it recognized the "high percentage of intermarried couples" in the community by calling itself "a congregation for Jews by birth, Jews by choice, and Jews at heart." In 2001, the congregation affiliated with the Reform movement. When Beit Am in Corvallis began a search for its "first-ever rabbi" in 2004, finding a religious leader who could work well with "a religiously diverse, unaffiliated Jewish community that recognizes patrilineal descent" was a top priority. The same demographic trends led Rabbi Emanuel Rose, the leading Reform rabbi in the state, to move relatively early toward performing interfaith weddings, under certain conditions. As he explained in a 1981 interview:

> I had to wrestle with this myself because the situation that I found was children that I taught here in this congregation would come into my office and tell me they wanted me to marry them and I would send them out with a no, one after another. And I did that for fifteen years and what I noticed was that I never had any more relationship with these kids. They didn't stick around. So I began reflecting on what I was doing. . . . Finally, I decided that I have to try something else. I've got to try, given the reality of the new Jewish circumstance. . . . I had to really take an honest look at this and see what I could do to help keep these kids close to Judaism. So I went through a process which took three years in working out until I finally came to the conclusion that I was going to officiate at mixed marriages. I set up a series of conditions. . . . Number one, the non-Jew cannot have any Christian theological commitment. Number two, there has to be an agreement to raise the children as Jews. Number three, there has to be an agreement to have

a Jewish home, and number four there has to be an agreement to study Judaism. They don't have to convert, short of conversion and under those circumstances, I would officiate at the marriage of a Jew and non-Jew. The result has been that I now see the kids. They stay close. They become members of the Temple and they are here.[26]

The issue clearly resonated in the region—when Rose's congregation hosted a meeting of the Pacific Northwest Council of the Union of American Hebrew Congregations (UAHC, the Reform movement) in 1974, one of the five study sessions was titled "Integrating Mixed Marriages into the Congregation."[27] Given that the call by UAHC president Rabbi Alexander Schindler for outreach to interfaith couples did not come until 1978 and that the movement did not endorse such marriages or recognize patrilineal descent until the early 1980s, this suggests that the region was ahead of the national group.[28] Although the compromise worked out by Rose later became widespread as the Reform movement shifted its position on intermarriage "from outrage to outreach," at the time it was relatively unusual. In the mid-1970s, as Rose was reevaluating his position, only about 10 percent of Reform rabbis were performing mixed marriages; even by the late 1980s, only about half did so.[29]

Rabbi Rose also worked together with Rabbis Joshua Stampfer and Yonah Geller to create an Introduction to Judaism class that served many couples exploring the possibility of having one partner convert. The three rabbis, who had cooperated in creating the Oregon Board of Rabbis, developed the Introduction to Judaism class as a joint venture and invited additional rabbis to participate as they joined the community. This allowed students to learn from rabbis of diverse backgrounds, representing the spectrum of Jewish movements. In developing the course, the three rabbis created a model for the country. As Stampfer explained, "I don't think there's another community in America which has a course, Introduction to Judaism, which is taught by rabbis of all different points of view, all different movements." The course's purpose, according to Geller, was "to spend twenty weeks with people who were potentially thinking about becoming Jewish." It is telling that *The Three Rabbis,* the 2005 documentary film focusing on the forty-plus-year careers of Stampfer, Rose, and Geller, features intermarriage as a central theme, profiling a couple, David and Amy Elkanich, as they experience the Introduction to Judaism class and explore the possibility of David's conversion. As Amy Elkanich reflects, "I think, especially in the Northwest—Seattle, Portland— we really are kind of the new face of Judaism in some ways, because there is one partner who just can't leave it behind and one partner who is . . . brought in." Rabbi Joey Wolf of Portland's Reconstructionist congregation Havurah Shalom, concurs on the importance of a welcoming posture: "Others are very much going to be walking in the door and they're going to need to be honored, so some of the distinctions and boundaries don't exist for us the way they once existed."[30]

Broader communal organizations recognized the challenges of outreach in a community with a very rapidly growing population of interfaith couples. In 1989, the Portland chapter of the American Jewish Committee instituted a program pairing intermarried couples with mentors. In the years that followed, the MJCC and Jewish Family and Child Services collaborated on a program of workshops on parenting issues for interfaith couples, an expansion of a similar program that JFCS had run for a number of years. Gesher [Bridge], a Portland-based outreach organization, was established in 1990 to serve unaffiliated Jews, with a particular focus on intermarried families. Its home-based, family-centered programs reached thousands of unaffiliated families over the years.[31] The *Jewish Review* added an advice column in 1996 that frequently focused on interfaith family issues and was authored by Lois Shenker, who, a few years later, wrote *Welcome to the Family*, a book intended to "help non-Jews feel at home with their new Jewish relatives." Shenker not only served for eight years as the coordinator of the Oregon Board of Rabbis' Introduction to Judaism course, but has also worked extensively with interfaith families through Mother's Circle, a group for women who were "new to Judaism through marriage or by choice" and raising Jewish children.[32]

Even as communal organizations responded to the growing number of interfaith couples, other outreach efforts were more geographic in focus, aiming squarely at the Eastside and its rapidly expanding young adult population. Although the east-west divide in the community generated much discussion in the early twenty-first century, it was not new. The flip side of community enrichment through clustering on the Westside in the 1960s and 1970s had been continued institutional neglect of the Eastside. Eastsiders—despite their significant numbers from midcentury on—have been consistently underserved by Jewish institutions. Congregations Ahavai Sholom, Neveh Zedek, Ahavath Achim, and Shaarie Torah all had substantial contingents that lobbied for relocation to the Eastside in the face of urban renewal. Despite these efforts, until the 1990s, there had only ever been one small congregation, Tifereth Israel, located east of the Willamette (in North Portland's Alberta neighborhood), and it had closed and been absorbed into Shaarie Torah in 1986.

With real estate values that were generally lower, the Eastside proved attractive to many young migrants. Although those who prioritized proximity to a synagogue, the Jewish day school, afternoon Hebrew school, or the JCC tended to congregate in Southwest Portland, the adjacent suburbs, or in Northwest, near Beth Israel, Havurah Shalom, and Shaarie Torah, many others were attracted to the Eastside. Some of them longed for a Jewish connection, yet felt alienated from the broader Jewish community. When the first meeting toward organizing the Eastside Jewish community gathered over forty prospective members in 1992, Chairman Jim Hilton captured this sense of alienation:

> It was a profoundly moving and gratifying experience for me. Community members spoke eloquently of the feeling of isolation Eastside Jews feel: most moving to me was the desire of parents to find Jewish playmates for their children. I sensed joy that our group exists and hope that we can begin to address the social and cultural needs of Eastsiders.[33]

As the Eastside Jewish Community of Portland (EJCoP) took shape, their activities suggested that, not surprisingly, Eastside Jewry reflected a pronounced version of secularism characteristic of the broader community. Their newsletter, the *Eastside Voice*, publicized a variety of social and cultural—but not religious—activities. The signature event was a monthly Shabbat dinner, usually held at either a Chinese or a pizza restaurant, without an accompanying service. Other events included summer picnics, fishing, ice skating, a ski party on Christmas day, a business networking group, family Chanukah parties, singles potlucks, a play group, a family social group, and craft workshops. The newsletter also published information on where to buy Jewish items, like challah and Chanukah *gelt*, on the Eastside.[34] There is no evidence in this period of religious services, aside from well-attended community Passover Seders. Indeed, the group's original mission was to address "the social and cultural needs of Eastsiders." It wasn't until 1997 that the group held its first Shabbat service, which led to a revision of the mission to address "religious and ritual needs" as well. A monthly Shabbat service was added in 1998.[35]

Still, the group continued to struggle, with newsletters admonishing members to step up and take responsibility for organizing and attending events. In the September-October 1998 newsletter, an article headlined "Whither EJCoP?" indicated that no one was willing to organize the annual summer picnic (which had to be canceled) and that only two members attended the most recent board meeting.[36] Although the group seemed reinvigorated by the following year, similar pleas and warnings would be issued periodically over the next several years.[37] After changing their name to Eastside Kehilla in 2009, they ceased regular programming and newsletter publication in 2010.[38] In the meantime, in 2002, a new congregation, Shir Tikvah, formed on the Eastside and invited Rabbi Ariel Stone, formerly associate rabbi at Congregation Beth Israel, to lead the independent, "post-denominational" congregation.[39] In addition, established congregations on the west side of the river tried to reach out to Eastsiders with initiatives like Neveh Shalom's Mizrach (East), which combined informal Shabbat services with summer potluck picnics and paired a bike ride with the Rosh Hashanah ritual of *tashlich* (the symbolic casting away of sins by throwing bread in the river).[40]

It became clear in 2011 that difficulties in establishing congregations on the Eastside were not caused by insufficient numbers. Until then, no one knew quite how many Eastside Jews there were. In 2011, a population study counted nearly twice as many Jews in the metro area as expected, including an unexpectedly large number on the Eastside. The results sent community leadership scrambling to determine who these Jews were and how to reach them. As an October 2011 article in *Tablet* explained,

> The "Lost Tribe"—a mass of younger, less affluent, largely unaffiliated Jews who turned up in the Federation's new census—can be found mainly in the city's eastern half. Hence, one major conclusion of the Federation's census: Jewish leaders in the city need to begin more outreach, "especially on the east side," the survey states, to engage this previously unknown, presently underserved mass of Jews.[41]

A special 2012 survey focusing on Eastside Jews found that they identified overwhelmingly in cultural rather than religious terms (73 percent versus 48 percent). Armed with the new survey information, the Federation set out to identify and attract the "lost tribe" through events like summer "Shabbat in the Park" and "Challahpalooza."[42] Also moving to the Eastside was Moishe House, a national nonprofit that serves twenty-somethings through an array of religious, cultural, and social activities organized by its residents, who receive rent subsidies. Initially locating in Southwest near the MJCC, Moishe House moved across the river in 2011. As Moishe House resident Jonathan Morgan explained, "We needed to go where the people are"—and young Jewish adults in Portland, increasingly, were on the Eastside.[43]

As Moishe House activities—emphasizing social gatherings, a Rosh Hashanah camping trip and other similar, environmentally themed programming—suggest, Jewish organizations trying to draw young Portlanders (on both sides of the Willamette) began to think outside the box in response to research confirming broader None Zone trends within the Jewish community: a population of recently arrived young adults who were not inclined to affiliate in traditional ways. Portland Jewish Events, a group launched in 2005 by Jodi Berris, who three years later would become a founding Moishe House resident, organized a series of gatherings for young Jewish adults and their partners (whether Jewish or not). Ranging from pub crawls and sports leagues (the Jewish Coed Dodgeball and Drinks League, for example) to offbeat holiday-themed parties, such as a "Macabees and Microbrews" Chanukah party and "Silent Night? Not!!!" (a party on Christmas Eve), the group sponsored a wide variety of events that played on Portland's hipster sensibilities and abundance of brewpubs. Over time, they expanded their age range, including

Yossi Shallman of Moishe House lights Shabbat candles in a Sukkah.
Courtesy OJMCHE

events for teens and for "masters"—those over forty. They also began sponsoring Birthright trips to Israel in 2009.[44]

Likewise, Portlander Sarah Liebman organized Machar (Tomorrow) in 2006 to reach out to young Jewish adults—college graduates who were not yet parents were the target population—with Jewish educational training through a partnership with Florence Melton Adult Mini School,[45] in addition to leadership training. The Machar cohort went on to create programming to reach out to their peers, launching events such as "'Succoth at the Farmer's Market,' a Jewish outreach education initiative on hunger." They also initiated a chapter of Mosaic, a Jewish environmental group, as well as hosting concerts, dialogues on peace in the Middle East, study groups, film festivals, and presentations. In October 2008, the *Jewish Review* reported that the previous year's Machar cohort had planned over forty events and grown their young adult LISTSERV from two hundred to seven hundred. In addition, Hineni, a group for the "post-college, pre-kid crowd" had five hundred on its (presumably overlapping) LISTSERV, and Liebman herself ran Urban Jews PDX, a LISTSERV focused on local Jewish events of interest to a young adult cohort.[46]

Trying to build on the outreach opportunities created by these groups, the Federation reached out to innovators such as Liebman and Berris and provided financial support for some of their programming. Liebman responded with a workshop titled "Talkin' About My Generation" that received

Alisha and Jacqueline Babbstein sit in a pomegranate-shaped sukkah at SukkahPDX, 2014. Courtesy OJMCHE

attention nationally (and internationally, in the *Jerusalem Post*) aiming to educate the Jewish establishment. Soon, Liebman was invited to address the national Reconstructionist convention as part of a panel on the future of the movement.[47]

Congregations and other communal organizations likewise experimented with new programs designed to draw young adults. Beth Israel's "Jews Next Dor" ("dor" is Hebrew for "generation") hosted "fun, informal, and inclusive" services for young adults on a monthly basis, as well as "special events and networking opportunities."[48] Such efforts complemented existing programs such as the annual Jewish film festival, Israel fairs, arts events, and other cultural activities designed to draw diverse Jews. The Oregon Jewish Museum's juried SukkahPDX competition created a space that attracted those interested in design, sustainability, and food security. The Jewish Theatre Collaborative, founded in 2008 and based on the Eastside, provided both touring and mainstage productions of Jewish-themed shows. All these programs were designed to reach a segment of the community uninterested in religious services and traditional educational and social programming, while at the same time creating greater visibility in a city where Jews remain a small minority. Coverage in the local secular press hinted at the broad appeal of such events, enabled unaffiliated Jews to learn about them, and, as in the case of a profile of the film festival in the *Willamette Week*, suggested that the Jewish community was not only visible to other Portlanders, but that a growing number of them were conversant in American Jewish culture:

> Portland Jewish Film Festival
> Off to the cinema, you schmuck.
>
> Ach, the Portland Jewish Film Festival. We've called it the least necessary of the film festivals—since the early 20th century, Jews haven't exactly been under-represented in cinema, and they've made immeasurable contributions to film—but like gefilte fish at Passover or that nosy aunt who won't stop asking when you're going to get married and start making lots of little Jewish babies, it just keeps coming back. With this quality of films, though, we're not kvetching.[49]

Although Jewish film festivals have gained popularity in many cities around the country,[50] fueled (or at least funded), in part, by efforts to reach out to unaffiliated Jews, the particular profile of Jewish Oregonians makes such efforts especially critical.

As outreach efforts proceeded, the question of how community and institutional life might shift to accommodate the changing population was still unfolding, as was the question of future leadership. As longtime community leader Arden Shenker reflected in a 2007 interview,

> If I go to meetings and gatherings of Jews today, I am in the minority of Jews who were born in Portland. If you look at the Jewish leadership of Portland today, the minority of those are people who have been here for more than twenty-five years. Transience is a fact in the Portland community. It also implies that, when we look for "new blood" we should assume that there will be people coming in from other communities with skills and interests, background and knowledge.

This requires a shift, Shenker argues, from the old mind-set, where the institutional leadership was groomed from within.[51] Moreover, the examples of Liebman and Berris suggest a new model for "do-it-yourself" programming and leadership that, at least initially, was independent of the organized community.

Beyond Portland

Although the overwhelming majority of the state's Jews continued to reside in the Portland area, smaller Jewish communities around the state also experienced growth in the late twentieth century—some for the first time since the pioneer era. Southern Oregon presents a particularly striking example. Jacksonville was home to one of Oregon's first Jewish communities, but there had been no Jewish life in that area in nearly a century when small groups began to organize themselves in the 1970s and 1980s. In Ashland—home to both the Oregon Shakespeare Festival and Southern Oregon University—a community emerged in 1973, when the Rogue Valley Jewish Community formed, serving congregants from Yreka in northern California to Grants Pass. In 1974, using a Torah borrowed from Portland, Los Angeles Rabbi Frank Rosenthal conducted the first rabbi-led High Holiday services conducted in Southern Oregon since 1883.[52] In a national Jewish population survey published in 1987, Medford, previously not listed as having a Jewish community at all, suddenly was "discovered" with a population of five hundred (including nearby Ashland).[53] The Ashland group held regular monthly services and ran a Sunday school even before organizing as Reform Temple Emek Shalom, purchasing a building, and hiring a part-time rabbi in the early 1980s. In 2003, the congregation dedicated a new, larger facility, and soon hired its first full-time rabbi.[54] By the early twenty-first century, the Chabad Jewish Center of Southern Oregon and Havurah Shir Hadash, a Renewal congregation, had also opened in Ashland. And Jewish communal growth in Southern Oregon in the new century was not limited to Ashland. An informal congregation (without fixed schedule or location), Anshe Shalom, was established in Klamath Falls, as was Mayim Shalom in Coos Bay on the southern Oregon Coast, and the Umpqua Valley Havurah in Roseburg, Douglas County.

In the northwest corner of the state, after decades of stagnation, Astoria's Jewish population also began to grow in the 1980s, when the community began to organize Passover Seders and, in 1983, celebrated a group b'nai mitvah for three community members ranging in age from thirteen to thirty-three—the first such ceremony celebrated in Astoria in thirty-five years. Regular services were not held on the North Coast until the 1990s, when a monthly Shabbat group was organized, including Jewish families from Astoria as well as Portlanders who either had second homes or had retired to North Coast communities like Cannon Beach and Seaside.[55] Among those former Portlanders who settled at the coast were retired Court of Appeals Judge Herbert Schwab and his wife Barbara Schwab, who took up residence in Cannon Beach, where he served as municipal judge, city councilman, and, from 1991 to 1994, mayor.[56]

Although more gradual than in Southern Oregon, growth also took place in the smaller communities of the Willamette Valley and in Central Oregon, east of the Cascades. The Salem congregation, which had long functioned as a lay-led community, finally hired its first rabbi in the late 1980s. Over the course of the next decade, the rabbinical position gradually expanded from part time to full time. Under the 1996–2006 leadership of Rabbi Gary Ellison, the congregation expanded and moved to a substantially larger building. Congregation Beit Am, in Corvallis, home of Oregon State University, was founded in 1974 and remained too small to support a rabbi until the turn of the century. Bend,

Table 3: Jewish Populations of Smaller Oregon Communities

	1972	1978	1986	1999	2012
Eugene	360	1500	2300	3000	3250
Salem	200	200	250	1000	1000
Corvallis	140	140	240	175	500
Medford/Ashland	NA	NA	500	1000	1000
Bend	NA	NA	NA	175	1000
Total non-Portland	1285	2100	3500	5500	6850

a central Oregon community that grew rapidly as a recreational hub in the late twentieth century, had, according to a Jewish communal history, "forty-six churches but no synagogues" as late as 1990. That summer, newcomers Gilead and Steve Leventhal met several other newly arrived Jewish families and a group of Jewish retirees who had begun to gather socially in the 1980s and organized a High Holiday potluck that drew sixty-four people. Out of this gathering, the Jewish Community of Central Oregon (JCCO) was born. Seven years later, about seventy-five families were involved in the new congregation, which ran a religious school that met twice a month, established a Jewish cemetery, and brought in Ashland Rabbi David Zaslow to lead services and programs six to eight times a year.[57] By 2012, Bend boasted a community religious school and two congregations, the independent JCCO (by then renamed Congregation Shalom Bayit) and Reform Temple Beth Tikvah, founded in 2008, as well as a Chabad center.

In Eugene, the expansion was most dramatic. Jews had resided in Eugene since the nineteenth century, and Jewish merchant Samson Friendly (after whom the University of Oregon's first dormitory was named) was elected mayor there in the 1890s. Yet it was not until the 1930s that a formal congregation, Temple Beth Israel, was established. After worshipping for two decades in a remodeled, donated home, the congregation built a synagogue in 1952 and hired its first rabbi soon after. Still, the community remained small. When the Goldschmidt family arrived in 1940, just before the birth of their son Neil—future Portland mayor and Oregon governor—there were still only a handful of families. Neil's bar mitzvah in 1953 was the first to take place in the synagogue.[58] The community grew slowly over the next two decades, and then suddenly exploded—counting only 360 Jews in 1972, Eugene was home to over four times that number in 1978, and doubled again over the next two decades. During these years, the congregation was served by two long-term rabbis, Louis Neimand (1963–1976) and Myron Kinberg, who served for seventeen years beginning in 1977. Kinberg's leadership was supplemented by the growing role of Yitzhak Husbands-Hankin, who began at Beth Israel as cantor and eventually became school director, assistant rabbi, and, in 1995, rabbi. In addition to Congregation Beth Israel, Eugene established its own Federation in 1992. At about the same time, an orthodox faction split off from Beth Israel to form Congregation Ahavas Torah. In more recent years, two additional unaffiliated congregations and a Chabad center have been established in Eugene, in addition to the Hillel that serves University of Oregon students.[59]

Judaism, Oregon Style

Among Jewish Oregonians who chose to join a congregation or otherwise express their identity in religious terms, contemporary patterns of affiliation and congregational styles reflect the Pacific Northwest context. As the Jewish population increased in the 1980s, and growth accelerated in the 1990s and 2000s, not surprisingly, many existing synagogues expanded and a number of new congregations were founded. Yet, in contrast to the early and mid-twentieth-century newcomers who tended to bolster mainstream institutions, the later migrants pushed communities in a less conventional, more "northwestern" direction. Oregon has far fewer Orthodox, Conservative, and Reform synagogues, and far more Reconstructionist, Renewal, and trans- or post-denominational congregations than Jewish centers elsewhere in the country. *Jewish Review* editor Paul Haist observed in 2006 that the number of new congregations was exploding. Where most Jewish Oregonians were served fifty years ago by three major Portland congregations, one Orthodox, one Conservative, and one Reform, by the early twenty-first century, "options abound[ed]."[60] Many of these new options—along with established institutions trying to reach out to a changing population—emphatically embraced the progressive, inclusive, and welcoming ethos associated with the Oregon Story.

Even as the Portland Jewish community doubled in size, and then doubled again, the number of traditional and Orthodox congregations shrank, reflecting migration patterns that brought less-embedded Jews to the region. In the mid-1980s, two decades after Shaarie Torah began calling itself "traditional" rather than Orthodox and merged with Linath Hazedek, it absorbed the Eastside congregation Tifereth Israel, which had similarly been transforming from an Orthodox into a Conservative congregation.[61] This left Kesser Israel as Portland's only Orthodox congregation (the Sephardic Ahavath Achim calls itself "traditional").

To be sure, Shaarie Torah's new identity as a Conservative congregation bolstered Kesser Israel, the only remaining Orthodox Union congregation in Portland. Kesser had been the sole synagogue in the old South Portland neighborhood to survive urban renewal, but did so only barely. With a small and mostly elderly membership and no rabbi, many predicted its demise. It was not until 1994 that, after decades as a lay-led congregation, the shul hired Rabbi Leonard Oppenheimer as its first full-time rabbi and began to expand its offerings to try to attract more members. By 1999, the congregation was offering a youth education program, including a small Sunday school and a youth group. When Rabbi Berel Wein visited the congregation that year, he reported optimistically on the "new young rabbi" and the "enthusiastic group of young couples that have revitalized the congregation," but warned that "decades of inactivity, neglect and lack of spirit and hope for the future are not erased in a few years."[62] As late as 2002, the congregation had fewer than ninety members, and Rabbi Oppenheimer, despite some optimism, reported that "making the morning *minyan* is always a struggle . . . [and] the evening *minyanim* are gasping for air."[63]

Yet as Shaarie Torah moved more decisively toward the Conservative movement, Kesser embraced its role as the sole remaining Orthodox congregation, adopting the tagline "the Orthodox Synagogue for All Jews" and emphatically reconfirming its commitment to Orthodox ritual. In 2006, under the guidance of a new rabbi, Kenneth Brodkin, the congregation began to offer services in rented quarters in Southwest Portland, in the Jewish hub anchored by the MJCC. As Brodkin explained, "if we are truly going to be 'The Orthodox Synagogue for All Jews,' we must be accessible. We must be in the center of the community."[64] They subsequently purchased a building, sold their historic synagogue in South Portland, and saw their membership increase. With only about 120 families, Kesser remains one of Portland's smaller congregations; and, aside from Chabad, it is today the only Portland congregation that defines itself as Orthodox. Eugene's Ahavas Torah is the only other such congregation in the state.[65]

As the number of Orthodox congregations dwindled, a variety of new institutions were founded. A few, such as Kol Ami in Vancouver, Washington (founded 1989), the South Metro Jewish Community (founded 1992, now called Beit Haverim and located in Lake Oswego), and Beth Tikvah in Bend (2008) affiliated with Reform Judaism. Yet what is most striking is the large number of congregations that chose options outside the three main branches of American Judaism, clustering at the progressive end of the spectrum. In the early twenty-first century, a plurality of the state's congregations either identify as Reconstructionist or Renewal, or are unaffiliated, describing themselves as "independent," "progressive," "Humanistic,"[66] or "egalitarian."

Portland's Congregation Havurah Shalom was founded in 1978 as an alternative to a traditional congregation. Initially an offshoot of Beth Israel and, like that congregation, identifying as Reform, it became Reconstructionist in 1997. From the beginning, the group was motivated by a desire to move away from the formality of a large, established synagogue. A visiting *Willamette Week* reporter explained in 1981:

the difference, it seems, is that its members don't feel they're part of an institution, in the Havurah, they feel like part of the community....

Havurah Shalom has grown out of a grassroots celebration of Jewishness by
a generation accustomed to doing things its own way. In this congregation, the
members aren't told how to worship; they conduct their own services. Nor are
there separate roles for men and women. All play an equal part in running the synagogue, which they don't plan to relinquish when they eventually hire a rabbi.[67]

One member claimed that, when they first met in 1978, "if anyone had mentioned forming a synagogue then, they would have been booed out of the room.
There was a strong sense among us of wanting no institution or organization."[68] Elden Rosenthal, part of the group of young professionals who founded
Havurah Shalom, recalled a sense that a "liberal alternative" was needed:
"There were the three big synagogues. And it hadn't changed in decades; it
hadn't changed since World War I."[69] Although antiestablishment attitudes
were fairly typical of the *havurah* (fellowship) movement—a growing national
movement at the time—the huge response almost immediately made Havurah
Shalom larger than the norm. One hundred fifty people showed up at their first
High Holiday services, and by 1981, 150 children were attending their Shabbat
school.[70] A profile in the *Oregonian* in 1989 emphasized that the congregation—
at that point still without a building of its own—offered a "much more intimate
kind of fellowship" and that it "specifically and intentionally wanted to get away
from a hierarchical kind of institution." In addition, the group was emphatic
in its egalitarian ethos and welcoming policy for "straights and gays, Jews and
non-Jewish partners."[71] It was this commitment that led the group to gravitate
toward Reconstructionism. President Carol Chestler explained in 1997 that
the vote to affiliate was "nearly unanimous" and cited "the Reconstructionist
movement's emphasis on egalitarianism" and "less formal structure" as moti-
vating factors.[72] The year before, they had moved into a renovated warehouse
in Northwest Portland. Given their original anti-institutional impulse, ironically, the congregation was the third largest in Portland by 2010.

Not surprisingly, one alternative congregation was not enough to satisfy
the quickly growing and notably progressive Portland community. Havurah
Shalom was joined in Portland by the Eastside Kehilla (founded, quite
emphatically as we have seen, not as a congregation but as a *community*,
1992), Kol Shalom (Humanistic, 1993), P'nai Or (Renewal, 1995), and Shir
Tikvah (independent/progressive, 2002), as well as by smaller groups without
fixed locations. Beyond Portland, Temple Beth Sholom in Salem and Temple
Beth Israel in Eugene—each at the time the only congregation in its city—both
affiliated with the Reconstructionist movement during the 1990s. Or haGan,
a small, independent congregation founded in Eugene in 2004, combined
Conservative and Renewal traditions. Beit Am, in Corvallis, another unaffiliated synagogue, describes itself as "inclusive" and "egalitarian." When they

hired their first rabbi in 2006, the congregation selected Rabbi Benjamin Barnett, a Reconstructionist.[73] "Inclusive" and "egalitarian" were descriptors that also appeared on the web pages of congregations and *havurot* in Bend, Coos Bay, Klamath Falls, and Ashland.

Even on the smaller, Orthodox end of the spectrum, the emphasis was also on exploration and outreach. For example, in the early 1990s, a group broke away from the (then) Conservative Temple Beth Israel in Eugene to form a new Orthodox congregation—the first to be founded in the state since the 1910s. Although there were other issues involved,[74] at the core of the split was an emerging interest among this faction in exploring traditional ritual, including the use of a *mechitza* (divider) to separate male and female worshipers. Meeting initially in a room within Beth Israel, and ultimately moving across the street to a house during a rather acrimonious split, this group began calling itself the Halachic Minyan and recruited an Orthodox rabbi in 1994. It later changed its name to Ahavas Torah. Sociologist Phil Zuckerman, who studied the split in the Eugene synagogue, grounds the growing interest among the breakaway group in immersing themselves in Orthodox Judaism in their increasing alienation as Beth Israel moved from Conservative Judaism and toward Reconstructionism. Beginning with the discomfort of some congregants with Rabbi Kinberg's increasingly progressive stance on issues ranging from gay rights to Israeli politics, as well as his move to shift the liturgy in Reconstructionist directions, this group gradually began to study and practice Orthodox Judaism.[75]

The greatest energy in the state in terms of fostering exploration of traditional practice came from Chabad.[76] Beginning in 1984, with the arrival of Rabbi Moshe Wilhelm to Portland, the Chabad presence in the state grew under his guidance to nine houses, including six in the Portland metropolitan area and one each in Salem, Ashland, and Bend. Chabad emphasizes spirituality and personal outreach, and has a practice of sending young rabbis and their families to peripheral and unlikely communities, where they operate houses or centers rather than formal synagogues. In Oregon, as elsewhere, Chabad tends to stand apart from the rest of the community, including the Orthodox community; as Arden Shenker explained in a 2007 oral history, "Chabad has not affiliated with the Jewish communal organizational apparatus in Oregon. . . . The rabbis of Chabad do not participate in the Oregon Board of Rabbis. Chabad did not participate with the Jewish Educational Association. It had a separate approach to its development and organization."[77] Initially, Chabad's public outreach efforts—such as its annual lighting of a giant Chanukah menorah in Pioneer Courthouse Square—were controversial in Oregon, as they were in Jewish communities across the nation. Over time, feelings have mellowed. As longtime Federation leader Henry Blauer mused in a 2008 interview, "Chabad people are doing an awful lot of outreach and it doesn't matter really what

Rabbi Moshe Wilhelm lights the Chanukah menorah in front of the Aleph Bet School. Courtesy OJMCHE

flavor of Judaism they sell as long as they are selling Judaism and keeping our children and grandchildren and great-grandchildren 'in the fold.'"[78] In a growing number of Oregon cities and towns, Chabad rabbis provide an opportunity for Jews—many with limited Jewish education and experience—to explore, connect, or reconnect with Jewish traditions.

Even with the addition of the Orthodox congregation in Eugene and the expanding Chabad presence, the affiliation choices of Jewish Oregonians tend firmly toward the progressive/liberal end of the Jewish spectrum, and set them apart from Jews in other regions. Rabbi Geller (by then retired from Shaarie Torah) noted both the extraordinary growth and the shift to the left when he observed, about the Oregon Board of Rabbis in 2006, "It has become very left wing. I don't know how many rabbis we've got now! Eighteen rabbis! I don't know what they know. I don't know where they stand. I know the majority of them are way out in left field."[79] Geller's impression of the direction of the shift is confirmed in studies, showing that Oregon's affiliation patterns deviate from national norms. A national study in 2006 found that the vast majority of synagogue members in the United States were affiliated with one of the three main streams of American Jewry, Reform (38 percent), Conservative (33 percent), or Orthodox (21 percent). Fewer than 10 percent of religiously affiliated American Jews belonged to a congregation not in one of those three movements: Reconstructionist (3 percent) and other (5 percent).[80] In contrast, in the 2009 Portland survey, among those who attended (or had a family member who attended) services, the Reconstructionist congregation Havurah Shalom had the third largest percentage of attendees (12.5 percent), after Neveh Shalom (Conservative, 24.5 percent) and Beth Israel (Reform, 21 percent). Fewer than 10 percent of those reporting participation in religious services indicated that they attended any of the congregations at the Orthodox/traditional end of the spectrum: Kesser Israel (Orthodox), Shaarie Torah (at that point still "traditional"), Ahavath Achim (traditional Sephardic), or one of the Chabad centers. Nearly as many named a congregation identifying itself as humanistic, renewal, egalitarian, or liberal.[81] It is not surprising therefore, that in a 2001 census of synagogues, the Portland metro area (in this case including Salem), stood out for having two Reconstructionist synagogues. Of the thirty-four American Jewish communities with populations between ten and one hundred thousand, Portland was one of only two that had more than one Reconstructionist congregation.[82] For the state as a whole, there were as many Reconstructionist as Reform congregations (three of each), and three additional renewal/humanistic/egalitarian congregations.[83]

National Affiliation—2006

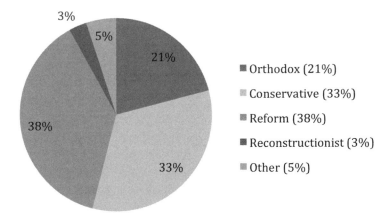

Portland Affiliation—2009

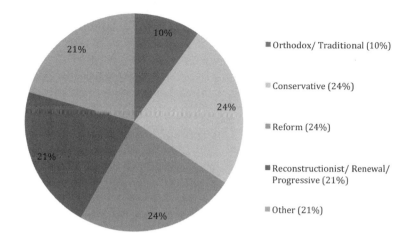

- Orthodox/ Traditional (10%)
- Conservative (24%)
- Reform (24%)
- Reconstructionist/ Renewal/ Progressive (21%)
- Other (21%)

As Richard Matza explained in a 2013 oral history, "We have everything here now. It was not like that when I was a kid. There were very defined segments of the community: Reformed [sic], Conservative, Orthodox, and Sephardic. And that was it. You know where you belonged. . . . Now it is all kinds of flavors."[84]

Beyond the synagogues, increasing numbers of Jewish Oregonians in the late 1990s and early 2000s began to connect religiously through nontraditional organizations. An excellent example is Gesher, founded in 1990, a Portland-based outreach organization established by Rabbi Gary Schoenberg and Rabbi Laurie Rutenberg, a married couple, aiming specifically to reach out to "Jews without memory and Jews on the move," by welcoming participants into their home and family, rather than by establishing a synagogue.[85] By 1999, Schoenberg and Rutenberg were being hailed nationally, listed in the *Forward* among the "top 50 Jewish leaders to watch in the years ahead." Gesher was held up as "a prototype for other such efforts around the country;" in ten years, over 6,500 unaffiliated Jews had participated in their Shabbat or holiday meals.[86] In 2002, Gesher's model was adopted by Shaarie Torah and Neveh Shalom, as both were awarded a grant by a national foundation to "encourage congregants . . . to start sharing Shabbat dinner experiences in each other's homes." The idea, inspired by Gesher, was to "create a growing circle of shared Jewish home life."[87]

A more singles-oriented religious outreach effort was founded by Jodi Berris of Portland Jewish Events. A self-described "super religious, yet super party girl," Berris set out to provide a noncongregational Shabbat outlet for

Gesher Rabbis Gary Schoenberg and Laurie Rutenberg leading an experiential Passover program. Courtesy OJMCHE

unaffiliated young adults. The first 1-800-Shabbat, in July 2005, started with Shabbat services, followed by hosted dinners for smaller groups of four to eight participants. After dinner, the group reconvened at Berris's house for a "cocktail and dessert party for all participants that featured kosher jello shots, among other yummy treats and drinks." The event drew seventy-six participants. By 2009, ten 1-800-Shabbat events had been held, and the group also offered a series of "MoDox [Modern Orthodox] Outdoor Adventure Shabbaton" weekends, along with its more purely social offerings, such as jBN (Jewish Bar Night).[88]

Outreach efforts such as 1-800-Shabbat and Gesher seem tailor-made for an area with a rapidly growing population of unaffiliated young Jews, including many who are disenchanted by, or unfamiliar with, traditional congregational life. They embody the Northwest style characterizing the "None Zone." As scholars Patricia O'Connell Killen and Mark Silk explain, the region's

low levels of religious "adherence," (i.e., affiliation with an organized religious community), coupled with the lack of a dominant denomination, render religious identity, commitment, and long-term belonging within a religious organization an ongoing problem. . . . Everyone who comes into the region must negotiate his or her own religious identity, because the meaning and style of religious belonging changes in a context where commitment, experimentation and indifference are equal.[89]

Local survey data demonstrates that this description is apt for the Jewish community—the 2009 survey found that nearly two-thirds of all Jews in the Portland metropolitan area "are in a different religious stream today compared to when they were growing up," a figure roughly double that in national polls.[90] The intense and personal brand of spirituality offered by groups like Gesher is an excellent fit for such a zone of experimentation; as Killen and Silk explain, "religious institutions that offer intense emotional and physical experiences of the divine" have been particularly successful.[91] Gesher's targeting of interfaith couples is also well-suited to the local scene. As we have seen, high intermarriage rates also contribute to the broader affiliation patterns in the region—like the Reform movement, Reconstruction, Renewal, Humanistic and other varieties of progressive Judaism are emphatic in their outreach to interfaith families and recognize patrilineal descent.

These movements' posture toward the welcoming of gay and lesbian Jews is also clearly a factor in their success in the region. Although there is no reason to assume that there is a significantly larger number of gay and lesbian Jews in the region than elsewhere (or, at least, than in other progressive cities that are home to substantial Jewish and LGBTQ communities), the strong presence of the Oregon Citizens Alliance (OCA) and its active use of the Oregon ballot made gay rights a prominent public issue beginning in the late 1980s, forcing Jews, and all Oregonians, to examine their positions on the issue. By the early 1990s, all the major congregations and Jewish organizations in Oregon had joined the fight against the OCA, participating in rallies, publishing statements in the state's *Voter's Pamphlet*, and otherwise actively taking part in the campaign to stop the various OCA-sponsored measures.[92] It is likely that the high profile of the public debate in the state, combined with the emphatically pro-gay rights stance taken by the community in the public arena, led to the early adoption of welcoming policies among the region's congregations and increased the affinity for movements like Reconstructionism and Renewal, which were early to take such positions.[93]

Therefore, it is clearly not coincidental that Havurah Shalom, the most emphatically welcoming congregation in Portland in the early 1990s, opted to affiliate with the Reconstructionist movement. Even before that formal affiliation took place, the congregation participated in Portland's Gay and Lesbian Pride Parade and dedicating the Shabbat service during Pride Week to that issue.[94] Renewal congregations such as Ashland's Havurah Shir Hadash were similarly apt to highlight welcoming messages; that congregation's Facebook page describes the group as "a Jewish Renewal community—an extended family of Jews by birth and by choice and friends from many different spiritual paths joining to infuse our lives with Torah & G-d. We are proud to be a LGBTQ Safe Zone."[95] And, despite the Conservative movement's stance on same-sex marriage, Portland's Neveh Shalom was early to initiate outreach efforts to the LGBTQ community. Holly Hart, local restauranteur, lesbian activist, and Neveh Shalom congregant, explained in a 1992 interview, "It's very gratifying to me that Neveh Shalom has done the outreach they're doing . . . . It caused me to enroll my daughter in Hebrew school there, and to opt for a more traditional Jewish education than I probably would have chosen otherwise."[96]

When Multnomah County began issuing same-sex marriage licenses for a brief period in 2004, Rabbi Ariel Stone-Halpern of Shir Tikvah, her (then) husband Rabbi Larry Halpern of the South Metro Jewish Community, and Rabbi Joey Wolf of Havurah all presided over weddings; in addition, Rabbi Kim Rosen (assistant rabbi at Beth Israel) and Rabbi Aryeh Hirschfield of P'nai Or indicated a willingness to do so. Among those married by Stone-Halpern on the first day of same-sex marriages in Multnomah County were Rivka and Lauren Gevurtz, renewing vows that they had made to one another before it was possible to get legal recognition. The front page of the *Jewish Review* featured both a story on local rabbis' participation in the wave of marriages taking place as the first licenses were issued, and a profile of the Gevurtzes, emphasizing the many legal benefits of marriage for the couple and for their daughter, a kindergartener at Portland Jewish Academy.[97] Rabbi Daniel Isaak of Neveh Shalom, according to the article, was still wrestling with the issue, as was the Conservative movement to which he belonged. The following month he announced a four-session seminar to study "Jewish views of homosexuality" at the synagogue, and by the summer of 2007, the congregation announced that it would "perform and recognize same-sex commitment ceremonies." As Isaak explained,

> We will allow such couples to receive a blessing at services as we do heterosexual couples and will congratulate such couples in our *Chronicle* [newsletter]. . . . This is an end of a process that started here a long time ago. We have had gay individuals and gay families who have been members as families for some time. We've had a gay and lesbian outreach group. We participated in the gay pride parade a few years ago. And we have long been listed as one of Portland's Welcoming Congregations.[98]

Rabbi Isaak would later officiate at the wedding of his own son, Misha Isaak and his partner.[99]

The Jewish community was not unanimous in its stance on the inclusion of members of the LGBTQ community—Rabbi David Rosenberg of Shaarie Torah and Rabbi Oppenheimer of Kesser Israel indicated at the time of these first legal same-sex marriages that they would not preside at such ceremonies (although the latter indicated an openness to same-sex civil unions). Still, these congregations made efforts to present themselves as welcoming. When Rabbi Steven Greenberg, the "first openly gay Orthodox rabbi," was invited to speak at the Judaic studies programs at Portland State University and University of Oregon, as well as at Neveh Shalom, in 2007, Kesser Israel Rabbi Kenneth Brodkin was emphatic about welcoming his colleague: "Our community has welcomed all Jews with open arms, including Rabbi Greenberg. . . . Kesser Israel, which we call 'the Orthodox Synagogue for All Jews' is a community which champions acceptance of all Jews. That is not just a slogan but a reality at Kesser which is acknowledged and appreciated by our members and guests."[100]

As with outreach to other key demographics, such as young adults and interfaith families, welcoming efforts went well beyond the congregations. For example, in the Portland area, JFCS organized a monthly LGBT potluck, called Keshet (rainbow), beginning in 2002. A feature story on Keshet's one-year anniversary in 2003 included a picture of Neveh Shalom's Rabbi Isaak presiding over a mezuzah hanging ceremony in the new home of a gay couple; along with Federation sponsorship (through JFCS, a Federation agency), this clearly communicated a message of inclusion of gays and lesbians in the mainstream community. At the same time, the article acknowledged that Keshet provided "needed connections and support" in a community where some still felt "a subtle feeling of not belonging."[101] Steering committee member Laney Kibel emphasized in a 2004 interview that "Portland is lucky to have a lot of gay-friendly congregations."[102] Nehirim, a national organization founded in 2004 and focusing on LGBTQ Jewish engagement, hired Rabbi Debra Kolodny, of Portland's P'nai Or, as executive director in 2013. While serving P'nai Or, Kolodny, a Renewal rabbi, codirected two Nehirim retreats and served on the national board. Working with Kolodny at Nehirim was Portlander Rivka Gevurtz, who serves as that organization's director of finance and administration.[103]

Spirituality in the "None Zone"

Historians such as Jonathan Sarna have noted the "awakening" or "renewal" that began to take hold in the American Jewish community in the final decades of the twentieth century. Sarna, who titles the final chapter of his tome, *American Judaism: A History*, "Renewal," explains that "the *havurah* movement and *The Jewish Catalog* anticipated and spurred" a shift toward more emphasis on "intimacy and worship in family-like settings" and a breaking down of the earlier focus on "decorum and solemnity."[104] As services became less performative and more engaging, there was a renewed emphasis on spirituality and a more personal religious experience that influenced many American Jews, across the spectrum of observance. Sarna explains,

> The renewal of traditional spiritual practices . . . owed a much greater debt to charismatic figures, several of the Holocaust refugees with ties to the Lubavitch movement, who ministered to Jewish religious seekers and became, in the process, Jewish spiritual revivalists whose influence spread from the counterculture to the mainstream. Taking advantage of a newfound interest in spiritual teachings, brought about by the emergence in America of Eastern religions like Buddhism, these "Jewish gurus" focused on music, meditation, and the power of prayer. They attracted legions of followers and paved the way for a full-scale renewal of Jewish spirituality across the spectrum of Jewish religious life.[105]

In tracing these shifts, Sarna points specifically to two influential rabbis, Shlomo Carlebach, "known as the Dancing Rabbi, the Singing Rabbi, and even the Hippie Rabbi," and Zalman Schachter-Shalomi, known as Reb Zalman. Through their students, the two rabbis' teachings and the Renewal movement in which they played central roles would have a particularly strong impact on Jewish spiritual life in Oregon.

Although Sarna uses the terms "renewal" and "awakening" to refer to a broad range of trends—from the expansion of Jewish cultural life in the form of film festivals and the founding of Jewish studies programs to indications of increased personal ritual practices—"Renewal" is also the name of a late twentieth-century movement within Judaism that places particular emphasis on spirituality and blends a personal religious experience with an embracing of full gender equality; a welcoming posture to the marginalized; a commitment to social justice and environmentalism; an openness to learning from other, particularly Eastern, spiritual traditions; and an embodied, kinetic ritual that includes chant, dance, and meditation.[106] Both through incorporation of Renewal teachings and practices in congregations affiliated with one of the mainstream movements or Reconstructionism, and through congregational decisions to affiliate with the new movement, Renewal's resonance in Oregon is striking. As a *Jewish Review* "Special Report on Oregon's Outlying Jewish Communities" observed in 1991, Eugene emerged as "one of the major West Coast magnets for ultra-progressive Jewish thought and life . . . [and was] widely considered a Northwest locus of the 'Jewish Renewal Movement.'"[107] Reb Zalman himself recognized Jewish Oregonians' embrace of Renewal: "I have a feel for it and they have a feeling for Jewish Renewal. What is it with Oregon and me that so many have felt they should study with me?" Until the year before his death in 2014 at age eighty-nine, Reb Zalman came to Ashland every year for a Shabbat retreat of "ecstatic music, deep learning, and prayer."[108]

Reb Zalman Schachter-Shalomi receiving blessings at Havurah Shir Hadash in Ashland, several months before his passing in 2014. Credit: Jim Young

That Oregon has proven fertile ground for a movement like Renewal is not surprising. The region is not notable just for its low level of formal religious affiliation, but also for the relatively large number of residents who, regardless of religious affiliation (or absence of affiliation) consider themselves "spiritual."[109] Religious sociologist Mark Shibley argues that "because Northwesterners are less tied to traditional religion, they are freer to explore alternative spirituality," and, while "institutionally unencumbered," they are not "a-spiritual."[110] Many who are "secular but spiritual" are attracted to either "New Age spirituality" or "earth-centered spirituality," both of which have a particularly strong presence in the region.[111] These forms of spirituality are outgrowths of the local countercultural influence, and have, in turn, influenced mainstream religions, including Judaism. As the Gesher example suggests, the Jewish communities of Oregon not only reflect the generally low affiliation rates of the region, but they also have incorporated—and used as outreach tools—many of the aspects of spirituality that have become so characteristic of the Pacific Northwest.

Given its association with the counterculture, it's not surprising that Eugene has played a central role in bringing Renewal Judaism to the region, driven by Yitzhak Husbands-Hankin and Aryeh Hirschfield (universally called "Yitz" and "Aryeh," respectively). Accomplished musicians, both came to Eugene in the 1970s and met at Temple Beth Israel. The two soon became close friends, connecting through music and Torah study. Their charisma and music drew others, and, before long, they were sharing a house in Eugene that quickly turned into a sort of commune for "quasi-Orthodox Jewish hippies." Dozens gathered for Friday night dinners and remained to sing into the evening.[112] A core group became involved at Beth Israel, then still a Conservative congregation. When Beth Israel Rabbi Louis Neimand died in 1976 after thirteen years of service, Aryeh and Yitz stepped up to provide spiritual leadership until a new rabbi could be hired. As Irwin Noparstak, a psychiatrist who arrived in Eugene in 1971 and became director of the White Bird Clinic, recalled, after Rabbi Neimand's death,

> I had heard that these two men were conducting services at Temple Beth Israel and it was an experience that I needed to experience. So I went and here were these two hippies leading the service—well, I called them Jewish Jesus freaks. I mean, they had the same energy as what I imagined Jesus freaks have—and they both were cloaked in my grandfather's *tallit*. And I sat there crying. . . . I was so amazed at what they were, what they were doing and that this was Jewish. Intellectually it didn't click in my brain that these very modern men were taking my grandpa—this *tallit*—and making something vital and alive and current about Judaism.[113]

Not everyone responded in this way. For some of the more conservative members, the Renewal style that was embraced at Beth Israel was off-putting. Nathan Fendrich objected strongly to what he called "counterculture" tendencies, explaining in a 2009 interview, "I want a guy who believes in more than just saying 'let's pray for peace' and strum a guitar and sing."[114] When Rabbi Myron Kinberg—who was quite open to innovation and would gradually gravitate toward Reconstructionism—was hired, Yitz continued serving Beth Israel, first as cantor and, later, as assistant rabbi, providing a regular, alternative Renewal service for those interested. During the early 1980s, both Yitz and Aryeh also led services on a monthly basis at Salem's Temple Beth Sholom, which did not have a rabbi or cantor of its own.

By this time, both Yitz and Aryeh were gravitating toward the emerging Renewal movement. Through musical circles, Yitz met Rabbi Shlomo Carlebach who later performed the ceremony when Yitz married Shonna Husbands. Soon, Yitz (now Husbands-Hankin) was studying with Carlebach, from whom he received his *smicha* (ordination) as a cantor in 1984. Aryeh and Yitz were, shortly thereafter, both ordained as rabbis by Reb Zalman, in 1985 and 1987, respectively. After Rabbi Kinberg's departure in the wake of the split at Beth Israel, Rabbi Yitz was hired as the spiritual leader of what was, by this time, an emerging Reconstructionist congregation. Meanwhile, Rabbi Aryeh became the founding rabbi at Ashland's Havurah Shir Hadash in 1985. When he left the Ashland congregation ten years later, the Renewal tradition would be continued by his successor, Rabbi David Zaslow, who also received

Rabbi Aryeh Hirschfield, 2009. Hirschfield was the founding rabbi of Ashland's Havurah Shir Hadash in 1985 and of Portland's P'nai Or in 1995. Courtesy OJMCHE

his ordination from Reb Zalman and was mentored by Rabbi Aryeh.[115] Rabbi Zaslow, in turn, spread Renewal teachings to Bend by serving as visiting rabbi, leading services six to eight times a year at the Jewish Community of Central Oregon (later named Congregation Shalom Bayit).[116] When that congregation hired its own rabbi in 2000, they selected Rabbi Jay Shupack, also ordained by Reb Zalman.[117] By 2002, Jean Zimmerman, longtime lay leader of the small Klamath Falls congregation, was seeking training through the Renewal movement's rabbinic pastor program.[118]

Rabbi Aryeh was also responsible for bringing Renewal to Portland. He was invited to lead a workshop at Gesher in 1991. Several of the participants were so inspired by his teachings that they continued to meet together for months afterward, and ultimately invited him to lead monthly services for an emerging group in Portland. That group, initially meeting in private homes, grew from just over a dozen participants to thirty to forty within a year. Soon Rabbi Aryeh was teaching a Thursday evening adult education class in addition to leading Friday night and Saturday morning services during his monthly visits to Portland. By 1994, they were renting larger spaces in the community for their services, and, in 1995, they brought Rabbi Aryeh to Portland full time as the founding rabbi of the new Renewal congregation P'nai Or.[119] Clearly, by the turn of the century, Oregon had become a center for Renewal: of fourteen Renewal congregations counted nationally in the 2001 census of synagogues, two were in Oregon—a striking number given that only 0.2 percent of all synagogues in the country are located in the state.[120] In addition, this figure counts neither Bend's Shalom Bayit, which has had a strong Renewal influence but is not formally affiliated, nor Eugene's Beth Israel, which, while led by Rabbi Husbands-Hankin, was officially affiliated with the Reconstructionist movement. In a 2013 interview, Reb Zalman noted that he had ordained eight of the state's thirty rabbis.[121] Since 2002, Portland Rabbi Debra Kolodny has served as executive director of ALEPH: Alliance for Jewish Renewal.[122]

There were several further Renewal connections in Eugene. As we have seen, Libby Bottero, of the Eugene mikvah, lived in Carlebach's San Francisco House of Love and Prayer in the late 1960s and studied with both Rabbi Carlebach and Reb Zalman. A 1991 story in the *Jewish Review* noted that Rabbi Hanan Sills who, starting in 1985 served for ten years as the founding rabbi of the University of Oregon Hillel, was also closely tied to the Renewal movement. Sills, described as a "genuinely mystical searcher," lived on a mountaintop in California with no running water or electricity while serving as a circuit rabbi in the Mendocino area. He visited people "in the communes and small towns like a country doctor, dispensing just the right dose of Judaism in each home." After leaving University of Oregon, Sills remained in Eugene, running a "synagogue without walls," which he described as "an inreach" program, designed to bring "the spirit of Jewish wellness' into homes."[123] It continues to offer High Holiday services described as "liberal, renewal, and inclusive in orientation" and drawing "from traditional and mystical sources."[124] Finally, Jonathan Seidel, a longtime Eugene resident who served at various times as adjunct professor of Judaic studies at UO and other Oregon universities, UO Hillel board member, prayer leader, and assistant rabbi at Eugene's Temple Beth Israel (2001–2003), received his ordination as a Renewal rabbi in 2004. Seidel, whose "spiritual journey was radically altered after meeting Rabbis Shlomo Carlebach and Zalman Schachter-Shalomi," became the founding rabbi of Or haGan in Eugene in 2004. The congregation, meeting at Eugene's Center for Spiritual Living, blended Conservative and Renewal teachings.[125]

Beyond these direct ties with Renewal Judaism, its approach—the emphasis on the spiritual and meditation, the embrace of both Eastern and Hasidic influences—clearly resonated more broadly in the community and was a key influence on a variety of institutions. As Rabbi Rose explained in the 2005 documentary *The Three Rabbis*, "There's sort of been a freeing up that is reflected in the Jewish community. . . . People who want to do things in a certain way, they don't necessarily want to be guided by the existing institutions, and therefore they create their own." Such institutions, Rabbi Stampfer concurred, demonstrate a new vitality: "I welcome it! I think it's a wonderful addition to the community in terms of the breadth and expanse of Jewish life."[126]

Such new options include a range, from formal institutions to grassroots efforts. In Portland, psychotherapist and student of Buddhist meditation Abby Layton founded Or Hadash (New Light) to "teach Jewish meditation and spirituality" in 2003. She would later be ordained as a Buddhist and become a teacher at the Mount Adams Zen Buddhist Temple.[127] Similarly, in 2006, Rabbi Kim Rosen, who had earlier served as assistant and associate rabbi at Portland's Beth Israel, opened Beit Midrash Eitz Chaim, a house of study "designed to meet the diverse religious, spiritual, educational and social needs of the Jewish community," with offerings that included courses and "one-on-one Jewish Spiritual Guidance sessions."[128] In Portland, the independent, progressive Shir Tikvah's rabbi, Ariel Stone, ordained as a Reform rabbi, is also a scholar of Jewish mysticism.[129] Likewise, the short-lived Eastside Kehillah Hadashah congregation (founded 2011), led by Reconstructionist-trained Rabbi David Kominsky, "reflect[ed] its inner eastside surroundings, with a focus on welcoming non-Jewish spouses and partners, and on those who blend Judaism with other teachings, like Buddhism and meditation."[130] Portland's Kollel (a national outreach group affiliated with the Orthodox Union's youth movement, NCSY), ran a series of seminars in the fall of 2006 that included speakers Roy and Leah Neuberger, who "explored Buddhism and Hinduism until they found their way back to their Jewish roots," and author Sara Rigler, whose "spiritual journey took her through India and fifteen years of teaching Vedanta philosophy and meditation," before her embrace of Torah Judaism.[131] After resigning from P'nai Or to lead Nehirim, Rabbi Kolodny announced that she would remain in Portland, leading "monthly mystical Torah study classes. . . . Rosh Chodesh groups . . . and LGBTQ Jewish gatherings," as well as partnering with a Sufi guide and two pastors to lead a bi-weekly gathering called "Bosom of Abraham, Rocking Our Sufi, Jewish and Christian Souls."[132] In Eugene, a Shabbat Chant Circle led by Lisa Kaye began to meet regularly in approximately 2009, affiliated with a broader network of "spiritually progressive" seekers in Eugene.[133]

Even within mainstream congregations, the influence of what some called "New Age Judaism" was apparent. For example, when the short-lived Orthodox Vermont Street Shul brought Rabbi Zecharya Tzvi Goldman to Portland to lead the congregation in 2004, he expressed optimism that he would "fit in well with Portland's political and environmental mindsets," noting "I am empathic [sic] to the political left and I have a background in ecology and alternative health and an appreciation of other spiritual traditions."[134] Likewise, Rabbi Joey Wolf of Havurah Shalom welcomed the new traditions of meditation and chanting to practice at that synagogue.[135] Even Neveh Shalom, then the only Conservative congregation in the state, announced in late 2004 that it was "opening the door to Jewish spirituality," by sending community leaders to retreats offered by the Institute for Jewish Spirituality, and introduced a variety of new elements to congregational practice. Cantor Linda Shivers began to include meditation as part of the Friday night service and, teens were offered the option of "yoga in lieu of attending regular Wednesday night services" before classes. As an article about the innovations explained, students could participate in "a kind of Jewish yoga in which the students are encouraged to focus on Jewish concepts while holding yoga poses and controlling their breathing and trying to stay emotionally or spiritually centered in the custom of yoga practice." Seventh-grade students were also encouraged to experiment "with meditation and different forms of praying."[136] In 2007, the congregation held a Shabbaton (weekend retreat) featuring Reconstructionist Rabbi Sheila Weinberg from the Institute for Jewish Spirituality. Titled "Healing the Heart, Healing the World, The Role of Meditation in Tikkun Olam," the weekend focused on Rabbi Weinberg's teachings on mindfulness and meditation practices.[137] By that point, both Rabbi Daniel Isaak and Cantor Linda Shivers were graduates of the institute's training course, which Rabbi Weinberg described as aiming to balance the "left-brain intellectual knowledge" emphasized in rabbinic training with "right brain, training the hearts and minds of rabbis and others looking for the pathways of meaning in their lives."[138] As the connection with the Institute for Spirituality suggests, this was part of a national trend—the institute runs retreats on both the West and East coasts; in addition, by the early twenty-first century, this type of spiritual training had been incorporated as an elective at mainstream rabbinical schools and was particularly popular at the Reconstructionist Rabbinical Seminary, where 75 percent of students chose this option. Yet it is clear that, in Oregon, where secular aspects of the counterculture, Reconstructionism, and Jewish Renewal all have had a strong presence, such movements found particularly fertile ground.

Blue, White ... and Green

Portland has become strongly associated with a particularly vigorous brand of environmentalism and sustainability. Carrie Brownstein and Fred Armisen's television series *Portlandia* makes this painfully clear in episodes exploring life in tiny houses, the challenges of verifying that a chicken featured as an entrée in a local restaurant was raised humanely, and the shaming of a man who has forgotten to bring his reusable bags to the grocery store. Since the days of Governor Tom McCall and the bottle bill, Oregon has developed a green reputation, despite strong countervailing forces in a state where economic development is often pitted against environmental policies. Although many Jewish communities across the country have taken up environmental causes as part of their embrace of *tikkun olam* (repairing or healing the world) in recent years, the incorporation of this cause into Oregon Jewish life is particularly strong, reflecting the local ethos. Just as the region's "New Age spiritualities" resonated with the emerging Renewal and other transdenominational Jewish influences in the region, the Pacific Northwest's "earth-centered spirituality" has also had a major impact on local expressions of Jewish community and identity.[139] Sustainability-themed Jewish programming has also become an important outreach tool, particularly for connecting with unaffiliated young people.

Although there certainly were many individuals with environmentalist proclivities and some community activity in this area earlier, green programming and an ethos of sustainability as a part of communal *tikkun olam* became prominent at the turn of the twenty-first century. Arden Shenker, a prominent Portland attorney whose practice had a strong focus on environmental law and who was a prominent leader of the National Jewish Community Relations Advisory Committee (NJCRAC), played a key role in bringing environmental causes onto the agenda of both national and local Jewish advocacy groups. When he served as NJCRAC chair, he found resistance to what some in the group called "Save the Whales" causes. In response, he worked to develop an "alternative mechanism for looking at Jewish interests in the environment." Shenker became the "godfather" of the Coalition on the Environment and Jewish Life (COEJL), a group that was founded in the early 1990s under the administrative umbrella of NJCRAC. He served as the group's founding vice chair, and later as its chair.[140] However, it was not yet a local, central communal cause; until the late 1990s, environmentalist activity was rarely mentioned in the *Jewish Review*. Within a few years, it became a major focus in many congregations and other organizations, and especially in the groups organized by or targeting young adults.

In November 1999, the Seattle-based Northwest Jewish Environmental Project (NJEP, a regional affiliate of COEJL), aiming to cast environmentalism as a Jewish issue, held its first Portland-based meeting. Thirty people came.[141] Three months later, the NJEP had opened a Portland office and was moving ahead with its agenda of teaching a "Jewish perspective on the environment" and providing opportunities for action. Soon, it was engaged in city- and statewide Earth Day celebrations and working with the Federation's Community Relations Council (CRC) to develop hands-on projects.[142] Very quickly, the broader Jewish community embraced the NJEP. In November 2000, the group took out a full-page ad in the *Review*, showcasing the "Northwest Rabbinical Statement on the Environment," signed by all the Oregon congregational rabbis and including an explanation of environmentalism as a Jewish value.[143] The community adopted a project called "Our

River, Our Future—*Mayim Chaim*: Living Waters." Sponsored by the CRC, NJEP, Shomrei Adamah Northwest (Guardians of the Land), and the Oregon Board of Rabbis, it focused on a campaign to "heal our river." Rabbi Stampfer keynoted the launch of the campaign, and Multnomah County commissioner Bev Stein explained that she was "honored to participate in this effort toward Tikkun Olam, repair of the world."[144] By June 2001, the NJEP had moved its main office from Seattle to Portland and was planning a workshop on global warming, a camping trip, lectures, an environmentally focused mission to Israel, and a ceremony with local Native Americans in conjunction with the river project. There was a "natural fit" between Judaism and conservation, the *Review* explained as it reported on the emerging agenda.[145]

Very quickly, environmental activism became a central communal cause, integrated into holiday events, congregational activities, and, increasingly, outreach efforts. In 2001, Tu B'Shvat, the holiday celebrating the first blossoming of trees in the spring, was marked with a tree planting and ecotour linked to the Our River, Our Future campaign. The following year, the MJCC and NJEP issued a challenge to sukkah builders, encouraging them to build an "eco-sukkah" either at home or on the MJCC campus. Eco-sukkahs would be judged based on "creativity, instructional message regarding the environment, and aesthetics."[146] Sustainability also was embraced in communal educational programs; Congregation Neveh Shalom dedicated the David A. Bernstein Library of Jewish Environmental Studies.[147]

By 2002, there was a torrent of stories in the *Jewish Review*, and it was clear that Portland's Jewish community had emerged as a national leader. The environmental mission to Israel, a ten-day trip sponsored by NJEP and the Jewish Federation of Portland, was touted by CRC director Bob Horenstein as "unprecedented;" he claimed, "No national Jewish organization has done this before." On Earth Day 2002, so many congregations and other Jewish organizations took part that environmental issues were divided up among them; each would "become the expert in their chosen field" and "develop an interactive project to educate people about the issue," as well as linking the issue to Jewish tradition and practice. It was suggested, "a look at water will include the uses of water in Jewish ritual, as well as rivers and drinking water." Other initiatives included CRC lobbying efforts on environmental issues and education about "eco-kashrut." As NJEP director Sandi Scheinberg explained, "Eating organically grown food that is not genetically altered and is picked by workers who are paid well is all part of ethical eating."[148]

The communal activity around environmental issues continued and expanded over the following decade, with programs including tree planting by Portland Jewish Academy schoolchildren, advocacy campaigns focused on issues like global warming, b'nai mitzvah service projects taking on environmental causes, educational programs tackling issues such as reducing one's carbon footprint, and congregations engaging in hands-on forest restoration projects. By the fall of 2002, under the directorship of Rivka Gevurtz, NJEP continued its lead role in these projects, as well as sponsoring an annual Shabbat in the Woods program designed to teach about "Jewish perspectives on the environment, ancient forest ecology, and current management practices on public lands," while modeling sustainable eco-kashrut practices. Rabbis admonished congregants that global warming was "a great moral issue," and the NJEP urged area Jews to join a Passover energy conservation drive to "remove the *chametz* (leavening) of energy consumption from our lives" and to "end idle worship on Sukkot" by turning off car engines rather than idling when stopped. When the NJEP sponsored a national Jewish environmental conference in 2003, the executive director of the national Coalition on the Environment and Jewish Life noted the leadership of the region, remarking on "Portland's unique tradition of upholding strong environmental values."[149]

As NJEP's emphasis on "eco-kosher" practices suggests—and not surprisingly in a city becoming known as a center of food culture with a particular zeal for the farm to fork movement—the emphasis on the environment shaped sensibilities about Jewish eating. Northwest Kosher, a kosher food cooperative formed in 2004, and the *Review* ran the first of several articles about Jewish farmers in the area, such as Shari Raider of Sauvie Island Organics. The article stressed the link between sustainability and Jewish values, and Raider's farm was the site for "Blackberry Shabbat," which became a Havurah Shalom annual event. During this same period, the short-lived Orthodox Vermont Street Shul hired Rabbi Goldman, the founder of Earth-Kosher, which he explained was "the only kosher certification agency that exclusively certifies health food companies and alternative medicines that show deep regard for human health, the environment and fair trade."[150] The enthusiasm for local food and farming was also evident in a joint Moishe House-Kesser Israel project to "Grow an End to Hunger," through which participants cultivated "fresh produce on a small plot adjacent to Kesser and in their own yards," with the harvest donated to food banks. The project provided an opportunity to combine community gardening with *tikkun olam* and connect to "Jews' agrarian beginnings."[151] By 2009, congregations Havurah Shalom and Neveh Shalom were teaming up with the MJCC and Sauvie Island Organics to launch Tuv Ha'aretz, a program that combined Jewish learning with the popular concept of a CSA (community-supported agriculture—through which local organic farms sell "shares" directly to consumers who pay a set fee in exchange for a weekly box of produce during the farming season). Tuv Ha'aretz, a national initiative started by Hazon, emphasizing Jewish connections to sustainability, encouraged participants to explore "the relationship of food and Jewish tradition," and "plant the seeds for community supported agriculture, gleaning and family education in Portland."[152] Through the program, participants could be involved in the harvest and other programming at the farm, rather than just receiving weekly boxes.

The potential of environmentalism as a recruiting tool was not lost on community leaders. Northwest Jewish Environmental Project Director Scheinberg explained at the 2002 Earth Day festivities, "Many unaffiliated Jews care keenly about the environment and they will come to an event like this. It's a way for them to learn about the family in the Jewish community that is available to them."[153] Not surprisingly, a number of the Jewish organizations targeting unaffiliated and minimally affiliated young adults quickly embraced environmentalism and sustainability as entrees into Jewish involvement. Most striking was Beit Kayam or "House of Sustainability," a Jewish "eco-house" founded in 2008 by Oregon native Shoshanna Krall, a graduate of the Portland Machar program, as well as of several Jewish farming programs on the East Coast. Beit Kayam—with support from a Federation grant—built on the Moishe House concept, with a more focused environmental mission. During its three-year existence, three twenty-somethings resided in the house in the Eastside Eliot neighborhood, with the goal of drawing Jewish young adults into their community through participation in projects focusing on the intersection between Judaism and sustainability. Modeling sustainable living, the residents, according to the *Review* profile, "hang their laundry to dry; . . . ride bikes or use public transportation whenever possible; their fridge contains only local, organic foods, eggs and dairy products from free-range, grass-fed animals and no meat. And the trio reuses and recycles everything possible, including rainwater for their garden." Among Bet Kayam's activities were a series of successful potlucks and "Taste of Melton," a text-based study of Jewish environmental ethics, cosponsored with Tuv Ha'Aretz and the Melton Adult Mini-School. More offbeat programs went even further in capturing the sustainable, creative, do-it-yourself Portland vibe. For example, a 2009 mezuzah-making event included the collection of "recyclables—such as beads, bike lights, feathers, glass, fabric and test tubes" on the streets of Portland, followed by a workshop in which they were refashioned into *mezuzot*. House resident and artist Claire Polansky led the workshop, after conducting research to create her own organic Torah ink, brewed out of "honey, vinegar, burnt willow, and crushed gallnut," for inscribing the mezuzah scrolls. "Kasher Your Cogs," a bike repair workshop led by Krall, was similarly in tune with the Portland scene. Beit Kayam, the *Review* profile proclaimed, placed Portland on the cutting edge of the Jewish sustainability movement. Even the Manhattan-based director of the Hazon program "hasn't heard of any Jewish eco-houses in the Big Apple. . . . In fact, she hasn't heard of anything around the country like Beit Kayam."[154]

Going beyond the bounds of a single house, a new idea for cooperative Jewish living emerged in Ashland in 2008, when the Renewal congregation,

Havurah Shir Hadash, announced plans for a new neighborhood, Aleph Springs. Surrounding the synagogue building, Aleph Springs would consist of "eight single-family homes and a complex of six condominium units 'wrapped around' the synagogue." The "new intentional community" according to Rabbi Zaslow, would be "aside from Orthodox enclaves . . . the first neighborhood of its kind where the homes are intended to expand the 'campus' of an existing synagogue." Although the community was planned as "a cousin to co-housing," it was also described as "the traditional country club community, where residents are drawn by common interests, and a clubhouse serves as the social hub." The difference, explained one of the developers, "is that here, our clubhouse is a synagogue."[155] Advertising itself as "Ashland's premier downtown neighborhood . . . where the synagogue's next door and Shakespeare's down the street," Aleph Springs, like the Eugene mikvah in a yurt, embraced much of what is quintessentially Oregonian. Combining the spiritually centered Renewal congregation with a commitment to a green and multigenerational ethos, the neighborhood was slated to include not only the synagogue, but a "village green," a community garden, a preschool, housing suitable for retirees as well as young families, and a bio-swale designed to purify storm water and runoff.[156] Although plans for Aleph Springs fell victim to the financial crisis of 2008–2009, it suggests the type of innovative, grassroots, sustainable experimentation that has become so characteristic of twenty-first-century Jewish community in Oregon.

By the end of the first decade of the twenty-first century, Oregon Jewry was very far from the staid, stodgy, and insular community it had been in the 1950s. As Rabbi Michael Cahana, who succeeded Rabbi Rose on the pulpit of Congregation Beth Israel, explained in a 2010 oral history,

> I think this is a time of unbelievable transition. We have not yet learned what it is a transition to, but the changes that have happened here over this past decade (only part of which I have seen but I am seeing the effects of it) are huge. The fact that there were three or four synagogues in this community for generations and now we are in an era where there are a multiplicity of synagogues here speaks to something in this community. It doesn't happen by itself. There is a desire for something. There is a need for an intimacy, for a certain kind of expression of identity. There is, frankly, a kind of anti-institutionalism that is around. And I think that the synagogues have gotten the message and are learning. As a leader of one of the largest synagogues in the community, I get it. I think the synagogues and all of the institutions are learning and are changing. We have to.[157]

Cahana's impressions were confirmed by the 2014 *Portland Jewish Tomorrow* study, commissioned by the Federation. The study found several defining characteristics shaping the community. First, it confirmed findings that migrants to places like Oregon "may either truly be psychologically more disinclined to connect with community and/or just less interested." In other words, the particular population of Jews in Portland, and presumably more broadly in Oregon, had a tendency to be "off the grid." Second, it emphasized that Jewish Portlanders preferred "hyper-specialization" to "big box" offerings—Portlanders wanted their craft beer, their organically grown food, and their Jewish engagements to be local and personalized rather than one-size-fits-all. Finally, the study confirmed the sense of geographic dispersion, with all the challenges dispersion creates for a community that had long been small and relatively concentrated. These three factors created a dichotomy in communal perceptions—on the one hand, some viewed the community as "diverse," "ready for reinvention," "vibrant," "intelligent," "committed, passionate," and "young." On the other, some characterized it as "siloed, disconnected, segmented, disjointed, scattered," "unengaged," and "indifferent." The contradiction between the rapidly growing total Jewish population and the shrinking percentage of that total number engaged with—and willing to help financially support—communal organizations, suggested that the community was "at a crossroads."[158]

As it has since the days of pioneer settlement, Oregon presents to its small Jewish population both the promise and the challenges of maintaining identity and community in a region that is rapidly growing, welcoming, and unconventional. Challenged in recent decades by an influx of newcomers who, like their non-Jewish peers, tend to be disconnected from traditional institutions, the Jewish community has responded by embracing the progressive ethos, sense of place, and stewardship over that place that has become so emblematically Oregonian. Although some of the experiments in creating progressive, personalized, spiritual, environmentally sensitive, and welcoming communities—like Aleph Springs, some of the short-lived congregations, or the Beit Kayam eco-house—have fallen short of full realization or have not proven sustainable in the long run, these models and their ethos have been welcomed and embraced by the community and suggest a path forward in continuing the Oregon Jewish story.

NOTES

Abbreviations

BB   B'nai B'rith
BBW   B'nai B'rith Women
JCC   Jewish Community Center
JEA   Jewish Education Association
JWF   Jewish Welfare Federation
LWV   League of Women Voters
NCJW   National Council of Jewish Women
OJM   Oregon Jewish Museum
OJMCHE   Oregon Jewish Museum and Center for Holocaust Education
SAC   Social Action Committee (of Portland's Congregation Beth Israel)

Preface

1   Steven Lowenstein, *The Jews of Oregon, 1850–1950* (Portland: Jewish Historical
     Society of Oregon, 1987).

2   A challenge of writing about women in the 1950s–1970s is that they are usually
     referred to by their husbands' names (as in Mrs. Alan Rosenfeld) in correspon-
     dence, in the press, and in community records. I have made every effort to recover
     not only women's given names but also their original ("maiden") last names.
     Wherever possible, I indicate women's original names in parentheses the first
     time they are mentioned in the text. This is one way of recovering the fuller sto-
     ries of women who married in an era when retaining one's original name was not
     a choice open to them. It also allows readers to connect women to their families
     of origin.

3   David Peterson del Mar, *Oregon's Promise: An Interpretive History* (Corvallis:
     Oregon State University Press, 2003), 8–9.

Chapter 1

1 The *American Jewish Yearbook* reported that there were 9,085 Jews in Oregon, including 7,800 in Portland, and a total of 700 in Salem, Corvallis, and Eugene combined. Alvin Chenkin, "Jewish Population in the United States, 1972," *American Jewish Yearbook* (1973). Accessed online, Berman Jewish Database, www.jewishdatabank.org.

2 *Jewish Review*, June 1971, 1.

3 Ibid., October 1968, 1.

4 Harold Schnitzer oral history (n.d., 1977), 17.

5 *Jewish Review*, December 1964, 7.

6 For more on Chabad, see chap. 6.

7 Carl Abbott, *Portland: Planning, Politics and Growth in a Twentieth Century City* (Lincoln: University of Nebraska Press, 1983), 209–10.

8 Craig Wollner, John Provo, and Julie Schablishky "Brief History of Urban Renewal in Portland, Oregon" (n.d.), Urban Renewal Subject File, OJMCHE.

9 Rabbi Yonah Geller, quoted in the documentary *The Three Rabbis: Three Men, Half a Century, One Community*, DVD (Portland: Oregon Public Broadcasting, 2005). Geller meant Neveh Zedek and Ahavai Shalom—the two congregations would subsequently merge to form Neveh Shalom.

10 Abe "English" Rosenberg oral history (July 20, 1977), 11.

11 Neveh Zedek's membership in the years before the merger dropped from 300 to 170 families, and members' average age was sixty. Gary Miranda, *Following a River: Portland's Congregation Neveh Shalom, 1869–1989* (Portland: Congregation Neveh Shalom, 1989), 119.

12 Transcript, *City of Portland v. Ahavath Achim.* Ahavath Achim, Organization 26, Box 5, Relocation Records, OJMCHE, 47–48.

13 Barry Itkin, quoted in "The Center: Our Presidents Remember," by Judith Aftergut. JCC records, Organization 5, Box 2, 80th Anniversary Event (1990).

14 Abbott, *Portland: Planning, Politics and Growth*, 170.

15 Milt Carl oral history (October 27, 2004), 27.

16 JCC Records, Org. 5, Box 3.

17 Miranda, *Following a River*, 123–25.

18 JCC Records, Org. 5 Box 3. For more on this nostalgia for Old South Portland and the emergence of that moniker for the neighborhood, see chap. 2.

19 Edward S. Shapiro, *A Time for Healing: American Jewry since World War II* (Baltimore: Johns Hopkins University Press, 1992), 147.

20 Like other American cities with significant Jewish populations, Portland has long had a Federation—an umbrella organization that runs community-wide agencies and conducts fundraising both for local communal needs and for international Jewry and Israel. Communal agencies that are part of the group supported by a federation are referred to as "constituent agencies" and serve broad communal needs in terms of social services, such as refugee resettlement or Jewish Family Services, or institutions such as a Jewish Community Center or a community school. Federations also often serve as a communal representative and include

a Community Relations Council. Synagogues, although working closely with federations, are not constituent agencies and fundraise separately. In Portland, the Federation was founded in 1920 as the Federated Jewish Societies. It has gone through a series of name changes over the years, becoming the Jewish Welfare Federation, the Jewish Federation of Portland, and, finally, the Jewish Federation of Greater Portland. In Portland as in many other communities, it is often called, simply "Federation."

21 "Jewish Census—Portland Urbanized Area—1957," Jewish Welfare Federation of Portland, 1. Rabbi Yonah Geller papers, Box 27, OJMCHE. Hereafter referred to as "1957 Census."

22 "The Portland Jewish Community—1971," Jewish Welfare Federation (December 31, 1972), 7. Jewish Welfare Federation collection, 5, OJMCHE. Hereafter referred to as "1971 Census."

23 1971 Census, 67.

24 Ibid., 67–69.

25 Ibid., 69.

26 Ellen Eisenberg, *Embracing a Western Identity: Jewish Oregonians, 1849–1950* (Corvallis: Oregon State University Press, 2015), chap. 1. See also Lowenstein, *Jews of Oregon,* 41.

27 Robert Neuberger oral history (September 23, 2009), 4.

28 Robert Levinson, *The Jews of Jacksonville Oregon* (master's thesis, University of Oregon, 1962), 22. Ellen Eisenberg, *Embracing a Western Identity: Jewish Oregonians, 1849–1950* (Corvallis: Oregon State University Press, 2015), chap. 1.

29 Lowenstein, *Jews of Oregon,* 89–91.

30 Rabbi Joshua Stampfer, quoted in *The Three Rabbis.*

31 Rabbis Rose, Stampfer, and Geller, and Lorraine Rose, quoted in *The Three Rabbis.*

32 Quoted in *The Three Rabbis.*

33 There are a number of inconsistencies in population studies caused by variations in methodology and scope. The 1957 Census included two hundred Jews living in Clark County, Washington, as well as those in Oregon suburbs of Portland. In the 1971 Census, "institutionalized" individuals, including those in the Robison Home, were not counted in the total (1971 survey, 5). Because both censuses were based on lists of Jews known to the community, there is no count of those who, while considering themselves Jewish by religion and/or ethnicity, were neither members of a congregation nor contributors to the Federation. On the evolving methodology of such surveys, see Elizabeth Tighe et al., "American Jewish Population Estimates: 2012 (Brandeis University, Steinhardt Social Research Institute, 2013), 11.

34 Jack Segal, "The Jews of Portland, Oregon: Their Religious Practices and Beliefs" (master's thesis, Oregon State University, 1965), 4. The study was conducted in 1961–1962. This study only included synagogue-affiliated Jews, but did make an effort to represent a range of members by reaching out through organizations like sisterhoods and brotherhoods, rather than only among service goers. The interview included ninety questions.

35   1957 Census, 1–3.

36   Ibid., 4.

37   The smaller population reported in the 1971 Census may be due to a difference in scope or methodology rather than an actual population decline.

38   1957 Census, 5. The 1957 Census reported that 6 percent of married couples included a non-Jew, a rate slightly lower than the national figures of 7 percent.

39   1971 Census, 7.

40   Ibid., 9.

41   Segal, "The Jews of Portland, Oregon," Table 32, 63.

42   Ibid., Tables 33, 34, 64.

43   Ibid., Tables 26, 58, and Tables 37, 67.

44   1971 Census, 33, 47.

45   Ibid., Census, 52.

46   Ibid., 9.

47   Ibid., 36.

48   Miranda, *Following a River*, 101–2.

49   Richard Matza oral history (January 20, 2013), 1–5. Richard Matza served as Ahavat Achim's president in the early 1990s and again from 2002–2009. In 2014, he was one of the key organizers of the Vida Sefaradi celebration of the centennial of Sephardic life in Portland.

50   Allocations, Jewish Welfare Federation, Box 3, OJMCHE.

51   Miranda, *Following a River*, 99–101.

52   Ibid., 103. For more on the Portland Friendship Club, see John Miller oral history (August 10, 1976), 16–17.

53   Lydia and Bernard Brown oral history (November 26 and December 14, 1975), 21.

54   Joy Alkalay oral history (February 15, 1976), 6–9. Joe worked first at White Stag and then at Schnitzer Steel; Joy's first position was with David Robinson at the Anti-Defamation League, she later worked at Congregation Beth Israel.

55   An exception in the 1970s and 1980s were the Soviet refuseniks, who came as sponsored immigrants. For more on Soviet immigrants, see chap. 5.

56   Joy Alkalay oral history (March 10, 1981), 7–8.

57   Martin Acker oral history (February 5, 2008) (Lane County Oral History Project of the Oregon Jewish Museum), 12.

58   Leon Gabinet oral history (June 28, 2010), 6.

59   Renee Holzman oral history (June 3, 2005), 4–5.

60   Harry Stein, *Gus J. Solomon* (Portland: Oregon Historical Society Press, 2006), 203–6. For a discussion of this process, see chap. 4.

61   Henry Blauer oral history (October 1 and 14, 2008), 3.

62   Ibid., 1.

63   Arden Shenker oral history (June 20, 2007), 18.

64   Leonard Goldberg oral history (June 3, 2010), 10–11. Note that this refers to Jack B. Schwartz, attorney and longtime community activist.

65   Rabbi Emanuel Rose oral history (March 10, 1981), 7–8.

66   On the earlier migration to the Eastside, see William Toll, *The Making of an Ethnic Middle Class* (Albany, NY: State University of New York Press, 1982), 137, 154–55.

67 Sura Rubenstein, Remarks for "South Portland History Pub," McMenamin's Kennedy School, June 2011. Old South Portland subject file, Oregon Jewish Museum.

68 Lila Goodman oral history (October 5, 2005), 5–6.

69 William Gordon oral history (January 6, 1977), 9; and (January 28, 1975), 7.

70 Shirley Gittlesohn oral history (September 24, 2008), 1, 10.

71 Ernie Bonyhadi oral history (December 4, 2007), 10. See also, Shirley Gittlesohn oral history, 10. Much later, Ernie Bonyhadi and Shirley Gittlesohn married each other.

72 Shaarie Torah 1957 roster, Shaarie Torah, Org. 25, Administration file, OJMCHE. Shaarie Torah instituted mixed seating in this era, and given this information on residential patterns, it is clear that a substantial portion of the community did not live within walking distance. It wasn't until later that the congregation would formally disaffiliate from the Orthodox movement. For more on this transition, see chap. 6.

73 Miranda, *Following a River,* 123. Rabbi Stampfer perceived that the community was "decidedly" shifting away from downtown and toward the Westside, and on this basis strongly supported the Peaceful Lane site.

74 William Gordon oral history (January 28, 1975), 7.

75 Minutes, Task Force on the Transmission of Jewish Heritage, January 18, 1977. Jewish Education Association (JEA), Box 2, Engleson papers, OJMCHE.

76 Notes, Engleson file, April 11, 1977. JEA, Box 2, Engleson papers, OJMCHE.

77 Minutes, Federation Task Force on the Transmission of Jewish Heritage, March 8, 1977. Engleson papers, JEA, Box 2, "Jewish Welfare Federation memos, correspondence" folder, OJMCHE.

78 Minutes, Bureau of Jewish Education, May 20, 1973. JEA, Box 2, Engleson papers.

79 Position Paper on Jewish Education in Portland, September 1973. JEA, Box 2, Engleson papers.

80 Minutes, Bureau of Jewish Education, 1973–75. JEA, Box 2, Engleson papers.

81 Jim Meyer oral history (March 22, May 2, and May 25, 2005), 8–10.

82 Minutes, Joint meeting of JWF with Congregations, November 17, 1975; Plan for Merger of the Hillel Academy of Portland and the JEA (May 10, 1977). JEA, Box 2.

83 Plan for Coordinating JEA and Hillel, April 10, 1975. JEA, Box 2, Engleson papers.

84 Jewish Federation of Portland, Community Planning Group, "Program Priority Proposals, 1977–1980," JEA, Box 2.

85 Jewish Federation of Portland, Executive Committee Meeting (October 5, 1984); Federation Executive Committee to Federation Board of Directors (October 8, 1984), JEA, Box 2. See also *Jewish Review* (August 1985), 1.

86 Toll, *Making of an Ethnic Middle Class,* 136, 138. Lowenstein, *Jews of Oregon,* 161. For more on Men's Camp, see http://bbcamp.org/bnai-brith-mens-camp/. An NBC News feature story on the BB Men's Camp can be viewed there.

87 Stampfer's summer at Brandeis Camp in 1943 was critical to his later development. Stampfer met his future wife, Goldie, there, and the experience also played a key role in his decision to shift his career trajectory from chemistry to the rabbinate. Rabbi Stampfer, "Reflections on 36 Years with Neveh Shalom," 2–3. Rabbi Stampfer file, OJMCHE.

88 William Gordon oral history (January 6, 1977), 14.

89 Irene Balk oral history (November 11, 1981), 9.

90 Jewish Historical Society, "Account of Origins," by Shirley Tanzer, 1974. OJMCHE. These developments will be discussed further in chap. 2.

91 http://judaicstudies.org/history.html.

92 "The Oregon Story" was a catchphrase coined by Tom McCall. See below.

93 Brent Walth, *Fire at Eden's Gate: Tom McCall and the Oregon Story* (Portland: Oregon Historical Society Press, 1994), 4.

94 Quoted in Peterson del Mar, *Oregon's Promise*, 240–41.

95 Walth, *Fire at Eden's Gate*, 5.

96 Governor Vic Atiyeh (1979–87) had McCall's pointed "Welcome to Oregon, We Hope You Enjoy Your Visit" sign replaced with "Welcome to Oregon," symbolically signaling the end of the emphasis on cautious, measured growth. Walth, "Prologue: The Sign," in *Fire at Eden's Gate*, 1–12. On the state slogan see "Sequential Identities," *Oregonian* (February 14, 2009). Accessed online.

97 Peterson del Mar, *Oregon's Promise*, 248.

98 The engagement of Jewish Oregonians in these efforts is discussed in detail in chap. 4.

99 William G. Robbins, *Landscapes of Conflict: The Oregon Story, 1940–2000* (Seattle: University of Washington Press, 2004), chap. 7.

100 Ibid., 216.

101 On the Klamath forest lands issues see Walth, *Fire at Eden's Gate*, 121–24; Robbins, *Landscapes of Conflict*, 227–31. McCall was heavily involved in this effort as a journalist/advocate. It has been fairly noted that, in this episode, Neuberger's concern lay far more with the forests and the local economy than with the welfare of the Klamath Tribe.

102 For a brief summary of Goldschmidt's career, see Wayne Thompson, "Neil Goldschmidt," http://oregonencyclopedia.org/articles/goldschmidt_neil/#.Vub 9kvkrLcs.

103 Carl Abbott, *Portland: Planning, Politics and Growth*, 209.

104 Arnold Cogan oral history (March 10, 1999). PSU College of Urban and Public Affairs. Accessed at OJMCHE, 1–2.

105 "Gussie Reinhardt Has Led Life of Jewish Service," *Jewish Review*, February 1, 2000, 3, 19; "Lair Hill Historical Tag Sought," *Oregonian* (April 24, 1977), C-1. Both in "Clippings File," Box 1, Augusta Reinhardt Collection, OJMCHE. See also, Abbott, *Portland: Planning Politics and Growth*, 183–85.

106 Carl Abbott, *Portland in Three Centuries: The Place and the People* (Corvallis: Oregon State University Press, 2011), 144.

107 Wollner, "Brief History of Urban Renewal." See also Abbott, *Portland: Planning, Politics and Growth*, chap. 9.

108 Abbott, *Portland in Three Centuries*, 145–46. See also Steve Johnson, "The Transformation of Civic Institutions and Practices in Portland Oregon, 1960–1999" (PhD diss., Portland State University, 2002).

109 *Jewish Review*, October 1971, 3.

110 Amanda Suutari, "USA-Oregon (Portland)-Sustainable City," (The EcoTipping Points Project: Models for Success in a Time of Chaos), http://www .ecotippingpoints.org/our-stories/indepth/usa-portland-sustainable-regional -planning.html.

111 Abbott, *Portland in Three Centuries*, 146.

112 Thompson, "Neil Goldschmidt," http://oregonencyclopedia.org/articles/gold-schmidt_neil/#.Vub9kvkrLcs.

113 "The Goldschmidt Era," reprinted online for the 25th Anniversary Issue, *Willamette Week*, http://wweek.com/__ALL_OLD_HTML/25-1976.html.

114 Steven Reed Johnson, "The Bicycle Movement" http://stevenreedjohnson.com /stevenreedjohnson/civicpdxbikes.html.

115 Elaine Cogan oral history (December 18, 2002), Portland State University College of Urban and Public Affairs. Accessed at OJMCHE, 5–6, 10. Elaine and Arnold Cogan became two of the principals of Cogan Owens and Cogan, a top land use planning firm.

116 Abbott, *Portland: Planning, Politics and Growth*, 200.

117 Eliza Canty-Jones, "HB2930, Anti-Discrimination Bill," *The Oregon History Project*, http://oregonhistoryproject.org/articles/historical-records/hb-2930 -anti-discrimination-bill/#.VucKP_krLcs. George T. Nicola, "Early Attempts at Oregon Gay Civil Rights," *GLAPN Northwest LGBTQ History*, http://glapn. org/6110earlyattempts.html.

118 *Jewish Review*, February 14, 1993, 1, 17. On the Yellow Bike Project, see "Portland Journal; Where Trust Rides a Yellow Bicycle," *New York Times*, December 8, 1994, accessed online.

119 Personal recollection by Paul Meyer, shared with the author (December 27, 2014). See also Thomas M. Hard, "Portland Symphonic Choir," http://oregonencyclopedia .org/articles/portland_symphonic_choir/#.VucLafkrLcs.

120 Helen Johnson Kintner, "Ernest Bloch," *Oregon Encyclopedia*, http ://oregonencyclopedia.org/articles/bloch_ernest_1880_1959_/#.VucMN_krLcs. See also "Ernest Bloch, 1880–1959," Milken Archive of Jewish Music, http://www .milkenarchive.org/#/people/view/composers/567/Bloch%2C+Ernest.

121 Grace Kook-Anderson, "Inside the Studio with Mel Katz," *Oregonian*, May 28, 2015. Accessed online.

122 Mel Katz, artist lecture (June 5, 2015), Hallie Ford Museum, Willamette University, Salem, Oregon.

123 Grace Kook-Anderson, "Inside the Studio with Mel Katz," *Oregonian*, May 28, 2015. Accessed online.

124 Randy Gragg, "The Arlene Effect," *Portland Monthly* (April 27, 2012), http://www .pdxmonthly.com/articles/2012/4/27/arlene-schnitzer-art-collector-may-2012.

125 Brian Ferriso, "The Impact and Legacy of Arlene and Harold Schnitzer," in Guenther, *In Passionate Pursuit: The Arlene and Harold Schnitzer Collection and Legacy*, Bruce Guenther, ed. (Portland: Portland Art Museum, 2014), 15. See also Greg Chaille and Kristin Anderson, *State of Giving: Stories of Oregon Volunteers, Donors, and Nonprofits* (Corvallis: Oregon State University Press, 2015), 26–27.

126 "In Passionate Pursuit: An Interview with Arlene Schnitzer," in Guenther, *In Passionate Pursuit*, 25.

127 Harry Glickman, *Promoter Ain't a Dirty Word* (Forest Grove, Oregon: Timber Press, 1978). On Blazermania, see 150–51.

128 James J. Kopp, *Eden within Eden: Oregon's Utopian Heritage* (Corvallis: Oregon State University Press, 2009), 134.

129 William G. Robbins, "Vortex I Music Festival," http://oregonencyclopedia.org /articles/vortex_i/#.VucRfPkrLcs. See also Abbott, *Portland in Three Centuries*, 140–42.

130 Steven Reed Johnson, "Building Sustainable Communities through Community Governance: The Story of Portland, Oregon," 176. (revised version of Steven Reed Johnson, "The Transformation of Civic Institutions and Practices in Portland, Oregon, 1960–1999" (PhD diss., Portland State University, 2002), http://www .stevenreedjohnson.com/stevenreedjohnson/PdxDownloads.html.

131 "Houseful of hippies" was attorney George Rives's description of Goldschmidt's mayoral election celebration in 1972. Quoted in Steven Reed Johnson, *Building Sustainable Communities*, 78.

132 For more information on the CRC and Portland-area Middle East dialogue, see chaps. 4 and 5. For more on Albert, see Stew Albert, *Who the Hell Is Stew Albert? A Memoir* (Los Angeles: Red Hen Press, 2004).

133 "The 30-Year Secret," *Willamette Week*, May 12, 2004, accessed online. See also "Editors Notebook: Willamette Week Enters Middle Age," *Daily Astorian*, November 7, 2014, accessed online. Meeker is married to Oregon attorney general Ellen Rosenblum, and they attend Congregation Beth Israel, as does the Goldschmidt family.

134 From the 1950s through the 1980s, Jews consistently made up between 0.4 and 0.5 percent of the state's total population, according to figures reported in the *American Jewish Yearbook*. During the 1990s, the population share doubled, to 1 percent. In 2010, it was estimated at 1.3 percent.

135 *American Jewish Yearbook* (2000), 244. Accessed via www.jewishdatabank.org.

136 A revised 2009 report, published in 2010, reported that 47,481 Jews lived in the Greater Portland Area, with 25,943 in Multnomah County. Jewish Federation of Portland, *Demographic and Needs Assessment Study* (Revised Report, February 2010), 13–14.

137 Sidney Goldstein and Alice Goldstein, *Jews on the Move: Implications for Jewish Identity* (Albany: SUNY Press, 1996), Table 2.2, 38–39.

138 Ira Sheskin and Arnold Dashefsky, "Jewish Population in the United States, 2012" (American Jewish Yearbook Reprint, 2012), 20, Table 2. Accessed online at www.jewishdatabank.org.

139 Goldstein and Goldstein, *Jews on the Move*, 89.

140 Cited in Goldstein and Goldstein, *Jews on the Move*, 43.

141 Cited in Goldstein and Goldstein, *Jews on the Move*, 99.

142 Goldstein and Goldstein, *Jews on the Move*, 175.

143 There are several competing explanations of this process. See Goldstein and Goldstein, *Jews on the Move*, 4–8.

144 See Patricia O'Connell Killen and Mark Silk: *Religion and Public Life in the Pacific Northwest: The None Zone* (Lanham: Rowman & Littlefield, 2004).

145 Patricia O'Connell Killen and Mark Shibley, "Surveying the Religious Landscape: Historical Trends and Current Patterns in Oregon, Washington and Alaska," in Killen and Silk, *Religion and Public Life in the Pacific Northwest*, 29.

146 "Jews in the West," National Jewish Population Survey, United Jewish Communities Presentation of findings, 2000–01.

147 Jim Schwartz, Jeffrey Scheckner, and Laurence Kotler-Berkowitz, "Census of U.S. Synagogues, 2001," American Jewish Committee (AJC), 2002, 124.

148 Sam Zidell obituary (clipping), *Oregonian* (October 7, 1967), Zidell file, OJMCHE. The Zidell family owned companies expanded from machinery to ship scrapping after World War II, to ship building and tube forging, and, more recently, real estate development.

149 *Jewish Review* (April 1, 2004), 1, 21.

Chapter Two

1 *Whatever Happened to Old South Portland?* (1969), JCC collection, Box 2, OJMCHE.

2 "Theatre: Notes from the Director," *Scribe* (reproduction in conjunction with the 1969 show, *Whatever Happened to Old South Portland?*, dated November 4, 1920), 1.

3 "An Anti-Semantic Song," *Whatever Happened to Old South Portland?*, 30.

4 "Theater: Notes from the Director."

5 *JCC Ace* (November 1969), 1. JCC collection, OJMCHE.

6 Rabbi Joshua Stampfer, *Pioneer Rabbi of the West: The Life and Times of Julius Eckman* (Portland: 1988).

7 *Historical Scribe* (Portland: May 1976). Jewish Historical Society of Oregon, Box 6: Historical Scribe Newsletter. See also Bicentennial Planning Committee meeting minutes, January 12, 1976, Jewish Historical Society of Portland, Box 6, "Memory Is Survival."

8 "Memory Is Survival" script.

9 Lillie Kugel oral history (February 15, 1974), 7.

10 Lillian Kobin oral history (August 30, 1977), 9

11 Besse Harris oral history (February 2, 1975), 7–8.

12 Rabbi Yonah Geller oral history (October 2006), 2.

13 Frances Bricker oral history (May 18, 1977), 21.

14 Kathryn Kahn Blumenfeld oral history (November 26, 1979), 10.

15 Shirley Tanzer, undated handwritten account of the oral history project. Tanzer file, OJMCHE.

16 *JCC Ace* (October 1968), 1, and insert.

17 Ibid. (December 1968), 1, 4.

18 Ibid. (March 1969), 1.

19 Ibid. (November 1969), 1.

20 Productions in the two years leading up to *Whatever Happened* included works

by George Bernard Shaw, Harold Pinter, and Dylan Thomas, as well as the performance of plays based on the stories of Yiddish writer Isaac Leib Peretz. *JCC Ace*, 1967–68.

21 *JCC Ace*, 1970.

22 Matthew Frye Jacobson, "A Ghetto to Look Back To: World of Our Fathers, Ethnic Revival, and the Arc of Multiculturalism," *American Jewish History* 88, no. 4 (2000): 463.

23 Shapiro, *A Time for Healing*, 151–52.

24 Seth Wolitz, "The Americanization of Tevye or Boarding the Jewish *Mayflower*," *American Quarterly* 40, no. 4 (December 1988): 514.

25 Hasia Diner, *Lower East Side Memories* (Princeton: Princeton University Press, 2000): 7. Beth Wenger also traces this sacralization of the Lower East Side, demonstrating its emergence as early as the interwar years. Beth Wenger, "Memory as Identity: The Invention of the Lower East Side," *American Jewish History* 85, no. 1 (March 1997): 3.

26 Diner, *Lower East Side Memories*, 8. See also, Hasia Diner, *Jews of the United States* (Berkeley: University of California Press, 2004): 285–86.

27 Catherine Rottenberg, ed. *Black Harlem and the Jewish Lower East Side: Narratives out of Time* (Albany: SUNY Press, 2013), 7.

28 Diner, *Lower East Side Memories*, 128–29.

29 *Congregation Beth Israel Bulletin*, April 10, 1953.

30 Samuel Suwol obituary, *Oregonian* (February 22, 1980), F8.

31 Samuel Suwol, *Jewish History of Oregon* (Portland: 1958), 1–2.

32 Rabbi Julius Nodel, *The Ties Between: A Century of Judaism on America's Last Frontier* (Portland: Temple Beth Israel, 1959), 5.

33 Ibid., 47.

34 Ibid., 51.

35 Ibid., 47.

36 Ibid., 48.

37 Shirley Tanzer, "Recollections," unpublished account, 1979. Originally intended as the introduction to a proposed collection of oral histories. "Tanzer," People file, OJMCHE.

38 For an interesting discussion of this, see Hasia Diner, "American West, New York Jewish," in *Jewish Life in the American West*, Ava Kahn, ed. (Seattle: University of Washington Press and the Autry Museum of Western Heritage, 2002). 33–52.

39 Diner, *Lower East Side Memories*, 9, 12.

40 Author's notes on session held at Temple Beth Sholom, Salem, Oregon (October 18, 2009).

41 Wenger, "Memory as Identity," 5.

42 Jenna Weissman Joselit, "Telling Tales: Or, How a Slum Became a Shrine," *Jewish Social Studies* 2, no. 2 (Winter 1996): 54.

43 David Kaufman, "Constructions of Memory: The Synagogue of the Lower East Side," in *Remembering the Lower East Side*, Hasia Diner, Jeffrey Shandler, and Beth Wenger, eds. (Bloomington: Indiana University Press, 2000), 114, 117.

44 Wenger, "Memory as Identity," 26.

45 Diner, *Lower East Side Memories*, 38.

46 Ibid., 163.

47 Alisa Solomon, *Wonder of Wonders: A Cultural History of Fiddler on the Roof* (New York: Metropolitan Books, 2013), 172.

48 Solomon, *Wonder of Wonders*, 3.

49 Nate Director oral history (June 7, 2005), 1.

50 "Whatever Happened to Shirley Blum?" *Historical Scribe,* May 1976. Jewish Historical Society of Oregon collection, Box 6, OJMCHE.

51 *Whatever Happened*, 2.

52 Using the Historic Oregon Newspaper digital database, a search was conducted for the word combinations "Portland" and "pushcart" in proximity to one another. When searched alone, "pushcart" appears sixty six times between 1890 and 1920 in the *Sunday Oregonian*. The vast majority of these cases are either stories about New York or fictional accounts. Pushcarts in Portland are mentioned only a handful of times, twice in advertisements. None of these place pushcarts in the South Portland neighborhood or connect them with Jewish peddlers.

53 "The Changing Face of Chinatown in Portland," Museum of the City website: http://www.museumofthecity.org/the-changing-face-of-chinatown-in-portland-oregon/.

54 *Whatever Happened*, 5.

55 Arthur Markewitz oral history (March 11, 1977, and May 10, 1977), 21.

56 Lillie Kugel oral history (February 15, 1974), 2.

57 Julius Zell oral history (December 18, 1974), 3.

58 Manley Labby oral history (January 27, 1975), 4.

59 Harold Schnitzer oral history (October 17, 1977), 5.

60 *Memory Is Survival*, 1, 11.

61 Lowenstein, *Jews of Oregon*, 97.

62 Ibid., 75.

63 Manley Labby oral history (January 27, 1975), 4; Dan Labby oral history, (November 12, 2004), 2.

64 *Whatever Happened*, 5, 19.

65 Lowenstein, *Jews of Oregon*, 96.

66 Polina Olsen, *Stories from Jewish Portland* (Charleston: The History Press, 2011), 52.

67 *Memory Is Survival*, 17.

68 On the Portland Hebrew School, see Lowenstein, *Jews of Oregon*, 118–20; Toll, *The Making of an Ethnic Middle Class*, 104–5.

69 *Whatever Happened,* 19.

70 Lowenstein, *Jews of Oregon*, 94.

71 Dora Levine oral history (1969), 6. Conducted by Shirley Tanzer, this is one of the few interviews in the collection dated before the creation of the Oral History Project in the early 1970s. It was likely an interview conducted as part of the research for *Whatever Happened*.

72 Augusta Reinhardt oral history (December 7, 1973), 2.

73 Frieda Gass Cohen oral history (April 25, 1975), 2.

74   Dan Labby oral history (November 12, 2004), 2–3.

75   Robison Jewish Home Sisterhood, program notice (February 6, 1996). Gussie Reinhardt papers, Box 7.

76   *Memory Is Survival*, 15–16. There is a handwritten margin note in the script attributing this statement to Diane Nemer, but it is not in the oral history transcript available at the OJM. Perhaps it comes from research notes that have not been preserved.

77   *JCC Ace* (February 1969).

78   Martin Clark, "Italians Make Gesture," *Oregon Journal* (undated clipping). JCC, Box 2, press clippings for *Whatever Happened*.

79   See discussion of selective migration in chap. 1.

80   Ellen Eisenberg, "Transplanted to the Rose City: The Creation of East European Jewish Community in Portland, Oregon," *Journal of American Ethnic History* 19, no.3 (Spring 2000): 82–97.

81   Toll, *Making of an Ethnic Middle Class*, 125.

82   *Scribe*, May 1976 (published in conjunction with *Memory Is Survival*), 6–7.

83   1971 Jewish Welfare Federation Survey, 67. See discussion of the survey and community response to it in chap. 1.

84   Kaufman, "Constructions of Memory," 117.

85   "Death of a Neighborhood," *Oregon Journal* (November 22, 1976), clipping file for *Whatever Happened*, JCC, Box 2: Events, OJMCHE.

86   Stephen Y. Leflar, *A History of South Portland*. Southwest Neighborhoods, Inc. http://swni.org/ahistoryofsouthportland (accessed October 10, 2014).

87   Richard Matza oral history (January 20, 2013), 6.

88   Arden Shenker oral history (June 13, 2007), 3.

89   Howard Marcus oral history (August 27, 2009), 16.

90   Wendy Liebreich oral history (April 14, 2005), 10.

91   Dora Levine oral history (n.d.,1969).

92   Exceptions include oral histories from Jack Hecht (1974), 4; Milton Margulis (February 9, 1974), 18; Manley Labby (January 27, 1975), 8.

93   Frieda Gass Cohen oral history 1, 10.

94   Manley Labby oral history 8.

95   Since the interviews were oral, it was the transcribers who chose to capitalize "Old."

96   Abe "English" Rosenberg oral history (July 20, 1977), 3.

97   Joanna Menashe oral history (March 17, 1975).

98   "Whatever Happened to Shirley Blum?"

99   Lowenstein, *Jews of Oregon*, chap. 11, "The Community of Old South Portland"; Polina Olsen, *The Immigrants' Children: Jewish and Italian Memories of Old South Portland* (Portland: Smart Talk Publications, 2006).

100   Tanzer, "Recollections," 2.

101   "Whatever Happened to Shirley Blum?" 4.

102   Information on the founding can be found in Box 1, Administrative Records, Jewish Historical Society of Oregon, OJMCHE. In addition to the bylaws and articles of incorporation, this collection contains a document titled "How the Idea for a Jewish Historical Society Grew."

103 For a brief history of the Sephardic community in Portland, see Ellen Eisenberg, "Portland's Sephardic Scene," in *Vida Sefaradi: A Century of Sephardic Life in Portland* (Portland: Ahavath Achim and Oregon Jewish Museum, 2014), 24–35. For a history of the congregation, see Sura Rubenstein, "Ahavath Achim: A History" in the same volume, 37–42.

104 *Whatever Happened,* 23–24.

105 Ezra and Joya Menashe oral history (part 2, November 24, 1975).

106 Rabbi Michael B. and Mrs. (Naile Teranto) Albagli oral history (May 15, 1985) and Sam and Sarah Menashe and Ogeni Babin oral history (May 20, 1985). Unlike the oral histories from the 1970s, the interviewers' and transcribers' names are not included on these transcripts.

107 *Memory Is Survival* script, 4–5.

108 Jonathan Sarna, "American Jewish History," *Modern Judaism* 10, no. 3, (October 1990), 356.

109 Aviva Ben-Ur, *Sephardic Jews in America: A Diasporic History* (New York: New York University Press, 2009), 2.

110 Ben-Ur, *Sephardic Jews in America,* 7.

111 *Vida Sefaradi: A Century of Sephardic Life in Portland.*

112 Judith Margles. Conversation with the author, October 30, 2014.

113 David Augusto Canelo, *The Last Crypto Jews of Portugal* (Portland: Institute for Judaic Studies, 1990), revised edition, edited by Rabbi Joshua Stampfer.

114 "About Us" and "Conferences" Institute for Judaic Studies website: judaic-studies.org. Accessed October, 2014.

115 Rabbi Joshua Stampfer, quoted in "A Vision Is Realized for the Oregon Jewish Museum," *The Downtowner* (March 1990), clipping, OJM, Series IV, Exhibitions, Box 9, *Jews of Greece.*

116 *Jews of Greece* exhibit file, Series IV, Box 9, OJMCHE.

117 Mission Statement (1990), Box 1, Administration, OJMCHE.

118 Judith Margles, conversation with author, October 30, 2014.

119 Rabbi Joshua Stampfer, quoted in "A Vision is Realized for the Oregon Jewish Museum," *The Downtowner* (March, 1990), clipping, OJM, Series IV, Exhibitions, Box 9, "Jews of Greece."

120 Mission Statement (1995), Box 1, Administration, OJMCHE.

121 Judith Margles, conversation with author, October 30, 2014.

122 Flyer, *In the Footsteps of Columbus,* publicity, OJM Series IV, Box 9.

123 *In the Footsteps of Columbus: Jews in America, 1654–1880,* exhibit catalog, Yossi Avner, ed. (Tel Aviv: Beth Hatefutsoth, The Nahum Goldmann Museum of the Jewish Diaspora, 1986–7).

124 "*In the Footsteps of Columbus,* publicity, event, and publication files, OJM Series IV, Box 9.

125 "Storyline," *In the Footsteps of Lewis and Clark,* planning file, OJM Series IV, Box 9.

126 Oregon Holocaust Resource Center, subject file, OJMCHE.

127 OHRC annual reports. OHRC collection, Box 1, OJMCHE.

128 Hans Biglajzer oral history (May 30, 1990), 50.

129 Rochella "Chella" Velt Meekcoms oral history (January 27–28, 1976), 63.

130   Charlotte Brown oral history (October 18 and 30, 2006), 15.

131   *Jewish Review*, June 15, 2001, 12.

132   Oregon Holocaust Memorial brochure, (City of Portland), Oregon Holocaust Resource Center Box 1, OJMCHE.

133   Diner, *Lower East Side Memories*, 129.

Chapter Three

1   *Jewish Review*, November 1971, 9. "Sub Debs" was a high school sorority.

2   Hasia Diner, Shira Kohn, and Rachel Kranson, eds. *The Jewish Feminine Mystique: Jewish Women in Postwar America* (New Brunswick: Rutgers University Press, 2010), 3-4.

3   1957 Census, 3–4.

4   Summary based on the January 1962 edition of the *Jewish Review*.

5   Summary based on the February 1975 edition of the *Jewish Review*.

6   Rabbi Stone-Halpern and her husband Rabbi Larry Halpern of the South Metro Jewish Community later divorced; after their divorce, she used the name Rabbi Ariel Stone.

7   Summary based on the January 2001 edition of the *Jewish Review*.

8   Deborah Lipstadt, "Feminism and American Judaism: Looking Back at the Turn of the Century" in Pam Nadel and Jonathan Sarna, eds., *Women and American Judaism: Historical Perspectives* (Hanover: Brandeis University Press, 2001), 291.

9   Diner, Kohn, and Kranson, *Jewish Feminine Mystique, 3–4.

10   Paula Hyman, "Ezrat Nashim and the Emergence of a New Jewish Feminism," in Robert Seltzer and Norman Cohen, *The Americanization of the Jews* (New York: NYU Press, 1995), 285.

11   Shirli Brautbar, *From Fashion to Politics: Hadassah and Jewish American Women in the Post World War II Era* (Boston: Academic Studies Press, 2013), 4–5.

12   Hasia Diner and Beryl Lieff Benderly, *Her Works Praise Her: A History of Jewish Women in America from Colonial Times to the Present* (New York: Basic Books, 2002), 380.

13   Helen Stern oral history (April 28, 2005), 12.

14   Evelyn Maizels oral history (April 6, 2010), 6.

15   Margaret Labby oral history (March 22, 2005), 2.

16   Toinette Menashe oral history (November 10, 2004), 8.

17   Elaine Cogan oral history (December 18, 2002), 2. For discussion of Cogan's involvement with urban planning and the Model Cities program, see chap. 1.

18   Sylvia Davidson oral history (July 29, 2010), 10. For more on Davidson, see chap. 4.

19   Fanny Friedman oral history (May 4, 1974), 17.

20   Joyce Loeb oral history (September 3, 2008), 10.

21   Sylvia Stevens oral history (August 29, 2009), 3, 8.

22   "Profiles in the Law: Sylvia Stevens Takes the Helm," *Oregon State Bar Bulletin*, December 2010, http://www.osbar.org/publications/bulletin/10dec/profiles.html.

23 "Legal Ladies," *Oregon Jewish Life* (December 1, 2014), http://orjewishlife.com/legal-ladies/.

24 Evelyn Maizels oral history, 6.

25 Eve Rosenfeld oral history (September 8, 2004), 6, 7.

26 Toinette Menashe oral history, 8.

27 Lois Shenker oral history (November 4, 2013), 29.

28 Ruth Schnitzer oral history (April 17, 1975), 4.

29 Helen Blumenthal oral history (March 3, 1977), 13, 31.

30 Madeline Nelson oral history (September 22, 2004), 1.

31 Bernice Gevurtz oral history, 7–9.

32 Cecille Beyl oral history (August 6, 2009), 8.

33 Sylvia Stevens oral history, 3.

34 Ruth Schnitzer oral history, 6.

35 Margaret Labby oral history, 5

36 Rosemarie Rosenfeld oral history (July 19, 2004), 9.

37 Nina Weinstein oral history (n.d., 2010), 6.

38 Evelyn Maizels oral history (March 13, 2013), 16.

39 For more on involvement in the League of Women Voters, see chap. 4.

40 Carrie Hervin oral history (May 3, 1974), 7. Hervin passed that sense of responsibility to her daughter Barbara (Hervin) Schwab, who was elected first vice president of the LWV in 1952, less than a decade after her mother's term as president.

41 Ahavath Achim Ladies Auxiliary records, Congregation Ahavath Achim, Box 4, OJMCHE.

42 Miriam Rosenfeld recounts this project, 13. The project was also featured in "Temple Sisterhood aids blind," *Jewish Review* (September 1978), 8. See also Beth Israel Sisterhood, "Projects," OJMCHE.

43 Project and Event files, Beth Israel Sisterhood, OJMCHE.

44 "Biographical notes," Gussie Reinhardt collection, Box 1, OJMCHE.

45 Lena Holzman oral history (April 22 and May 15, 1974).

46 Alice Meyer, personal account via e-mail to author (August 12, 2015).

47 Lois Shenker oral history, 28.

48 Linda Singer oral history (July 1, 2005), 5–6.

49 Ruth Schnitzer oral history, 5, 6.

50 Lois Shenker oral history, 28.

51 *Hadassah Newsletter*, March 1962. The awardees were for arts, Jacob Avshalomov the conductor of the Portland Junior Symphony; for public relations, Tom McCall for his defense of civil rights and liberties and work on the Metropolitan Youth Commission; for education, PSU president Branford Millar; for human relations, Mark Smith of the Civil Rights Division of the Department of Labor; for medicine, OHSU's Dr. Albert Starr, who invented the first artificial heart valve; and for international relations Mrs. Beatrice Stevens, Portland high school teacher.

52 Ruth Schnitzer oral history, 4.

53 Shirley Nudelman oral history (November 17, 2009), 24.

54 *B'nai B'rith Women Newsletter*, see for example "Percolatin' with Perkel," a social news column. September 1954. B'nai B'rith Collection, Box 11, OJMCHE.

55 All these are themes throughout the minutes and clippings files from the 1960s. NCJW Records, Administration, Box 12; Clippings, Box 18. For more on NCJW civil rights efforts, see chap. 4.

56 *B'nai B'rith Women Newsletter*, December 1957, 2. B'nai B'rith Collection, Box 11, OJMCHE.

57 Hadassah, *Northern Pacific Coast Region Bulletin*, November 1974, 4. Hadassah records, Box 1, OJMCHE.

58 Brautbar, *From Fashion to Politics*, 85–86.

59 Undated flyer, circa 1960s, Hadassah, Box 1. For an analysis of Hadassah fashion shows, see Brautbar, chap. 5.

60 Hadassah, *Northern Pacific Coast Region Bulletin*, April 1965, 2. Hadassah Box 1.

61 Ibid., 1.

62 Ibid., November 1974, 5.

63 Undated press release, circa 1960s. Hadassah, Box 1.

64 *Hadassah Newsletter*, May 1966. Hadassah, Box 6.

65 *B'nai B'rith Women Newsletter*, October 1956, 2, 4. B'nai B'rith Collection, Box 11.

66 For example, a BBW communique in December 1956 reprinted a telegram urging emergency meetings in response to the persecution of Jews in Egypt. B'nai B'rith Women district to chapter presidents, correspondence, December 13, 1956, "Middle East Crisis." B'nai B'rith Collection, Box 11.

67 Rosemarie Rosenfeld oral history, 13.

68 Alvin Rackner oral history (May 11, 2005), 2.

69 Ibid., 4.

70 *Hadassah Northern Pacific Coast Bulletin* (Portland, October 1973), 2, 4.

71 *B'nai B'rith Women Newsletter*, September 1957, 4. B'nai B'rith Collection, Box 11.

72 Jeanne Newmark oral history (February 23, 2007), 11.

73 Meryl Haber oral history (April 10, 2013), 5.

74 Jewish Welfare Federation Yearbook, 1967. JWF, Box 3.

75 B'nai B'rith Women bylaw committee report, n.d., circa 1950s. B'nai B'rith Collection, Box 11.

76 *Hadassah Newsletter*, May 1965. The panel featured Solomon Menashe, Herbert Newmark, and Jerome Parker, and was moderated by Dr. Gerald Cogan.

77 Robison Sisterhood, "Commemorating 60 Years of Service: Generation to Generation: The Robison Jewish Home Sisterhood" (1988), Robison Home File, OJMCHE.

78 Linda Veltman oral history (September 6, 2011), 8.

79 Eve Rosenfeld oral history, 7.

80 *Jewish Review* clipping, January 1969, Holzman File, OJMCHE.

81 "Changing Female Role Topic," *Oregonian*, April 28, 1963, 77. The review of the book, which also referenced the forum, ran in the same issue on p. 39. Ruth Saltzman recounts the process of organizing the event in her oral history, 15.

82 Paula Hyman, "Jewish Feminism Faces the American Women's Movement:

Conversion and Divergence," in *American Jewish Identity Politics*, Deborah Dash Moore, ed. (Ann Arbor: University of Michigan Press, 2008), 222–23.

83 Faith Rogow, *Gone to Another Meeting: The National Council of Jewish Women, 1893–1993* (Tuscaloosa: University of Alabama Press, 1993), 188.

84 Linda Veltman oral history, 8.

85 *Portland Section Bulletin*, NCJW, September 1968, Box 28.

86 Ibid., October 1970.

87 Ibid., September 1971.

88 Letter reprinted in *Portland Section Bulletin*, NCJW, February 1973, Box 28.

89 *Portland Section Bulletin*, NCJW, October 1976.

90 *Jewish Review*, January 1972, 10.

91 *Hadassah, Northern Pacific Coast Bulletin* (October 1973), 3.

92 *Hadassah Newsletter*, October 1983.

93 *Jewish Review*, September 1977, 17–18.

94 Rose Rustin oral history (August 25, 2005), 6–7, 9. The first female president of Beth Israel was Bernadine Brenner, who served from 1981 to 1983.

95 Rogow, *Gone to Another Meeting*, 190–91.

96 "Jewish ERA delegate attacks 'militant faction,'" *Oregonian*, May 6, 1977, NCJW clipping file, Box 18.

97 *Portland Section Bulletin*, NCJW, May 1979.

98 Robison Sisterhood, "Commemorating 60 Years of Service" (1988), Gussie Reinhardt Collection.

99 Lois Shenker oral history, 29.

100 Ibid., 28.

101 "Active Volunteer Knows It Pays Off," *Oregon Journal* (1978). Clippings file, NCJW Box 18.

102 *Jewish Review*, July August 1984, 13.

103 Evelyn Maizels oral history (March 13, 2013), 16.

104 *Jewish Review*, December 1976, 10.

105 Ibid., December 1976, 10.

106 Rosemarie Rosenfeld oral history, 6.

107 Calendars, Beth Israel Sisterhood, Activities (unprocessed box), OJMCHE.

108 "Evening Groups," Beth Israel Sisterhood, Activities.

109 *Hadassah Newsletter*, May/June 1989.

110 *Hadassah Newsletter* (December–January 1988–89), back page.

111 *Neighborhood House Bulletin*, September 2000.

112 *Jewish Review*, July–August 1984, 12, 13, 10. Anderson became editor of the *Review* in 1968 and served for seventeen years; she was followed by Elaine Cogan, who served by 1985–1987.

113 Emily Georges Gottfried, obituary, *Oregon Jewish Life* (February 1, 2013), accessed online.

114 Miranda, *Following a River*, 142.

115 "Biographical notes," Gussie Reinhardt papers, Box 1.

116 *Jewish Review*, December 15, 1994, 8.

117 Ibid., August 15, 1999.

118 *Jewish Welfare Federation Yearbook*, 1967, 1968. JWF, Box 3.

119 Federation campaign coverage from *Jewish Review*, November 1975; December 1975; January 1976.

120 *Jewish Review*, January 1977, 10.

121 Event advertisement, *Jewish Review*, February 1976, 6; February 1978, 3.

122 As noted above, Eve Rosenfeld chaired the Allocations Committee in 1984–1985.

123 *Jewish Review*, December 1983, 9.

124 Ibid., *Jewish Review*, December 1983, 9.

125 "Conference Schedules Feminist, Rabbi" *Oregonian*, October 14, 1984, 11.

126 The spirituality workshops are discussed in the next section of this chapter.

127 "The Emerging Jewish Woman: Workshop Information and Resource Kit," October 28, 1984, Portland, Oregon. Jewish Welfare Federation, Box 4, Organizational Records and Research.

128 *Jewish Review*, April 1, 1994, 5.

129 Ibid., May 15, 1994, 1.

130 Ibid., May 15, 1996, 5.

131 Ibid., December 15, 1993, 1.

132 Ibid., November 1, 2004, 10.

133 *Jewish Review* clipping, 2007, Holzman file, OJMCHE.

134 Shirley Nudelman oral history, 24.

135 Helen Blumenthal oral history, 27.

136 Meryl Haber oral history, 10–11.

137 Judith Hauptman, "Conservative Judaism: The Ethical Challenge of Feminist Change," in Seltzer and Cohen, *Americanization of the Jews,* 296.

138 Deborah Waxman, "'A Lady Sometimes Blows the Shofar': Women's Religious Equality in the Postwar Reconstructionist Movement," in Diner, Kohn, and Kranson, *The Jewish Feminine Mystique*, 88–89.

139 Quoted in Jonathan Sarna, *American Judaism: A History* (New Haven: Yale University Press, 2004), 339.

140 Diner and Benderly, *Her Works Praise Her*, 399–400.

141 Ibid., chap. 16.

142 Sura Rubenstein, "Conference Focuses on Role of Women in Jewish Religion," *Oregonian*, October 29, 1984, B8.

143 Workshop titles and descriptions are found in "The Emerging Jewish Woman: Workshop Information and Resource Kit," October 28, 1984, Portland, Oregon. Jewish Welfare Federation, Box 4, Organizational Records and Research.

144 For a detailed discussion of how migration and an increasingly progressive environment affected synagogue affiliation, see chap. 6.

145 Traditionally, Judaism is passed through the mother, so that any baby born to a Jewish mother is considered Jewish by birth. Recognition of patrilineal descent, adopted by the more liberal branches of Judaism, allows children of Jewish fathers to also be recognized as Jews by birth, regardless of their mothers' status. A *minyan* is the required ten adults needed to hold a formal prayer service and

read from the Torah. Traditionally, the requirement was for ten Jewish men; all branches of Judaism except for the Orthodox now count women in a *minyan*.

146 The tale of this split is told, using pseudonyms for all involved, including the city and congregations, in Phil Zuckerman, *Strife in the Sanctuary: Religious Schism in a Jewish Community* (Walnut Creek, CA: Alta Mira Press, 1999). Additional detail on this split can be found in chap. 6.

147 An exception to this is the expanding Chabad movement in the state. For a discussion of Chabad in Oregon, see chap. 6.

148 *Jewish Review*, November 1986, 10.

149 For a fuller discussion of these affiliation patterns, see chap. 6.

150 Dina Feuer oral history (December 4, 2007), 26–27. The group disbanded after about eight years.

151 Note that Kol Ami grew out of the Southwest Washington Jewish Community Association based in Vancouver, Washington. In 1998, that group formed a congregation; in 2001 they adopted the name Kol Ami; in 2004, they affiliated with the Reform Movement. Rabbi Dunsker, who arrived in 2008, was preceded by two female spiritual leaders, Jan Rabinovitch and Rabbi Aviva Bass. jewishvancouverusa.org/about-us/our-history.

152 *Jewish Review*, August 1, 2002, 8.

153 On Ariel Stone-Halpern see *Jewish Review*, July 15, 1996; June 1, 2002; on Shoshana Dworsky see *Jewish Review*, August 15, 2001. As noted earlier, Stone-Halpern was known as Rabbi Stone after her divorce.

154 Ellen M. Umansky, "Feminism and American Reform Judaism," Seltzer and Cohen, *The Americanization of the Jews*, 267–68.

155 Umansky, "Feminist and American Reform Judaism," 268.

156 "Cantor's Contributions," *Oregon Jewish Life* (June 1, 2012), http://orjewishlife.com/cantors-contributions.

157 Sarna, *American Judaism*, 287.

158 Paula Hyman, "Bat Mitzvah," *Jewish Women's Archive Encyclopedia*, online www.jwa.org/encyclopedia.

159 Paula Hyman, "Ezrat Nashim," 285–86.

160 Hauptman, "Conservative Judaism," 297–98, 301–2. See also Hyman, "Ezrat Nashim," 286; Hyman, "Jewish Feminism Faces the American Women's Movement," 224–25. For the debate within the Conservative movement, see Sarna, *American Judaism*, 340–42.

161 Miranda, *Following a River*, 142.

162 Date for the first Beth Israel bat mitzvah comes from the exhibit notes for *Bat Mitzvah Comes of Age in Oregon*, Oregon Jewish Museum exhibit, 2013. For more on the Reform Movement's tradition of confirmation over bar/bat mitzvah, see Sarna, *American Judaism*, 287.

163 "Introduction," *Bat Mitzvah Comes of Age in Oregon*, Oregon Jewish Museum exhibit, 2013.

164 Goldie Stampfer oral history (August 15, 2005), 12.

165 Miranda, *Following a River*, 142–43.

166 Goldie Stampfer oral history, 12.

167 Ibid., 11. This event occurred around the time of Nehama's bat mitzvah, approximately 1971.

168 Milton Horenstein oral history (November 14, 2003), 18.

169 Rabbi Yonah Geller, quoted in *The Three Rabbis* DVD.

170 *The First Hundred Years of Shaarie Torah, 1905–2005* (Portland: Congregation Shaarie Torah, 2005), 1. Shaarie Torah collection, OJMCHE.

171 For example, in the listing of synagogues in the *Jewish Review* in the mid-1980s, the congregation was listed as Modern Orthodox.

172 Rabbi Baruch Shapiro to Mark Schnitzer, August 6, 1962. Rabbi Geller papers, correspondence files, OJMCHE.

173 Rabbi Israel Klavan to Rabbi Yonah Geller (Corpus Christi), November 25, 1955, Rabbi Geller papers, correspondence files, OJMCHE.

174 Account of the bat mitzvah of Michelle Goldberg. *Jewish Review*, December 1971, 4.

175 *Jewish Review*, November 1985, 15.

176 Ibid., March 14, 1997, 1; January 1, 1999, 15.

177 Rabbi Yonah Geller oral history, 13.

178 Rabbi Arthur Zuckerman oral history (June 19, 2014), 23–24. See also "Shaarie Torah Rabbi Finds Balance in Transition," *Northwest Examiner*, April 2013, 18–19.

179 Marshal Spector to Rabbi David Rosenberg and President Barry Benson, Shaarie Torah, January 9, 2006. Rabbi Geller papers, Box 27, "Non-Rabbi Correspondence."

180 Milt Carl and Rabbi Yonah Geller, quoted in *Three Rabbis* DVD.

181 Milton Horenstein oral history, 18.

182 Lorraine Rose, quoted in *Three Rabbis* DVD.

183 Rabbi Michael Cahana oral history (October 28, 2010), 13.

184 For background on both Rabbi Michael Cahana and Cantor Ida Rae Cahana, see "Our Clergy," www.bethisrael-pdx.org/about/clergy.

185 For more on Gesher see chap. 6.

Chapter Four

1 "Statement of Portland Jewish Community Relations Committee to the Committee on Race and Education," *Jewish Review*, May 5, 1964.

2 This has been widely documented by historians including Jonathan Sarna, Hasia Diner, Stuart Svonkin, Marc Dollinger, and Cheryl Greenberg.

3 Eisenberg, *Embracing a Western Identity*, chap. 6; Eisenberg, *The First to Cry Down Injustice? Western Jews and Japanese Removal during World War II* (Lanham, MD: Lexington Books/Rowman & Littlefield, 2008), chap. 2.

4 Stuart McElderry calls the City Club's 1945 report "The Negro in Portland," "Portland's version of *An American Dilemma*." Stuart J. McElderry, "The Problem of the Color Line: Civil Rights and Racial Ideology in Portland, Oregon, 1944–1965" (PhD diss. University of Oregon, 1998), 119.

5　The city of Vanport was hastily built on a floodplain along Columbia River to house shipyard workers during World War II. At the time of the flood in 1948, Vanport was home to approximately 40,000, about 40 percent of them African American, making it the largest African American community in the state. For a discussion of Jewish involvement in desegregation efforts, see Eisenberg, *Embracing a Western Identity*, chap. 6.

6　Irene Balk oral history, 9.

7　*Portland 1952: One Ethnic Group Supporting Another* (1962); David Robinson to Hyman Balk (October 3, 1952), Congregation Tifereth Israel collection, OJMCHE. This folder also contains a number of undated newspaper clippings about the incident.

8　McElderry, "The Problem of the Color Line," 364. See also Ethan Johnson and Felicia Williams, "Desegregation and Multiculturalism in the Portland Public Schools," *Oregon Historical Quarterly* 111, no. 1 (Spring 2010): 6–37.

9　McElderry, "Problem of the Color Line," 365–73.

10　See Herbert M. Schwab, *Race and Equal Educational Opportunity in Portland's Public Schools* (Report to the Board of Education, Portland, October 29, 1964). Lawyer and Jewish community leader Roscoe Nelson also served on the Schwab Committee.

11　"Statement of Portland Jewish Community Relations Committee to the Committee on Race and Education," published in *The Jewish Review*, May 5, 1964. Although Congregation Beth Israel was not a signatory, their Social Action Committee did approve the statement and the Congregation did later issue an endorsement of the Schwab Report.

12　McElderry, "Problem of the Color Line," 372.

13　Marc Dollinger, *Quest for Inclusion: Jews and Liberalism in Modern America* (Princeton: Princeton University Press, 2000), 188–89.

14　Dollinger, *Quest for Inclusion*, 186.

15　There is vigorous debate over this apparent conflict. Some historians flatly label this migration as hypocritical. Other historians offer more sympathetic readings. See Lila Corwin Berman, "Jewish Urban Politics in the City and Beyond," *The Journal of American History* 99, no. 2 (September 2012): 495–96; Cheryl Greenberg, "Liberal NIMBY: American Jews and Civil Rights" *Journal of Urban History* 38, no. 3 (May 2012): 452; Gerald Gamm, *Urban Exodus: Why the Jews Left Boston and the Catholics Stayed* (Cambridge: Harvard University Press, 1999), 15.

16　According to the Schwab report, Irvington School was 30 percent African American in 1960, 42 percent in 1963–64, 48 percent in 1964–65. Sabin was 15 percent African American in 1960, 26 percent in 1963–64, and 33 percent the following year. Schwab report, 31–34. The Portland Hebrew School roster, 1960, indicates which public school each of the enrolled children attended.

17　McElderry, "Problem of the Color Line," Appendix A, 398.

18　Whereas over a third of the Jewish community lived in North/Northeast in 1957, that number shrank to 14 percent by 1971. See Tables 1 and 2 in chaps. 1 and 6. It is important to note that the Portland Jewish Academy (day school) did not open until 1986.

19   Beth Israel separately voted to support the plan. *Jewish Review* (June 1970): 1, 8, 14.

20   Johnson and Williams, "Desegregation and Multiculturalism," 24. Newman resigned from the school board in 1979, in the midst of conflict over the desegregation plan.

21   For a detailed discussion of the Jordan case see Eisenberg, *Embracing a Western Identity*, chap. 6. See also Michael Munk "Oregon's Scottsboro Case," *The Portland Alliance* (February 2001), http://college.lclark.edu/programs/political _economy/student_resources/past/ (accessed October 12, 2012).

22   Eisenberg, *The First to Cry Down Injustice*, chap. 2.

23   Eisenberg, *Embracing a Western Identity*, chap. 6.

24   Harry Gevurtz narrative, 1974, 4. See also, Eisenberg, *Embracing a Western Identity*, chap. 6.

25   Elinor Shank oral history (January 23, 2007), 8.

26   Paul Meyer oral history (August 18, 2009), 7. Alice Meyer, personal account via e-mail to author (August 12, 2015). Maure Goldschmidt was the uncle of future Portland mayor and Oregon governor Neil Goldschmidt.

27   An excellent account of this phase of the movement can be found in McElderry, "Problem of the Color Line," chap. 4. For a discussion of Jewish involvement in this phase of the movement, see Eisenberg, *Embracing a Western Identity*, chap. 6.

28   Michael Munk, *The Portland Red Guide: Sites and Stories of our Radical Past* (Portland: Ooligan Press, 2007), 106.

29   Munk, *The Portland Red Guide*, 106, 138. On Robison, see Munk, "Oregon's Scottsboro Case."

30   Lowenstein, *Jews of Oregon*, 177. See also "In Tribute to Harry M. Kenin," *Oregon Democrat* (April 1954): 13, Harry Kenin individual file, OJMCHE. On Robinson's role, see Gerald Robinson resume, Robinson file, OJMCHE.

31   Lowenstein, *Jews of Oregon*, 170.

32   Paul Meyer oral history (August 18, 2009), 7. See also Sid Lezak oral history (August 2, 2005), 14–15. Among the founders and early officers of the ACLU were Jonathan Newman, Paul Meyer, Herbert Schwab, and Sid Lezak. Note that, although Richard Neuberger briefly attended law school, he did not complete his degree or practice law.

33   George Bodner oral history (June 26, 2007), 10.

34   Robert Litin oral history (January 19, 2010), 6–7.

35   Richard Littman oral history (May 17, 2007), 10.

36   Morris Galen oral history (May 23, 2010), 7–8.

37   Lowenstein, 179–80. Stein, *Gus J. Solomon*, 34.

38   Alice Meyer, personal account via e-mail to author (August 12, 2015).

39   Leon Gabinet oral history, 10–11. Hart, Spencer would eventually become Stoel Rives, the largest law firm in Oregon.

40   Meyer Eisenberg, recounted to the author via e-mail, June 7, 2013 (Eisenberg is the author's father). See also Stein, *Gus J. Solomon*, 202–3.

41   Joy Alkalay oral history (February 15, 1976), 8.

42 Leon Gabinet oral history, 2.

43 The earliest members of MAC, including several members of the Goldsmith family, a Lipman, a Wasserman and a Friedlander, are listed in Kristyn McIvor, Joel D. Freeman, and Luana Hellman Hill, *Legacy of the Twenty-Six: A Celebration of the First 100 Years of the Multnomah Athletic Club* (1991), 19. On the restrictive admissions policy, see *Perfectly Fit: The Multnomah Athletic Club, 1891–2016*, Oregon Historical Society. The exhibit notes that the restrictive policy began in "the 1920s or earlier."

44 Stein, *Gus Solomon*, 205–6.

45 On the "Jewish committee," see Hal Saltzman oral history (December 20, 2006), 8. A number of informants mention quotas at the MAC see, for example, Ilaine Cohen oral history (August 29, 2008), 4; Harry Turtledove oral history, (December 6, 2004), 12.

46 Video testimony from Robert Liberty for the memorial service for Roger Meyer, shared with the author via e-mail by Paul Meyer (brother of Roger Meyer), November 2014.

47 Henry Blauer oral history (October 1, 2008), 3.

48 Toll, *Making of an Ethnic Middle Class*, 142.

49 *B'nai B'rith Bulletin*, April 1957. B'nai B'rith records, Box 9, OJMCHE.

50 Rabbi Stephen Wise (1874–1949) served Portland's Beth Israel from 1900 to 1906 and then went on to establish New York's Free Synagogue and to become one of the foremost leaders of the Reform movement and of American Zionism in the country.

51 Eisenberg, *Embracing a Western Identity*, chap. 6.

52 *Beth Israel Bulletin* (October 20 and November 3, 1950). Nodel continued such activities in subsequent years. For example, he spoke on "Prejudice—Its Causes and Cures" at a joint service of five churches. *Beth Israel Bulletin* 2 (14), January 18, 1952. Similar titles appear throughout Nodel's tenure, 1950–1959.

53 *Beth Israel Bulletin* (May 18, 1962). The committee included another member of this group of Jewish activists, Hans Linde, who at the time was a professor of law at the University of Oregon. Serving with them were the managing editor of the Medford *Mail Tribune*, the president of the City Club, a past president of the Oregon Council of Churches, and former Governor Charles Sprague.

54 Ibid. (February 10, 1961).

55 Ibid. (July 5, 1963 and August 30, 1963).

56 Joshua Joe Bryan, Portland, "Oregon's Long Hot Summers: Racial Unrest and Public Response, 1967–1969" (master's thesis, Portland State University, 2013), 68.

57 *Beth Israel Bulletin* (February 5, 1954).

58 Ibid. (January 18, 1965).

59 *Jewish Review* December 1963.

60 *Neveh Shalom Chronicle* (March 12, 1964). It is difficult to document the level of activity at Neveh Shalom because much of the congregation's archive has not survived; the *Chronicle* did not generally announce sermon topics.

61 Rabbi Geller, undated 1963 sermon, Shaarie Torah collection, OJMCHE.

62   Rabbi Geller, "Shabbaos Behar Behukos" (May 9, 1964), Shaarie Torah collection. This sermon coincided with the joint communal letter to the School Board.

63   Sarna, *American Judaism*, 309.

64   For more on Neighborhood House's commitment to intergroup work, see Eisenberg, *Embracing a Western Identity*, chap. 3.

65   McElderry, "Problem of the Color Line," 143.

66   Ibid., 148–51, 155.

67   Jacob Tanzer oral history (April 20, 2010), 4.

68   Jacob Tanzer, "1964, My Story of Life and Death in Mississippi." Jacob Tanzer people file, OJM, 2.

69   Sid Lezak oral history, OJMCHE, 13.

70   Paul Meyer oral history (August 18, 2009), 9.

71   *B'nai B'rith Bulletin*, April 1957. On Willner's sponsorship of the bills, see *Oregonian*, April 9, 1957, 2.

72   *Beth Israel Bulletin*, May 18, 1962.

73   *B'nai B'rith Bulletin*, April 1957. The minutes of the March 27, 1957, Lodge meeting show that Hershel Tanzer's proposed resolution to support "wholeheartedly" these measures passed unanimously.

74   *B'nai B'rith Bulletin*, March 1959, 4.

75   Ibid., September 1961; October 1961.

76   Ibid., February 1961; February 1962.

77   The group also included lawyer Ossie Georges and economist Mike Katz. Paul Meyer, personal interview with the author, November 26, 2014.

78   Although Dick Neuberger was Jewish, his wife, Maurine, was not.

79   The major shift toward the Democratic Party occurred in the mid-1950s; in addition to Neuberger's US Senate seat, Democrat Edith Green won election to the US Congress. Two years later, maverick Republican US Senator Wayne Morse switched his party affiliation to the Democratic Party, and was then reelected. Paul Meyer oral history (July 28, 2009), 9.

80   Paul Meyer oral history (August 6, 2009), 2–3. See also *Sidney I. Lezak: An Oral History*, Oregon Historical Society, SR 1220 (Portland: US District Court of Oregon Historical Society), 21–22. Willner and Mike Katz each served a term as president of the Young Democrats during this period. Ossie Georges and Ernie Bonyhadi were also involved in the group.

81   Sylvia Davidson, 8, 10. See also, Spokane *Spokesman Review*, July 31, 1959, 2. Davidson was a key player in Edith Green's Congressional campaign, as well as in the Oregon campaigns of presidential candidates Adlai Stevenson and John F. Kennedy. She attended Reed in the late 1940s, as did Bonyhadi, Georges, and Linde.

82   Leon Gabinet oral history, 6.

83   Jacob Tanzer oral history, 11–20.

84   Sid Lezak obituary, *Oregonian* (August 2, 2005).

85   "Guiding Principles," *Oregon Jewish Life* (November 1, 2012), http://orjewishlife.com/guiding-principles.

86   "Legal Ladies," *Oregon Jewish Life* (December 1, 2014), http://orjewishlife.com/legal-ladies.

87   Ben Padrow obituary, *Oregonian*, February 10, 1986, 3M.

88   "Neil Goldschmidt," *Oregon Encyclopedia*, Oregon Historical Society, http ://oregonencyclopedia.org/articles/goldschmidt_neil/#.VvrHBuIrLcs; and Ron Buel, "The Goldschmidt Era," *Willamette Week*, 25th Anniversary Edition, accessed online. See also "Fate of Rights Bill Crucial Test," *Eugene Register-Guard*, February 25, 1964, B1. For more on Goldschmidt, see chap. 1.

89   Jonathan Newman obituary, *Oregonian*, October 25, 1991.

90   Paul Meyer oral history (August 6, 2009), 5.

91   Elden Rosenthal oral history (June 17, 2010), 10.

92   Tanzer, "1964," 2.

93   Ibid., 15.

94   *Jewish Review*, September 1985, 6–7. Note that this is not Jack B. Schwartz, long-time community leader, mentioned in chap. 1, who was also an attorney.

95   Ibid., March 15, 1993, 8.

96   April Baer, "What Is Cesar Chavez's Connection to Oregon," Oregon Public Broadcasting, July 17, 2012, http://www.opb.org/news/article/what-cesar -chavezs-connection-oregon.

97   Jacob Tanzer oral history, 1. Tanzer is emphatic in saying that being Jewish did not create any professional barriers for him.

98   Hasia Diner, *Jews in the United States*, 266; Eric Goldstein, *The Price of Whiteness: Jews, Race, and American Identity* (Princeton: Princeton University Press, 2006), 218.

99   For an extensive treatment of this phenomenon among white ethnics (including Jews), see Matthew Frye Jacobson, *Roots Too: White Ethnic Revival in Post-Civil Rights America* (Cambridge: Harvard University Press, 2006).

100 Goldstein, *The Price of Whiteness*, 213.

101 Camille Debreczeny, "Jewish Racialization and the National Council of Jewish Women, Portland Section" (Willamette University, Liberal Arts Research Collaborative project, Summer 2014), 7.

102 Debreczeny, "Jewish Racialization," 8.

103 Jennifer Stevens, "Feminizing Portland, Oregon: A History of the League of Women Voters in the Postwar Era, 1950–1975," in *Breaking the Wave: Women: Their Organizations, and Feminism, 1945–1985*, Kathleen A. Laughlin and Jacqueline L. Casteldine, eds. (New York: Routledge, 2011), 155–72.

104 Margaret Labby oral history, 5.

105 *Scribe*, June 1952, 9. Barbara Schwab was married to Judge Herbert Schwab. City commissioner Mildred Schwab was his sister.

106 Alice Meyer, personal account via e-mail to author (August 12, 2015).

107 Elinor Shank oral history (January 23, 2007), 6.

108 Steve Reed Johnson, "Perseverance of the League of Women Voters," Civic Portland, online http://stevenreedjohnson.com/stevenreedjohnson/pdx.league-women.html. See chap. 1.

109 Tara Watson and Melody Rose, "She Flies with Her Own Wings: Women in the 1973 Oregon Legislative Session," *Oregon Historical Quarterly* 111, no. 1 (Spring 2010): 38–63.

110 Watson and Rose, "She Flies with Her Own Wings."

111 *Jewish Review*, February 15, 1993, 17.

112 Elinor Shank oral history (July 31, 2007), 1–2.

113 Martin Acker oral history, 12–13.

114 Richard Littman oral history, 7, 10.

115 Merritt Linn oral history (July 24, 2008), 2.

116 Dina Linn oral history (August 2, 2004), 3, 6.

117 Don Zadoff oral history (October 20, 2009), 7.

118 *Jewish Review*, March 15, 1999, 1.

119 Alvin Rackner oral history, 8.

120 *Jewish Review*, February 15, 1996, 1.

121 Anonymous, doctor's personal account shared with the author, July 3, 2015. The mother here is the author.

122 *Hadassah Newsletter*, November 1963, 2.

123 The *Jewish Review* began publication in 1959 under Padrow's editorship. His tenure as editor lasted until 1962, when a publications committee took over this responsibility. See Howard Temkin, "Portland Jewish Newspapers (1893–2012): An Overview," research document, Oregon Jewish Museum (February 2012), 17–18.

124 *Jewish Review*, March 1960, 5.

125 Ibid., July 1960, 7.

126 Ibid., January 1962, 8.

127 Ibid., November 1962, 4; December 1962, 2, 3.

128 A full run of the paper is not available. For volume 1 (1959–60), ten of the paper's sixteen editions are available. Of these, about half carried stories on race relations/civil rights themes, none of them local.

129 *Jewish Review*, June 1963, 2.

130 Ibid., October 1963, 1, 2.

131 Ibid., October 1961, 2.

132 Ibid., June 1963, 3, 5.

133 Ibid., December 1963, 7.

134 Ibid., May 1965, 2.

135 The story of Neighborhood House's evolution is told more fully in Eisenberg, *Embracing a Western Identity*, chap. 3.

136 NCJW, *Bulletin* (January 1963); Portland section, Minutes, April 1964.

137 NCJW, Portland section, Minutes, May 28, 1969.

138 NCJW, Letter to School Board, March 12, 1970.

139 Patricia Rumer, "Citizen Advocacy Groups—An Intervention Strategy: A Case Study of the Community Coalition for School Integration in Portland, Oregon" (PhD diss., Portland State University, 1981), appendix E. See also *City Club of Portland Bulletin* 60, no. 56 (May 30, 1980): 339.

140 Debreczeny, "Jewish Racialization," 5; numerous statements of support for Affirmative Action can be found in Section records, up through the turn of the twenty-first century.

141 NCJW Portland section, Minutes May 26, 1965. There are mentions of the Albina preschool program in the minutes as late as 1969.

142 NCJW, Portland section minutes, December 7 1969.

143 See, for example, Sarna, *American Judaism,* 306–23. Dollinger, *Quest for Inclusion,* chap. 8; Stuart Svonkin, *Jews against Prejudice: American Jews and the Fight for Civil Liberties* (New York: Columbia University Press, 1977), chap. 8. This focus on worldwide Jewry will be explored in chap. 5.

144 *Jewish Review,* June 1970, 8.

145 NCJW Portland section, Minutes, Special Consultation Meeting, January 17, 1969.

146 NCJW, Portland section, Minutes, May 28, 1969. Organizational records demonstrate that the Section remained engaged with this issue for many years afterward; for example, Council had a representative on the Desegregation Monitoring Advisory Committee for the School District well into the 1980s. See NCJW *Bulletin,* November 1983.

147 NCJW, Portland Section minutes, October 20, 1969. See Debreczeny, "Jewish Racialization," 10–12. Quoting Eric Goldstein's *The Price of Whiteness,* Debreczeny notes how this episode reveals the white privilege under which councilwomen operated and that, as Jewish women had become fully accepted as white members of the middle class, they used "blacks and black causes as surrogates for concerns that had become less immediate in their own lives, but to which they retained a strong emotional connection."

148 NCJW, Letter to School Board, March 12, 1970.

149 NCJW, "Green Circle 1977–1989," Projects, Box 24.

150 NCJW "Defining Justice for Children" report, 1982, Juvenile Justice file.

151 *Beth Israel Bulletin,* November 18, 1960, 1.

152 SAC minutes (January 25, 1961). Congregation Beth Israel, Board of Trustee Committee files. SAC Report, Congregation Beth Israel annual meeting, June 2, 1961.

153 As noted earlier, the congregational board did not pass this resolution until later that year. CBI Board minutes, April 16, 1964, and December 21, 1964. The reason for this delay is not clear.

154 SAC minutes, June 27, 1967.

155 Ibid., June 11, 1968.

156 Ibid., January 5, 1968.

157 Ibid., May 14, 1968.

158 Ibid., 1970. In 1970–1971, the SAC developed two major subcommittees, one dealing with Jewish affairs and the other with "the problems of the black and other minority communities in Portland." SAC minutes, July 7, 1970.

159 The SAC minutes show numerous instances in which the committee affirmed its commitment to addressing local racial issues and/or took a stand on local issues. See Social Action Committee records, "The Black Jewish Dialogue."

160 SAC minutes, June 11, 1968.

161 Ibid., May 14, 1968.

162 Ibid., June 11, 1968.

163 *Jewish Review*, April 1968, 1.

164 Project Equality letter, August 21, 1972, SAC file.

165 SAC minutes, July 14, 1977.

166 NCJW Project Records, Boxes 24–26.

167 SAC minutes, October 8, 1968; February 11, 1968; September 9, 1969; August 21, 1972.

168 NCJW "Indo-Chinese Cultural," 1979–84, Box 8.

169 SAC minutes August 8, 1979.

170 *Jewish Review*, July/August 1979, 1, 10.

171 Ibid., March 1981, 3.

172 Ibid., February 1986, 16–17.

173 1971 Census, 43.

174 "Community Relations Committee Summary," *Jewish Federation of Portland Annual Report*, 1986–7. Arden Shenker Collection, Box 4.

175 Rosenthal oral history, 13, 20.

176 *Jewish Review*, March 1, 1993, 10.

177 "About Us," Coalition Against Hate Crimes, http://www.againsthate.pdx.edu /about.htm.

178 Emily Simon papers, OJMCHE.

179 Elden Rosenthal oral history, 6.

180 "Queer Heroes NW—Featured Hero: Sanford Director" (June 25, 2014), Q Center, www.pdxqcenter.org. The Imperial Sovereign Rose Court of Oregon was the state's first LGBTQ organization.

181 Peter Boag, "Gay and Lesbian Rights Movement," http://oregonencyclopedia.org /articles/gay_lesbian_rights_movement/#.VvxQk-IrLcs.

182 *Oregon Voters Pamphlet*, 1992, 115, 116, 107. On the formation of the PAC see *Jewish Review*, September 1, 1992, 5.

183 Steve Wasserstrom, "Measure 9 Threatens All," *Jewish Review*, September 1, 1992, 9. An example of such a profile is that of Holly Hart, lesbian activist and restaurant owner, on the front page of the *Jewish Review*'s February 15–29, 1992 issue.

184 *Jewish Review*, October 15, 1992, 1.

185 Ibid., June 15, 1993, 5.

186 For the joint statement, see *Oregon Voters Pamphlet*, 1994, 92. Horenstein and Haist op-ed pieces, *Jewish Review*, November 1, 1994, 10. For additional coverage see *Jewish Review*, September 15, 1994, 6; October 15, 1994, 6.

187 *Jewish Review*, June 15–30, 1990, 4; August 1990, 4; September 1990, 4.

188 *Oregonian,* September 22, 1992, C4.

189 Josh Kardon's remembrance of this incident was originally shared on Facebook, and then published by BlueOregon.com, http://www.blueoregon.com/2013/03 /how-ron-wyden-became-first-us-senator-ever-endorse-marriage-equality/

190 See discussion in chap. 6.

191 Harris was spokesperson for an interfaith coalition, the Religious Response

Network, which submitted anti–Measure 36 arguments for the *Voters' Pamphlet*. 2004 *Voters' Pamphlet*, 95.

192 *Amicus Brief in Support of Motion for Summary Judgement*, http://www .millernash.com/files/News/1c94b19b-1221–4b3b-b368-3f3f04aeb31a /Presentation/NewsAttachment/c3159faf-65d4-4c26-8603-43386b2537ed /OAJC%20Amicus%20Brief.pdf.

193 Peter Zuckerman, "How Reedies Helped Oregon Win the Freedom to Wed," *Reed Magazine* (June 17, 2014), http://www.reed.edu/reed_magazine/collg portal /posts/2014/how-reedies-helped-oregon-win-the-freedom-to-marry.html.

194 In the *Portland Jewish Tomorrow* report, Federation director Marc Blattner articulated the goals of making Jewish community more "accessible, inclusive, meaningful/inspiring, and fun." Under "inclusive," welcoming the LGBTQ community, as well as interfaith families and people with disabilities, was the main priority. Blattner, "Marc's Remarks," Addendum A, 65.

195 Jewish Federation of Portland, Executive Summary, 2009 Population Study; Revised Report, February 2010 (Yacoubian Research), question 8, 50. This compared to only 7.5 percent who believed Israel should be the first priority and 15.8 percent who listed "fighting anti-Semitism." Among those who were "known Jews"—meaning they were affiliated with the Jewish community—"promotion of civil rights and tolerance" still received a plurality among the individual choices, although with only 17 percent of the respondents. "All of them" was also a possible response, and among the "known Jews," 40 percent chose this response.

Chapter Five

1 Just a few months earlier, Rose had been the subject of an extensive feature profile in the *Oregonian*'s Sunday magazine. Stan Federman, "Rabbi Rose: Man for All Seasons," *Oregonian, Northwest Magazine,* March 19, 1967, 8, 13.

2 Rabbi Rose letter to congregation, May 24, 1967. Beth Israel Correspondence file.

3 Noam Stampfer to Elton Adler (May 26, 1967), reprint in the *Neveh Shalom Chronicle*, June 13, 1967, 3.

4 Rabbi Joshua Stampfer, "Diary of an Israelite" *Oregonian, Northwest Magazine,* August 20, 1967, 8. Because the *Jewish Review* took a summer hiatus, publishing in early June, before the war's outbreak, and not again until September, these accounts did not appear in that publication.

5 Goldie Stampfer to congregation (May 23 or 24, 1967), in *Neveh Shalom Chronicle,* June 8, 1967, 2.

6 Rabbi Stampfer to congregation (May 25, 1967), *Neveh Shalom Chronicle,* June 13, 1967, 4.

7 Federman, "Rabbi from Portland," *Oregonian*, June 7, 1967, 8.

8 Rose, "A Report from Israel," *Oregonian, Northwest Magazine,* June 18, 1967, 6.

9 Stampfer, "Diary," 8.

10 Federman, "Rabbi from Portland," 8.

11 Stampfer, "Diary," 8.

12 Rose, "Report from Israel," 6.

13 "Portland Rabbi Airs Peace Hope in Wake of Victory by Israel," *Oregonian*, June 18, 1967, 23.

14 Stampfer, "Diary," 13.

15 Rose, "A Report from Israel," 6.

16 "Portland Rabbi," *Oregonian*, June 18, 1967, 23.

17 Diner, *The Jews of the United States*, 323.

18 Heschel, quoted in Sarna, *American Judaism*, 315.

19 Urofsky, quoted in Theodore Sasson, *The New American Zionism* (New York: New York University Press, 2014): 21.

20 Sarna, *American Judaism*, 315–16.

21 Sasson, *New American Zionism*, 20.

22 "Special Campaign Issue," *Jewish Review*, March 1967, 1.

23 Hershel Tanzer, "A Message from the Federation President," *Jewish Review*, June 1967, 1.

24 *Jewish Review*, September 1967, 1.

25 Sasson, *New American Zionism*, 21.

26 Jewish Welfare Federation of Portland, *The Challenge 1970* (campaign issue), Jewish Federation of Portland, Organizational Records, Box 3.

27 Diner, *Jews of the United States*, 324.

28 Susan Abravanel, op-ed. *Jewish Review*, March 15, 1998, 13.

29 Dollinger, *Quest for Inclusion*, 201.

30 Sarna, *American Judaism*, 315–17.

31 Alice Mandler oral history (n.d. 1978), 6.

32 Arden Shenker oral history (June 13, 2007), 14.

33 See discussion of the 1971 Census in chap. 1.

34 1971 Census, 16

35 Ibid., 33–35.

36 *Jewish Review*, November 1967, 1, 3, 4.

37 Ibid., November 1967, 3.

38 Rabbi Yonah Geller, *Jewish Review*, February 1970, 2.

39 Anti-Defamation League ad, *Jewish Review*, July-August 1976, 10.

40 *Jewish Review*, December 1975, 1.

41 Morris Stein, "Musings," *Jewish Review*, December 1975, 2.

42 According to the 1971 survey of known Jews in Portland, 30 percent of those over the age of 65 had visited Israel; only 17 percent of those 45–64 and 13 percent of those ages 25–44 had done so. Question 48, 1971 survey.

43 Sasson, *New American Zionism*, 13–14.

44 *Jewish Review*, September 1971, 2.

45 Shenker speech, reprinted in *Jewish Review*, April 1976, 1.

46 Shenker Collection, Box 4 correspondence.

47 Morris "Moe" Stein oral history (August 16, 2004), 2.

48 For example, see Morris Stein, "Musings," *Jewish Review*, May 1976.

49 *Jewish Review*, May 1978, 2.

50 Jewish Federation of Portland, Annual Report, 1986–7, Shenker collection, Box 4.

51 *Jewish Review*, March 1984, 4.

52 Ibid., Summer 1986, Calendar announcement.

53 Sarna, *American Judaism,* 318–19.

54 The earlier Hillel Day School had been affiliated with the Orthodox movement.

55 Sarna, *American Judaism*, 317.

56 William Orbach, *The American Movement to Aid Soviet Jews* (Amherst: University of Massachusetts Press, 1979), 4.

57 Charlie Schiffman oral history (February 14, 2013), 7.

58 Dollinger, *Quest for Inclusion*, 221.

59 Sarna, *American Judaism*, 318.

60 *Congregation Beth Israel Bulletin*, May 8, 1964.

61 *Jewish Review*, May 1964, 2. See discussion of the school desegregation issue in chap. 3.

62 Ibid., March 1966, 2; November 1966, 3.

63 *Congregation Beth Israel Bulletin*, January 1, 8, and 22, 1965; February 12, 1965; March 19 and 26, 1965; and April 30, 1965. The *Bulletin* only occasionally printed sermon titles; often it simply indicated that Rabbi Rose would present an "inspirational sermon," without specifying the topic.

64 Social Action Committee minutes, June 11, 1968.

65 Social Action Committee, February 3, 1970.

66 Ibid., July 7, 1970.

67 Social Action Committee minutes, February 23, 1971; April 6, 1971; October 13, 1971.

68 For an account of the Stampfers' mission, see David Michael Smith, *To Learn and to Teach: The Life of Rabbi Joshua Stampfer* (Portland: Institute for Judaic Studies, 2003), 242–58.

69 *Jewish Review*, May 1970, 1.

70 Jewish Welfare Federation, letter, April 15, 1971. Box 3, Correspondence Re: Soviet Jewry, 1969–1973.

71 Jewish Welfare Federation, letter, October 3, 1972. Box 3, Correspondence Re: Soviet Jewry, 1969–1973.

72 *Jewish Review*, May 1971, 1.

73 Governor Neil Goldschmidt, "Proclamation" (December 6, 1987). Jewish Federation of Portland organizational chart (1987). Arden Shenker Collection, Box 4, CRC materials.

74 Annelise Orleck, "Soviet Jewish Immigration," in *Encyclopedia of American Jewish History*, vol. 1, Stephen Norwood and Eunice Pollack, eds. (Santa Barbara: ABC-CLIO, 2008), 47.

75 *Jewish Review*, June 1, 2000, 1.

76 "Community Relations Committee summary," Jewish Federation of Portland, *Annual Report*, 1986–87 (Ardern Shenker Collection, CRC materials, Box 4).

77 *Oregon Journal* clipping (n.d., 1974). NCJW collection, Box 26, Projects, "Russian Resettlement, 1971–1980). This file also contains thank-you letters from JFCS to council section president Sharon Tarlow, noting the council's work in setting up apartments and orienting new families.

78 *Jewish Review*, September 1976, 22. See also Alvin Rackner oral history, 6.

79   *Jewish Review*, June 1977, 1.

80   "Many Soviet Jews Settle in Portland," *Oregonian*, September 18, 1978, 13.

81   Alvin Rackner oral history, 5.

82   *Jewish Review*, April 1988, 15. Emphasis in original.

83   Ibid., September 1989, 41.

84   Ibid., April 1990, 1.

85   Ibid., August 1990, 1.

86   *Oregon Journal* clipping (n.d., 1974). NCJW collection, Box 26, Projects, "Russian Resettlement, 1971–1980).

87   Tanya Lifshitz, *In the Beginning: An English-Russian Guidebook for New Immigrants* (Portland: JFCS, March 1981). Jewish Family and Child Services collection, OJMCHE.

88   NCJW (national) "Moments in History" (1993), in NCJW-Portland *Bulletin* (January 1993). NCJW Records, Publications, Box 29.

89   Clipping (n.d., 1974), in "Russian Resettlement, 1971–1980," NCJW Records, Projects, Box 26.

90   Diner, *Jews of the United States*, 317–18.

91   *Jewish Review*, September 1976, 19.

92   *Oregonian*, December 19, 1976, 76.

93   Eugene *Register-Guard*, September 18, 1978, 4.

94   Carol Chestler's comments appear in a paper by Scott P. Anderson, "Acclimation and Adjustment: Russian Jews in Oregon, 1970s-1980s." (University of Oregon, unpublished paper, June 2007). "Soviet Jews" subject file, OJMCHE.

95   Alvin Rackner oral history, 6.

96   Yulia Libov was a featured speaker at the June 2000 annual Federation meeting celebrating "Ten Years of Russian Resettlement." By then, she had graduated from the University of Oregon. *Jewish Review*, July 1, 2000, 6.

97   *Jewish Review*, June 1, 2000, 1.

98   Ibid., December 1975, 15.

99   Ibid., April 1989, 5.

100   Ibid., September 1987, flyer insert.

101   Ibid., October 1989, 4.

102   Ibid., November 1, 1991, and February 1, 1992, 1.

103   Sasson, *New American Zionism*, 13.

104   Ibid., 14.

105   Ibid., 28.

106   The new editorial policy was announced in April 1977, on the *Jewish Review*'s front page. The "Question of the Month" feature began that summer.

107   *Jewish Review*, July-August 1977, 3.

108   Sasson's account aims to refute the widely held perception that American Jews have "distanced" themselves from Israel, positing instead that the relationship with Israel has actually intensified, becoming more personal and diverse.

109   This section was greatly informed by discussions with undergraduate Cathryn Priebe through Willamette's Liberal Arts Research Collaborative in the summer

of 2014. See Cathryn Priebe, "Zionism in Oregon" (Willamette University, Liberal Arts Research Collaborative, Summer 2014).

110 *Jewish Review*, October 1977, 2.

111 Ibid., December 1977, 14.

112 Ibid., May 1982, 15 and 21.

113 Ibid., June 1982, 6.

114 Ibid., December 1981, 17.

115 Events Files, JCC organizational records, Box 1.

116 *Jewish Review*, November 1982, 2.

117 Ibid., October 1989, 1.

118 Breira means choice or alternative in Hebrew. It is an implicit response to the frequent assertion that Israel had "no choice" (*ain breira*), asserting that Israel did have options about how to move forward toward peace.

119 Jack Wertheimer, "Breaking the Taboo: Critics of Israel and the American Jewish Establishment," in *Envisioning Israel: The Changing Images and Ideals of North American Jews*, Allon Gal, ed. (Detroit: Wayne State University Press, 1996): 397–419.

120 Sasson, *New American Zionism*, 32. See also Steven Rosenthal, *Irreconcilable Differences: The Waning of the American Jewish Love Affair with Israel* (Hanover: Brandeis University Press/University Press of New England, 2001).

121 Quoted in Wertheimer, "Breaking the Taboo," 410.

122 *Jewish Review*, December 1983, 11, 19.

123 Ibid., July-August 1984, 1, 10, 11.

124 Temkin, "Portland Jewish Newspapers," 21–22.

125 *Jewish Review*, February 1984, 15, 23.

126 Ibid., February 1984, 15, 23. For an article on the founding of the Israel Committee, see *Jewish Review*, September 1983, 17.

127 Jewish Americans for Middle East Understanding was another similar group founded in Portland in January 1986. *Jewish Review*, February 1986.

128 *Jewish Review*, April 1986, "Letters to the editor."

129 Ibid., May and June 1986, "Letters to the editor."

130 Ibid., October 1986, "Letters."

131 Ibid., November 1988, 11.

132 Ibid., January-June 1988, letters. Among the letters are many from local rabbis, community leaders, and other readers.

133 Ibid., June 1988, 1, 12.

134 For details on Stampfer's story, see Smith, *To Learn and to Teach*.

135 Joshua Stampfer, "Reflecting on 36 Years with Neveh Shalom" (unpublished manuscript, 1989), Rabbi Joshua Stampfer, individual file, OJM, 6.

136 Smith, *To Learn and to Teach*, 171.

137 Ibid., 280–81.

138 *Oregonian*, February 16, 1988, B3; September 18, 1988, L1.

139 *Oregonian* stories on the mission to Israel ran in 1989 on January 30, B1; February 13, A9; February 15, A7; February 17, C9; and March 1, 1989, A2.

140 On Kinberg, see Eugene *Register-Guard*, April 20, 1996, 1, 16. See also Gary Tepfer oral history (Eugene, January 19, 2007), 15. When Rabbi Stampfer's group invited Ron Young back to Portland in May 2008, he also made a stop in Eugene to meet with the Eugene Committee for Peace in the Middle East, in which Kinberg was centrally involved. *Oregonian*, June 19, 1988, C1.

141 *Oregonian*, December 1, 1988, C9.

142 *Jewish Review*, June 1989, 9.

143 *Oregonian*, January 30, 1989, B1.

144 Rabbi Emanuel Rose, "Rabbinic Forum," *Jewish Review*, March 1989, 12.

145 *Oregonian*, March 25, 1989, B1.

146 Rabbi Joey Garon-Wolf, "Rabbinic Forum," *Jewish Review*, January 1989, 13; Rabbi Yonah Geller, "Rabbinic Forum," *Jewish Review*, February 1989.

147 *Oregonian*, April 9, 1989, B9.

148 Wertheimer, "Breaking the Taboo," 417–18.

149 *Jewish Review*, October 1989, 1.

150 Ibid., November 1989, 6.

151 "Dayenu," Hebrew for "it would have been enough for us," comes from a Passover song recounting a series of miracles God performed during the Exodus from Egypt; after each, the chorus "dayenu," is sung, signifying that each miracle would have been enough. In this instance, however, the usage suggests a sentiment of "enough already."

152 *Jewish Review*, November 1989, 8; December 1989, 4; January 1990, 2.

153 Paul Meyer oral history (August 6, 2009), 10.

154 The first column in this series showcased the views of Shirley Tanzer, publisher of the local newsletter of Parents of North American Israelis; Stew Albert of Portland New Jewish Agenda, Sarah Mendlovitz of the CRC, and Rabbi Joseph Wolf of Havurah.

155 *Jewish Review*, August 1, 1992, 1.

156 Ibid., 7.

157 Ibid., August 1, 1993; September 15, 1994, 9.

158 Ibid., August 15, 1992, 8.

159 Jack Wertheimer, "Jewish Organizational Life Since 1945," *American Jewish Yearbook* (1995), 43.

160 *Jewish Review*, September 15, 1992, 10.

161 Ibid., April 15, 1996, 13; May 15, 1996, 11.

162 Ibid., May 15, 1996, 5, 13.

163 Ibid., March 15, 1997, 12.

164 Ibid., June 1, 1997, 1.

165 *Oregonian*, June 28, 1998.

166 *Jewish Review*, July 15, 2000, 1.

167 Ibid., April 15, 2002, 15–16. The series of articles conveying the group's responses to questions on Israel ran in three successive issues, from April 1 to May 15, 2002. These were followed in the two June editions by an unusually large number of letters to the editor.

168 Ibid., April 15, 2002, 1; May 1, 2002, 1, 17.

169 Ibid., April 1, 2002, 21.

170 Ibid., April 15, 2002, 16.

171 Ibid., June 1 and 15, 2003, 3.

172 See chap. 4.

173 Sasson, *The New American Zionism*, 65. On the Oregon-Israel Fund's establishment see *Jewish Review*, December 15, 1998, 7.

174 Priebe, "Zionism in Oregon."

175 Eliezer Don-Yehiye "Orthodox and other American Jews and their Attitude to the State of Israel" *Israel Studies* 17, no. 2 (Summer 2012): 123. On the affiliation patterns of Jewish Oregonians, see chap. 6.

176 Jack Wertheimer "American Jews and Israel; A 60-Year Retrospective," in *American Jewish Yearbook* (2008), 63. For extended treatment of this trend, see Ofira Seliktar, *Divided We Stand: American Jews, Israel and the Peace Process* (Westport: Praeger, 2002).

177 The United Jewish Appeal (UJA, founded 1939) was the umbrella organization into which federation funds for overseas Jewry flowed. The UJA's funds were allocated mostly to Israel through the United Israel Appeal (UIA), with a smaller portion going to the American Jewish Joint Distribution Committee (JDC) for support of other world Jewish communities. In 1990, the UJA merged with the Council of Jewish Federations and the UIA to form the United Jewish Communities (UJC). In 2009 this organization would change its name to the Jewish Federations of North America. See Sasson, *New American Zionism*, 63–65.

178 For Portland figures, see *Review* (June 1991), 5, and (June 2005). For national, see Sasson, 64.

179 Jewish Federation survey, 2009; National Jewish Population Survey, 2000; Pew Survey, 2014.

Chapter Six

1 Mayan Miriam dedication, http://www.homemikveh.org/construction/constr _24.html.

2 Ibid.

3 Libby Bottero, phone interview with the author, June 1, 2015.

4 Ibid.

5 Libby Bottero, "My American Jewish Life," personal essay written to be shared at Temple Beth Israel, Eugene, April 24, 2015 (unpublished).

6 http://rebaryeh.com/biography.html.

7 http://www.homemikveh.org/construction/constr_24.html.

8 Libby Bottero, phone interview with the author, June 1, 2015. It is notable that the much larger Mayyim Hayyim mikvah in the Boston area, with a similar philosophy of welcoming, spirituality, and innovation, opened a year after Mayan Miriam. Bottero was in communication with the group in Boston as they formulated their plans.

9   The slogan was an adaptation of "Keep Austin Weird."

10   For a discussion of Jewish engagement in the fight against the OCA, see chap. 4.

11   Peterson Del Mar, *Oregon's Promise*, 248.

12   Jewish population in Oregon grew by 363 percent between 1970 and 2012. Ira
     Sheskin and Arnold Dashefsky, *Jewish Population in the United States, 2012* (Storrs,
     CT: Mandell L. Berman Institute, North American Jewish Data Bank, 2012), 19, 24.

13   Goldstein and Goldstein, *Jews on the Move*, chaps. 5 and 6. See also *Portland
     Jewish Tomorrow Final Report* (Dynamic Change Solutions, for the Jewish
     Federation of Greater Portland, May 29, 2014), 1.

14   Joyce Loeb oral history, 15.

15   Killen and Silk, *Religion and Public Life in the Pacific Northwest: The None Zone*,
     11. Goldstein and Goldstein, *Jews on the Move*, 99.

16   Pew Research Center, *A Portrait of Jewish Americans: Overview* (Washington,
     DC: Pew Center, 2013), 7.

17   Pew, *Portrait of Jewish Americans*, full report, 46. http://www.pewforum.org
     /files/2013/10/jewish-american-full-report-for-web.pdf.

18   Jewish Federation Survey, 2009, 19.

19   See discussion in chap. 1.

20   "Major Objectives of the JCC" (1943). Jewish Community Center Collection, Box
     1, OJMCHE.

21   See discussion of the 1971 Census in chap. 1.

22   *Jewish Review*, January 15, 2008, 1.

23   "Demographic and Opportunity Study," 2011 (Jewish Federation of Greater
     Portland), slide 19. Note that this study was the second phase of a study. The first
     phase was the "Demographic Needs and Assessment Study," conducted in 2009;
     a revised report on this study was issued by Federation in February, 2010. Here,
     the two are referred to as the 2009 and 2011 surveys.

24   Jewish Federation Survey, 2009, 23.

25   National Jewish Population Survey, Special Report: Jews in the West, 2000–
     01. Note that a marriage is only counted as an interfaith marriage if the non-
     Jewish partner does not convert. http://www.bjpa.org/Publications/details.
     cfm?PublicationID=855.

26   Rabbi Emanuel Rose oral history, 16.

27   Program, Pacific Northwest Council of the UAHC (November 22–24, 1974),
     Pacific Northwest Council, Beth Israel Collection.

28   Egon Mayer, "A Demographic Revolution in American Jewry," in *American
     Jewish Identity Politics*, Deborah Dash Moore, ed. (Ann Arbor: University of
     Michigan, 2008), 272. Hasia Diner, *Jews of the United States*, 309.

29   Shapiro, *A Time for Healing*, 238. For more on this sort of outreach, see Egon
     Mayer, "A Demographic Revolution," 267–99.

30   *The Three Rabbis* DVD.

31   "A Short History of Gesher," Gesher website, ourjewishhome.net.

32   *Jewish Review*, December 1989, 6; March 15, 1995, 8; September 1, 2001, 26. On
     Mothers' Circle, see www.joi.org/motherscircle.

33 Jim Hilton in the *Eastside Voice* newsletter, September 1992. Eastside Jewish Community of Portland collection, Oregon Jewish Museum.

34 *Eastside Voice* newsletter, various editions, 1992–1995.

35 *Eastside Voice* newsletter, 1998. Although the online history of the congregation indicates that the monthly services started in 1999, the newsletters show that they began occurring on a monthly basis in 1998.

36 Ibid., September/October 1998.

37 The December 2005 edition contains similar articles, expressing concern about lagging memberships and participation.

38 The last newsletter and web update were in spring 2010. http://www.ejcop.org /history.html.

39 Shir Tikvah website, http://shirtikvahpdx.org/about_shir-tikvah/; *Jewish Review*, May 15, 2007, 9.

40 Mizrach/Eastside, Neveh Shalom website, www.nevehshalom.org/our -communiity/mizrach-east-side.

41 http://www.tabletmag.com/tag/bridgetown October 19, 2011.

42 Ibid.

43 "Jewish Community Embraces Portland's East Side," *Oregonian*, September 23, 2011, accessed online.

44 Portlandjewishevents.com. They also sponsored Shabbat programming. See discussion below.

45 The Florence Melton Adult Mini-School is a two-year Jewish adult education program centered on text-based study in a transdenominational and open learning environment. Based at Hebrew University and founded in 1980, Melton programs are available in many communities worldwide, and are offered in Oregon in both Portland and Eugene.

46 Elizabeth Kellog, "PDXPlosion: Portland Is Good for the Jews," *Presentense* (e-magazine: presentense.org), Issue 5. Accessed online. For more on environmentally focused programming, see below. See also *Jewish Review*, October 15, 2008, 5, 11.

47 Ibid. See also *Jewish Review*, December 15, 2008, 9.

48 Ibid., *Jewish Review*, October 15, 2008, 5.

49 *Willamette Week*, June 18, 2014, 1. Accessed online.

50 There were, as of 2014, approximately eighty Jewish film festivals in the country. "The Best Jewish Film Festivals of 2014," *The Forward*, January 3, 2014. Accessed online.

51 Arden Shenker oral history (June 20, 2007), 23.

52 "Rabbi's Presence Marks S. Oregon Milestone," *Oregonian*, September 14, 1974, 19.

53 Barry Kosmin, Paul Ritterband, and Jeffrey Scheckner, "Counting Jewish Populations: Methods and Problems; Jewish Population in the United States, 1987" (North American Jewish Data Bank, Council of Jewish Federations and the Graduate School and University Center of the City University of New York), 22. Accessed online via www.jewishdatabank.org.

54 "A Short History of Temple Emek Shalom," www.emekshalom.org/about-us/history/

55 Carol Newman (Astoria), interview with the author, January 19, 2015. Joan Steele, "The Jews of Astoria: Diaspora and Disappearance," *Cumtux* (Clatsop County Historical Society) 12, no. 4(1992): 2–19.

56 "Community Service No Sacrifice," *Oregon Jewish Life* (November 2012): 22.

57 Deborah Seldner, "JCCO: The Emerging Jewish Community of Central Oregon," *Western State Jewish History* 30, no. 2 (January 1998): 133–37. Reprint from *Jewish Review*, July 16, 1997.

58 Annette Goldschmidt oral history (December 9, 2009), 6 (the informant is Neil Goldschmidt's mother).

59 Information on the Jewish community in Eugene can be found on the Jewish Federation of Lane County website.

60 Paul Haist, "Oregon Synagogues," *Jewish Review*, September 1, 2006, insert.

61 *Jewish Review*, November 1986, 10. In the March 1985 listing of congregations in the *Jewish Review*, Tifereth Israel was listed as Conservative, 16. Shaarie Torah formally joined the Conservative movement in 2013.

62 *Kesser Messer* (Kesser Israel bulletin) (February-March 1999). Kesser Israel collection, OJMCHE.

63 Kesser Israel directory, 2002. Rabbi Oppenheimer in *Kesser Messer*, November-March 2002–2003, 1. Kesser Israel collection.

64 Rabbi Brodkin in *Nu's & Shmooze* (Kesser Israel bulletin), October 2006, 1.

65 Although a new Orthodox congregation, the Vermont Street Shul, was founded in 2004, it apparently was short-lived, folding after Kesser moved to the same neighborhood near the MJCC. See *Jewish Review* (June 1, 2003), 21. The Jewish Federation of Greater Portland lists all synagogues on its Community Resources page, searchable by affiliation, www.jewishportland.org (accessed December 29, 2015).

66 Humanistic Judaism describes itself as "non-theistic" and serves secular Jews who want to participate in congregational life as well as many interfaith couples.

67 Suzie Boss, "Rediscovering What's Good About Judaism," *Willamette Week*, January 19–26, 1981. Congregation Havurah Shalom subject file, OJMCHE.

68 Boss, "Rediscovering."

69 Elden Rosenthal oral history, 17–18.

70 Boss, "Rediscovering."

71 "A New Way to an Old Faith," *Oregonian*, October 6, 1989. Congregation Havurah Shalom subject file, OJMCHE.

72 *Jewish Review*, July 1, 1997, 5.

73 Ibid., September 1, 2006, 20.

74 For example, some congregants were displeased with Rabbi Kinberg's early endorsement of a two-state solution in the Middle East. See chap 5.

75 Zuckerman, *Strife in the Sanctuary*. Zuckerman uses pseudonyms for the city, congregations, and all participants.

76 For an account of Chabad's expansion, including some coverage on Portland's Chabad presence, see Sue Fishkoff, *The Rebbe's Army: Inside the World of Chabad-Lubavitch* (New York: Schocken Books, 2003).

77 Arden Shenker oral history (June 13, 2007), 17.

78 Henry Blauer oral history (October 1, 2008), 8.

79 Rabbi Yonah Geller oral history, 12.

80 Steven M. Cohen, "Members and Motives: Who Joins American Jewish Congregations and Why," *S3K Report* (S3K Synagogue Studies Institute) Fall 2006, no. 1, accessed online. This breakdown is similar to that in the Pew Foundation 2013 survey, which found 39 percent Reform, 29 percent Conservative, 22 percent Orthodox, 4 percent Other, and 6 percent no denomination.

81 Jewish Federation Survey, 2009, 65A, appendix, 74.

82 2001 Census of U.S. Synagogues, table 3, 19–20.

83 Ibid., table 5, 32. Note that in this study, only congregations with permanent locations, scheduled services, and leadership (ordained or lay) were counted.

84 Richard Matza oral history, 17.

85 "A Short History of Gesher," Gesher website, ourjewishhome.net

86 *Jewish Review*, December 15, 1999, 6.

87 Ibid., October 1, 2002, 7.

88 http://portlandjewishevents.com/.

89 Killen and Silk, *Religion and Public Life in the Pacific Northwest: The None Zone*, 11–12.

90 Jewish Federation Survey, 2009, 20. For national comparison, the 2013 Pew Foundation Survey of American Jews found roughly a quarter to a third of Jews from each denomination has switched to a different stream.

91 Killen and Silk, *Religion and Public Life in the Pacific Northwest: The None Zone*, 11–12.

92 For a discussion of the Jewish community's involvement in the public debate in the state, see chap. 4.

93 Renewal has welcomed gays and lesbians from the outset, and Reconstructionism affirmed gay marriage in the 1992 *Report of the Reconstructionist Commission on Homosexuality,* stating, "As we celebrate the love between heterosexual couples, so too we celebrate the love between gay or lesbian Jews." Although the Reform movement was emphatic in opposing federal, state, and local measures to restrict gay rights or ban gay marriage and endorsing civil unions, it took longer to embrace the idea of Jewish weddings for same-sex couples, only approving them in 2000, subject to the rabbi's discretion. Although both groups joined in opposing discrimination in the public sphere (and, in Oregon, joined the rest of the Jewish community in opposing the OCA measures), the issue remained more controversial in Conservative and Orthodox circles, with Conservative permitting same-sex commitment ceremonies in 2006, and gay marriage in 2012; only a few Orthodox rabbis have performed gay marriages or civil unions, and their organized bodies have rejected them. Rabbi Amber Powers, "Same-Sex Marriage" (2012), myjewishlearning.com.

94 *Jewish Review*, July 15, 1992, 1.

95 https://www.facebook.com/HavurahShirHadash?sk=info.

96 *Jewish Review*, February 15–29, 1992, 1.

97 Ibid., March 15, 2004, 1.

98 Ibid., August 1, 2007, 1. By this time, the Conservative Jewish Theological Seminary had recently announced that it would admit openly gay students.

99   Melissa Binder, "Welcome to My World: A Retired Rabbi Talks Teaching, Translating and Interpreting God's Word," October 5, 2015. http://www.oregonlive.com/living/index.ssf/2015/10/welcome_to_my_world_rabbi.html.

100   *Jewish Review*, January 1, 2007, 13; March 1, 2007, 14.

101   *Jewish Review*, May 15, 2003, 10.

102   Ibid., December 1, 2004, 6.

103   www.nehirim.org/staff.

104   Sarna, *American Judaism*, 324.

105   Ibid., 345.

106   Rabbi Marcia Prager, "What is Jewish Renewal?" (Kol Aleph, Alliance for Jewish Renewal website) kolaleph.org.

107   *Jewish Review*, March 15, 1991.

108   John Darling, "Reb Zalman," *Oregon Jewish Life* (April 2013), 56–57, and (August 2015) online.

109   Killen and Silk, *Religion and Public Life in the Pacific Northwest: The None Zone*, 24–25.

110   Mark Shibley, "Secular but Spiritual in the Pacific Northwest," in Killen and Silk, *Religion and Public Life in the Pacific Northwest*, 140.

111   Ibid, 142. Shibley also points to "apocalyptic millennialism" as a third "alternative spirituality," but this is not relevant to the discussion here as it has little if any resonance for Jews.

112   Zuckerman, *Strife in the Sanctuary*, 49–51.

113   Irwin Noparstak oral history (July 22, 2009), Lane County Oral History Project, 13–14.

114   Nathan Fendrich oral history (September 8, 2009), 17.

115   "Our Rabbi" Havurah Shir Hadash, www.havurahshirhadash.org.

116   Seldner, "JCCO: The Emerging Jewish Community of Central Oregon," 133–37.

117   John Darling, "Reb Zalman," *Oregon Jewish Life* (April 2013): 56–57.

118   *Jewish Review*, August 1, 2002, 8.

119   "History of P'nai Or," P'nai Or, www.pnaiorpdx.org. Rabbi Aryeh would serve there until his tragic death in a snorkeling accident in Mexico in 2009.

120   Schwartz, Scheckner, and Berkowitz, "Census of U.S. Synagogues, 2001," 129, 131.

121   John Darling, "Reb Zalman," *Oregon Jewish Life* (April 2013): 56–57.

122   *Oregon Jewish Life* (January 2015): 13.

123   *Jewish Review*, April 15, 2004.

124   Ad Olam Mishpacha website, http://www.adolam.org/.

125   "About Us" and "Rabbi Biography," Or haGan website, www.orhagan.org. The name Or haGan means Light of the Garden, and was chosen because of its phonetic similarity to "Oregon."

126   *The Three Rabbis* DVD.

127   *Jewish Review*, January 1, 2003, 8. Newsletter, Mount Adams Zen Buddhist Temple (September 2012), http://archive.constantcontact.com/fs027/1103604989501/archive/1110062074051.html.

128   *Jewish Review*, July 1, 2006, 10.

129   Shir Tikvah website, http://shirtikvahpdx.org/about-shir-tikvah/affiliation/.

130 "Jewish Community embrace Portland's East Side," *Oregonian*, September 23, 2011, online.

131 *Jewish Review*, October 15, 2006, 22.

132 *Oregon Jewish Life* (January 2015): 13.

133 Shabbat website, http://www.spiritpathnow.com/shabbat/about.html.

134 *Jewish Review*, June 15, 2004, 5.

135 *The Three Rabbis* DVD.

136 *Jewish Review*, December 15, 2014, 8.

137 Ibid., January 1, 2007, 23.

138 Ibid., February 1, 2007, 8, 22.

139 Shibley, "Secular but Spiritual in the Pacific Northwest," 140–42.

140 Arden Shenker oral history (June 13, 2007), 21.

141 *Jewish Review*, November 1, 1999, 1.

142 Ibid., March 15, 2000.

143 Ibid., November 1, 2000, 20.

144 Ibid., November 15, 2000, 13.

145 Ibid., June 1, 2001, 5.

146 Ibid., August 1, 2002, 17.

147 Ibid., January 15, 2001, 8.

148 *Jewish Review*, February 1, 2002, 23.

149 Ibid., February 1, 2003, 23; March 1, 2002, 5, 12; July 15, 2002, 8; October 15, 2002, 6; January 1, 2003, 9; November 1, 2002, 12; April 1, 2003, 5; September 15, 2003, A12; August 1, 2003, 11.

150 Ibid., June 1, 2004, 5, 11; August 1, 2005, 24; June 15, 2004, 5.

151 Ibid., April 15, 2009, 10.

152 Ibid., February 1, 2009, 1, 19.

153 Ibid., February 1, 2002, 23.

154 Ibid., July 15, 2009, 10; December 1, 2008, 27.

155 Ibid., June 15, 2008, 1; June 15, 2009, 10.

156 *Aleph Springs Shofar* (Summer 2009), http://rosenbergpr.com/Aleph%20Springs%20Shofar%205-29-09.pdf.

157 Rabbi Michael Cahana oral history, 14.

158 *Portland Jewish Tomorrow*, 11–12, 13, 1.

BIBLIOGRAPHY

Periodicals:

American Jewish Yearbook (accessed via www.jewishdatabank.org)
Beth Israel Bulletin
The Bulletin (Portland Section, Council of Jewish Women newsletter)
Eastside Voice
Historical Scribe (Jewish Historical Society of Oregon)
The JCC Ace
The Jewish Review (Portland, 1959–2012)
The Jewish Scribe (Portland, 1919–1953)
Kesser Messer
Neveh Shalom Chronicle
The Oregonian
Oregon Jewish Life
Portland Monthly
Willamette Week

Manuscript Collections:

Oregon Jewish Museum and Center for Holocaust Education (OJMCHE):
   Ahavat Achim Congregation
   Beth Israel Congregation
   B'nai B'rith (Portland)
   Council of Jewish Women, Portland Section
   Eastside Jewish Community
   Morris Engleson Collection
   Rabbi Yonah Geller Collection
   Hadassah, Portland Chapter
   Jewish Community Center
   Jewish Education Association
   Jewish Family and Child Services

Jewish Federation of Greater Portland
Jewish Historical Society of Oregon
Jewish Service Association
Jewish Welfare Federation of Portland
Kesser Israel Collection
Neighborhood House
Oregon Émigré Committee
Oregon Holocaust Resource Center
Augusta "Gussie" Reinhardt Collection
Shaarie Torah Congregation
Tifereth Israel Congregation
Emily Simon papers

Community Censuses and Population Studies:

1957: "Jewish Census—Portland Urbanized Area—1957," Jewish Welfare Federation of Portland, 1. Located in Rabbi Yonah Geller papers, Box 27, OJMCHE.

1971: Jewish Welfare Federation: "The Portland Jewish Community—1971" (December 31, 1972). Jewish Welfare Federation collection, Box 5, OJMCHE.

2008–2010: Jewish Federation of Portland, Executive Summary, 2009 Population Study; Revised Report, February 2010 (Yacoubian Research) Jewish Federation of Portland, *Demographic and Needs Assessment Study* (Revised Report, February 2010)

State of Oregon:

Voters' Pamphlet Collection

OJMCHE Oral Histories:

Martin Acker (February 5, 2008)
Rabbi and Mrs. Albagli (May 15, 1985)
Joy Alkalay (February 15, 1976, and March 10, 1981)
Irene Balk (November 11, 1981)
Cecille Beyl (August 6, 2009)
Hans Biglajzer (May 30, 1990)
Henry Blauer (October 1, 2008, and October 14, 2008)
Kathryn Kahn Blumenfeld (November 26, 1979)
Helen Blumenthal (March 3, 1977)
George Bodner (June 26, 2007)
Ernie Bonyhadi (December 4, 2007)
Frances Bricker (May 18, 1977)
Charlotte Brown (October 18 and 30, 2006)
Lydia and Bernard Brown (November 26 and December 14, 1975)
Rabbi Michael Cahana (October 28, 2010)
Milt Carl (October 27, 2004)

Frieda Gass Cohen (April 25, 1975)

Ilaine Cohen (August 29, 2008)

Sylvia Davidson (July 29, 2010)

Nate Director (June 7, 2005)

Nathan Fendrich (September 8, 2009)

Dina Feuer (December 4, 2007)

Fanny Friedman (May 4, 1974)

Leon Gabinet (June 28, 2010)

Morris Galen (May 23, 2010)

Rabbi Yonah Geller (October, 2006)

Bernice Gevurtz (October 10, 2005)

Harry Gevurtz (narrative, April 3, 1974, and April 10, 1974)

Shirley Gittleson (September 24, 2008)

Leonard Goldberg (June 3, 2010)

Annette Goldschmidt (December 9, 2009)

Lila Goodman (October 5, 2005)

William Gordon (January 28, 1975, and January 6, 1977)

Meryl Haber (April 10, 2013)

Besse Harris (February 2, 1975)

Jack Hecht (n.d. 1974)

Carrie Hervin (May 3, 1974)

Renee Holzman (June 3, 2005)

Lena Holzman (April 22 and May 15, 1974)

Milton Horenstein (November 14, 2003)

Lillian Kobin (August 30, 1977)

Lillie Kugel (February 15, 1974)

Dan Labby (November 12, 2004)

Manley Labby (January 27, 1975)

Margaret Labby (March 22, 2005)

Dora Levine (n.d. 1969)

Sid Lezak (August 2, 2005)

Wendy Liebreich (April 14, 2005)

Dina Linn (August 2, 2004)

Merritt Linn (July 24, 2008)

Robert Litin (January 19, 2010)

Richard Littman (May 17, 2007)

Joyce Loeb (September 3, 2008)

Evelyn Maizels (April 6, 2010, and March 13, 2013)

Alice Mandler (n.d. 1978)

Howard Marcus (August 27, 2009)

Milton Margulis (February 9, 1974)

Arthur Markewitz (March 11, 1977, and May 10, 1977)

Richard Matza (January 20, 2013)

Rochella "Chella" Velt Meekcoms (January 27–28, 1976)

Ezra and Joya Menashe (November 24, 1975)

Joanna Menashe (March 17, 1975)

Sam and Sarah Menashe and Ogeni Babin oral history (May 20, 1985)

Toinette Menashe (November 10, 2004)

Jim Meyer (March 22, May 2, and May 25, 2005)

Paul Meyer (July 14, 2009; July 28, 2008; August 6, 2009; and
    August 18, 2009)

John Miller (August 10, 1976)

Madeline Nelson (September 22, 2004)

Robert Neuberger (September 23, 2009)

Jeanne Newmark (February 23, 2007)

Irwin Noparstak (July 22, 2009)

Shirley Nudelman (November 17, 2009)

Alvin Rackner (May 11, 2005)

Augusta Reinhardt (December 7, 1973)

Rabbi Emanuel Rose (March 10, 1981; February 20, 2011; and
    March 2, 2011)

Abe "English" Rosenberg (July 20, 1977)

Eve Rosenfeld (September 8, 2004)

Rosemarie Rosenfeld (July 19, 2004)

Elden Rosenthal (June 17, 2010)

Rose Rustin (August 25, 2005)

Hal Saltzman (December 26, 2006)

Charlie Schiffman (February 14, 2013)

Harold Schnitzer (n.d., 1977 and October 17, 1977)

Ruth Schnitzer (April 17, 1975)

Elinor Shank (January 23, 2007 and July 31, 2007)

Arden Shenker (June 20, 2007 and June 13, 2007)

Lois Shenker (November 4, 2013)

Linda Singer (July 1, 2005)

Goldie Stampfer (August 15, 2005)

Morris "Moe" Stein (August 16, 2004)

Helen Stern (April 28, 2005)

Sylvia Stevens (August 29, 2009)

Jacob Tanzer (April 20, 2010)

Gary Tepfer (January 19, 2007)

Harry Turtledove (December 6, 2004)

Linda Veltman (September 6, 2011)

Nina Weinstein oral history (n.d., 2010)

Don Zadoff (October 20, 2009)

Julius Zell (December 18, 1974)

Rabbi Arthur Zuckerman (June 19, 2014)

Additional oral histories:

> Arnold Cogan (March 10, 1999; PSU College of Urban and Public Affairs)
> Elaine Cogan (December 18, 2002; PSU College of Urban and Public Affairs)
> *Sidney I. Lezak: An Oral History* (Portland: US District Court of Oregon Historical Society/Oregon Historical Society).

Secondary Sources:

Abbott, Carl. *Portland: Planning, Politics and Growth in a Twentieth Century City.* Lincoln: University of Nebraska Press, 1983.

——. *Portland in Three Centuries: The Place and the People.* Corvallis: Oregon State University Press, 2011.

Albert, Stew. *Who the Hell Is Stew Albert? A Memoir.* Los Angeles: Red Hen Press, 2004.

Anderson, Scott P. "Acclimation and Adjustment: Russian Jews in Oregon, 1970s–1980s." University of Oregon, unpublished paper, June, 2007. "Soviet Jews" subject file, OJMCHE.

Avner, Yossi, ed. *In the Footsteps of Columbus: Jews in America, 1654–1880.* Exhibit catalog. Tel Aviv: Beth Hatefutsoth, The Nahum Goldmann Museum of the Jewish Diaspora, 1986–87.

Ben-Ur, Aviva. *Sephardic Jews in America: A Diasporic History.* New York: New York University Press, 2009.

Berman, Lila Corwin. "Jewish Urban Politics in the City and Beyond." *Journal of American History* 99, no. 2 (September 2012): 495–96.

"Ernest Bloch, 1880–1959." Milken Archive of Jewish Music. http://www.milkenarchive.org/#/people/view/composers/567/Bloch%2C+Ernest.

Boag, Peter. "Gay and Lesbian Rights Movement." http://oregonencyclopedia.org/articles/gay_lesbian_rights_movement/#.Vt-N7EIrLIU.

Brautbar, Shirli. *From Fashion to Politics: Hadassah and Jewish American Women in the Post World War II Era.* Boston: Academic Studies Press, 2013.

Bryan, Joshua Joe. "Portland, Oregon's Long Hot Summers: Racial Unrest and Public Response, 1967–1969." Master's thesis, Portland State University, 2013.

Canelo, David Augusto. *The Last Crypto Jews of Portugal.* Portland: Institute for Judaic Studies, 1990 (revised edition), edited by Rabbi Joshua Stampfer.

Canty-Jones, Eliza. "HB2930, Anti-Discrimination Bill," *The Oregon History Project.* Portland: Oregon Historical Society, 2007. http://oregonhistoryproject.org/articles/historical-records/hb-2930-anti-discrimination-bill/#.Vt-JlkIrLIU.

Chaille, Greg, and Kristin Anderson. *State of Giving: Stories of Oregon Volunteers, Donors, and Nonprofits.* Corvallis: Oregon State University Press, 2015.

Chenkin, Alvin. "Jewish Population in the United States, 1972" *American Jewish Yearbook* (1973). Accessed online, Berman Jewish Database. www.jewishdatabank.org.

Cohen, Steven M. "Members and Motives: Who Joins American Jewish Congregations and Why" *S3K Report* (S3K Synagogue Studies Institute) Fall, no. 1 (2006), accessed online.

Debreczeny, Camille. "Jewish Racialization and the National Council of Jewish Women, Portland Section" (Willamette University, Liberal Arts Research Collaborative project, Summer 2014).

Diner, Hasia. "American West, New York Jewish," in *Jewish Life in the American West*, edited by Ava Kahn, Seattle: University of Washington Press and the Autry Museum of Western Heritage, 2002.

——. *Jews of the United States.* Berkeley: University of California Press, 2004.

——. *Lower East Side Memories.* Princeton, NJ: Princeton University Press, 2000.

Diner, Hasia, and Beryl Lieff Benderly. *Her Works Praise Her: A History of Jewish Women in America from Colonial Times to the Present.* New York: Basic Books, 2002.

Diner, Hasia, Shira Kohn, and Rachel Kranson, eds. *The Jewish Feminine Mystique: Jewish Women in Postwar America.* New Brunswick, NJ: Rutgers University Press, 2010.

Diner, Hasia, Jeffrey Shandler, and Beth Wenger, eds. *Remembering the Lower East Side.* Bloomington: Indiana University Press, 2000.

Dollinger, Marc. *Quest for Inclusion: Jews and Liberalism in Modern America.* Princeton, NJ: Princeton University Press, 2000.

Don-Yehiye, Eliezer. "Orthodox and Other American Jews and Their Attitude to the State of Israel." *Israel Studies* 17, no. 2 (Summer 2012): 120–28.

Eisenberg, Ellen. *Embracing a Western Identity: Jewish Oregonians, 1849–1950.* Corvallis: Oregon State University Press, 2015.

——. *The First to Cry Down Injustice? Western Jews and Japanese Removal during World War II.* Lanham, MD: Lexington Books/Rowman & Littlefield, 2008.

——. "Portland's Sephardic Scene," in *Vida Sefaradi: A Century of Sephardic Life in Portland*, 24–35. Portland: Ahavath Achim and Oregon Jewish Museum, 2014.

——. "Transplanted to the Rose City: The Creation of East European Jewish Community in Portland, Oregon." *Journal of American Ethnic History* 19, no. 3, (Spring 2000): 82–97.

Eisenberg, Ellen, Ava F. Kahn, and William Toll. *Jews of the Pacific Coast: Reinventing Community on America's Edge.* Seattle: University of Washington Press, 2010.

Fishkoff, Sue. *The Rebbe's Army: Inside the World of Chabad-Lubavitch.* New York: Schocken Books, 2003.

Gamm, Gerald. *Urban Exodus: Why the Jews Left Boston and the Catholics Stayed.* Cambridge, MA: Harvard University Press, 1999.

Glickman, Harry. *Promoter Ain't a Dirty Word.* Forest Grove, OR: Timber Press, 1978.

Goldstein, Eric. *The Price of Whiteness: Jews, Race, and American Identity.* Princeton, NJ: Princeton University Press, 2006.

Goldstein, Sidney, and Alice Goldstein. *Jews on the Move: Implications for Jewish Identity.* Albany: SUNY Press, 1996.

Greenberg, Cheryl. "Liberal NIMBY: American Jews and Civil Rights" *Journal of Urban History* 38, no. 3 (May 2012); 452–66.

Guenther, Bruce, ed. *In Passionate Pursuit: The Arlene and Harold Schnitzer Collection and Legacy.* Portland: Portland Art Museum, 2014.

Hard, Thomas M. "Portland Symphonic Choir." http://oregonencyclopedia.org
/articles/portland_symphonic_choir/#.Vt-Q_EIrLIU.

Hauptman, Judith. "Conservative Judaism: The Ethical Challenge of Feminist
Change," in *Americanization of the Jews,* edited by Seltzer and Cohen. New York:
NYU Press, 1995.

Hyman, Paula. "Bat Mitzvah," *Jewish Women's Archive Encyclopedia,* online. www.jwa
.org/encyclopedia.

———. "Ezrat Nashim and the Emergence of a New Jewish Feminism," in Robert
Seltzer and Norman Cohen, *The Americanization of the Jews.* New York: NYU Press,
1995, 284–95.

———. "Jewish Feminism Faces the American Women's Movement: Conversion and
Divergence," in *American Jewish Identity Politics,* edited by Deborah Dash Moore,
221–42, Ann Arbor: University of Michigan Press, 2008.

Jacobson, Matthew Frye. "A Ghetto to Look Back To: World of Our Fathers, Ethnic
Revival, and the Arc of Multiculturalism," *American Jewish History* 88, no. 4
(December 2000): 463–474.

———. *Roots Too: White Ethnic Revival in Post–Civil Rights America.* Cambridge, MA:
Harvard University Press, 2006.

Johnson, Ethan, and Felicia Williams. "Desegregation and Multiculturalism in the
Portland Public Schools." *Oregon Historical Quarterly* 111, no. 1 (Spring 2010): 6–37.

Johnson, Steven Reed. *Building Sustainable Communities through Community
Governance: The Story of Portland Oregon* (revised version of Steven Reed Johnson,
"The Transformation of Civic Institutions and Practices in Portland, Oregon, 1960–
1999." PhD diss., Portland State University, 2002.

———. "Perseverance of the League of Women Voters." Civic Portland, online. http
://stevenreedjohnson.com/stevenreedjohnson/pdx.leaguewomen.html.

———. "The Transformation of Civic Institutions and Practices in Portland
Oregon, 1960–1999." PhD diss., Portland State University, 2002. http://www
.stevenreedjohnson.com/stevenreedjohnson/PdxDownloads.html.

———. "The Bicycle Movement." http://stevenreedjohnson.com/stevenreedjohnson
/civicpdxbikes.html.

Joselit, Jenna Weissman. "Telling Tales: Or, How a Slum Became a Shrine." *Jewish
Social Studies* 2, no. 2 (Winter 1996): 54–63.

Katz, Mel. Artist lecture (June 5, 2015). Hallie Ford Museum, Willamette University.
Salem, Oregon.

Killen, Patricia O'Connell, and Mark Silk. *Religion and Public Life in the Pacific
Northwest: The None Zone.* Lanham, MD: Rowman & Littlefield, 2004.

Kintner, Helen Johnson. http://oregonencyclopedia.org/articles/bloch_ernest_1880
_1959_/#.Vt-UmUIrLIU.

Kopp, James J. *Eden within Eden: Oregon's Utopian Heritage.* Corvallis: Oregon State
University Press, 2009.

Kosmin, Barry, Paul Ritterband, and Jeffrey Scheckner. "Counting Jewish
Populations: Methods and Problems; Jewish Population in the United States,
1987." North American Jewish Data Bank, Council of Jewish Federations and the

Graduate School and University Center of the City University of New York. www
.jewishdatabank.org.

Leflar, Stephen Y. *A History of South Portland.* Southwest Neighborhoods, Inc. http
://swni.org/ahistoryofsouthportland.

Levinson, Robert. "The Jews of Jacksonville Oregon." Master's thesis, University of
Oregon, 1962.

Lipstadt, Deborah. "Feminism and American Judaism: Looking Back at the Turn of the
Century," in *Women and American Judaism: Historical Perspectives,* edited by Pam
Nadel and Jonathan Sarna. Hanover: Brandeis University Press, 2001.

Lowenstein, Steven. *The Jews of Oregon, 1850–1950.* Portland: Jewish Historical
Society of Oregon, 1987.

Mayer, Egon. "A Demographic Revolution in American Jewry," in *American Jewish
Identity Politics,* edited by Deborah Dash Moore, 267–300. Ann Arbor: University
of Michigan, 2008.

McElderry, Stuart John. "The Problem of the Color Line: Civil Rights and Racial
Ideology in Portland, Oregon, 1944–1965." PhD diss. University of Oregon, 1998.

McIvor, Kristyn, Joel D. Freeman, and Luana Hellman Hill. *Legacy of the Twenty-
Six: A Celebration of the First 100 Years of the Multnomah Athletic Club.* Portland:
Multnomah Athletic Club, 1991.

Miranda, Gary. *Following a River: Portland's Congregation Neveh Shalom, 1869–1889.*
Portland: Congregation Neveh Shalom, 1989.

Munk, Michael. "Oregon's Scottsboro Case." *Portland Alliance* (February 2001).
http://college.lclark.edu/programs/political_economy/student_resources/past
/ (accessed October 12, 2012).

——. *The Portland Red Guide: Sites and Stories of Our Radical Past.* Portland: Ooligan
Press, 2007.

National Jewish Population Survey, Special Report: Jews in the West, 2000–01.

Nicola, George T. "Early Attempts at Oregon Gay Civil Rights." *GLAPN Northwest
LGBTQ History.* Portland: Gay and Lesbian Archives of the Pacific Northwest.
http://glapn.org/6110earlyattempts.html.

Nodel, Rabbi Julius. *The Ties Between: A Century of Judaism on America's Last
Frontier.* Portland: Temple Beth Israel, 1959.

Olsen, Polina. *The Immigrants' Children: Jewish and Italian Memories of Old South
Portland.* Portland: Smart Talk Publications, 2006.

——. *Stories from Jewish Portland.* Charleston, SC: The History Press, 2011.

Orbach, William. *The American Movement to Aid Soviet Jews.* Amherst: University of
Massachusetts Press, 1979.

Orleck, Annelise. "Soviet Jewish Immigration," in *Encyclopedia of American Jewish
History,* vol. 1, edited by Stephen Norwood and Eunice Pollack, 47. Santa Barbara:
ABC-CLIO, 2008.

Peterson del Mar, David. *Oregon's Promise: An Interpretive History.* Corvallis: Oregon
State University Press, 2003.

Pew Research Center. *A Portrait of Jewish Americans: Overview.* Washington, DC: Pew
Center, 2013.

Portland Jewish Tomorrow Final Report. Dynamic Change Solutions, for the Jewish Federation of Greater Portland, May 29, 2014.

Powers, Rabbi Amber. "Same-Sex Marriage," 2012. myjewishlearning.com.

Prager, Rabbi Marcia. "What Is Jewish Renewal?" Kol Aleph, Alliance for Jewish Renewal website. kolaleph.org.

Priebe, Cathryn. "Zionism in Oregon." Willamette University, Liberal Arts Research Collaborative, Summer 2014.

"Queer Heroes NW—Featured Hero: Sanford Director" (June 25, 2014), Q Center. www.pdxqcenter.org.

Robbins, William G. *Landscapes of Conflict: The Oregon Story, 1940–2000*. Seattle: University of Washington Press, 2004.

——. "Vortex I Music Festival." http://oregonencyclopedia.org/articles/vortex_1/#.Vt-bRUIrLIU.

Rogow, Faith. *Gone to Another Meeting: The National Council of Jewish Women, 1893–1993*. Tuscaloosa: University of Alabama Press, 1993.

Rosenthal, Steven. *Irreconcilable Differences: The Waning of the American Jewish Love Affair with Israel*. Hanover, NH: Brandeis University Press/University Press of New England, 2001.

Rottenberg, Catherine, ed. *Black Harlem and the Jewish Lower East Side: Narratives out of Time*. Albany: SUNY Press, 2013.

Rubenstein, Sura. "Ahavath Achim: A History," in *Vida Sefaradi: A Century of Sephardic Life in Portland*, 37–42. Portland: Ahavath Achim and Oregon Jewish Museum, 2014.

——. Remarks for "South Portland History Pub." McMenamin's Kennedy School, June 2011. Old South Portland subject file, Oregon Jewish Museum.

Rumer, Patricia. "Citizen Advocacy Groups—An Intervention Strategy: A Case Study of the Community Coalition for School Integration in Portland, Oregon." Phd diss. Portland State University, 1981.

Sarna, Jonathan. "American Jewish History." *Modern Judaism* 10, no. 3 (October 1990): 343–65.

——. *American Judaism: A History*. New Haven, CT: Yale University Press, 2004.

Sasson, Theodore. *The New American Zionism*. New York: New York University Press, 2014.

Schwab, Herbert M. *Race and Equal Educational Opportunity in Portland's Public Schools*. Report to the Board of Education, Portland, October 29, 1964.

Schwartz, Jim, Jeffrey Scheckner, and Laurence Kotler-Berkowitz. "Census of U.S. Synagogues, 2001." American Jewish Committee. 2002: http://www.bjpa.org/Publications/details.cfm?PublicationID=3162.

Segal, Jack. "The Jews of Portland, Oregon: Their Religious Practices and Beliefs." Master's thesis, Oregon State University, 1965.

Seldner, Deborah. "JCCO: The Emerging Jewish Community of Central Oregon." *Western State Jewish History* 30, no. 2 (January 1998): 133–37. Reprint from *Jewish Review*, July 16, 1997.

Seliktar, Ofira. *Divided We Stand: American Jews, Israel and the Peace Process*. Westport, CT: Praeger, 2002.

Shapiro, Edward S. *A Time for Healing: American Jewry since World War II.* Baltimore, MD: Johns Hopkins University Press, 1992.

Sheskin, Ira, and Arnold Dashefsky. *Jewish Population in the United States, 2012.* Storrs, CT: Mandell L. Berman Institute, North American Jewish Data Bank, 2012.

Smith, David Michael. *To Learn and to Teach: The Life of Rabbi Joshua Stampfer.* Portland: Institute for Judaic Studies, 2003.

Solomon, Alisa. *Wonder of Wonders: A Cultural History of Fiddler on the Roof.* New York: Metropolitan Books, 2013.

Steele, Joan. "The Jews of Astoria: Diaspora and Disappearance." *Cumtux*, Clatsop County Historical Society 12, no. 4 (1992): 2–19.

Stampfer, Rabbi Joshua. *Pioneer Rabbi of the West: The Life and Times of Julius Eckman.* Portland: 1988.

Stein, Harry. *Gus J. Solomon: Liberal Politics, Jews and the Federal Courts.* Portland: Oregon Historical Society Press, 2006.

Stevens, Jennifer. "Feminizing Portland, Oregon: A History of the League of Women Voters in the Postwar Era, 1950–1975" in *Breaking the Wave: Women, Their Organizations, and Feminism, 1945–1985*, edited by Kathleen A. Laughlin and Jacqueline L. Casteldine, 155–72. New York: Routledge, 2011.

Suutari, Amanda. "USA-Oregon (Portland)-Sustainable City" The EcoTipping Points Project: Models for Success in a Time of Chaos. http://www.ecotippingpoints.org /our-stories/indepth/usa-portland-sustainable-regional-planning.html.

Suwol, Samuel. *Jewish History of Oregon.* Portland: 1958.

Svonkin, Stuart. *Jews Against Prejudice: American Jews and the Fight for Civil Liberties.* New York: Columbia University Press, 1977.

Temkin, Howard. "Portland Jewish Newspapers (1893–2012): An Overview." Research document, Oregon Jewish Museum (February 2012).

Thompson, Wayne. "Neil Goldschmidt." http://oregonencyclopedia.org/articles /goldschmidt_neil/#.Vt-lFUIrLIV.

The Three Rabbis: Three Men, Half a Century, One Community. DVD. Portland: Oregon Public Broadcasting, 2005.

Tighe, Elizabeth *et al.* "American Jewish Population Estimates: 2012." Brandeis University, Steinhardt Social Research Institute, 2013.

Toll, William. *The Making of an Ethnic Middle Class.* Albany, NY: State University of New York Press, 1982.

Umansky, Ellen M. "Feminism and American Reform Judaism," in *The Americanization of the Jews,* edited by Seltzer and Cohen. NY: NYU Press, 1995.

Vida Sefaradi: A Century of Sephardic Life in Portland. Portland: Oregon Jewish Museum and Congregation Ahavath Achim, 2014.

Walth, Brent. *Fire at Eden's Gate: Tom McCall and the Oregon Story.* Portland: Oregon Historical Society Press, 1994.

Watson, Tara, and Melody Rose. "She Flies with her Own Wings: Women in the 1973 Oregon Legislative Session." *Oregon Historical Quarterly* 111, no. 1 (Spring 2010): 38–63.

Wenger, Beth. "Memory as Identity: The Invention of the Lower East Side." *American Jewish History* 85, no. 1 (March 1997): 3–27.

Wertheimer, Jack. "American Jews and Israel: A 60-Year Retrospective." *American Jewish Yearbook* (2008): 3–79.

——. "Breaking the Taboo: Critics of Israel and the American Jewish Establishment," in *Envisioning Israel: The Changing Images and Ideals of North American Jews,* edited by Allon Gal, 397–419. Detroit: Wayne State University Press, 1996.

——. "Jewish Organizational Life Since 1945," *American Jewish Yearbook* (1995): 3–100.

Wolitz, Seth. "The Americanization of Tevye or Boarding the Jewish *Mayflower.*" *American Quarterly* 40, no. 4 (December 1988): 514–36.

Wollner, Craig, John Provo, and Julie Schablishky. "Brief History of Urban Renewal in Portland, Oregon" (n.d.) Urban Renewal Subject File, OJMCHE.

Zuckerman, Peter, "How Reedies Helped Oregon Win the Freedom to Wed," *Reed Magazine* (June 17, 2014). http://www.reed.edu/reed_magazine/sallyportal/posts/2014/how-reedies-helped-oregon-win-the-freedom-to-marry.html.

Zuckerman, Phil. *Strife in the Sanctuary: Religious Schism in a Jewish Community.* Walnut Creek, CA: Alta Mira Press, 1999.

INDEX

Maizels, Lois, 77
Mandler, Alice (Fried), 170
March on Washington, 128–129, 133, 146, 176–177
Marcus, David, 103
Marcus, Howard, 62
Marcus, Susan (Woolach), 64, 101
Margles, Judith "Judy", 66, 67–68, 72, 78
Markewitz, Arthur, 55
Matza, Aaron, 14–15
Matza, Richard, 14–15, 62, 233, 254n49
Mayan Miriam (Miriam's Well), xiv, 208–211, 213, 242, 249, 285n8
Mayfield, Brandon, 156
Mayim Shalom (Coos Bay), 225
Mayors. See Harry Steinbock; Neil Goldschmidt; Vera (Pistrak) Katz; Terry Schrunk;, Bud Clark
Mayors Commission on Human Rights, 125
May Terrace Apartments. See Cedar Sinai Park
Mayyim Hayyim mikvah, 285n8
McCall, Tom, 25–27, 31, 36, 174, 179, 212, 244, 256n96, 256n101, 265n51
McElderry, Stuart, 121
Medford, OR, 11, 225, 226
Meekcoms, Rochella "Chella", 70
Meeker, Richard, 37, 258n133
Meier and Frank, 27, 124
Meier, Julius, 23
Melman, Rabbi Baruch, 114
Memory is Survival, 43, 46, 55–57, 58, 60, 61, 64–65, 66, 69–70, 72
Menashe, Ezra, 66
Menashe, Joanna (Capeluto), 63, 66
Menashe, Joya, 66
Menashe, Liz (McBride), 104
Menashe, Solomon, 266n76
Menashe, Toinette (Rosenberg), 80, 81, 144–145, 179, 186
Menashe, Victor, 22, 69, 179, 186
Men's Division. See Jewish Welfare Federation of Greater Portland, Men's Division
Mesher, Harriet, 77
Mesher, Shirley, 112
Meyer, Alice (Turtledove), 64, 85–86, 136, 139
Meyer, Jim, 174
Meyer, Paul, 31–32, 89, 124, 125, 126, 133, 134, 136, 199, 272n32

Meyer, Roger, 127
Meyers, Clay. See Myers, Clay
middle class, 6–8, 13, 46, 138, 147, 161, 177, 277n147
Millar, Branford, 265n51
minority consciousness, 117–144, 149, 155–156, 158. See also anti-Semitism; discrimination; intergroup work
Min Zidell Education Building, 39
Miranda, Gary, 14
Mittleman, Harry, 1, 39
Mittleman, Helen, 1
Mittleman Jewish Community Center (MJCC). See Jewish Community Center
MJCC. See Jewish Community Center
Model Cities Program, 30, 139
Moe and Izetta Tonkon chair in Jewish Studies, 25
Moishe House, 221–222, 247, 248
Morgan, Jonathan, 221
Morse, Wayne, 174, 274n79
Mosaic, 222
Mosler's Bakery, 44, 45, 55–56, 62
Mothers' Circle, 219
Mothers' Club, 112
Multnomah Athletic Club (MAC), 16–17, 127, 273n43, 273n45
Munk, Michael, 125
Muslim-Jewish relations, xv, xvii, xviii, 36–37, 87, 90, 156, 162–175, 172–173, 187–207. See also Friends of Israel for a Palestinian State; Intifada; Israeli-Palestinian conflict; Palestine Liberation Organization; Palestinians
Myrdal, Gunnar, 119
Myers, Clay, 174
Myers, Eleanor, 94

N

NAACP. See National Association for the Advancement of Colored People
Napom, Leah, 77
National Association for the Advancement of Colored People, 120–121, 124, 131, 133, 137
National Community Relations Advisory Committee (NCRAC), 121, 146, 174
National Conference of Christians and Jews, 124, 131

National Council of Jewish Women (NCJW), 28, 64, 76, 77, 78, 83–84, 85, 87, 89, 91, 93–97, 99, 102, 105, 117, 118, 123, 130–131, 138, 139, 147–154, 157, 176 181, 183–184, 277n147
National Jewish Community Relations Advisory Council, 174, 195, 198, 245
National Organization for Women (NOW), 75
National Organization of Women for Equality (NOWE), 145
Native Americans, 137, 246
NCJW. See National Council of Jewish Women
Nehirim, 237, 243
neighborhood associations, 29, 105
Neighborhood House, 28, 47, 87, 99, 119, 131, 147, 150, 154, 175
Neimand, Rabbi Louis, 226, 240
Nelson, Madeline (Brill), 82
Nelson, Roscoe C., 24–25, 82, 151, 271n10
Nelson, Roscoe C., Jr., 32, 151
Nemer, Diane (Holzman), 60, 112
Nemer, Sylvia, 88
Netanyahu, Benjamin, 201–202
Neuberger, Maurine (Brown), 19, 132, 134, 135
Neuberger, Richard "Dick", 26 27, 125, 131–134, 256n101, 272n32, 274n78
Neuberger, Robert, 10
Neveh Shalom (Portland), 1–2, 3, 4, 12, 19, 20, 24, 42–43, 64, 78, 86, 100, 108–112, 115, 130, 147, 156, 158, 159, 160, 163, 165, 170, 171, 182, 184, 185, 195, 203, 220, 232, 233, 236, 237, 243–244, 246, 247, 252n9
Neveh Zedek (Portland), 2, 4, 5, 11, 14, 20, 41, 45, 219, 252n11
New Israel Fund, 190–191, 204
New Jewish Agenda (NJA), 36, 157, 190–193, 195, 196–200
Newman, Jonathan, 123, 124, 125, 129, 130, 133, 134, 135–136, 272n20, 272n32
Newman, Rabbi Louis, 135–136
Newman Plan, 123
Newmark, Herbert, 266n76
Newmark, Jeanne (Mittleman), 91
New Odessa, OR, 11